SPIRIT MATTERS

The Washington Institute for Values in Public Policy

The Washington Institute sponsors research that helps provide the information and fresh insights necessary for formulating policy in a democratic society. Founded in 1982, the Institute is an independent, non-profit educational and research organization which examines current and upcoming issues with particular attention to ethical implications.

ADDITIONAL TITLES

The Economics of Mass Migration in the 20th Century
Edited by Sidney Klein (1987)

The Terrible Meek: Essays on Religion and Revolution
Edited by Lonnie D. Kliever (1987)

The Dissolving Alliance: The United States and the Future of Europe
Edited by Richard L. Rubenstein (1987)

Human Rights in East Asia: A Cultural Perspective
Edited by James C. Hsiung (1986)

Beyond Constructive Engagement: United States Foreign Policy Toward Africa
Edited by Elliott P. Skinner (1986)

The Nuclear Connection: A Reassessment of Nuclear Power and Nuclear Proliferation
Edited by Alvin Weinberg, Marcelo Alonso and Jack N. Barkenbus (1985)

Central America in Crisis
Edited by Marcelo Alonso (1984)

Global Policy: Challenge of the 80's
Edited by Morton A. Kaplan (1984)

SPIRIT MATTERS

The Worldwide Impact of Religion on Contemporary Politics

EDITED BY
RICHARD L. RUBENSTEIN

with an introduction by
HUSTON SMITH

A WASHINGTON INSTITUTE BOOK

PARAGON HOUSE PUBLISHERS
New York

Published in the United States by

Paragon House Publishers
90 Fifth Avenue
New York, New York 10011

A Washington Institute for Values in Public Policy book

Library of Congress Cataloging-in-Publication Data

Spirit matters.

"A Washington Institute book."
Includes bibliographies and index.
1. Religion and politics—History—20th century.
2. World politics—1945- I. Rubenstein, Richard L.
BL65.P7S74 1986 291.1′77 86-25172
ISBN 0-88702-203-0
ISBN 0-88702-211-1 (pbk.)

Contents

Acknowledgments

As a multi-authored effort, this book is the work of many hands. The editor wishes to express his thanks to the contributors for their essays and for their participation in the original task force which undertook the project of exploring the worldwide implications of religion on contemporary politics. He is especially grateful to those contributors who felt the need and were willing to update their essays in light of events occurring since the conference, where the essays were originally presented, in Washington, D.C., October 15–17, 1982. Professor Szymon Chodak did not participate in that conference, but was invited to submit his paper at a later time. The project itself was initiated by the Professors World Peace Academy of America, the original sponsor of The Washington Institute for Values in Public Policy. When the Institute became an independent, public-policy research institution incorporated in the city of Washington, it took over responsibility for the entire project. The editor wishes to thank Hugh Spurgin, formerly Secretary-General of PWPA-USA, and his staff, for their efforts in initiating the project. He wishes to express his gratitude to Neil A. Salonen, Director of The Washington Institute, for his administrative supervision of the entire project. The editor is further indebted to Jonathan Slevin, Director of Publications of The Washington Institute; Robert Rand, Production Consultant; and Helen Driller, Production Manager of Paragon House Publishers, for their patient, diligent and expert work in seeing this book through production.

RLR

INTRODUCTION

Does Spirit Matter? The Worldwide Impact of Religion on Contemporary Politics

HUSTON SMITH

There are some who will see the tension in this book's title—spirit joined to matter, its opposite—as an author's device to catch the reader's eye, but that is not the whole story. The *double entendre* in the word "matter" captures the book's thesis precisely. Spirit matters in making a difference, but it also "matters" in that the difference it makes occurs partly in the material realm. It affects the course of history, enlivening and shaping it, ambiguous in its power to both redeem and destroy. One thinks of the lines from the *Bhagavad-Gita* that occurred to Oppenheimer as the first atomic bomb exploded over the sands of New Mexico:

> I am come as Time, the waster of worlds,
> Ready for that hour that ripens to their ruin.

From Liberation Theology to the New Right, America is aflame with debate over the actual and appropriate applications of faith; Ayatollahs, abortion, creationism, and bishops-on-the-bomb jostle one another for front page billing. A journalist recently wrote that he had been trained to think first in terms of power—who's got the guns and the money to buy them? Now, though, he concluded, it's back to Religion 101. Irving Kristol cites the collapse of Christianity as the most important political fact of the twentieth century; for Malcolm Muggeridge that fact is the Soviet Union's inability to stamp out the Orthodox Church. They differ on specifics, but both nominate a religious occurrence for the most important political fact of our time. Spirit matters.

As the emphasis of this book is on specifics—the way individual religions are currently affecting politics in regions like Eastern Europe, Latin America, and the Middle East—I shall use this introductory statement to dub in some general points that could throw these detailed studies into sharper relief. Background affects foreground; what is timeless affects what is timely. My hope is that the frighteningly immediate topics that are taken up in the papers that follow will emerge in clearer outline if some historical, cross-cultural truths about the relation between religion and politics are first set in place.

Historical Background

Religion is about power quite as much as is politics. Archaeologists have found no ancient city which does not have a ceremonial center as its oldest layer—an altar, a megalith, whatever. It is as if a divine intrusion into history was required to provide the energy—in this case a centripetal, focusing energy—for pastoral and agrarian societies to gather and concentrate themselves in urban centers. Within the full light of history, we have the instance of Islam. The Qur'an's incursion into history occasioned the greatest political explosion the world has ever seen, one that produced in a century an empire that stretched from the shores of the Atlantic to the confines of China. We tend to associate religion with the invisible, but it would be a mistake to think the invisible is impotent. If we can trust what the physicists tell us, it makes more sense to link it with power. A thimbleful of vacuum, that shows us nothing at all, contains more energy than do all the atoms in our visible, thirteen billion lightyear universe.

Initially, religion's power was all-embracing, blanketing society as a whole. Nowhere in the primitive world was there a meaningful distinction between the political and the religious. Civilization could not have gotten off the ground without priest-kings whose temporal power derived from sacred sanction. Without the Mandate of Heaven, the Chinese emperors were no more than commoners, while Islam's most effective political years were those in which the caliphate, an office in which sacred and secular were combined, was a reality. In Europe, once the doctrine of the Divine Right of Kings was abandoned, kingship was no longer taken seriously. This permeation of the secular by the sacred was not (in early times) restricted to heads of state. Not just secular societies but secular components *of* society are recent developments. At their start, the great historical religions looked more like civilizations than like religions as currently conceived; they were prescriptions for ordering the entire range of human affairs: economics, politics, ethics, law, philosophy, art, and diet. There was a time when, in a large sector of the world, everything from the smallest drinking cup to the most impressive Mamluk or Mogul palaces carried the stamp of Islam, a point which holds for the other great religio-civilizations as well.

Today, of course, only tribes provide us with examples of religion-saturated societies. In civilizations, the passing of centuries brings complexity and role differentiation. Religion ceases to blanket the whole of life, and takes its place as one of life's compartments. The interface between religion as one of life's compartments and politics as another compartment—both compartments concerned with power, let us not forget—is the focus of this book, so to that interface I now turn.

Personal Religion

Religion affects politics at two levels: an individual or personal level, and a collective or institutional level. The second is the more visible of the two, being where religion can become a lobbying force, so to speak; and as it is also the guise most related to the object of this book, I shall give it most of my attention. But I have already suggested that invisible does not necessarily mean unimportant, and here is a case in point. Before turning to institutionalized religion, we need to take a sharp, if brief, look at the way individual or personal religion impacts politics.

By personal religion, I mean it to be what I think Whitehead had in mind when he defined religion as "what an individual does with his own solitariness." In religion at this level, we are not concerned with institutional affiliation—whether the individual in question belongs to a church or engages in collective rites and observances. Our eye is on the unique and radically private dimension of his existence. To help us get a grip on that dimension we might imagine him in moments when he is most alone. Perhaps he is involved in a period of soul-searching and has driven off for a day by himself. Or he may be lying on his deathbed, engaged in his final withdrawal from his social identity. What goes on in the deepest interior of a self at such moments—moments when, as it were, an individual steps into life's voting booth, closes the curtains behind him, and casts his ballot: for his egoistic interests only or for those of others as well; for resentment or gratitude as his response to life; for hope or despair as his stance towards the future? I shall not answer that question. All I need say is that what does go on is what I mean by "personal" in the phrase "personal religion." The drama takes place in every moment of our lives, but for the most part subliminally. Institutions and history itself are but aggregates of the micro, capillary responses which, moment by moment, are enacted in the personal dimensions of our lives. Which is why this intimate dimension of religion, obscure though it is, cannot be omitted, even when the focus, as in this book, is on religion's most visible consequences, in politics. The word "religion" in "personal religion," indicates the direction in which the individual's decisions move. *Morally,* religion stands for love of neighbor; *aspirationally,* for hope over despair; and *conceptually,* for the conviction that goodness is more deeply rooted in reality than is evil. Personal religion is that within the deepest recesses of the self which, in difficult situations, enables it to decide and act in these religious directions.

Unlike the descriptive approach to religion that characterizes most of this book, the definition of religion just given is normative, for at this basic, personal level it seems difficult to finesse the question of religion's worth. The problem with defining religion normatively, of course, arises from the discrepancy between profession and practice; it could be protested that the foregoing definition may accurately describe what religions preach, but what about their actual behavior? Almost invariably, the behavior the objecters have in mind here are public, collective ones like the Inquisition or Crusades. I shall speak to these when, after the present section, I proceed to institutional expressions of religion, the focus of this book. Here these institutional aspects of religion must take their place alongside its private, personal yield. Religion would hardly have persisted, as perpetual as play, as universal as song, had it not, on balance, served some important human need. Even scientists who admit to having no religious beliefs of their own concede that, in the long run, religion is "probably adaptive"; that is, life furthering,[1] and the fact that no society has been found without it seems to support that point. Human life requires more meaning than it routinely perceives, and more altruism than is built into its genes. From an evolutionary standpoint, religion has the look of a supplementary diet that compensates for these deficiencies.

The bearing of this on politics, the companion pole of this book, is not far to seek. Governments require of their constituents what they cannot themselves provide: meaning and motivation, including motivation that is directed toward the public good. It used to be taken for granted that religion was an important custodian of such motivation; John Locke's *Essay on Toleration* is one of the most powerful defenses of that virtue ever penned, but he thought it would be a mistake to tolerate atheists because, as he said, they could not be counted on to keep their word. What has become evident, though, is that, since the disestablishment of religion, the West has been unable to come up with a convincing theory of political responsibility. Many versions of utilitarianism have been proposed, but they have not gained wide acceptance. This is not surprising, for no merely utilitarian definition of civic loyalty is going to persuade anyone that it makes sense for him to die for his country or even report his taxable income honestly. For over a century now, social critics have been warning us that the West is living off the accumulated moral capital of traditional religion and traditional moral philosophy. These critics were never popular because, as Irving Kristol points out, "the educated classes . . . simply could not bring themselves to believe that religion or philosophy was that important to polity." "Well," he continues, "I think it is becoming clear that religion and a moral philosophy associated with religion, is far more important politically than the philosophy of liberal individualism [under which we currently operate] admits."[2] Philip Rieff likens faith to the glue that holds communities together, adding that Dostoevsky's question, "Can civilized men believe?" has become, "Can unbelieving men be civilized?"[3]

We do not have to try to determine here how far our moral capital has been depleted. Rising crime and suicide rates are not reassuring,[4] and social critics tend, on the whole, to be pessimistic. Solzhenitsyn describes the West as being in a state of "spiritual exhaustion,"[5] and in his important recent book, significantly titled *After Virtue,* Alasdaire MacIntyre concludes that "morality has to some large degree disappeared."[6] Our object here is not to diagnose, but rather to register an abiding point. Politicians tend to regard religion as a nuisance, an annoyance that must be dealt with, but in its micro, personal workings it eases their tasks enormously. On this underside of the tapestry where, like happiness, religion has no history, it strengthens the meaning, the motivation, and the altruism that collective life requires. And it provides an alternative to demands which, if they were directed entirely to the public sector, would create discontents which governments would have difficulty handling. In all societies, the overwhelming majority of people lead lives of considerable frustration. Religion provides two resources for coping with this frustration: hope that it can have an end, and assurance that it provides the prod for spiritual growth. No amount of harping on the way these can be turned into instruments for exploitation—Marx's belief that religion is the "opiate of the masses"—will cause another, more basic, fact to go away: Remove religion's two internal ways of coping with frustration, and what is left is an external way that asks society to relieve it. One consequence of the decline of faith and growing skepticism about "the consolations of religion" has been that the demands placed on society and government in the name of temporal happiness have become ever more insistent and ever more unreasonable. So modernity, having spiritually expropriated the masses of its citizenry, finds their demands for material compensations becoming as infinite as the ontological, religious Infinity that has been denied them. A regime which has to pacify a populace that is seeking fulfillment in the wrong place, will find its problems insuperable.

Institutional and Communal Religion

In personal religion, I was concerned with a generic phenomenon; namely religion as source and custodian of virtues that are so important that even avowedly secular regimes spawn civil religions to nurture them. When we move to religious organizations, we are obviously in a world that is different in being pluralistic from the start. There may be something corresponding to "religion" in the singular, but religious institutions and communities are perforce multiple.

Of the two, institutions are more palpable than communities. They consist of buildings, texts, rites, officiants, and beliefs that are relatively easy to identify. Religious communities derive from religious institutions, but are broader in scope and less tangible; in ways they are like shadows that institutions cast. One can belong to a religious community in this extended sense (we could equally say to a religious culture) without belonging to its institutions or even subscribing to its tenets—the secular Jew is an obvious example. All that is required are certain "habits of the heart," as De Tocqueville called them, that bind us to those who share those habits, while making persons who don't, seem foreign. The habits may have been acquired through family rituals and other shared practices of childhood, or simply assimilated (as naturally as the air we breathe) from our primary culture, that "artificial, secondary environment" consisting of language, habits, ideas, beliefs, customs, artifacts, and values that human beings superimpose on the natural world. Considered sociologically, religion, in Tillich's aphorism, is the substance of culture, culture the form of religion.

It is through its communities and institutions that religion's impact on politics becomes visible, so the rest of this introduction will deal with it in these twin guises. The safest generalization that can be made about institutional and communal religion is that they are at once inevitable and morally ambiguous. The second of these inevitabilities leads many to reject organized religion while granting it a place in private life; kept to oneself it can be useful, these privatists argue, but institutional religion is a scourge and abomination. The position is understandable—Cardinal Newman's "O how we hate one another for the love of God" carries us to its point immediately—but as a considered stand it fails because institutions are the primary channels by which ideas take hold in history. Institutionalization counters death and demise; without it ideas and essences evaporate. So we must accept the inevitability of religion's becoming institutionalized, and the equal inevitability of the ambiguities and compromises that attend this move. Nowhere are religion and politics more alike than in these twin inevitabilities, which is why emperors and popes understand each other so well. Samuel resists the Israelites' demands for a king, foreseeing with uncanny prescience the evils that will follow: "You will cry out because of your king, whom you have chosen for yourselves" (I Sam. 8:18). In the end, though, he yields. The human condition being what it is—"It is not you [Samuel] they have rejected, but they have rejected me [God] from being king over them" (I Sam. 8:7)—the move was inevitable.

As for the ambiguities that plague institutionalized religion, they all derive from the fact that we live in what Arthur Koestler calls a holarchic universe, a universe that is made up of a hierarchy of holons. Everything is a "holon" or whole in its own right, a stable, integrated structure, equipped with self-regulatory devices and enjoying a considerable degree of autonomy or self-government; thus cells, muscles, nerves and organs all have their intrinsic rhythms and patterns of activity. At the same time, each is a part of a larger whole. So holons are Janus-faced. Each turns upward, towards the higher levels on which it depends; concomitantly, it faces downward, towards its own constituents, in which respect it is a whole of remarkable stability.

It is easy to place our individual selves in this holistic framework. Each of us is a holon that needs to discover and maintain its identity while, at the same time, participate deeply and meaningfully in communities in which we are embedded and without which we could not live. And communities are comparably Janus-faced. They, too, have their consolidating needs; their need to keep their boundaries intact—keep their fences mended—to maintain their self-definition: here, issues of orthodoxy and heresy, loyalty and treason, inevitably arise. But communities also have outgoing impulses. They not only need, but want to traffic with the world, through diplomatic missions and embassies to be sure, but also in ways that are intrinsically ecumenical. Balancing the adage that "good fences make good neighbors," are ones that proclaim an open door policy: "Don't fence me in," and "something there is that doesn't love a wall."

Religion lies on the cusp of these centripetal/centrifugal, self/other propensities. In both individuals and communities, it provides a reference for self-definition and identity, while at the same time pressing towards deep reaches of consciousness where our selfhood opens onto our shared humanity and we find our lives by losing them.

The ambiguities that attend religious institutions derive directly from these opposing, self/other pulls which all life must accommodate and learn to live with. Four of these ambiguities are relevant for the present study.

1. The group identity that religious institutions generate is both good and bad. It is good in binding members into larger holons or wholes, inspiring in each community a healthy self-image and group morale. But the dark side of this virtue is the exclusion that identity requires. Things are defined as much by their edges as their contents; as much by what they differ from as by what they positively present.

2. The preceding point—that there can be no group without edges that prompt both in-group and out-group feelings—leads into a second ambiguity. The feelings that are directed towards outsiders can be either positive or negative. From the fact that religion is a major force for in-group cohesion (and, by the same token, for out-group exclusion), it would be wrong to conclude that it only (or even mostly) builds walls. It levels them as well. The Buddha renounced caste; Jonah enlarged "Yahweh's" horizons to include an enemy, Assyria; and Christ's parable of the Good Samaritan changed the definition of "neighbor." In *The Two*

Sources of Morality and Religion, Bergson makes the tension between religion's constricting and expanding propensities the focus of his entire study. Max Weber does something of the same when he argues that "shattering the fetters of the sib" was the great achievement of ethical religions. These religions established the superior community of faith and a common ethical way of life in opposition to the community of blood; in extreme circumstances they even sanction opposition to the family. Again we encounter ambiguity. Religion pulls in opposite directions. Either impulse can carry the day and, historically, according to time and place, has done so.

3. The ambiguities continue if we narrow our focus to the role religious institutions play in their own societies and cultures. They can become ingrown, centering their energies on institutional preservation and self-aggrandizement, or they can look beyond themselves to the needs of others.
4. Finally, on the conserving–innovating continuum, religion again works both sides of the street: it has both priestly and prophetic roles. Clifford Geertz sees religion as essentially pattern-maintenance, but Dean Inge was fond of claiming that Mary's *Magnificat* contains more social dynamite than the *Communist Manifesto.* Religion is a conservative force, and it is profoundly subversive; it is opiate *and* catalyst. It creates enclaves and levels social barriers. Too often we find it raising church budgets, but it has also raised the oppressed. It makes peace with iniquity, and, to the extent that the world can be redeemed, it redeems the world.

A recent exchange may help to illustrate the points this section has outlined abstractly. I had been asked to lecture on religion in a history course entitled *The Middle East Today,* and in the discussion that followed, it became evident that the students were puzzled. They had hoped to find, in the teachings of Judaism, Christianity and Islam differences that were commensurate with the political differences that have made the region a combat zone for centuries; ethical or doctrinal differences which, if they did not justify the reigning antagonisms, would at least explain them. It became my task to argue that if it was causes of conflict they were looking for, it would be unwise to expect much from a religious historian. As far as teachings go, Jesus considered himself a Jew to the end, and it surprised Muhammad that the Jews did not recognize him as a true successor to Abraham. To be sure, the differences in the way the two men were perceived by their contemporaries quickly produced distinct communities that elongated into different religions. But once their separate identities were in place, the religions became, in their historical interactions, primarily touchstones for social identity. The hurts that each collectivity suffered at the hands of the others were plastered onto the originating revelations until (again, if it is historical interplay our eye is on) the differences in revelational content scarcely mattered, only the overlay being visible. Even if the differences in content were visible, would they matter: would spirit matter? Yes, but in political confrontations between religious communities, not much. That brothers were raised not only in the same religion but in the same family doesn't keep them from going to court if they have a falling out over their inheritance.

A Case Study

Approaching the matter from an historical and comparative angle, I have tried to abstract some general features of religion that bear on the way it interacts with politics. The other essays in this book examine concrete instances of this interaction that are currently taking place around the world, and to provide a bridge to them I shall speak more concretely in my remaining pages. There is room for one short case study, which I have drawn from the United States. After this single brush with a specific problem, I shall move halfway back towards generalities, concluding this essay with several observations that are broad but not (as were the earlier ones) universal, for they will be related to specific geographical regions.

Of the places in America where religion is overtly rubbing shoulders with politics, I pass over Right-to-Life, school prayer, the "Moral Majority," and bishops on poverty and nuclear war, in favor of the Creationist controversy. I choose this last as being the only one in this list where there is a chance of showing, in brief compass, what is causing the disturbance and what might be done about it.

More than half a century after the Scopes Trial, with carbon dating established almost beyond dispute, to find, in our 1980s West, Americans who still believe that our planet is only about 10,000 years old is almost embarrassing. But more: it is an affront. That a tiny handful of persons who consider the Bible a sourcebook for science has been able to muster enough support to (a) introduce into more than twenty state legislatures bills that would require Creationism to be taught in public schools, (b) persuade reputable scientists to witness for certain aspects of their case, and (c) rack up opinion polls that show an appreciable portion of the nation as favoring equal teaching time for their position—this is a challenge to liberal premises which, when one factors in its unexpected show of strength, turns embarrassment into humiliation. How is it possible that a position that is backed by modern science (and has had more than a century in which to make its case) has failed to persuade the American public? We sense the affront that mainline America feels in the ill-concealed outrage of the American Civil Liberties Union, the National Council of Churches, and the media generally, for as Annie Dillard has pointed out,

> fundamentalist Christians have a very bad press. . . .They live and work in the same world as we, and know the derision they face from people whose areas of ignorance are perhaps different, who dismantled their mangers when they moved to town and threw out the baby with the straw.[7]

At a deeper level, the affront felt by sophisticated America shows itself in its inability to see any validity whatsoever in the Creationists' position. There is some validity there, though, and of proportions that will, I suspect, cause intellectual historians to look for psychological explanations for why liberal America is refusing to see it. They may even think of the lines from one of Robert Penn Warren's poems:

> How once I had lied to my mother and hid
> In a closet and said, in darkness, aloud: "I hate you."

For there is something in the Creationists' case that is true, and one suspects that deep down, America knows that it is true. The "down" here, though, is so deep that the knowing is unconscious. So the guilt that derives from denying and opposing the partial truth in Creationism gets projected on the conscious level in anger and abuse.

The truth in the Creationists' position, buried to be sure under mountains of absurdity, is that our lives are meaningful and derive that meaning from having issued from a meaningful source. It holds as much for meaning as for other things that from nothing, nothing can emerge. But science cannot deal with existential meanings, whence Steven Weinberg's point in *The First Three Minutes* that "the more the universe seems [scientifically] comprehensible, the more it also seems pointless." And as the scientific account of human origins is the only one that can be taught in public schools, meaningless causes for human life are the only ones our children are offered. We want our lives to make sense, but this no longer seems possible if we follow the thinking of our recent Western intellectual ancestors, with Darwin prominent among them. Gertrude Himmelfarb brings this out clearly. "When George Eliot was asked to define her idea of duty," she writes,

> she said that it was the "recognition of something to be lived for beyond the mere satisfaction of self, which is to the moral life what the addition of a great central ganglion is to animal life." What Darwinism did was to imperil that moral faith by making the "great central ganglion" of animal life the nerve center of human life as well. This was the traumatic effect of Darwinism: it did not so much displace God by man as displace man by nature, moral man by amoral nature.[8]

To relate these points to the Creationist controversy syllogistically:

The question of human origins—and origins generally, for that matter—is a religious one, which is why the Doctrine of Creation is theologically important. The United States is ostensibly a religious nation; a recent Gallup Poll showed 94% of Americans professing to believe in God. Yet we seem to have worked ourselves into a position where only an irreligious account of how we got here can officially, in public schools, be taught our children.

God-including answers are debarred twice over. They are debarred by law because they would violate the First Amendment, and by science because they don't fit the scientific method. "The cornerstone of scientific method," Jacques Monod has written, "is the *systematic* denial that 'true' knowledge can be got at by interpreting phenomena in terms of . . . 'purpose'."[9] Science *ad*mits only non-theistic evidence because that is the only kind its method *per*mits.

So truth becomes a secondary consideration in what American children are taught. The determining question has shifted to what they are allowed to be taught, with courts setting the limits on one side and the scientific method on the other. In something of the unforeseen way the 1954 Supreme Court decision, written to *prevent* a child from being bussed out of her neighborhood school district, has come to *require* that children be so bussed; or that Affirmative Action regulations, written to *allay* race and sex as job criteria, have in ways *resurrected* them in "goals," "timetables" and "quotas"—so, too, in the case at hand. A Constitution that was written to prevent ideologies from getting a stranglehold on our nation is, in unwitting alliance with the scientific method, currently working to *help* tighten an ideology's stranglehold. It is abetting the secular humanism, or scientism, which Nobel laureate Elias Canetti says has "grabbed our century by the throat."

The distinction between "what is true" and "what may be taught" did not arise as long as Darwinism seemed unquestionably true, but today Darwinism is fighting for its life. This is not widely recognized, for the theory is so firmly entrenched that the shock-waves that are threatening it will have to reach high proportions before they penetrate the wall of complacency that surrounds it. But they are already more than lapping that wall. Within the citadel of Darwinism itself, Stephen Jay Gould admits that "neither of Darwinism's two central themes will survive in their strict formulation,"[10] and that "it could be false that [natural selection] is as strong a determinant of evolutionary events as we think."[11] Arthur Koestler was not a scientist, but he was an astute reporter, and he concluded his investigation of Darwinism by calling it "a citadel in ruins."[12] In all six of the fields of science on which Darwinists rely for their evidence—the fossil record, population breeding, natural selection, embryology and vestigial organs, biogenesis, and mathematical biology—there is heated argument today as to whether the balance of evidence favors Darwin or challenges him.[13]

Important for understanding what is going on is the distinction between evolution as description and evolution as explanation. As *description*—of the sequences in which life-forms have appeared, with complex forms appearing later than simpler ones—"evolution" (if we can shift the accent in that word from "out of" to "after") remains firmly in place. But as *explanation*—the hypothesis that natural selection working on chance mutations accounts for how and why the sequences occurred—Darwinism is far weaker than for a century we have supposed. Jeremy Rifkin is probably right in predicting that our children will not be Darwinists in this explanatory sense.

Which brings us back to the important truth in the Creationists' position. On the question of human origins, school children should either be introduced to alternatives to the Darwinian hypothesis, or be shown clearly how far short of settling the issue that hypothesis falls. How different this would be from the way evolution is now presented, can be gathered from the way the article on the subject in the current (1979) edition of *The New Encyclopedia Britannica* concludes:

> Evolution is accepted by all biologists *and natural selection is recognized as its cause. . . .*
>
> Darwin did two things: he showed that evolution was a fact contradicting scriptural legends of creation and that its cause, natural selection, was automatic with no room for divine guidance or design (Vol. 7, p. 23, italics added.)

Can the general points that were entered in the earlier sections of this paper help us to understand this one concrete issue into which we have ventured? Is there anything the religious analyst can say, to judges or legislators or school boards, that might help them cope with the Creationist controversy?

Perhaps something like this:

Because religious sentiment continues at a significant level in the United States and the question of human origins is a religious one, governments can continue to expect opposition if public schools pull against a religious answer to how we got here. Some of the forms of this opposition are overt: bills entered into state legislatures, campaigns that support candidates who favor those bills, a burgeoning private school movement, and parents who illegally keep their children home from school to teach them themselves. Backstage, however, in corridors that are quiet and largely hidden from public view, opposition is proceeding on a different front, where the instrument is not votes, but truth. I refer to the Creationist scientists who, for all the distortion their Biblical literalism introduces, are scientists still. The Creation Research Society claims more than 650 members who have either doctoral or master's degrees in the natural sciences, some from institutions as prestigious as Harvard and the University of California. These are not the "know nothings" of the Scopes trial. They are, as *The Sciences* (April 1981) conceded, "a very different breed," adding: "in fact, they may have found and hit the Achilles' heel of modern evolutionary biochemistry" (p. 17). Until mainline America acknowledges the element of truth in the Creationist position, its political expressions will continue to catch us off-guard. For truth, surfacing here as a synonym for spirit, matters. We would not *have* Creationism today had we not accorded Darwinism-as-explanation more status than it deserves. One enormity has produced another. When fundamentals are lost, Fundamentalism tries to replace them.

Regional Differences

From the specifics of the case study just concluded, I shall (in this brief closing section) move halfway back towards the universals with which I began. How are politics and religion differently aligned in the major geographical regions of the contemporary world?

The West tries to separate the two terms, church and state, and accord rights to each. Once the separation is effected, there is the question of their relationship. A modicum of tension between Caesar and God is built into the arrangement, and periodically it erupts in open conflict. Still, each basically respects the other, even while at times opposing it.

Almost the opposite situation pertains in the Soviet Bloc. For more than half a century, Communism has sought to abolish the religion-politics polarity by removing its religious term. But as man is by nature *homo religiosus*[14]—his religious element cannot be completely repressed—so, too, in Marxism we find it surfacing, though in disguise. The phenomenological parallels between Christianity and Communism were visible almost from the start, with the historical process doubling for God, *Das Kapital* and *The Communist Manifesto* for Bible and Creed, the Communist Party for the Church, Marxist orthodoxy for Christian theology, revisionism for heresy, purges for Inquisitions, and the classless society for the Second Coming. It is a truism that Communism cannot be understood apart from its religious zeal, its messianic consciousness, and its salvific claims. But if phenomenologically, in appearance, Communism looks in many ways like a religion, ontologically, in its vision of reality, it remains relentlessly atheistic, despising the theism of the Orthodox Church. For fifty years this Church has been politically helpless, but we have noted Malcolm Muggeridge's contention that the inability of the Soviets to stamp it out is the most revealing historical lesson of our century.

If, according to Marxist Leninism, religion shouldn't interface with politics because there should be no religion, the opposite pertains in Islam: there should be no secular state. The rationale for this is that the Qur'an orders collective life—its social, legal, economic, and political structures—as much as it regulates private devotion. This orthodox view of the matter, though, is theoretical rather than actual. Not since the death of Ali, Muhammad's nephew, has the Caliphate managed to provide an inclusive political umbrella for Islam. As a consequence, Islamic history presents a picture not radically different from that of Europe up to the Enlightenment. It is a picture of constantly shifting patterns of partnership, confrontation, and compromise between political leaders and the *ulema* (Doctors of the Law) in a relationship that is basically symbiotic. There is an important difference, though, in the way the two great branches of Islam, Sunni and Shi'ite, envision the relationship. The Shi'ites, who represent 15% of Islam and are concentrated in Iran and Iraq, hold that political leaders should be descendants of Muhammad who carry spiritual, as well as political endowments, almost in their genes, we might say; whereas the Sunnis have always held that rule should be lodged with the most capable political leader as determined by representatives of constituent groups. This difference makes Shi'ites more suspicious of secularized political, military, and administrative power than are Sunnis. Western political analysts who were not aware of this difference, or who doubted that spirit could "matter" decisively in an economically prosperous Iran governed by a Westernized Shah who was backed by an immense army, paid the price of their ignorance.

In China, religion and politics are interacting in a way that presents yet a different pattern. No more than in Soviet Communism is there room for either supernaturalism or religious institutions that might challenge the state's absolute sway, and the two communisms are also alike in the way politics assumes the trappings of a civil religion. What is different is the degree to which Chinese Communism has been, and is continuing to be, shaped by China's cultural, specifically Confucian, past. If we consider traditional Chinese culture to be religious, as in a profoundly humanistic way we should, the impact of religion on politics in contemporary China is the impact of the past upon the present; Confucius characterized himself as "a lover of the ancients," and Mao could almost have done the same—the harsh things he *said* about the ancients are beside the point here. China's this-worldly emphasis and preoccupation with the social problem made her receptive to Marxism in the first place, as did her yin/yang dialectic into which Marx's dialectic slipped as hand into glove. The Confucian virtues of filial piety, loyalty, respect for authority, and self-discipline were ready-made for Mao. As Robert Lifton observed, "the Chinese became filial Communists." Langdon Gilkey states the general point here in words I cannot improve on:

> The embeddedness of the individual in and his or her responsibility to the community, the ineradicability and value of relationships and their obligations, the priority, therefore, of community obligations over obligations to the self, the absolute importance of the category of the "common good" as a balance to that of the person—all of these communal emphases are peculiarly oriental, as the Confucian tradition in both China and Japan witnesses. They reappear in modern, progressive, and creative form in Maoist thought and in the reality of the new life in China: in the principles of the Mass Line, of the polarity of elite and peasant, in the emphasis on the social origin and character of knowing and theory, and in the identity of the substance of China with the whole *People* of China.[15]

We see the hand of religion—in the Chinese configuration, to repeat, religion appears in the presentness of her past—in the subordination of technology to the embracing of ideology, the subordination of the expert and technician to the political and moral goals of society, and the insistence that theory be reinterpreted through praxis. These are not just the politization of life and absolutizing of an ideology, as Gilkey rightly remarks. They represent the continuing impact of a tradition that was, and remains, importantly religious in ways we are still trying to clearly discern.

More than anywhere else, South America is the place where the principles of liberation theology are currently being explicitly worked out and tested, so this is where religion faces politics in a posture most directly challenging and confrontational; I refer not to South America as a whole, but to what, for our purposes, are its most important pockets. As that continent is treated extensively elsewhere in this book, I shall pass over it to my last characterization, which is of India.

Such a fascinating, bewildering, paradoxical complex of currents and cultures! Who can presume to speak of India? Yet there she is: *a propos* our topic, the most overtly religious country in the world and, at the same time, its largest working democracy. It is enough here to point out the obvious: the distinctive element India introduces into the study of politics and religion is caste. There is no hope of understanding the interface between those two forces in South Asia without understanding caste, and that is a task which (despite the best effort to date, namely, Louis Dumont's *Homo Hierarchicus*) has yet to be accomplished, if indeed the Indians understand caste themselves. If in the West, the church is viewed as the sacred social structure, and in the Soviet Bloc, the Communist Party in ways fills that role, in India, caste is the social institution by which spirituality takes on social form. Political, economic, educational, cultural, and legal functions are determined by it quite as much as are religious ones. Today almost no one outside India says a good word about caste, and in India, parliament, drawing heavily on its British inheritance, has moved concertedly against it. But at the village level, where most Indians still live, it remains the order of the day. At that level, elder representatives of the various castes and sub-castes continue to meet and adjudicate in India's age-old *panchiat* tradition. And in many respects, the delegates to modern parliamentary bodies continue to represent castes or coalitions of castes in that ancient "council of five" tradition.

So, religion and politics are arrayed in six distinguishable patterns in the world today. In the West, they are *partners.* The Soviet Bloc tries to *deny religion,* while orthodox Islam tries to *deny the secular state.* In China, religion (without the name) enters politics through her *present-informing past.* In test points in South America, church *confronts* the state. In India, religion, through caste, *sets conditions* through which democratic processes work.

Clearly, it is time to move to the specifics in these several arrangements.

NOTES

1. Alex Comfort, *I and That* (New York: Crown Publishers, 1979), p. 69. The full statement reads: "Religious behaviors are . . . probably adaptive; [their] dialog with 'nature' . . . is an important integrator of [man's] whole self-view in relation to the world and to activity."
2. *Two Cheers for Capitalism* (New York: Basic Books, 1978), p. 66.
3. *The Triumph of the Therapeutic* (New York: Harper & Row, 1968), p. 4.
4. In *New Rules,* Paul Yankelovich notes that the suicide rate among teenagers in the United States has risen 200% in the last thirty years (Toronto: Bantam Books, 1982), p. 184.
5. Alexander Solzhenitsyn, *A World Split Apart* (New York: Harper & Row, 1978), p. 35.
6. Notre Dame: University of Notre Dame Press, 1980, p. 21.
7. *Teaching a Stone to Talk* (New York: Harper & Row, 1982), p. 121.

8. *The American Scholar* (Autumn 1981), p. 453.
9. *Chance and Necessity* (New York: Vintage Books, 1972), p. 21.
10. *Science* (April 23, 1982).
11. *Unitarian-Universalist World* (February 15, 1982), p. 8.
12. *Janus: A Summing Up* (New York: Viking Books, 1978), p. 166.
13. Cf. Norman Macbeth, *Darwin Retried* (Boston: Gambit, 1971); Jeremy Rifkin, *Algeny* (New York: Viking Press, 1983); and Gordon Rattree Taylor, *The Great Evolution Mystery* (New York: Harper & Row, 1983).
14. Even sociobiologists, who as a group seem not overly pleased by the finding, tend to concede that religion probably has a genetic base. Edward O. Wilson says that the religious impulse in humans is "in all probability ineradicable" (*On Human Nature* [New York: Basic Books, 1978], p. 176).
15. *Society and the Sacred* (New York: Crossroad Books, 1982), p. 145.

1

Reflections on Religion and Public Policy

RICHARD L. RUBENSTEIN

The bitter and divisive public debates concerning nuclear armament, nuclear energy, environmental pollution, human rights, abortion, and prayer in public school are but a few of the policy issues around which religious leaders have come to play important roles in the formation of public opinion.[1] Nor is the involvement of religious leaders in matters of public policy confined to one segment of the political spectrum. Both right and left are represented. If fundamentalists have tended to support the current administration on a rapid build-up of America's defense establishment and have sought the reinstatement of prayer in the public schools, the leaders of mainstream Protestantism have tended to favor a nuclear freeze and have been wary of the "right to life" movement.

Although there have always been religious leaders who have sought actively to influence public policy, the current wave of political activism can be seen as an outgrowth of the civil rights struggles of the 1960s and of the Vietnam War. Until the upheavals of the sixties, an American religious leader who took an active part in the political arena, or who even gave expression to strong opinions on political matters, ran the risk of incurring the disfavor of powerful elements in his community for not "sticking to religion." The idea that religion and politics were discrete realms was deeply rooted in the minds of most Americans. Yet, there was a certain naiveté about it. Both religion and politics are concerned with power and the ways in which men and women come to terms with power.

In the ancient Near East, the office and person of the ruler was held to be sacred and there was no separation between religion and politics. The king was considered to be an incarnate god, or at the very least, a sacred mediator between the community and its gods. Until the end of World War II, an aura of divinity was said to rest in the person of the Emperor of Japan. The idea of divine kingship, which represents the ultimate union of religion and politics, has had a long and continuing history in human civilization.

Yet, if the institution of divine kingship has proven durable over millenia, it is also true that the Judeo-Christian tradition had its beginnings in a successful revolt against that institution, and that both Judaism and Christianity have been its implacable opponents since their inception. It is the opinion of many of the best contemporary biblical scholars that the beginnings of the biblical idea of God, originally an utterly novel idea in the ancient Near East, as well as mankind's obligations to that God, are to be found in the decisive encounter between the Hebrew slaves and their Egyptian masters at the time of the Exodus.[2] In any consideration of religion and public policy in the United States, it is important that we understand what is at stake politically and socially in the biblical idea of the ultimate source of power in human affairs. More than any other major civilization, the culture of the United States has been shaped by those religious communities, the dissenting Protestant denominations, that placed greatest stress on the authority of the Bible as a source of values in human affairs. It is possible to reflect on the problems of religion and public policy without considering biblical ideas when discussing Japan or India, for example, but not the United States. Let us, therefore, consider the ways in which biblical thought and experience are relevant to our topic.

As is well known, the ancient Egyptian state depended upon a system of corvée labor for many of its most important projects, such as the building of pyramids and temples. Because Pharaoh was considered to be a living God, he was regarded as the sole proprietor of all of the goods and services within the nation. In theory, there was no such thing as private property in the ancient Egyptian state. As was the case with most of the other rulers of the ancient Near East, one of Pharaoh's chief social functions was to redistribute the community's wealth. Since the Egyptians lacked any conception of either personal freedom or private property, they did not regard any service they rendered to Pharaoh, whether in the form of goods or labor, as a form of slavery. However, this was not true of those non-Egyptians who had been condemned to corvée labor because they were prisoners of war, hostages or had experienced a radical degradation in status, such as occurred to the Hebrews after the Semitic Hyksos' domination of Egypt had been overthrown in the thirteenth century B.C.[3] We have terse evidence of this degradation of status in Scripture:

And there arose a King who knew not Joseph (Ex. 1:11).

Scripture further tells us that the Hebrews were condemned to slavery, and, when their numbers increased beyond the labor requirements of the slavemasters, all male Hebrew infants were ordered put to death at birth (Ex. 1:16). Apparently, extermination was a method of eliminating a surplus population in ancient as well as modern times.

As the story is told in Scripture, it would appear at first glance that the Hebrews enslaved by the Egyptians shared a common religious and ethnic background. This is, of course, the way they are normally regarded within the Judeo-Christian tradition. In reality, Scripture offers hints that the group that escaped with Moses did not share a common inheritance. Referring to the band of Moses' followers in the wilderness, Scripture tells us:

Now there was a mixed company of strangers who had joined the Israelites (Num. 11:4).

For several centuries before the Exodus, people from Palestine and Syria had entered Egypt, some as prisoners of war, some who were forced to take up residence by the Egyptians after engaging in activities hostile to Egypt in their home communities, others who were merchants. Not all were slaves, but the situation of all resident aliens tended to deteriorate as time went on. It is thought today that each group within the resident aliens retained something of its own identity, particularly insofar as its religious traditions involved some elements of ancestor worship.[4] Scripture identifies the resident aliens as "Hebrews," but that name designated a number of peoples who shared a common condition and social location but were of diverse origins.[5] In some respects, the situation of the Hebrews had some similarities to that of members of a modern multi-ethnic metropolis, in which diverse groups share common problems in the present but remain distinct from each other because of differences in origin, religion and culture.

When the time came for the escape from Egypt, the Hebrews shared a common yearning for liberation and a common hatred of their overlords, but little else. This was enough to unify them so that they could escape. However, as soon as they were beyond the immediate reach of the Egyptians, a compelling basis for unity beyond shared hatred and a desire to escape had to be found if the band of fugitives and outcasts was to survive the natural and human hazards of the wilderness. Fortunately, the escape provided a further shared experience, the Exodus itself.

An important function of any new religion that originates in a radical break with past tradition is to facilitate the founding of a community for those who share no community. This was later to be the case with both Christianity and Islam.[6] In any event, there could be only one basis for communal unity in the ancient Near East, where the distinction between group membership and religious identity was unknown. The diverse peoples could only become a single people if they were united by a common God. Moreover, the God had to be a new God whose power was greater than that of the Egyptian god-king. It would have been difficult for any of the peoples among the escapees to assert that its particular ancestral god ought to be the God of the entire band without arousing the mistrust and hostility of the others. *The Hebrews shared a common historical experience rather than kinship.* Ancestral gods were an impediment to unity. Only a God who was the author of their shared experience could have unified them. Of course, *after* the new God had unified them, it was natural for the assorted peoples to read back elements of continuity between the new God and their ancestral gods. That process is visible in Scripture.[7]

We know that under Moses, the new God and the new unity were found. It also appears that, within a relatively short time, the united escapees experienced an extraordinary increase in numbers and energy and that the enlarged group was able to gain control of much of the territory of Palestine and Jordan. The details of the conquest are unimportant for our purposes. What is important is that we understand something of the nature of the new God and his utterly novel relationship to his people.

From the very beginning, the followers of this God were convinced that he shared his power with no other being, human or divine. All human power was thought to be subordinate and accountable to his power. Moreover, the new God was thought to exercise his power in a manner that was both rational and ethical. It was rational in that there was nothing gratuitous, arbitrary or purposeless in its exercise; it was ethical in the sense that it was fundamentally concerned with the *well-being of persons* rather than the maintenance of political, social or even religious institutions. His power was also thought to be ethical and rational in the sense that he gave his followers the assurance that there was a predictable and dependable relationship between their conduct and the way he exercised his power over them.

The structure by means of which the new God offered the followers of Moses a secure relationship was, as we have indicated, utterly novel. It resembled a form of treaty that had been used in the ancient Near East, especially among the Hittites, in international relations in order to define the relationship between a suzerain and his vassals. It had, however, never been employed by a God to define his relationship to a people whom he had adopted as his own. This treaty form was that of a *covenant.*[8]

Modern biblical scholarship has given us a relatively accurate picture of the origins of the covenant form. There were two types of covenant, one between equals, and the other the suzerainty type, which was a pact imposed by a powerful lord upon a vassal, stipulating what the vassal must do to receive the lord's protection. These Hittite instruments were basically devices for securing binding agreements in international relations. The Hittite overlords were trying to cope with a problem that continues to plague nations to this day. Although there are means of enforcing agreements, once made, within a nation, there is no effective, impartial institution capable of enforcing the keeping of promises between sovereign states if one of the parties to the agreement should conclude that its interest is no longer served by so doing. In such a case, the injured party has no choice but to accept the breach of faith or to resort to military force to enforce the pact. The purpose of the Hittite covenant was to give international agreements a binding character. This was done by the lord binding the vassal by an oath to meet the obligations stipulated in the agreement. An oath is a conditional self-curse, in which the person appeals to his own gods to punish him should he break the agreement. In the ancient Near East, oaths were initially effective in guaranteeing that a promise would be kept. In time, they lost their effectiveness. A covenant can also be seen as a means of achieving unity of purpose between groups that were bound to each other neither by ties of kinship nor by common ancestral gods. It was this aspect of the covenant that was to prove so important in its use in religion.

According to George Mendenhall, perhaps the preeminent authority on the subject, the Hittite covenants had an elaborate form which was later used in the biblical covenant. Among the elements that are of interest are the following: (a) a preamble identifying the king who was the author of the convenant; (b) a review by the king, speaking in the first person, of the past benefits he had bestowed upon the vassal, as well as an assertion that these benefits were the basis for the vassal's future obligation to the suzerain. Both in the Hittite documents and the biblical covenant, *historical events* rather than the magic qualities of the lord were the basis of obligation. Since history is the record of the ways in which men have used power that are considered worthy of memory, it was the lord's possession of and past use of power that constituted the basis of obligation; (c) a statement of the precise nature of the obligations incumbent upon the vassal. Moreover, in the Hittite treaties, the vassal was explicitly excluded from entering into a relationship with any other suzerain, just as in the biblical covenant Israel is excluded from having any God other than Yahweh.

It is impossible to reconstruct fully what happened at Sinai, but there is no reason to doubt that Moses had a revelatory experience at a sacred desert mountain and that the experience became the basis for a covenant between the new God and the escapees, whereby the God stipulated the conditions under which he would accept and protect the former slaves as his people. The novelty of the encounter with the new God can be expressed sociologically: Before Sinai there had been high gods, nature gods, ancestral gods and gods of the polis, but there had never been a high God of escaped slaves and declassed fugitives. Moreover, by his election of the outcasts as his people, his "peculiar treasure," the new God was seen as overturning all existing social hierarchies, in principle if not yet in fact. This was something utterly novel in human history and was to have revolutionary consequences. The Bible does not confirm social hierarchies.

The escapees had witnessed the dark side of Egyptian sacral kingship, a political system, incidentally, that was not without merits in offering its people a kind of stability and security unknown in the modern world. Nevertheless, the escapees had concluded that there were ethical and political values in the Egyptian system that had to be overthrown. Briefly stated, the new tradition asserted the primacy of personal ethical values, legitimated as expressions of the will of the God of the covenant, over political values. In Egypt, where the ruler was a divinity, the interests of the state had a claim that transcended the claims of any of its subjects. There was, of course, a strong note of social protest in the new values. Escaped slaves, who had been the object of abusive power, were far less likely to give priority to the state's monopoly of force than were members of the ruling class. It is not surprising that oppressed classes have frequently identified themselves with Israel in Egypt and at Sinai. This can be seen in contemporary liberation theology. Because the stories of Israel in the wilderness form such a familiar part of our inheritance, we seldom give thought to the sociopolitical significance of the transformation wrought at Sinai.

Like the Hittite pacts, the Sinai covenant has a prologue in which Yahweh, the divine author, identifies himself and states his past benefits to those with whom he is to enter a covenant. "I am Yahweh your God who has brought you out of Egypt out of the land of slavery" (Ex. 20:2) identifies the author of the covenant, and states the basis of obligation. As in the Hittite document, the memory of concrete historical events within the human world is the basis of the vassal's obligation. Similarly, just as the vassal is prohibited from fealty to more than one lord, so the Hebrews are excluded from loyalty to any other God. "You shall have no other gods to set against me . . . for I am Yahweh, your God, a jealous God" (Ex. 20:3–5). Yahweh's insistence on exclusive worship had both political as well as religious import. It united those who accepted it into a community and effectively barred them from giving their loyalty to any of the sacralized kingships of the ancient Near East.

The second set of covenantal obligations dealt not with God, but with the relations between man and man. Scholars identify several very old collections in Scripture that offer slightly different accounts of these obligations, but in all these collections the *ethical relations between individuals have a priority over both political and cultic values.*[9] Moreover, all accounts of the covenantal obligations are based on a *new conception of the place of power in human affairs.* The functions and the authority that had normally been ascribed to human rulers are depicted in Scripture as the prerogative of God alone.

When, as in ancient Egypt, the ruler is declared to be a god, the state and its institutions are thought of as both ultimate and self-legitimating, a view rejected by Scripture. Where such is the case, whether in ancient sacralized kingdoms or modern secular states, there is no effective limit to the actions that can be committed and legitimated by those who control the state's monopoly of power. This does not mean that those in command will invariably abuse their power. Nevertheless, when political power is self-legitimating, in principle there is no value or institution that can serve as an effective check on those in command. Even in the United States, with its constitutional system of checks and balances, in a national emergency the normal checks on the executive branch of government can be suspended. The programs of mass enslavement, extermination and expulsion initiated by such governments as Nazi Germany, the Soviet Union, the Cambodian Pol Pot regime, Castro's Cuba and North Vietnam are among the contemporary examples of the extremes to which the exercise of power can go when the authority of the state is regarded as self-legitimating. In the contemporary world, the balance of nuclear terror is the only credible restraint upon sovereign states that recognize no value as overriding their own requirements for security and self-maintenance.

Those who truly accepted the covenant at Sinai as binding upon them, rather than as mere pious rhetoric, were bound unconditionally by values that transcend and sometimes contradict the state's requirements for self-maintenance. Murder, adultery, theft, false testimony and coveting are forbidden by the covenant, although such categories of behavior can at times become legitimate means of maintaining or enhancing the power of the state. This is evident in the difference between the kind of behavior a state will tolerate in its citizens in peacetime and the kind of behavior it will not only tolerate, but reward when carried out by members of its armed forces and intelligence agencies under conditions of emergency. Violent behavior, often carried out in stealth, can be legitimated as being in the national interest, a claim that cannot easily or realistically be disputed.

The case of the double agent highlights some of the more complex dilemmas of the assertion of the primacy of the interests of the state. In order to establish his credibility, a double agent may have to act as if he were a traitor and even be responsible for the death of many of his fellow citizens. Sometimes governments may knowingly sustain attacks on their own citizens rather than permit an agent to be uncovered. Thus, when the maintenance of the power of the state is self-legitimating, there can be situations in which there is no predictable relationship between the loyalty and trust of citizens and the actions of their government. In ancient times, rituals of human sacrifice were a regular part of the life of almost every community. To this day, the state's insistence on human sacrifice, at least in emergency situations, has not and probably cannot entirely be done away with. There are situations even in peace time when the state's requirements for self-maintenance may compel its leaders to endanger or imperil the lives of some of its loyal citizens. Undoubtedly, the age-old belief in the ultimacy of the state's interests provided the rationale for such questionable programs as the Army's secret introduction of dangerously infectuous micro-organisms into the ventilating systems of a number of American cities a generation ago, thereby making innocent citizens involuntary guinea pigs in biological warfare experiments. The list could be multiplied. It includes the involuntary administering of harmful doses of LSD to unknowing citizens by intelligence agents who were curious about the psychological effects of these drugs. As is well known, a number of these experiments resulted in the death of the unknowing subjects. It could be said that the government agents were "playing God" by virtue of their life-and-death power over others. It is not surprising that ancient man regarded those who possessed such power as gods.

Regrettably, there appear to be no viable alternatives to the idea that the state's requirements for self-maintenance ultimately override all other claims, at least in times of national emergency. Nevertheless, Israel's ancient covenant with Yahweh was an attempt to create just such an effective alternative to the state's claim to ultimacy. By positing a God who possessed neither human image nor human incarnation as the power to whom the community owed its fundamental fidelity, the covenant had the effect of rejecting both the doctrine and the institutions that affirmed the ultimacy of the political order. Moreover, by insisting on the primacy of the ethical over the political in the new community's obligations to its God under the covenant, it imposed unconditional standards on the behavior of men and nations alike. Moreover, there was a harsh corollary to the idea that the community's obligations to its God were based upon the fact that he had redeemed them from Egypt and had constituted them a nation: if ever the new community failed to meet the ethical and religious obligations of the covenant, their God would withdraw his protection from them and they would be destroyed as a nation. In contrast to the sacralized kingdoms that assert the security and stability of the community to be cosmically grounded, Israel's existence as a nation was conditional on her keeping the covenant.

In the Sinai covenant, many of the most significant features of Israel's later religious life can already be discerned. Because of the decisive importance of the Bible for the religious life of America, the values embedded within the covenant have been of overwhelming importance to American religious life as well. By subordinating the political order to the obligations of the covenant, the Sinai covenant laid the foundation of the prophetic protest against the ethical and religious abuses of the period of the monarchy, as well as the prophetic idea that men and nations alike stand under the judgment of the God of the covenant. Over and over again, Israel's prophets reiterated their warnings that the very survival of the nation was dependent upon its keeping the covenant.[10]

In a country such as the United States, where the Bible has played so central a role in both religious and cultural life, it is not surprising that there are many voices that proclaim that the nation's survival is dependent upon its acting in a way that is acceptable to God. Representative religious figures, such as the Rev. Jesse Jackson on the left and the Rev. Jerry Falwell on the right, are far closer to each other in their basic theological presuppositions than is generally realized. *Both religious leaders reject the ultimacy of political values* in the life of the nation and insist that the nation must unconditionally subordinate its political interests to a standard which is said to derive its authority and legitimacy from God. Their critique of contemporary American politics has its roots in the prophets' condemnation of Israel's political leaders for their failure to keep the covenant. In Jackson's case, America has failed to keep the covenant by its exploitation of the Third World in the foreign arena and its exploitation of its minorities, largely of Third World origin, at home. For Falwell, and those who think as he does, America's failure is largely to be found in the power of "secular humanism" to destroy American moral life. Both Jackson and Falwell would, of course, insist that they have not subordinated the state's need to maintain itself to religious and ethical values. They would argue that it is in America's political interest to behave in what they regard as a religiously appropriate way, since America's survival depends upon her ability to be a Godly nation. Here again, both men echo the warnings and denunciations leveled by the prophets at Israel's political leaders. Mendenhall has expressed the prophetic message succinctly and accurately:

> . . . The rejection of those ethical controls that were identified with the rule of God and constituted the rejection of God Himself, and therefore the corporate existence brought about by that divine rule could no longer by legitimized by appeal to Yahweh. On the contrary, it must be destroyed as the enemy of Yahweh. But there is nothing in the prophetic message that would prescribe the death penalty for all persons; rather it is

the social institutions of state and temple that must go, once they have ceased to be responsible either to Yahweh or to those in society who most need protection.[11]

If we compare this message to that offered by the religious left and right today, we will notice the similarities.

There is yet another feature of covenant religion which continues to influence American religious thinking about power to this day: When the Assyrians destroyed the Northern Kingdom in 722 BC and the Babylonians destroyed Judea in 586 BC, the prophets saw the national catastrophes as evidence of the majesty and sovereignty of the God of the covenant. Although they could not help but be moved by the disaster that befell their people, they nevertheless saw the terrible events as a vindication of their value system.[12] It is no exaggeration to say that a certain apocalyptic thread continues to manifest itself in contemporary American life because of the continuing influence of the prophetic theology of power. Sometimes, one discerns in the religious left a kind of guilt-ridden insistence that America does not deserve to survive unless it repents of its alleged past political sins and becomes a leader in the struggle for liberation of the oppressed peoples of the world. Translated into simpler language, the message becomes: A capitalist America deserves to perish. It is not surprising that the religious left has not only been a consistent opponent of mainstream American foreign policy, but has had a tendency to take sides with the rivals of the United States in almost every international conflict. Instead of seeing America as seeking to maintain its security in a world in which all nations give priority to their own interests, the left sees capitalist America as rebelling against God by her selfishness. Like such prophets as Jeremiah, who regarded Babylonia's destruction of Jerusalem as God's judgment against a sinful Israel, the religious left has had a tendency to view America's recent defeats as chastisements the country richly deserves.[13] To say the least, this is a highly problematic subordination of the political imperative of national security to a religiously inspired ideology.

A catastrophic and apocalyptic note is also sounded by the religious right. Here the message in its simplest terms is that an unbelieving, unrepentant, un-christian America is in danger of perishing. Once again, the religious takes priority over the political. There is, however, an important difference between the religious right and left: the religious right does not insistently favor the rivals and opponents of America in every international conflict. Moreover, on national defense issues, the religious right has had a far more realistic understanding of the defense requirements of the United States than has the left.

The perceptions of the religious right also seem more on target than those of their opponents in their claim that there must be a religious basis for community. Here the experience of the Hebrews at Sinai is instructive. Let us recall that the escaped fugitives did not share either common kinship or common religion before Sinai. That which gave them the unity that made their existence as a people viable was their unity in a common God and a common set of obligations. As we have suggested, without that unity, they would have been an anomic horde with little possibility of long-term survival. Scripture records a second occasion when a number of previously diverse tribal groups united themselves by accepting the God of the covenant, the meeting at Shechem when Joshua demanded of the tribes that they forsake their ancestral gods and serve Yahweh alone (Joshua 24:1–28). According to contemporary biblical scholarship, on that occasion, the original community of Israel was augmented by the addition of a number of new groups from the land of Canaan.[14] Once more, diverse peoples were able to unify themselves by common service of a single God where there had been no other shared community.

We have already noted that the United States is also a country that includes a very large number of groups of diverse origins. Perhaps no other country in the world has so great a measure of diversity. Unfortunately, in addition to our diversity of origin, we are beset by an absence of any kind of value consensus. Regretably, without some basis for unity beyond the fact that we all think of ourselves as Americans, there is the danger that the country might splinter apart, not in normal times when sheer inertia prevents national fragmentation, but in times of radical crisis. Historically, common faith or common origin have been the most viable basis for national unity. The religious right intuits that we are in danger of having neither. People who do not share common values are not likely to feel bound by shared obligation. In a time of crisis, the absence of any shared basis of value and community could constitute a national peril.

It is, however, this writer's conviction that the religious right adds to national disunity by its insistence that political leaders be evaluated largely in terms of what the right regards as non-negotiable moral issues, such as abortion, sex education and school prayer. The real dangers that confront the United States today require that our political leaders be men and women of uncommon ability. To judge their fitness on the basis of single issues, or even on the stand they took on issues a decade ago, as was the case in attacks by some members of the religious right against Justice Sandra Day O'Connor when she was nominated by President Reagan for her current position on the Supreme Court, is to run the risk of excluding capable and dedicated men and women from public office and diverting the attention of the nation from the overwhelmingly difficult economic, diplomatic and military problems that confront it to single issues which, no matter how important they may be, must be weighed in the balance with the other problems that confront us. Moreover, it does not follow that because America requires a non-secular basis for community, we shall find it in the foreseeable future. Although the religious right sees the roots of contemporary moral relativism in what it identifies as "secular humanism," even the most elementary study of the history of Western civilization will demonstrate that secularism and the religio-ethical problems that attend it have been with us with ever-increasing force since the beginning of the modern period. Events such as the Protestant Reformation, the Enlightenment, and the rise of capitalism have all contributed to the rise of modern secularism. Almost all responsible social theorists have been painfully aware of the dangers of the moral relativism that is an inevitable consequence of secularism.[15] It is, unfortunately, easier to identify a disorder than it is to find an effective cure. Moreover, while the cure is being sought, there are urgent tasks which await the nation as a whole. Those of us who believe that the internal and external problems confronting our country have grown in severity in recent years cannot rejoice in the kind of divisive politics that has become the style of both the religious left and the religious right.

If the religious right is internally divisive, the religious left is positively myopic when weighing the relative merits of the United States and the Eastern European bloc. Recently, the Central Committee of the World Council of Churches met in Dresden, East Germany, where it was welcomed by Erich Honecker, the head of the Communist Party of the GDR. According to the liberal *New Republic,* "a practically infallible predictor of who will be singled out by the WCC . . . for condemnation is a country's ideological affinity with the US."[16] Such hostility to the US and willingness to break bread with the leader of one of the more repressive regimes in the Eastern bloc can make sense only to those who long ago committed themselves to a religiously-legitimated political ideology, with an inexhaustible fund of apologies for the abuses of left-wing governments, and an utter intolerance of even the smallest failings in the capitalist world. Unfortunately, the anti-Americanism of the religious left is more likely to grow stronger for the foreseeable future. Most mainstream religious organizations, including the major denominations and the WCC, are administered bureaucratically. Since bureaucracies tend to be self-perpetuating, once the religious left gains control of a denominational or an organizational bureaucracy, it is very likely to select its decision-making personnel on the basis of the compatibility of their political views with that of those in control of the apparatus.

Both within the religious left and the right, the conception of power implicit in the biblical covenant continues to exert a powerful influence in our own day. Perhaps, the influence of biblical ideas has never been stronger because of the ability of religious leaders to reach mass audiences through electronic communication. Nevertheless, there may be some serious limitations involved in the unreflective use of biblically-derived norms to evaluate contemporary political decision-making. As we have noted, the covenant accorded primacy to a religiously-legitimated personal ethic over the interests of the state.

Fifty years ago, Reinhold Niebuhr criticized the liberals of his day for their failure to discern the difference between "the morality of individuals and the morality of collectives, whether races, classes or nations."[17] Niebuhr held that the distinction between these two moralities often "justifies and necessitates political policies which a purely individual ethic must always find embarassing."[18] An important reason for Niebuhr's distinction is that normally, conflicts between individuals can be adjudicated peacefully by an impartial arbiter. There is no impartial arbiter that can be trusted to adjudicate between conflicting nations. States, therefore, must adopt very different modes of behavior than do individuals if they are to survive. This simple distinction has not been taken seriously by either the religious left or the right. It is, of course, understandable that this should be so, since the biblical source of inspiration for their approach to politics implicitly rejects the distinction.

It has been emphasized in this paper that the covenant was functional in its original situation and that it facilitated the creation of a new community for a group of tenuously united fugitives who had been without access to the normal levers of power within an established community. Nevertheless, once the covenant community was established and in possession of its own territorial base, it found itself confronted by the same dilemmas of power and national interest as all of the other kingdoms of the ancient Near East. The Israelite kingdoms had to defend themselves, sometimes by making war, sometimes by making alliances with their neighbors. Often, these alliances were ratified by the marriage of an Israelite king and a pagan princess. The covenant's demand for rendering exclusive homage to Yahweh simply could not be maintained by Israel's rulers without dangerously offending their allies and putting at hazard the security of the state. Of course, the prophets insisted that exclusive fidelity to Yahweh constituted the real security of the state, but which of us, had we been a ruler, would have deliberately endangered our nation's security in order to meet the prophetic demand for religious exclusivity? Similarly, the prophets accused the kings of favoring the rich over the poor, an accusation that is still heard in the land. Nevertheless, is it not possible that there are times when those who control large resources are a greater source of strength for the state than those who have no competence in the control of resources? It is not my intention to advocate that the rich be favored over the poor. My purpose is to suggest that there are times when the state must make decisions that do not always conform to our customary ideas of what is fair and equitable between individuals.

It is not surprising that, faced with similar political and social problems, the rulers of the Israelite kingdoms began to respond as did the other rulers in the area. Political values, especially the state's fundamental requirement that it maintain its monopoly of force against both internal and external opponents, took precedence over individual ethical values; the religion of the landless, escaped slaves was found to be less functional than the agrarian religion of Canaan to men who now possessed and had to defend their own turf.

We know how the prophets reacted to this development. We also know that the prophets' response formed the basis for much of the contemporary criticism of the state in countries with a strongly biblical culture, such as the United States. What we regard as a natural and perhaps inevitable political and social evolution in ancient Israel was regarded by the prophets as unpardonable idolatry for which Israel deserved the worst kind of punishment. It can, however, be said in defense of Israel's rulers that *a very different set of values is necessary to create a community, where none had previously existed, than is required to maintain that community.* As soon as the problems of maintenance displaced those of creation, some means had to be found to legitimate the interests of the state. One can dethrone the old gods when one is rejecting the old order. When one seeks a psychologically effective and cost-effective means of maintaining the new order, there will almost always be the strong compulsion to resacralize political institutions, or at the very least, to ascribe primacy to the state.

It can, of course, be argued that Israel's trust in political institutions proved futile, that both the kingdoms of Israel and Judah fell to the assaults of their enemies. Much of the continuing authority of the prophets came from the fact that their prophecies of doom proved accurate. Nevertheless, it does not follow from the fact that the prophets were correct in predicting disaster, that they were also correct in their analysis of its causes. This observation also applies to the contemporary would-be prophets who offer their judgments on American politics. Is it reasonable to believe that the kingdoms of Israel and Judah would have been able to withstand the assaults of the Assyrians and the Babylonians if they had scrupulously maintained the personal and religious obligations of the covenant? What destroyed the two small kingdoms was their relative military weakness. If permitted to develop, such a flaw might someday destroy the United States as well. Undoubtedly, national morale in ancient Israel would have been higher had the prophets' warnings against the exploitation of the poor been heeded, but even a perfectly just Israelite state could not have withstood the assaults that were directed against it.

There is a measure of irony in the fact that the religious values that originated in the needs of escaped slaves have perennially been the basis of so much of the religious criticism of politics in countries with a Judeo-Christian heritage. Yet on reflection, this phenomenon is not so strange. Normally, those who have turned to the prophetic critique of politics have been men and women with no realistic access to decision-making power within the political arena. A hierarchy of values originally formulated by the powerless has been more symmetrical with the condition and social location of most of the religious critics of politics than with those who possess effective means to influence the decision-making process. It is also interesting to note that, when those who use the ethic of the powerless do gain power, they invariably become just as insistent, even ruthless, in maintaining their power as those whom they have displaced. They can and do claim that their exercise of power, not excluding murder on a large scale, is in the service of a higher righteousness. How often have we seen that process at work in the revolutions of our own era!

The powerless are always more likely to emphasize individual ethical values than those with power, because their lives are essentially private; whereas those with decision-making power must act in the public realm, enduring the risks and responsibilities of their station. Perhaps the problem of religion and politics in contemporary America can best be summed up by the fact that the majority of Americans have little understanding of the difference between the risks and responsibilities of the public and private realms. That distinction was clearly understood by the Greeks, but it could not have been understood by the escaped slaves at Sinai, for the slave was ever a stranger to the public realm.[19] That is perhaps the final paradox of religion and politics in America. Our religious leaders tend to evaluate the public realm in terms of values that derive from escaped slaves who had no place in the public realm. But we are incapable of taking seriously the fact that when the descendants of the escaped slaves entered the public realm, they realized the limitations of the slaves' original values. Instead of learning from their experience, we discredit it, because the original experience of the escaped slaves has been decisive in forming our permanent image of mankind's obligations to God. Still, we in America have no choice but to take the awesome responsibilities of the public realm seriously. It is a mistake to evaluate that realm according to norms that are appropriate only between private individuals. We have power in greater measure than any other community has ever had before. Unfortunately, so, too, do our potential enemies. Perhaps the time has come to reexamine the foundations of the religious critique of American politics.

NOTES

1. An earlier version of this paper was published by The Washington Institute for Values in Public Policy in 1984.
2. See George E. Mendenhall, *The Tenth Generation: The Origins of the Biblical Tradition* (Baltimore: 1973), pp. 1–31.

3. See Moshe Greenberg, "The Hab/Piru," *American Oriental Series,* Vol. 39 (New Haven: 1955), pp. 55–57.
4. See Gerhard von Rad, *Old Testament Theology* (London: 1973), Vol. 1, pp. 8–9, 20.
5. See Greenberg, "The Hab/Piru," loc. cit.
6. On Islam, see Montgomery Watt, *Muhammed at Mecca* (Oxford: 1953), p. 153 ff.
7. See, for example, Exodus 3:13. After God reveals himself, Moses is depicted as asking him, "If I go to the Israelites and tell them, and they ask me his name, what shall I say?" See also Exodus 6:2,3 in which God is depicted as saying to Moses, "I am the Lord. I appeared to Abraham, Isaac and Jacob as God Almighty. But I did not let myself be known to them by the name of Yahweh."
8. See article, "Covenant" in *Encyclopedia Judaica* (Jerusalem: 1972) V., pp. 1012–22; George E. Mendenhall, *Law and Covenant in Israel and the Ancient Near East* (Pittsburgh: 1955).
9. On the collections in Scripture that are said to derive from the encounter at Sinai, see von Rad, *Old Testament Theology,* Vol. 1, pp. 197 ff. On the ethical character of the contents, see Mendenhall, *The Tenth Generation,* pp. 29–30.
10. For a comprehensive discussion of the theology of covenant in the Bible, see Dennis J. McCarthy, S.J., *Old Testament Covenant* (Richmond, Va.: 1972).
11. Mendenhall, *The Tenth Generation,* p. 30.
12. See article, "Prophecy," *The New Encyclopedia Britannica* (1981), Vol. 1, p. 645.
13. Jeremiah 26:1–24 describes Jeremiah's prophecies of doom and the reaction of his hearers.
14. See George Mendenhall, "The Hebrew Conquest of Palestine" in *The Biblical Archaeologist Reader* (Garden City, N.Y.: 1970), pp. 25–53.
15. See Anthony Giddens, *Capitalism and Modern Society Theory* (Cambridge, Ma.: 1971), pp. 178–184.
16. Charles Krauthammer, "Holy Fools" in *The New Republic,* September 9, 1981, pp. 10–13. For a discussion of the movement towards an anti-American bias on the part of the WCC, see Ernest W. Lefever, *Amsterdam to Nairobi: The World Council of Churches and the Third World* (Washington: 1979).
17. Reinhold Niebuhr, *Moral Man and Immoral Society* (New York: 1932), p. XI.
18. Niebuhr, *Moral Man,* loc. cit.
19. See Hannah Arendt, *The Human Condition* (Chicago: 1958). pp. 22 ff.; and Giddens, *Capitalism and Modern Society Theory*, pp. 178–84.

2

Who Speaks for America? Religious Groups and Public Policy Formation

LEO SANDON

Introduction

Paul Tillich maintained that "Religion is the substance of culture, culture is the form of religion."[1] Tillich's aphorism implies two important points, the first being that at the heart of culture is religion—our understanding of ultimate reality and our articulation of the values by which we live. The second implication is that religion, in both its social and personal aspects, is culturally formed. Religion and culture, therefore, are inextricably related in a dialectical way.

Politics is ubiquitous to culture in both normative and functional ways. When Aristotle maintained that humans are political animals, he did not mean that we have a political instinct or an inborn knowledge of politics. Aristotle meant that political life belongs to human fulfillment and that it conforms to human nature. For Aristotle, politics were normative and ubiquitous to culture in a functional sense: government is inherent in the nature of the social order. The truth of R. M. MacIver's observation is fundamental to an understanding of the role of politics in all group life:

> Wherever man lives on earth, at whatever level of existence, there is a social order, and always permeating it is government of some sort. Government is an aspect of society.[2]

Politics is the human enterprise by which things get done. There are many factors which limit the range of political possibilities. Historical, economic, and biological forces are obvious checks on the number of options for policy formulation. There is, nevertheless, a priority which belongs to politics as the only way in which some options are selected and others rejected. The political framework of economic life, for example, is easily demonstrated even though the universal economic reality is the scarcity of resources. Decisions concerning the use of scarce resources are political in nature. The "eternal laws" of classical or Marxist economics thus are valid only under certain historical, social, and political conditions. There is a logical and functional priority of the political order over the economic order, logical because the very definition of property is provided by the political order, and functional because decisions regarding the production and distribution of goods, finally, are political decisions. The same priority of the political order over other basic human institutions can be demonstrated.

Religion relates to the political order in both normative and functional ways. It relates normatively to politics because the structure of the political order is as much a matter of integration as it is domination. Force alone cannot hold social groups together. The political order needs authority—legitimated power—as well as raw force. Religion seeks to provide the ultimate legitimation for the social order.[3] The final explanations and justifications for institutional arrangements traditionally have been provided by religion. In addition, religion frequently relates in a functional way to the political order because political decisions are shot through and through with assumptions about human nature and human social good—assumptions which are important to religious communities.

The question which we pose in this essay is: "Which religious groups are currently attempting to provide the moral legitimation for the American experience?" The problem of finding a legitimate religious perspective from which America can be both affirmed and judged is made difficult by the modern phenomenon of pluralism.[4] Peter Berger observes that:

> In a pluralistic situation, for reasons that are readily visible to historical and social-scientific observation, the authority of all religious traditions tends to be undermined.[5]

American society, always theoretically pluralistic, is now radically pluralistic. Richard John Neuhaus correctly observes that the current contest is not between the Moral Majority and the immoral minority but, rather, between "moral minorities in conflict."[6] Many religious groups presume to speak either for, or at least to, the essential meaning of the American experience. One useful way of classifying a number of these religious communities is the designation, "mainline."

Mainline Religious Groups

The term is derived from railroad culture where the mainline is the principal route, as contrasted to a branch line or a side track. Mainline has an elitist connotation in American social history in that originally it connoted the aristocratic district just outside Philadelphia, served by the Pennsylvania Railroad. Those of us who write about religion in America use mainline to refer to those religious groups which are viewed as established and traditional and which commonly are designated mainline by journalists, historians, and sociologists. For many years, mainline meant white Protestant, but Roman Catholicism and Judaism—Reform and Conservative Judaism—are now on the religious mainline in America. Mainline bodies tend not to be exclusivist in their religious claims and are therefore ecumenical in outlook.[7] Mainline religious groups include: Reform and Conservative Judaism; the United Church of Christ; the United Methodist Church; the recently reunited Presbyterian Church, USA; the new Lutheran denomination—the Evangelical Lutheran Church in America; the American Baptist Convention; the Episcopal Church; the Roman Catholic Church, and the Reformed Church in America.

Some of the older mainline groups, more or less descendants of the Puritans, compiled an impressive record of articulating the ultimate meaning of the American experience. Martin E. Marty and Robert T. Handy described their efforts in *Righteous Empire* and *A Christian America,* respectively.[8] The influence of these groups has been declining the past thirty years. Mainline liberals have given up building a Christian America for more modest enterprises. As a Presbyterian social ethicist recently remarked to me, "H. Richard Niebhur's idea of transforming culture is now unrealistic; the appropriate understanding is subverting culture—Christ subverting culture."

Mainline Protestant bodies have been losing members throughout the 1970s, although there are indications of a slowdown in membership losses the past five years.[9] Each denomination has experienced conflict among its members over confessional issues, the understanding of the Church's mission, and the nature of religious authority.[10] In the 1970s, most mainline groups were preoccupied with matters of institutional reorganization. The National Council of Churches of Christ in America, for over thirty years the voice of mainline ecumenical social action, is under seige today both from internal and external critics for allegedly promoting policies which do not reflect the position of its member communities. The credibility of mainline Protestant leadership has been in decline as part of the general declension of the liberal political establishment with which it has been closely identified for the past forty years.

Mainline Protestant leaders have enlisted a number of their constituents in a peace movement which is proving to be their first significant social action effort since the civil rights movement of the 1960s. Effectiveness in influencing public policy formulation has, nevertheless, shifted from Protestant mainliners to the Roman Catholic hierarchy. Roman Catholic initiative on the nuclear arms issue has had more impact than its Protestant counterparts.

Catholic inclusion in the religious mainline is one of the important developments of the past thirty years in American religion and culture. The fact that the Roman Catholic bishops have written a pastoral letter condemning nuclear war and calling for a nuclear freeze is not without irony. American bishops heretofore had been known for their largely uncritical and unstinting support of United States military policy. It was an important event, then, when on May 3, 1983, the bishops voted 238–9 in favor of a pastoral letter which called upon Catholics to rid the world of nuclear weapons.[11]

The preparation of the pastoral letter spotlighted the United States Roman Catholic hierarchy as no other issue in American history. Critics from within the Reagan Administration sought to modify certain statements between the second and third drafts of the letter. Conservative Catholics were openly critical of the various drafts. The bishops, undaunted by such significant opposition, produced a document which blazed new paths in the church's teaching on social justice. The letter's influence has been pervasive. Kenneth A. Briggs assessed the letter's probable impact with the comment: "These themes will now echo throughout homilies, classrooms and conferences, for the letter has provided an instrument for analyzing not only the moral standards that underlie it, but a range of prudential solutions with which Catholics may agree or disagree."[12] The American bishops have also prepared a pastoral on distributive justice—economics—which has proved to be as provocative as the peace pastoral. Among religious mainliners the initiative and momentum for political influence currently is with the United States Roman Catholic hierarchy.

The only other members of the religious mainline who have the potential to speak for and to America is the Lutheran contingent. The Lutherans have a distinctive theological tradition from which they can speak and, with the decision of three Lutheran bodies to merge into a new denomination of 5½ million members, they now have the numbers. Lutheran energy in America has thus far focused on liturgical and pastoral concerns with less attention to justice issues. Some theologians argue that the Lutheran distinction between Law and Gospel does not provide a rationale for societal formation or transformation. Others maintain that it is precisely the "two realm" tradition in Lutheran social ethics which equips Lutherans to contribute to political discussion. Lutheran influence on American public policy formation remains potential.

In the 1980s, attention has not been so much on the American religious mainline as it has been on the new religious political right. The generic storyline for mainline journalists is one or another version of "the fundamentalists are coming."

The New Religious Political Right

The most dramatic development in American religion and politics has been the political mobilization of ultraconservative evangelicals; the New Religious Political Right. The Moral Majority, Inc., is the core of the movement, but there are other significant organizations which compose the militant evangelical political coalition.

There is also the Religious Roundtable composed of 56 members—corresponding to the 56 signers of the Declaration of Independence—which includes prominent television evangelists and many of the politicians who are associated with the far right. The Roundtable, which functions as a coordinating body for the militant evangelicals, sponsored the famous National Affairs Briefing in Dallas, Aug. 21–22, 1980. The Briefing was attended by approximately 12,000 conservative ministers who heard Ronald Reagan call for a return to the "old time religion" and the "old time Constitution."

Yet another organization is Christian Voice, a political organization of ultra-conservative evangelical ministers that was organized in 1979. The formation of Christian Voice was occasioned by the IRS's investigation of evangelical schools in 1978. In the recent national election, Christian Voice compiled a rating system of the voting records of congressmen, with special reference to homosexuality, abortion and pornography.

The Moral Majority, now absorbed into the newly titled "Liberty Federation," has attracted much attention and is credited with having a significant impact on recent presidential and congressional elections. Since its founding, the organization's national membership has grown to over 400,000, 72,000 of whom are ministers.

The politically aroused evangelicals believe that America is morally adrift and that time is running out to restore national righteousness. They are against abortion, pornography, the acceptance of homosexuality and the Equal Rights Amendment—the pro-family package. They are for prayer in public schools, unconditional support for Israel as a nation, unrestricted private enterprise and a superior national defense. They will support candidates who are right on these issues and pray for those who are wrong.

The rubric for all that is evil in American life is humanism—secular humanism. "The little tugboat of humanism is pulling America into moral degradation." Humanists, according to the ultraconservative evangelicals, are persons who believe in atheism, evolution, situational ethics, the autonomous person and socialistic one-worldism. The Moral Majority argues that the official religion of the public schools is humanism. To many, they explain, the word religion means a belief in God. Religion, however, really means that which is basic and ultimate. That which is most important to us is our religion. What we have in the public schools (or government schools) is religious humanism: a militant, anti-Christian faith.

There is nothing particularly new about religious and political conservatism operating together in the United States. Christian anti-communist crusades flourished in the 1950s and the early 1960s. The late J. Howard Pew, founder of the Sun Oil Company, established and financed The Christian Freedom Foundation, which is engaged in the advocacy of the free enterprise system. I once heard the founder and first chairman of the Florida Moral Majority offer a prayer at a George Wallace rally, in which he described Wallace's 1972 Presidential campaign as "God's man and movement for this hour." There are, however, four new factors which are present in current conservative evangelical political activism.

First, there is the new breed of an American religious type, the independent evangelist: Today's version of the independent evangelist is the big-time television preacher, the televangelist. The Reverend Falwell's "Old Time Gospel Hour" is carried on 304 television stations in this country and 69 abroad. In Lynchburg, Virginia, Falwell presides over the Thomas Road Baptist Church, a private Christian academy, the Liberty Baptist College and the headquarters of his vast electronic empire. Other prominent television evangelists are Pat Robertson of the 700 Club (Virginia Beach, Virginia), Jimmy Joe Swaggart (Baton Range, Louisiana) and the Reverend James Robinson of Hurst, Texas, vice-president of the Religious Roundtable, whose television program, "Man with a Message," is popular in the Southwest. These preachers have created a mammoth electronic constituency.[13] The television congregations have proved to be a reservoir of financial resources for incredible fund–raising feats as has become evident in the scandals which resulted in the downfall of Jim Bakker.

A second important factor is the linkage between these ministries and leaders of the New Right. Men who are former school administrators, business executives and political organizers have organized the conservative evangelical constituency into a cohesive coalition. The three key leaders of New Right political activity have been Richard Viguerie, the professional fund raiser and publisher of the *Conservative Digest;* the late Terry Dolan of the National Conservative Political Action Committee (NCPAC); and Paul Weyrich, director of the Committee for the Survival of a Free Congress (CFSFC). Weyrich and Viguerie founded the CFSFC and the Heritage Foundation, the conservative think tank, in 1974. Weyrich, a political conservative and Eastern Rite Catholic, discovered "The Sleeping Giant" of the ultra-conservative constituency. Two other names of some importance are the Religious Roundtable's president, Ed McAteer, and Howard Phillips, the head of the Conservative Caucus. Weyrich organized Christian Voice in 1979, giving the New Right access to the religious fundamentalist constituency. McAteer introduced Phillips to Falwell, and soon thereafter Falwell organized Moral Majority with the Reverend Bob Billings as the executive director. Up until that time, Billings had been Weyrich's deputy at CFSFC.

Falwell thus founded Moral Majority on the advice of, and in consultation with, a group of New Right veterans who are professional organizers and managers. These men know how to use computer mailing lists and they are skilled in organizational development. The constituency is no longer a diffuse Bible Belt population led by charismatic leaders who are short on organizational competence.

A third factor contributing to the movement's success is the willingness of militant evangelicals to enter into coalition with those who do not share the same theological beliefs. In the past, the fundamentalists' obsession for doctrinal purity hampered their ability to form alliances or enter into coalition. A Utah Moral Majority chapter recently has been organized, even though Mormon theology is a scandalous heresy to an independent Baptist. Mormons, as politically conservative Americans, are right on all of the key moral issues. Ultraconservative evangelicals now are willing to enter into political coalition with those with whom they cannot enter into full religious fellowship. Cooperation with Roman Catholics, which in the past would have been problematical if not unthinkable, has become part of the working strategy. Weyrich refers to this development as reverse ecumenism "because the original ecumenical movement was a very liberal movement. And now we have cooperation among . . . all kinds of people who frankly didn't speak to each other."

A fourth factor, and the most important one that has given impetus to evangelical politics, is the establishment over the past 25 years of a network of private Christian academies. There are over 20,000 Christian schools in the United States, and they have both defined and consolidated the conservative evangelical subculture. Leaders of the Christian school movement claim that a new Christian school is birthed in the United States every seven hours.[14] Certainly the movement is a significant force in American society. It is my thesis that the interests of the private evangelical academy both provoked the ultraconservative evangelical political movement and provided its leadership network.

The 1978 decision of the Internal Revenue Service to challenge the tax-exempt status of private Christian schools—especially segregated schools in the South—provoked a strong response. Weyrich moved quickly to express the New Right's sympathy and support for the schools. One of Moral Majority's admonitions to its members is that they must resist the government interference that would "stifle and harass" them in their Christian education mission. The leadership of Moral Majority consists largely of men who were administrators of private Christian schools.

The core membership of Moral Majority can be described as fundamentalist in heritage, belief, and lifestyle. Fundamentalism emerged as a movement in the late 19th century and became a more militant and narrowly gauged expression of Protestant Christianity than mainstream evangelicalism.

The Moral Majority's message is appealing to millions of Americans who do not belong to the fundamentalist subculture. Belief in the importance of personal morality, a devotion to free enterprise capitalism and a conviction that we must maintain military superiority are positions held by what probably is a majority of Americans.

Marion G. "Pat" Robertson's all but announced presidential candidacy is not so much a candidacy for the presidency as it is for the leadership of the new religious right. Robertson is attempting to replace Falwell as the chief spokesman for the ultra-conservative evangelicals. He will probably be a political broker when the Republicans choose a vice-presidential candidate in 1988, just as Falwell was in 1980.

By far the best educated of the prime-time preachers, Robertson is a Phi Beta Kappa graduate of Washington and Lee University and the Yale Law School. He has been giving erudite lectures on a variety of subjects for years and has an impressive command of the facts. As a founder of the Christian Broadcasting Network, he is one of the leading televangelists—a master of his medium. He can hold his own with most candidates on the platform and in debate, as well as on the tube. Robertson is off and running and he runs well.

The new version of the religious political right is probably going to be a significant force in American politics throughout and beyond the 1980s. A particular electorate has been organized, its views on specific issues have been shaped, a common language has been learned and a network of communication has been established. Money is being raised to support candidates and to influence policy at federal, state, and local levels. Workers are being trained in the techniques of political organization. The new religious political right's leaders, while not learned men, are nonetheless shrewd, industrious, and wise in the ways of organizational development.

It is unlikely that the religious right will capture either political party. But the politically mobilized fundmentalists are achieving a level of mass-media attention in the 1980s that they have not enjoyed since the 1920s, a result of their involvement in national politics.

Other Evangelicals

Not all evangelicals are members of the New Religious Political Right. The largest evangelical denomination in America, the Southern Baptist Convention, with 14 million members, is moving closer to the New Religious Political Right, but many of the 43 denominations which comprise the National Association of Evangelicals have not endorsed the NRPR.

Evangelicals are so diverse and diffuse in America that it is inappropriate to treat them as one group. Many evangelicals are not politically inclined. Among the politically active are those who are liberal or even radical in their politics. There is an evangelical left. Jim Wallis, the editor of *Sojourners* magazine, has been arrested for anti-nuclear protest in the Capitol Rotunda in Washington, D.C. In a recent evangelical conference, Wallis said that "it is increasingly clear that the nuclear arms race will not be ended by the use of traditional political channels alone. It will take a powerful movement of nonviolent direct action, as powerful as the civil rights movement or Gandhi's Indian independence movement."[15] At the same conference, Ed Robb, head of the Institute on Religion and Democracy, gave an impassioned plea for military and nuclear preparedness: "The Japanese attacked Pearl Harbor because we were unprepared. Argentina attacked the Falklands because they didn't think Great Britain had the will or the ability to fight."[16]

There is no simple evangelical consensus on the meaning of America in the 1980s. Evangelicals, as is the case with mainliners, are in a period of agonizing reappraisal of their social agenda.

Jewish Contributions to Public Policy Formulation

American Jews constitute a self-conscious religious minority, the views of which have been determined by two thousand years of life in an abnormal situation. As a minority with a long and heavy history, American Jews, to use Jacob Neusner's felicitous phrase, are "strangers at home." Neusner is correct in identifying the foci for American Jewish reflection as the Holocaust and the establishment of the State of Israel.[17]

Preoccupation with Zionism and with various levels of anti-Semitism sometimes leads toward single issue politics on the part of members of the American Jewish community. American policy in the Middle East and issues monitored by the major Jewish defense agencies—the Anti-Defamation League, the American-Jewish Committee and the American Jewish Congress—provide much of the agenda for Jewish political life. There is, to be sure, an impressive degree of Jewish participation in American political and intellectual life, but there is little evidence of a distinctively Jewish perspective on the meaning of America.

Black Religious Groups

The Black Church has been the central institution of Afro-American life since the post-Civil War era, and was the institutional base for the civil rights movement in the 1960s. Much of Martin Luther King, Jr.'s rhetoric was based on his version of the American dream—"I have a dream." It is important to note that the civil rights effort in the 1960s was a social movement which transcended any particular Black denomination.

Since the 1960s, the Black Church in America has not been able to articulate a compelling vision for American policy. The largest black denomination, the National Baptist Convention, USA, with 5.5 million members, currently is undergoing a change in leadership and direction which may make it a more progressive force in American religious life. The AME denominations, that is, black Methodist Churches, work closely with white denominations in the ecumenical mainstream. Other black denominations, largely independent evangelicals and pentecostals, have a sectarian view of religion which does not include a rigorous social ethic from which they can speak to public policy issues.

In 1983, the Reverend Jesse Jackson mounted a campaign, ostensibly for the Democratic presidential nomination, but really to become a serious broker in the 1984 Democratic convention. Jackson was spokesman for a coalition of interest groups, taking a position left of center in behalf of a tradition of liberal idealism. While not likely to receive the 1988 presidential nomination, Jackson may be able to compel the Democrats to nominate him for Vice-President, thereby alienating conservative whites, or risk losing his powerful minority coalition. The presidential candidacies of Robertson and Jackson, two ordained ministers, one right of center and one left of center, is an intriguing phenomenon which invites a commentator to compare their similarities and differences.

New Religious Movements

Neither the older "new" religions—Hinduism, Buddhism, and Islam—nor the new religions seem to have the numbers, credibility, or religious concepts to speak on the meaning of America. Of the forty or more Hindu groups which are in America today, none have taken a stand on articulating a public philosophy. There are probably 500,000 Buddhists in America with the diversity of liberal and conservative factions which characterizes other religious groups. With the exceptions of Hawaii and California, Buddhist influence is not significant in American culture. Islam is more visible in America as a result of the economics and politics of oil. The Islamic revolution in Iran, accompanied by the taking of American hostages in November, 1979, also increased American interest in Islam. Orthodox (Sunni) centers were organized as early as 1912. Orthodox (Shi'a) Muslims organized in the 1970s as Iraqi and Iranian immigrants arrived in large numbers in the United States. The Black Muslims have now become the World Community of Islam in the West. There are several other Muslim groups, including the Muslim offshoot, Baha'i World Faith, an eclectic religion originating in Persia in the nineteenth century. None of these groups are in a position to speak for and to the meaning of America.

Most of the new religious movements, with the possible exception of Sun Myung Moon's Unification Church, have no significant political component to their mission. The Unification Church has a theological commitment to political transformation and it remains quite visible as probably the most controversial new religious movement in America. The publication of *The Washington Times* and the successful establishment of a public policy institute and sponsorship of symposia are significant activities. The future influence of the Unification Church upon public policy is largely dependent upon its achievement of acceptance in American society, a goal toward which the church is making measurable progress.

Doctrinal Humanism and Practical Humanism

As noted above, "humanism" is an important code word for the new religious political right. The reference usually is to "secular humanism" or to "religious humanism." Typical of the antihumanist rhetoric is the warning issued by Francis Schaeffer, a theologian often quoted in conservative Protestant circles: "Unless humanism is stopped it intends to beat to death the Christian base which made our culture possible."

We can assume that the new religious political right is not referring to academic humanists, those linguists, lexicographers, historians, philosophers, critics, novelists, poets, essayists, and artists who comprise humanities faculties. Neither do the opponents of humanism target the Christian humanist tradition associated with Thomas Aquinas, Erasmus, and Thomas More, more recently with Jacques Maritain and C. S. Lewis. The humanists the new religious right have in mind are those aggressive humanists I call "doctrinal humanists."

Doctrinal humanism is principally expressed in three documents: *A Humanist Manifesto* (1933); *Humanist Manifesto II* (1973); and *The Secular Humanist Declaration* (1980). While differing in tone and emphasis, all three documents affirm the following:

Philosophical Naturalism: The natural world is the only one we know and, consequently, it is the only one that matters. Persons should learn to live in the here-and-now, forsaking the supernatural and all hopes of personal immortality.
Scientific Rationalism: Appeals to divine revelation, mystical insight and intuition must pass the bar of reason. Truth is best discovered rationally.
Anthropocentrism: Human beings possess ultimate worth. Humans are the sole source of morals and values, and the highest human achievement is always the improvement of the human condition.
Evolutionary Optimism: History demonstrates that human progress and the future will be better than the past if human beings proceed ethically and rationally.
Democratic Autonomy: No decision-making system has proved superior to democracy. Humanists would implement democratic procedures in business, politics, religion and education, with the expectation that this would enhance personal freedom and individual security.

For some individuals, these ideals have become the basis for a humanistic faith replacing traditional Judaism or Christianity. These persons are doctrinal humanists.

There is another type of humanism which I will call "practical humanism." The practical humanist is a person who thinks and acts humanistically while maintaining a more conventional religious identity. The practical humanist believes in the efficacy of technology, accepts a scientific-rational approach to problem-solving, finds the theory of evolution credible, and sees the improvement of the human condition as life's most worthy goal. This same individual may attend a conventional church, accept certain moral laws as eternally valid and tell George Gallup that s/he believes in God and personal immortality. Doctrinal humanists, no longer finding humanism and traditional theism compatible, replace traditional religious identity with a surrogate religion. Practical humanists live with both ideologies, sometimes in uncritical inconsistency, sometimes in uneasy tension.

Doctrinal humanists probably are not the source of threat to traditional American values that the religious right claims. In a sense, both doctrinal humanists and the ultra-conservative evangelicals need each other: they thrive on polemical exchanges. Doctrinal humanists in the U.S. number about 150,000 at most, and can claim few supporters in the upper echelons of business and government.

Humanist themes are nonetheless pervasive in American culture. A nation with a high-technology infrastructure is a fertile breeding ground for practical or *de facto* humanism. Rational, optimistic, human centered, and naturalistic attitudes contribute to the nature of practical humanism. The attractions of traditional religious commitment are still great, however, and many persons will continue to proclaim faith in God, while behaving as humanists in daily life. The conservative evangelicals are at least half right in their identification of humanism as the problem, but the problem is posed by practical humanism rather than by theoretical or doctrinal humanism.

Conclusion

The most significant groups speaking to, and for, the American experience today are (1) the United States Roman Catholic hierarchy which, along with mainline Protestant groups, has placed the moral and ethical dimensions of nuclear arms in the center of national debate and (2) the New Religious Political Right which is calling for a restored America governed by the principles of conservative evangelical Protestantism. We can speculate that any new group or coalition of groups which attempts to speak for the ultimate meaning of America must effectively engage the reality of practical humanism. For the foreseeable future, any successful articulation of the American vision will be a religious position which is biblically based, probably Christian, though open to elements from other major religious traditions. An effective formulation of a new public philosophy must be built on both a serious theological tradition and an attractive spirituality. To speak for, or to, America at the conclusion of the twentieth century, the effective philosophy should probably be culturally conservative, politically liberal, and economically pragmatic.

NOTES

1. Paul Tillich, *Theology of Culture* (London: Oxford University Press, 1969), p. 42.
2. R. M. MacIver, *The Web of Government* (New York: The Macmillan Company, 1947).
3. See Peter L. Berger, *The Sacred Canopy: Elements of a Sociological Theory of Religion* (Garden City, New York: Anchor Books, 1969), pp. 29 ff.
4. In the 1960s and 1970s theologians tended to identify the phenomenon of secularity as the problem. Today there is an emerging consensus that the problem with religious legitimations is not so much secularity, but pluralism.
5. Peter L. Berger, *The Heretical Imperative* (Garden City, New York: Anchor Press/Doubleday, 1979), p. xi.
6. Richard John Neuhaus, "Who, Now, Will Shape the Meaning of America?" *Christianity Today* (March 19, 1982), pp. 19–20.
7. See Dean M. Kelley, *Why Conservative Churches Are Growing* (New York: Harper and Row, 1977), p. 89. Kelley provides an Exclusivist-Ecumenical Gradient which is instructive.
8. Martin E. Marty, *Righteous Empire: The Protestant Experience in America* (New York: The Dial Press, 1970); Robert T. Handy, *A Christian America: Protestant Hopes and Historical Realities* (New York: Oxford University Press, 1971).
9. *Yearbook of American and Canadian Churches* (Abingdon, 1983).
10. See Jeffrey K. Hadden, *The Gathering Storm in the Churches* (Garden City, New York: Doubleday, 1970).
11. *The Challenge of Peace: God's Promise and Our Response* (Washington: National Catholic Documentary Service, May 19, 1983, Vol. 13: No. 2).
12. Kenneth A. Briggs, *The New York Times* (May 8, 1983), p. E5.
13. Nielson and Arbitron reports, as cited in Samuel S. Hill and Dennis E. Owen, *The New Religious Political Right in America* (Nashville: Abingdon Press, 1982), p. 143.
14. Glenn E. Fox, *Encyclopedia for Christian Schools,* "Foreward" by Morris Sheats (Dallas, Texas: Life Inc., 1980).

15. As reported in *The Christian Century* Vol. 100, No. 22 (July 20–27, 1983), pp. 668–669.

16. *Ibid.*, p. 669.

17. See Jacob Neusner, *Stranger at Home* (Chicago: The University of Chicago Press, 1981).

3

Religion and the Democratization of Culture

LONNIE D. KLIEVER

Historians and social scientists would warn us to approach our theme, "The Worldwide Impact of Religion on Contemporary Politics" with caution. Religion is not one thing worldwide, but many different things. Nor is the impact of religion on politics the same worldwide; it differs widely from society to society. The ideological forms, institutional embodiments and social strategies of the world's religions vary immensely from time to time and from place to place. The impact of religion on politics sometimes inhibits and sometimes promotes change, sometimes enhances and sometimes thwarts justice. To be sure, historians and social scientists have succeeded in reducing this immense variety to manageable proportions through typological comparisons and structural analyses. Thus, religions can be broadly grouped into supernatural or historical world views, church or sect collectivities, world-affirming or world-denying ethics. Nevertheless, our theme can best be explored if we concentrate on particular religious traditions and political systems.

Accordingly, I propose to explore the impact of theistic religion on political democracy, particularly in the American context. In anticipation of fuller discussion below, by "theism" I mean those religious systems which distinguish a sacred realm from the secular world and conceive of that sacred realm in a personalistic and unitary way. Put in less guarded and technical terms, theistic religion believes in a transcendent personal God who is the ultimate source of the world's being and value. By "democracy" I mean those political systems which rest on the formative principle that all governmental power emanates from the people, whether that power issues in a unitary or a republican form of government. Each individual in a democracy is entitled to contribute his or her share to the determination of governmental policies. Put in the popular, though somewhat misleading phrase, political democracy means "rule by the people." Understood in this way, there is a close historical and philosophical connection between theistic religion and political democracy in the West. Some scholars argue that the latter necessarily grew out of and rests on the former. For them, theistic religion is the central historical cause and necessary philosophical basis underlying all democratic forms of government. I personally am not prepared to argue either that historical or philosophical thesis. Mine is a more modest one: Historically, theism and democracy have emerged together in the West and are thus vitally implicated in one another's development. Philosophically, some principle of radical individuation and iconoclasm is necessary for the survival and completion of democracy. From these two theses, I draw the conclusion that a socially privatized and politically neutralized theism does have an important role to play in maintaining political democracies.

Democratization as Cultural Process

To correctly understand theism's historical and philosophical relation to political democracy, we must place these political forms within the context of Western culture as a whole. As Karl Mannheim has brilliantly argued, the "democratization" of politics is but one expression of a wider, ongoing process in the culture at large.[1] Indeed, the democratization of the political order could not have begun apart from these wider cultural transformations. Thus we can see a democratic principle at work, not only in politics but in all expressions of cultural life—in manners, language and education as well as in art, religion and philosophy. In Western culture as a whole, the sheer number of individuals actively participating in cultural life, both as its *creators* and *recipients,* has become increasingly more inclusive and intensive. In other words, the growth of autonomous individualism is more than a mere political phenomenon in the West. Democratization is the pervasive principle of the whole of Western culture.

Mannheim argues his case anecdotally by showing how the democratic ideal has penetrated all areas of culture. In each case, he contrasts an aristocratic to a democratic sensibility. In an aristocratic culture, a class of elites is elevated above the mass and this "distantiation" is reflected in all expressions of culture. But the process of democratization levels down the distance between these elites and the masses. Moreover, this leveling occurs in every area of cultural life—in manners, speech and education, in philosophy, art and religion as well as in politics and economics. In manners, the hereditary superiority of the upper classes and the genteel professions has given way to egalitarian relationships and bureaucratic labor. Democratic sociology accepts the dignity of ordinary persons and everyday work. In speech, the elevated language of cultured breeding and humane wisdom has given way to vernacular discourse and common sense. Democratic linguistics affirms the virtue of candid talk and free discussion. In education, the authoritarian relationship between teacher and pupil has given way to a collaborative pursuit of the truth. Democratic pedagogy assumes the plasticity of all minds and the availability of all knowledge. In reflection, dogmatic appeals to private channels of knowledge have given way to public methods of articulation and verification. Democratic philosophy stresses the unlimited accessibility and communicability of all truth. In art, the classical conventions of monumental art have given way to the intimate realism of perspectival style and easel painting. Democratic aesthetics celebrates the simple beauty of everyday activities and commonplace objects. In religion, the sacral mystique of an uncontestable priesthood and a magic liturgy has given way to lay involvement and private piety. Democratic theology shrinks the distance between the individual believer and the central symbols and rituals of the faith. Mannheim insists that these trends reveal a radical negation of aristocratic distance in every realm of culture. This "de-distantation" opens the way for individuals to find an ever-widening scope for influencing the political, economic and cultural life.

What role has theistic religion played in this culture-wide process of democratization? Certainly not the singular role that many defenders of theism would claim. Throughout most of its history, theism has been aristocratic through and through. Yet the emergence of the great theistic religions did prepare the way for the democratization of culture. Theism's sharp distinction between God and the world, especially evident in the historic religions of Judaism, Christianity and Islam, contributed decisively to the gradual secularization of powers and equalization of persons which fueled the democratization process by "leveling down" the elite and "leveling up" the mass. Viewed in historical perspective, the various cultural shifts which Mannheim catalogues are but the latest stage of a long series of interdependent changes in religion and culture.

Sociologist Robert N. Bellah marks out five such stages of religious symbolization and sociocultural order—primitive, archaic, historic, early modern, and modern.[2] Primitive religion envisioned a mythic world inhabited by ancestral figures, some human and some animal, who were the progenitors of all significant natural occurrences, and the exemplars of all fixed social roles. Primitive religious life was not focused on worshiping these ancestral figures so much as on ritually acting out their heroic deeds and lives. There were no priests and no spectators in primitive ritual enactment. All present were involved, and each participant became one with the mythic heroes and totems. In other words, in primitive cultures there were no *special* religious roles and organizations that were separated from ordinary social roles and organizations. Religious roles and organizations were fused with other cultural tasks and institutions. As such, religion reinforced social solidarity and transmitted social roles from one generation to the next. As a "one-possibility thing," primitive religion furnished little opportunity or inclination to change the world.

Archaic religion elaborated primitive myths and rituals into a systematic complex of gods, priests, worship, sacrifice and, in some cases, divine kingship. For the archaic mind, there was still only one world acted upon by mythical beings who dominate particular parts of it. But those beings were now conceived as actively and willfully controlling the natural and the human world. Moreover, relations among the gods were hierarchically arranged according to their relative prestige and power. Especially important were the "high gods" whose knowledge and power were thought to be vast. Archaic religious institutions were still largely merged with social structures. But the geographical multiplication of worshiping cults and the sociological monopolization of priestly functions signaled the emergence of a "two-class system" that differentiated religious roles and rituals from everyday life. Although archaic religions still grounded traditional social structures and roles in the cosmic order of things, the very notion of gods acting over and against mortals, and of priests mediating between them, introduced an element of openness lacking at the primitive level. Struggles between rival cults created new social alignments and required new religious symbolizations. In other words, the problem of maintaining increasingly complex religious and social orders in some sort of balance tended to undermine the very patterns of archaic religion and culture.

Historic religion, which emerged in societies that were more or less literate, broke through the "cosmological monism" of the earlier stages by affirming a transcendent realm of universal reality. Though articulated in a variety of symbol systems in the Orient and the Occident, the historic religions were all hierarchical and universalistic. In the West, both the earthly and the heavenly worlds were ordered by a personal God that radically transcended the ordinary world of things and of persons. This theistic worldview led for the first time to a conception of a "core self" that was ultimately separable from all conditions of finite existence—from all ignorance, suffering and death. This religious "separation from the world" was, in turn, clearly reflected in the social order that accompanied historic religion. The emergence of a religious elite alongside a political one created a delicate balance of powers between political and religious leadership. This balance was complicated by a corresponding separation of the role of the believer and the role of the citizen among the masses. Given these tensions, balance often became imbalance between power elites, and separation often became opposition between social roles. To be sure, such imbalance and opposition were comparatively rare because the historic religions, like their earlier counterparts, typically sanctioned and stabilized the sociocultural order. But on occasion, the historic religions provided the ideology and inspiration for revolutionary changes in that order.

The last two stages of religious evolution have only emerged in the West from that congeries of events known as the Protestant Reformation and the Enlightenment. The stage of early modern religion retained the dualistic separation of this world and the next, but collapsed all hierarchical structuring of them. The Reformation, followed in turn by the Enlightenment, brought a decisive break with all hierarchical legal and sacramental systems of salvation. This early modern emphasis on the direct relation between the individual and God opened the door to autonomous individualism. Though individual autonomy was still severely limited in religious and moral matters by a rigid orthodoxy and ecclesiastical discipline, individuals were freed to assume increasing control over their own political and economic affairs. The resulting appearance of a variety of worldly organizations free of both ecclesiastical and governmental control multiplied the possibilities for social change. Thereby, early modern religion played a key role in the full emergence of the multi-centered, self-revising social order that characterizes today's democratic societies.

Bellah sees still another stage of religion, profoundly different from the religion of all the earlier stages, emerging out of the last two centuries of intellectual, technological and political change. Modern religion's central feature is the elimination of all vestiges of the hierarchical thinking that were carried over from historical religion into the early modern stage. Modern religion leaves behind all dualistic and authoritarian definitions of reality. Responsibility for making sense out of the ultimate conditions of existence has, in the modern context, shifted more and more to the individual. The church as collective embodiment of a religious perspective survives for many modern men and women, but with far greater fluidity of membership and flexibility of organization. The role of enforcing standards of doctrine and morality has been largely dropped, with the church now serving as a supportive community for those involved in the search for meaningful solutions to individual concerns. The underlying assumption of these trends and changes is that culture and personality are endlessly and individually revisable. In the modern context, religion and culture have become an "infinite-possibility thing" rather than the "one-possibility thing" of the primitive past.

Bellah's descriptive analysis of the sweeping changes in religion and culture over the centuries helps us pinpoint both the gains and the losses in the cultural process of democratization. What has been gained is an immeasurable increase in personal and social freedom. Democratization allows both individuals and groups wide latitude for experimentation with new models of reality and new forms of life. But we have paid an enormous price for this Faustian power. In the aristocratic past, groups were rigidly structured by an authoritarian tradition. Individuals were totally controlled by a hierarchical system. While there was little room for innovation and independence in these stratified societies, there was equally little room for individual anxiety and social turmoil. In contrast, the automatic security and solidarity provided by these predemocratic patterns of order has been lost in the process of democratization. In democratic societies, security and solidarity must be continually reestablished through conflict and compromise between the autonomous individuals and competing groups that constitute the society. In other words, democratization is always an *imperiled* achievement.

Democratization as Imperiled Achievement

We are so prepared to defend the virtues of democracy that we seldom question its vices. We are so accustomed to enjoying the strengths of democracy that we seldom recognize its weaknesses. To be sure, the least reflective truck driver and the most successful financier are both painfully aware of the failings of "the system." But these complaints are passed off as failures to put real democracy into practice. There is, of course, a certain truth to such criticisms of our democratic institutions. Our cultural approximations of the democratic ideal are far from perfect and complete—especially in the realm of politics. But passing off the vices and weaknesses of "the system" as failures to live up to the ideal of democracy obscures the deep structural tensions and innumerable self-neutralizing factors within the process of democratization itself. Democratic cultures are constantly imperiled by either succeeding too well in leveling all differences (what Mannheim calls "massification"), or falling too short of unifying all interests (what Mannheim calls "totalitarianism").

To understand the inherent precariousness of modern democracies, we must grasp the fundamental structural principles of democracy, both in the narrow sphere of politics as well as in the broad context of culture. Following Mannheim again, there are three such principles. The first fundamental principle of democracy is *the equality of all persons.*[3] In predemocratic societies, social authority is linked to the idea of the inherent superiority of the person, the family or the party wielding authority. Kingship is the most obvious example of such inherent superiority, but we see the same stratification in notions of magic charisma, inherent genius, social caste, racial privilege, divine election. But democratic societies deny all such essential vertical distances between the leaders and the led. Political democracy, in fact, extends the sharing of governmental power to all because it is convinced of the essential equality of all human beings.

Of course, the process of democratization has by no means eliminated all the vertical divisions of higher and lower orders in today's world. Nor does the principle of the equality of all human beings imply a mechanical leveling of all quantitative differences within modern society. The point is not that all persons possess equal abilities and endowments, nor even that they all deserve equal recognitions and rewards. But—all embody the same value of *humanness* as such. The democratic principle of equality need not prevent some individuals from becoming superior to others under the conditions of competition. It only demands that the competition be fair as well as free—that no person, class or caste be given greater opportunity and higher status by the accident of birth alone.

The second fundamental principle of democracy is *the autonomy of each self.*[4] In predemocratic societies, social order is regulated and enforced strictly from above. Most individuals are simply denied an autonomous life of their own. The family, the guild, the state and the church are all authoritarian regimes which rule by divine right or hereditary privilege. Exacting obedience from the masses is no problem since these absolute rulers can count on the docility of the common man. But democratic societies extend to the many, rather than reserve for the few the freedom to challenge leaders, to question traditions and to change institutions. In democracies, social consensus is fashioned from below out of discussion and compromise rather than being imposed from above by entitlement and force.

Once again, in today's world the process of democratization still falls far short of mobilizing the vital energies of individuals in shaping the social will. Moreover, the principle of the autonomy of every self does not mean that every individual can constantly make full use of his or her right to influence public decisions. Orderly social life would be impossible if each individual constantly influenced every public decision. Every democratic society must somehow find ways to limit the exercise of individual freedom. But the healthy democracy finds ways to insure that these renunciations of individual freedom are essentially *voluntary* in nature. Thus, for example, representative democracies limit individual freedom by vesting power in the hands of an elected elite, but individuals and groups are still able to make their aspirations and grievances known through their elected representatives and the electoral process.

This brings us to the third fundamental principle of democracy—*the openness of ruling elites.*[5] Democracies no less than other ways of ordering social life are led by elites. Democratization does not do away with all differences between elites and masses. To be sure, there is a leveling of the distance between the two in democratic cultures, but even in political democracies there must still be small groups who explore new cultural possibilities, shape public policy and manage daily affairs. Social order in all but the smallest groups is unthinkable without the inspiration and leadership of elites.

Democratization does, however, bring about a new mode of elite selection and elite sensibility. In predemocratic societies, elites are formed and maintained by hereditary privilege, feudal monopoly, divine right or military prowess. Such aristocratic elites rigorously maintain a qualitative distance between themselves and the masses, even when they are disposed to champion the cause or heed the needs of the masses. Aristocratic elites remain resolutely closed to the masses both with respect to membership and accountability. By contrast, democratic elites are open to the masses in a double sense—members of democratic elites in some way rise out of the mass and are in some way answerable to the mass.

Democratic elites are chosen from the mass they represent and serve. Of course, there are different ways that democratic elites are selected and maintained. As Mannheim explains, people may rise into elite positions of social and especially political leadership by three different routes—bureaucratic advancement, unregulated competition or class pressures. Most democratic societies maintain their stability and continuity through managerial bureaucracies, which provide new leadership through a systematic pattern of bureaucratic advancement. But democratic leadership, particularly in the area of politics, may also arise out of popular competition. Still others are advanced to positions of democratic leadership through membership in some political party or militant minority. The most important thing in democratic elite selection is not the particular manner of choice so much as the breadth of the basis of selection. A system is democratic only if elite recruitment is not limited to some closed group within the larger society.

Democratic elites are also answerable to the mass they serve. Members of the elite are accountable to the mass in the obvious sense that there are mechanisms for their removal or replacement if they do not handle the leadership entrusted to them in an adequate way. But members of democratic elites are answerable to the mass in a more profound way. The elite is responsible for transmitting its new insights and sharing its highest achievements with the masses. This responsibility may lead to the broadening of the elite by including more people from more diverse backgrounds in places of leadership and privilege. But such broadening only proves successful when it represents a "leveling-up" of the mass rather than a "leveling-down" of the elite. Herein is the most distinctive feature of democratic elites—they reduce the distance between themselves and the masses by drawing the masses higher and higher toward their own vision and standard of life. The truly *democratic* elite seeks to cultivate among the masses the specialized knowledge, cultured taste and refined skills required for full access to the highest levels of achievement and leadership within the society. Ideally, democratic elites are self-neutralizing groups bent on sharing with others what they themselves have achieved.

In the light of these three formative principles, we can readily see the dangers *of* and the dangers *to* democracy. There is, within democracy itself, an inherent ambiguity or instability by virtue of a tension between the ideals of universal equality and individual autonomy.[6] As noted above, the equality of all is an affirmation of value rather than an estimate of ability or a calculus of achievement. In a democratic society, there are great individual inequalities of ability and achievement. The divergent interests and aspirations born of empirical differences between individuals can create severe problems for the democratic society precisely because, in principle, these differing individuals are granted the autonomous right to assert themselves within the political process. The principle of equality thus comes into conflict with the principle of autonomy—a contradiction which can never be resolved so long as individual ideals are radically divergent. Of course, the democratic elites bear the responsibility for neutralizing such chaotic conflicts and competition through short-term manipulation and long-term education of the masses. But as the elites themselves become more representative of a fragmented society, the same potential for chaotic conflict and competition is carried into the very heart of social order.

Faced with this unresolved antinomy between its own fundamental principles, democratization as an ongoing process swings precariously between two aberrant forms of democratic social order: *totalitarianism* and *massification.* Far from being the antithesis of democracy, totalitarianism, even in the extreme form of dictatorship, represents one of the ways a democratic society may try to overcome a governing elite's failure to achieve a workable consensus. Indeed, modern totalitarianisms are made possible by the fluidity of leadership and the precariousness of order within democracies, particularly in their early stages of formation or following some massive breakdown of the social order such as economic collapse or military defeat. In the early stages of the democratization of a given society, the reins of power may pass to a military junta or revolutionary cadre totally unprepared for orchestrating the free play of political and social forces within the society as a whole.

Democratization may then be short-circuited in favor of a totalitarian phase. Even if the political process passes into the hands of an experienced elite, their leadership is often taxed beyond capacity by new groups not yet familiar with political realities who use their universal sufferage to embark on wildly utopian schemes or dangerously partisan pursuits. Burdened by such demands, even dictatorship may seem like an acceptable way to discipline the mass and to restore order. Democracies that cannot mobilize or neutralize the divergent interests within their own society are always threatened by the rise of totalitarian elites who will take drastic measures to regain control of a society in shambles.

The other ever-present danger to an immature democracy is massification—the achievement of social solidarity through the radical homogenization of culture. As we have seen, democratization is a process of social and cultural "de-distantiation." In a democracy, the individual finds an ever-widening scope for influencing political, economic and cultural life. But a curious inversion of individual influence can occur if this process is carried to the extreme. As the distance between the typical individual and the social and cultural elites becomes less, the everyday perspective of the typical individual becomes more dominant. As earlier gradations between high and low, aristocrat and commoner, sacred and secular are leveled, social and cultural experience becomes ever more homogeneous. In a field of experience where every single thing carries equal weight, none retains a special dignity or distinctive character. If no object or person is respected above any other, the value of the individual disappears in the mass. Under these circumstances, some kind of "re-distantiation" is required to save the individual from disappearing in the mass.

Here then are the twin nemeses of the process of democratization, born of the unresolved conflict between the fundamental principles of democracy itself. The failure to achieve a consensus based on reasonable compromise because individual autonomy runs unchecked may lead to totalitarianism as the tragic price for restoring order. The individual then counts for nothing and universal *equality* is lost. The opposite peril is equally daunting. The failure to avoid a consensus based on homogeneity because universal equality reigns supreme may lead to massification as the tragic price for achieving order. Here, once again, the individual counts for nothing and individual *autonomy* is lost. Each of these aberrant forms of democracy undercuts one of its foundational principles.

Is there no way to avoid these twin perils? Can the developing democratic society avoid the expediency of totalitarianism and the extreme of massification? Is the fully democratic society impossible to achieve by the very nature of its inherent principles? These questions point us to the true character of democracy. At bottom, radical democratization is an "impossible possibility"—an inspiring vision of social order that ever eludes final completion. In other words, democratization is a *moral* ideal.

Democratization as Moral Ideal

Democratic societies are not self-regulating mechanisms which automatically balance out competing interests and conflicting procedures. To be sure, enduring democracies have built up a system of checks and balances which place limits on partisan power and levy penalties for social disruption. An elaborate system of procedural values, bureaucratic structures and technical mechanisms encourage and enforce socially responsible behavior. But these impersonal patterns of order are never fully effective or persuasive. Finally, these rational procedures operate only so long as the majority of people cooperate! Democratic societies are ultimately held together by a *moral* bond of public responsibility and disinterested goodwill. Democratic societies, no less than their aristocratic predecessors, depend upon the renunciation of power by the masses, with the one momentous difference being that in democracies this individual renunciation of power is *voluntary* and *conditional.* In democracies, individuals willfully delegate power to their ruling elites only so long as those elites skillfully maintain order and maximize justice. Thus, the process of democratization rests upon moral foundations, though housed within rational structures. Universal equality and individual autonomy, to say nothing of ruling elites responsive and responsible to the masses, are, in the final analysis, moral ideals rather than empirical facts.

Seen in this light, there is little wonder that many thoughtful people insist that democracy cannot endure without religion at its heart. Whence will come the civic consciousness—the public responsibility and disinterested goodwill that every democratic system of checks and balances requires—without religious supports and sanctions? Will individuals surrender their own private power and interests for the sake of the public order and good, without the threat of this-worldly punishments or the promise of otherworldly compensations? What, other than shared religious beliefs and practices, can unify a democratic society as complex and diverse as the United States?

Those who insist on a religious basis for every social order have the past on their side. As Bellah's analysis of religious evolution makes clear, religion *was* the sum and substance of social cohesion in the past. Primitive and archaic societies drew no sharp distinctions between "sacral" and "profane" roles and organizations. These small-scale societies were permeated with religious representations and rituals. Even the ensuing differentiation of religious from non-religious ideologies and institutions, which characterized the great historic religions, did not eliminate religion's role in maintaining social order. Religious institutions enjoyed parity and religious ideologies were given priority over their non-religious counterparts in the large-scale societies of the medieval and early modern period. But, increasingly in the modern period, the great historic religions have lost their social centrality and intellectual sovereignty. The modern world's self-understanding is deeply secular and its social order is highly differentiated. These interdependent changes in modern thought and life have squeezed religion into the "private areas" of human experience, and have thereby created a new relationship between religion and the social order.[7]

The historical causes and defining characteristics of secularization are topics of endless debate among interpreters of contemporary society. But most of these commentators agree that secularization involves a dramatic shift in the modern era from "otherworldly" to "this-worldly" thinking. Traditional societies, from the primitive to the early modern, have been built on sacral worldviews. For them, religious representations and presentations of an "other" world have illumined and guided life in this world. But such traditional interpretive schemes and action plans have become increasingly problematic, thanks to the new knowledge and power that modern science, technology, and politics have concentrated in human hands. Appeals to an extraordinary world alongside or above this world have become less necessary as we have learned more and more about the ordinary world around and within us. Transcendental grounds and goals have increasingly given way to immanent explanations and controls of the natural and human world.

Such mounting secularization of the modern world's self-understanding is closely tied to the increasing differentiation of the modern world's social order. Ideological secularization and structural differentiation are, in fact, two aspects of a single process. An increasing fragmentation of overarching systems of religious thought mirrors an increasing segmentation of institutional embodiments of human meaning. But this process loosens the connection between religious belief and social order. Religious worldviews have binding power only when they enjoy a monopoly over reality definition and are embodied in the primary public institutions of a society.

As we have seen, an "official" worldview was mediated through all the significant organizations and roles of primitive and archaic societies. Historic cultures differentiated religious from nonreligious institutions but did not totally separate them. Indeed, these specialized religious institutions maintained their hold on reality definition and personality formation well into the early modern era. But the traditional preeminance of religious roles and organizations has become increasingly problematic in the modern era as the forces of industrialization and urbanization spawned new tasks and new organizations. As social structures in general became increasingly specialized, religious institutions became decreasingly authoritative. New political, economic, military and educational organizations emerged, with each specialized institution generating its own goals of endeavor and pressing that rationale on its membership. But such specialized "performance demands" reached no further than the particular interests served and obligations incurred within a given group. As a consequence, life in the modern world is increasingly organized in segmented ways that neither call for nor receive any overarching religious meaning. Religious ideologies have become one among many other provisional interpretations of the world. Religious institutions have become merely one among many voluntary institutions catering to a specialized clientele. In this situation, religion has become ever more socially privatized and politically neutralized. Because we may believe anything we like, we are entitled to keep it to ourselves. Because others need not believe what we believe, we are expected to keep it to ourselves. Freedom *for* our own religion requires freedom *from* the religion of others!

How then has social order been maintained in the face of the increasing individualization of religious meaning in modern societies? Some commentators insist that modern societies, bereft of a dominant religion at their center, are rapidly disintegrating. The anecdotal evidence of massive social breakdown is marshalled in proof—increasing crime, mental breakdown, epidemic divorce, drug addiction, civil unrest, worker absenteeism. But a cooler reading suggests that whatever increasing social breakdown we are experiencing cannot simply be laid to the decline of religion. We have a fairly long history of modern democracies surviving without an established religion as their integrating center and legitimating source. Moreover, with only a few notable exceptions, social order has been maintained in these modern democracies without the exercise of brute force.

How has this been possible? There are two widely-championed answers which still hold on to the idea that religion remains the indispensable source of social order, whatever the declining influences of institutionalized religion in our day. One such answer to the question "Why is there order rather than chaos?" argues that we are still drawing on the spiritual capital of the past. Our religious heritage so permeated the political and economic order that we still pay some honor to those Christian values on which our society is based. But we are rapidly becoming a society without religious roots, and like all "cut-flower civilizations," we are doomed to wither and crumble. A more sophisticated answer to the question simply relocates society's religious center in an "invisible religion." The decline of traditional forms of religion is no evidence for religion's absence, since every society rests on some set of values. The operative religion of a given society is that shared system of values which stands at its center and legitimates its authority.

But these efforts to demonstrate religion's necessity by pointing to a dying or a hidden religion at the center of modern societies are unconvincing. The "cut-flower civilization" argument rests on debatable predictions of social disintegration. Even if such predictions are coming true, they may have other than religious causes. The "invisible religion" arguments rests on debatable assumptions about social integration. Even if social order requires a central core of shared values, those values need not be religious in nature. The question of religion's necessity cannot be settled by speculation or definition!

Other social scientists and political historians are prepared to see religion's relation to the social order in more varied terms. Religion has sometimes legitimated social order and other times justified revolutionary action. Religion has sometimes enforced standards of equity and other times reinforced structures of injustice. Whether religion plays a key role in maintaining social order and what the quality of that unity might be are historical questions that may be answered quite differently from place to place and time to time. But in all modern democratic societies, there is overwhelming evidence that religion plays less and less an official role in maintaining social order. The United States, with its constitutional separation of church and state, anticipated with remarkable prescience what was destined to happen sooner or later in every modern democracy. Institutionalized forms of religion have for the most part been confined to the private sphere of personal relationships and voluntary associations.

What then is religion's role in modern democratic societies? Is theistic religion totally irrelevant to the social order? Should organized religion be completely divorced from political involvements? These questions can only be answered in the light of how particular democratic societies actually work. In the case of the United States, biblical theism plays an ever-diminishing role in public life—a reduction already foreshadowed by the shift in grounds for public order from natural *religion* in the Declaration of Independence to utilitarian *philosophy* in the Constitution. This is not to deny all influence to organized religion. Jewish and Christian groups retain some political clout by influencing private attitudes and public opinion. But, even when social policies are inspired by religious agents, they are administered by secular agencies. Religious groups must remain content to work informally behind the scenes and indirectly through the system as one pressure group among others.

Despite this reduced public visibility and expanded private vitality, such modern religiosity may be more important to democratic societies than either doctrinaire secularists or reactionary theists imagine. Recall that democratic societies are continually prey to doing their job of containing diversity too well (thus swallowing the individual within a homogenous mass), or not doing their job of unifying interests well enough (thus throttling the individual through repressive elites). In other words, the individual is continually threatened by the tyranny of the mob (massification) or the tyranny of the party (totalitarianism). Ideologically, the best defense against these twin threats is the denial of finality to every system of beliefs about the social world and human good. Institutionally, the best check against these recurrent dangers is the diffusion of power through a network of competing interest groups. Of course, democracies structurally *are* such self-revising and multicentered societies. But the privatized and neutralized religion of modernity can also contribute directly to these protective strategies.

By limiting ultimate meaning to *personal* existence, privatized religion denies absolute status to any mass consciousness. By dividing communal loyalties among multiple associations, neutralized religion denies exclusive authority to any totalitarian elite. Put in Mannheim's terms, a socially privatized and politically neutralized religion combats totalitarianism by encouraging a "de-distantiation" of authority, while simultaneously contesting massification by legitimating a "re-distantiation"of individuality. Strange as it sounds, the very fragmentation of modern religion contributes to the maintenance of social order in democratic societies.[8]

Conclusion

What seems to be emerging in modern democratic societies is not only a new role for religion in the social order but a new model of cultural order itself. Culture has always sheltered us from the terrors and trials of existence. In the past, that shelter was always a *sacred* canopy, while increasingly in our day, culture has become a *secular* canopy.[9] But, in democratized cultures, that shift from a sacred to a secular canopy goes far deeper than simply the *idiom* of social order. There have been profound changes in the *structure* of the canopy as well. Modern societies are not simply societies which are organized around a secular, rather than a sacral center of integrating values and practices. Democratized societies have no center at all—whether sacred or secular![10]

Perhaps I can best capture these interdependent shifts from sacred to secular and from single center to absent center by contrasting two metaphors of social order—the tent and the geodesic dome.[11] In societies of the past, the cultural canopy was like a *tent.* The small-scale "tents" of the primitive and archaic past were supported by a single religious pole in the center. A religious stackpole of integrating and legitimating myths and rituals provided the integrating and legitimating basis of personal identity and social order. In the more encompassing and complex societies that emerged in antiquity and persisted until the initiation of the modern era, the cultural canopy remained a tent, though it is now more like a circus tent than a family shelter. Other "poles" were required to support and sustain the cultural order. Political, economic, military and educational support systems were erected as relatively freestanding cultural systems. But religion remained the center that held the entire cultural system together.

Today's self-revising and multi-centered societies can no longer be envisioned as a tent, even with a primary center around which other secondary centers help support the overarching canopy of culture. The more apt figure for emerging democratic societies is the geodesic dome—that marvel of modern construction that stands without apparent support. Of course, the geodesic dome is constituted by a system of balanced tensions. Similar practical applications of the science of statics can be seen in domes and arches. But, unlike these earlier spanning structures, the geodesic dome has no *keystone* that holds the entire structure in place. For the geodesic dome, no one segment plays the critical role in holding the system together. Modern society with its pluralism of and competition between meaning systems is like a geodesic dome. It shelters and endures only so long as its constituent parts remain in balance with one another. Modern religion can and does play a role—indeed, perhaps a double role—in this scheme of things. Religion is but one of the constituent parts of the social order and as such, exerts its own limited tension and contributes its own sheltering haven. But religion can also serve to unmask and rebuff all those efforts to claim more than a relative power and value for any of the constituent parts of the cultural order, including itself. As it turns out, in democratic societies the prohibition of *idolatry* is the first principle of politics as well as religion.

In keeping with the practical intentions of our joint effort, what are some policy implications of the view of religion and politics that I have sketched here? Restricting myself to the American situation alone, I offer five concrete recommendations:

1. Religious groups should uphold the strict separation of church and state.
2. Religious groups should eschew politicizing religious beliefs and practices.
3. Religious groups should lobby for broadly humanistic goals, but not seek control of humanitarian programs of government.
4. Religious groups should support those private and voluntary organizations which serve as a buffer between the individual and the state.
5. Religious groups should support the public school system and the Supreme Court, since these are our only "universal" value-educating institutions.

I am well aware that these policy recommendations envision a more indirect and less visible impact of religion on politics than some of my colleagues in this endeavor are proposing. But, for the historical and philosophical reasons set out above, less *is* more when it comes to modern religion and democratic politics.

NOTES

1. Mannheim, Karl, "The Democratization of Culture," in *From Karl Mannheim,* ed. Kurt H. Wolff (New York: Oxford University Press, 1971), pp. 241–346.
2. Bellah, Robert N., "Religious Evolution," in *Reader in Comparative Religion,* eds., William A. Lessa and Evan Z. Vogt (New York: Harper & Row, 1965), pp. 36–50.
3. Mannheim, Karl, "The Democratization of Culture," pp. 276–77, 280–88.
4. *Ibid.,* pp. 277–79, 288–99.
5. *Ibid.,* pp. 279–80, 300–29.
6. *Ibid.,* p. 326.
7. Luckmann, Thomas, *The Invisible Religion* (New York: Macmillan Co., 1967), pp. 50–117.
8. Elsewhere I have argued that religion pluralism embodies an iconoclastic principle of great importance for both personal identity and social stability (Kliever, 1982). I have yet to fully explore the relation between a *negative* iconoclasm (the continual dishabilitation of the absolute) and *positive* iconoclasm (the perpetual transfiguration of the relative).
9. Berger, Peter, *The Sacred Canopy* (Garden City, N.Y.: Doubleday, 1969).
10. Lamert, Charles C., "Social Structure and the Absent Center," in *Sociological Analysis* 36 (1975), pp. 95–107.
11. The metaphor of the geodesic dome is suggested by Swatos (1982).

REFERENCES

Kliever, Lonnie D., "Authority in a Pluralistic World," in *Modernization: The Humanist Response to Its Promise and Problems,* ed. Richard L. Rubenstein (Washington: Paragon House, 1982).

Swatos, William H., Jr., "Mysticism, Modernity, and the Definition of Religion: Bursting Old Skins" (unpublished manuscript) (1982).

4

The Prices of Peace: Religion and Politics in Western Europe

JOHN K. ROTH

The American son of German immigrants, and arguably the most perceptive religious ethicist the United States has yet produced, Reinhold Niebuhr kept a diary during the early years of his career when he was the pastor of a church in Detroit. In 1929 those entries became an aptly titled book, *Leaves from the Notebook of a Tamed Cynic.* One day during the year before, Niebuhr's musings had contained these lines: "Everyone must decide for himself just where he is going to put his peg; where he is going to arrive at some stable equilibrium between moral adventure and necessary caution."[1] Such words make a fitting epigraph for the 1980s, a decade savaged by terrorism and dangerously divided by Soviet-American strife. Especially where the latter ingredient is concerned, nuclear power plays a central part. Anxiety has been intensified in both the Western and Eastern blocs not only by President Reagan's Strategic Defense Initiative (SDI or, to some, "Star Wars"), but also by the Soviet nuclear accident at Chernobyl in April 1986. Understandably, the Western Europeans are particularly troubled by the calamities that a nuclear age may provoke, for continuing Soviet-American conflict puts them severely at risk.

In recent years, Western Europe, no less than the United States, has witnessed mass protests against nuclear weapons. It is reliably estimated, for instance, that just prior to the International Public Hearing on Nuclear Weapons and Disarmament, held November 23–27, 1981 in Amsterdam by the World Council of Churches, some 400,000 persons gathered in that Dutch city to dissent against the nuclear arms race and to advocate disarmament.[2] Before the autumn and early winter of 1981 had ended, some two million Western Europeans had participated in similar demonstrations. Though Western Europe's states remain diverse, where certain aspects of nuclear politics are concerned, a sufficient consensus exists to warrant speaking about a Western European Peace Movement. This paper describes and analyzes some of the religious elements that influence it. Because space will not permit an in-depth account of the situation in every country, instead, the goals will be: (1) to suggest what the Western European Peace Movement is like overall as far as its religious components are concerned; (2) to focus some specific practical problems that the religious elements in the Peace Movement bring out; (3) to reflect on some of the broader philosophical questions raised by the religious orientation of the Peace Movement; and (4) to summarize some public policy considerations that merit attention as one puts together the first three pieces of this puzzle.

I do not approach this four-part goal without some fundamental assumptions. Indeed my introductory remarks imply them, even as I hope those opening comments suggest that these assumptions are not unexamined, but, instead, are rooted in actual experiences about which I have thought a good deal. Although the list is not exhaustive—no enumeration of one's own assumptions in an inquiry ever can be—here are some of the most important.

- Even if it is a truism to say that nobody wants nuclear war per se, Hiroshima introduced a nuclear age that entails two things: first, we may not survive with nuclear arms, but, second, we are not going to live without them either.
- As the predicament of Third World and recently developing regions indicates, there are conditions that could trigger nuclear war—limited or total—and those conditions have everything to do with an irreducible fact, namely, that the world has too many people competing for too few resources.
- If Middle Eastern dilemmas are any indication, we occupy a world in which national interests, far from receding in favor of international harmony, are intensifying and thus creating mistrust that will be hard-pressed to resist temptations to break into violence, unless there is a balance of power that can maintain stability.
- Although Western Europe is a far more secular society than it once was, religion, specifically Protestant and Catholic Christianity, is anything but moribund. Its influence bears watching as we consider the prices of peace in the late twentieth century.

John K. Roth

Mobilizing for Peace

As far as its religious ingredients are concerned, how should the Western European Peace Movement be characterized? At least four traits stand out. First, from a religious perspective this Peace Movement is both substantial in its impact and yet varied in its intensity, the latter factor correlating largely with national boundaries. Next, the religious input within the Western European Peace Movement is not naive; instead it is well-informed by current research in political science, economics, military strategy, and the technologies of thermonuclear warfare. Third, if the religious voices in the Peace Movement at times advocate unilateral steps toward a nuclear freeze or other disarmament strategies, that stance is not held by all of them at all times. More generally pervasive, however, is the effort of each religious group to put pressure on the regime currently in power in its own state. Finally, the motivation behind the religious activism in the Peace Movement is based on humanistic-spirtual values that few people in the West would be likely, at least in principle, to question let alone to reject. This fact makes it difficult to criticize the religious thrust of the Peace Movement without running the risk of being portrayed as insensitive, intransigent, inhumane, or worse. Some additional points about each of these characteristics will fill in the picture.

Since the autumn of 1981, disarmament demonstrations have drawn as many as 150,000 persons in London, 200,000 each in Rome and in Brussels, and another 250,000 in Bonn, as well as the previously mentioned 400,000 in Amsterdam. Demonstrations do come and go, and thus in some quarters it is tempting to downplay their importance. To dismiss these activities too quickly, however, would be a serious miscalculation, for nobody can safely assume that the figures cited point to a peak of antinuclear sentiment in Western Europe. A better appraisal is that the demonstrations are more like the tip of an iceberg. One reason for saying so is that no thinking European can avoid understanding that he or she lives "on the most equipped battlefield in the history of humanity," a battlefield covered by NATO and Soviet missiles "capable of hitting targets within five minutes of launching."[3] As most Western Europeans perceive this dilemma, the launching of these missiles would destroy their civilization. Those well-grounded fears, though, do not entail desire to welcome warmly an alternative, namely, the expansion of Soviet influence in Western Europe, which could culminate in the "Finlandization" of the entire region. On the contrary, Western European life since World War II has emphasized deterring and even physically resisting Soviet incursions.

Most Western Europeans feel caught between a rock and a hard place. For many, however, fear of Soviet domination does take second place now to concerns about the potential nuclear battlefield in which they live. That tradeoff emerges from some complex factors. During much of the 1970s, for example, Western Europeans tolerated a policy of deterrence crafted by NATO and Soviet policies together. It was called "mutually assured destruction"—MAD for short. This strategy did indeed seem to produce a balance of terror, but one of the cunning ironies of nuclear competition is that it reinstates the threats of conventional warfare. That prospect kept the military strategists at work. The NATO perception has been that if the conventional forces of the Soviet Union and the Warsaw Pact, which are judged to be superior to NATO's, were mobilized against Western Europe, the line of defense could not be an all-out nuclear attack but would need to be a more controlled one. Hence the concept of limited or even isolated use of nuclear weapons asserted itself. This propect seems literally "mad" to many Western Europeans. They see little assurance that such use of nuclear devices would not trigger all-out nuclear war. Furthermore, the very concept of a controlled, limited use of nuclear weaponry appears unconvincing because any use of these weapons will unleash aftereffects that continue to kill long after the detonation. One result of Chernobyl is the reinforcement of these anti-nuclear convictions. Especially in Europe, people seem to equate the peril of nuclear accidents with the deadly potential of nuclear weapons. Some experts, moreover, had argued that accidents such as the one at Chernobyl could virtually never happen. The falsification of that argument will not make it easier to convince Europeans that their hopes for peace are best grounded in strengthened nuclear arsenals.

Faced by the prospect of nuclear war—limited or total—Western Europeans increasingly believe that they are the pawns, if not the hostages, in a struggle that is essentially between the United States and the USSR. President Reagan's SDI notwithstanding, conviction that the United States is able and willing to defend Western Europe recedes in favor of the view that this region has become the no man's land that stands between the Soviets and the Americans. If Western Europe cannot completely control its own fate in these circumstances, current feeling presently runs strong that it can and should take steps to assure the disarmament which will reduce, if not eliminate completely, the prospect of being bombed back into the Stone Age. Realigned Western European attitudes about self-interest are asserting themselves. They place more priority on erasing the threat of nuclear destruction than on checking Soviet domination. Ironically, many of the United States' Western European friends may be saying, however inadvertently or unintentionally, that they fear Washington more than Moscow.

Such attitudes exist throughout Western Europe, but nowhere are they more pronounced than in the Netherlands and in West Germany. Their intensity in West Germany is understandable simply because it is unimaginable that her territory would not figure centrally in any East-West confrontation involving nuclear arms in Western Europe. Before saying more about the German scene, however, some comments about the Netherlands are appropriate. In 1977 the Dutch Inter-Church Peace Council (ICK) initiated a campaign whose slogan was: "Free the world of nuclear weapons, and first of all our own country." Substantial, the ensuing sympathetic response did not occur in a vacuum. Organized in 1966 by nine churches whose membership includes more than ninety percent of all Dutch churchgoers, the ICK had carried on, for many years, an extensive program of peace activism and education, spearheaded by some 10,000 active members from 400 local chapters across the country. This organization could rightly claim credit for public opinion polls that found nearly three-quarters of the Dutch population opposed to the stationing of Cruise missiles in their nation. At the heart of the ICK's position has been the conviction that "the superpowers, left to themselves, will not be able on their own to find the way to liberate themselves from their deadly struggle."[4] Hope for breaking the deadlock, the ICK argued, might be found in a grassroots movement that could influence public policy in a small nation. Serving as a catalyst, the ICK hoped to set a Dutch example that would energize similar agencies elsewhere. To show the folly of underestimating what the small powers of the world are still capable of doing, one need only turn again to West Germany.

By the autumn of 1981, for example, the German Evangelical Church, largest and most powerful of the Christian churches in West Germany, had adopted many of the positions taken earlier by the Dutch Council.[5] One result was a huge rally in Bonn (October 10, 1981), where the speakers included a wide range of political and religious leaders. If they were predominantly left-of-center, it is important to note that none of the most important were Communists, let alone the Kremlin's agents. Nor, it must be added, were many of the Bonn demonstrators purely pacifists or advocates of unilateral antinuclear initiatives. They did wish, however, not to replicate the political passivity that characterized the German populace under Nazi government. Thus, these dissenters have worked to create an environment in which political decision-makers must reckon with their desires. Those aims include: "(1) resistance to the introduction of new nuclear weapons in Europe; (2) withdrawal of NATO support for the decision to deploy new medium-range missiles; (3) a decrease in the number of nuclear weapons in both Western and Eastern Europe, with the aim of arriving at a multilateral and global disarmament process; (4) a Europe in which nuclear weapons are neither manufactured, stored nor used; and (5) initiatives taken by European governments toward effective disarmament negotiations."[6] These goals are not simply those of the religious in West Germany. They are shared by a Peace Movement encompassing an array of political opinion, much of it non- or even antireligious. Yet the Peace Movement in West Germany and in the Netherlands could never enjoy the power and the respectability it possesses without the infusion of a religious spirit that is "more attracted to nonviolence, more broadly based, less marked by intergenerational hostility and more inclusive of the working class" than were any of the social protest movements of the 1960s.

No detailed overview of Western Europe can be offered here, but leaving aside countries such as Italy, Spain, and Austria, consider a few other crucial pieces in this puzzle. In Denmark and Norway, leadership in the Peace Movement has found it more difficult to attract the average citizen than has been true in the Netherlands or in West Germany. Nevertheless, religious voices have urged these countries to withdraw from NATO and to denounce development of the controversial neutron bomb and SDI, a sentiment expressed frequently elsewhere in Europe as well. Across the North Sea, Prime Minister Margaret Thatcher's willingness to have Cruise and Pershing missiles located in Great Britain, plus her approval of the neutron bomb and SDI, lent great intensity to the Peace Movement there, and once again religious spokespersons are in its vanguard. In France, the situation is quieter, owing partly to the fact that the French are committed to sustaining a nuclear force of their own. An additional factor not to be overlooked, however, is that France is not a NATO member and thus does not permit American nuclear weapons to be placed within its borders. The Western European Peace Movement, in general, and its religiously derived intensity, in particular, seem to be fueled nationally by nothing so much as the presence and future development of American weapons and the concomitant perception that those weapons are aimed less to defend Europe than to defend the United States, whose self-interest might deem Western Europe expendable were events to come to a nuclear showdown.

The Western European Peace Movement, especially in its religious dimensions, is not emanating from a lunatic fringe but from society's mainstream. Equally significant, this movement is not naive, at least not if one equates 'naive' with 'ill-informed.' Twice devasted by war in this century alone, Western Europe contains a historical consciousness that understands mass violence all too well. As both the United States and the Soviet Union carry on their military competition to become or to remain "Number One," that scenario seems increasingly absurd, and the sanity of striving instead for a reduction of arms in both Western and Eastern Europe appears increasingly sensible. Since the Western European nations have greater clout with the United States than with the Soviet Union, it is also understandable that they work in that direction to get the first steps toward limitation and reduction under way.

In Western European religious communities, however, more than a historical consciousness produces current antinuclear moods. For instance, well organized centers for peace studies and antinuclear strategies—the Stockholm International Peace Research Institute is one of the better known—are becoming commonplace. They have religious support. Headquartered in Western Europe, the World Council of Churches actively promotes similar activities, to date the most dramatic of which was the aforementioned International Public Hearing on Nuclear Weapons and Disarmament held in Amsterdam.[7] It attracted a distinguished group of politicians and scientists, as well as religious figures, and gave a considerable boost to delegitimizing human attitudes that place trust in the further development and stockpiling of nuclear devices. The sophisticated nature of the research done within the Peace Movement has vastly complicated the entire picture. Those who take exception to its positions can no longer afford to do so merely on grounds that the peace advocates have not done their homework. They have done and are continuing to do it. One outcome is that decisions about policy in these matters can no longer be regarded simply as a matter of lining up facts and making decisions based on what the facts clearly and obviously mean. For the facts no longer speak for themselves, if they ever did. They are so many and so liable to diverse interpretations that what we must contend with, at least as much as anything else, are some very basic and prior assumptions about people and politics. More about those assumptions shortly, but the point to underscore here is that it remains debatable whether the religiously motivated Peace Movement advocates or those who are skeptical of their aims are the greater realists.

Already noted, the specific policies that various religious groups advance in the Western European Peace Movement are essentially of two kinds, both aimed at reduction of arms in the short run and at total nuclear disarmament in Europe as the long range objective. Representative examples are provided by the Dutch and the Germans, although it would be incorrect to infer that opinion is undivided in either place. Dutch voices, especially within the ICK, urge Western European countries to commit themselves at least "to some unilateral initiatives in the field of arms reduction or arms control or in the political field."[8] Wearied by a strategy of arms control negotiations predicated on the principle of bargaining always from a position of strength, which seems to entail the paradox of arming in order to disarm, plus a refusal to disturb the balance of power, this perspective banks instead on the premise that "only carefully designed unilateral steps can stop the arms race and turn it around."[9] Negotiation is not to be tossed out as fruitless, but it will be carried out in a context where one side has broken a previous deadlock by acting concretely to reduce its nuclear forces, thus creating pressure, if not good will, to make the other side "put up or shut up" where its professed claims for disarmament and peace are concerned.

In West Germany, which has "the dubious distinction of having the heaviest concentration of nuclear weapons per square mile of any nation in the world,"[10] the strategy of unilateralism has its proponents in the religious communities, but the mood in German churches on nuclear questions has not been so single-minded as in the Netherlands. Indeed, antinuclear peace advocates are still a minority within West German churches, although their strength is enough to make some observers suggest that the peace question could fracture those communities irreparably.[11] To the extent that

West Germany's religious peace policies are less unilateral than those recommended by the Dutch, one factor in accounting for that position is a perception that both East and West Germany may still be influential *together,* even though hopes for a full unification are practically gone. In fact, some German church leaders call for a Central European neutralism in which West and East Germany would play dominant roles. How these views will be sifted and sorted in West Germany during the remainder of the 1980s remains a question that only the passage of time can answer. The unsettled political environment of that nation reflects its religious climate and vice versa. But it is crucial to see that, while the religious peace groups in Western Europe are not monolithically wedded to a single program, they are committed to nuclear arms reduction and elimination insofar as possible. Unexpectedly, this mixture of division and unity, far from making the movement vulnerable, is one of its assets since a single objective is being approached in considerable strength on a number of fronts. Those who question the wisdom of the religious motivations behind the Peace Movement have to make their case on multiple issues and levels, which complicates the task considerably.

Those complications are compounded because all of the religious motivations behind the Peace Movement take their stand upon humanistic-spiritual values that few persons in the West would be likely to question, at least in principle, let alone reject. No better example could be cited than the way in which the Peace Movement has turned the word 'peace' to good advantage. Who, in some sense or other, is not for peace? Skillfully, the Peace Movement has seized an initiative by keeping that ideal in the vanguard, which is a result that is *not* the most obvious when, as is so often true where these matters are concerned, discussion focuses instead on the latest weapons that are to be deployed or developed, the imbalances that may or may not exist between the nuclear superpowers, and the fears of nuclear holocaust that are played upon in order to generate support for defense spending. Those latter considerations have to be taken seriously if peace is to be kept or made more secure. Speaking words of peace is not enough to qualify anyone as a genuine peacemaker, but by keeping the peace ideal out in front, the Peace Movement has a lure that defense-minded proponents are hard-pressed to match.

Other examples could be listed at length. The ethical reflection and religious rhetoric undergirding the Peace Movement emphasize the need, as one representative statement has it, to accept "the risk of change that could reduce tensions, overcome inequities between peoples, and establish the basis for reconciliation that is grounded in justice."[12] Everything does depend on the risks one is willing to take, but without much question, such aims are noble. The Peace Movement doubtlessly has real advantages in this debate because it can more easily speak the language of religious faith and of moral idealism than can those who see the best chances for peace existing in the maintenance of strong military force that depends upon continued nuclear weaponry. The issue here is not to judge whether one perspective is right and the other wrong. It is to hold that public policy debates on such matters are not going to occur in a religious and moral vacuum. Those who contact the religious and moral sensitivities of men and women by using authentically the language that moves them possess a persuasive power whose potential influence can hardly be overestimated. A return to these points will make additional sense once the prices of peace are considered more concretely.

A Practical Dilemma

As the editors of *Christianity and Crisis* have asserted, two salient historical facts merit consideration. First, since the atomic bombing of Nagasaki on August 9, 1945, no nation has used nuclear weapons in a war. Second, although the world has witnessed scores of wars since that time, none has been on the scales of World Wars I and II. "We have not seen another Hiroshima," remind these writers, "neither have we experienced another Stalingrad or Dresden." It does not follow, they acknowledge, that an umbrella of nuclear terror has sheltered us from World War III or that a continuation of nuclear threats will go on to provide an admittedly fragile and precariously balanced protection. Moreover, they continue, the costs of these present arrangements are huge; the resources spent on nuclear defense could do boundless good elsewhere if it were feasible to redirect them. Still, if "Armageddon has not happened . . . yet; and there is some connection between that reality and the very awfulness of the Bomb," so far it remains a fact, too, that "the only system we have for preserving a measure of peace is a balance of terror."[13]

At this juncture the Peace Movement joins the issue. Here also lurks the most crucial practical dilemma that confronts any assessment of the prices of peace, and the case of Western Europe and her religiously sensitive peace proponents heightens the tension as well as any example that can be found. Those proponents' assumption is that there has to be, must be, a better way to make peace. Nearly everyone would share that premise as a hope, but opinion splinters over acting upon that supposition and well it should. Faced by what they see as a tremendously unstable situation, the religious leaders of the Western European Peace Movement want not merely to alter those circumstances, but to take what they acknowledge are considerable risks to do so. In short, to stabilize an unstable situation, they are advocating policies that will destabilize things even further, at least in the short run, in the expectation that a more genuine stability will emerge over the longer haul. The issue that looms large is this: In a world and particularly in a European environment that are clearly in a precariously peaceful situation, how much and what kinds of stress are tolerable before a breakdown ensues that will lead to things worse than we have now?

In response, one scenario could involve failure in the Peace Movement, the absence of arms negotiations, and a continuation of the arms race as we have seen it unfold in the past. If those eventualities transpire, how should Western Europeans—religious or not—want things to develop? Obviously they must answer for themselves, but it seems doubtful that most would desire a clear Soviet superiority in the arms field. Whether, on the other hand, they would like the United States to have an overwhelming advantage is hardly a self-evident truth. The temptations for both sides might simply be too great in either case; Western Europe's instability could then be lethally compounded. Only the lesser of evils, though it is the safest and sanest situation in such a scenario, might well be roughly what exists today, namely, a nuclear stalemate.

At the other end of a spectrum could be a situation in which the Western European Peace Movement, sparked by its religious components, is substantially successful in getting its policy implementation under way. As things stand today, that success would include not only bilateral negotiations but also a series of unilateral actions, the effect of which would be to weaken, for however short a time, the nuclear striking capacity of NATO. These advocates would assume that this momentary weakening of strength is a means to the end of a vastly more stable peace. The question is whether that outcome is the one most probable. Answers depend on how one analyzes the intentions of East and West, but history offers a record full of inconvenient facts for those who would take a sanguine view of Soviet goodwill. Soviet communism may not be the evil that Western demonology has made it out to be, but that system has slaughtered millions of its own citizens, and the world has witnessed what happened in Hungary, Czechoslovakia, and Poland. Hardly any Western Europeans would deny that they would feel much safer if the Soviets had no nuclear-armed missiles to point in their direction. Of course they do have such missiles in abundance, and the fact remains that even if a freeze on or the removal of some NATO counter forces were to occur, especially if those steps were to be taken unilaterally, there would still be more incentive than disincentive for the Soviets to keep their fire power in place as far as possible. To see why, it is important to remember two dimensions of the present nuclear dilemma.

Nuclear war is not simply a matter of firing or of not firing nuclear warheads. It is a matter of politics as well, and the battles waged without ever a shot's being fired are pivotal for what will happen to us all. As Michael Novak has observed: "Without being used militarily, nuclear weapons have powerful political utility. They frighten. They set in motion deep policy shifts. They intimidate. They may be used to freeze opponents in checkmate, while other actions elsewhere are launched. They may be used as blackmail."[14] The Western European Peace Movement, not least in its religious manifestations, is partly an assertion of European independence against the United States. Ironically, however, these stirrings of nationalistic or continental autonomy play into the hands of increased Soviet hegemony in Western Europe because the Soviets are unlikely to settle for less than a covert domination of Western Europe by military threat if they can get away with it. Hence, unless the Western European Peace Movement is predicated on well-founded assurances from the Soviet Union and the Warsaw Pact that demonstrate their unwillingness to make Western Europe their satellite, the Movement operates on a premise about the future that appears to be less realistic than its well-informed understanding of the volatile predicament a nuclear stalemate involves.

The Western European Peace Movement may be too close to the trees to see the forest. So long as they can take their steps with impunity, the Soviet bloc has everything to gain and very little to lose by seeking domination over Western Europe in whatever form they can acquire it. If that is what Western Europeans want, as religious people or otherwise, they should embrace the Peace Movement wholeheartedly. To the degree that they are leery of such an outcome, they will be skeptical of its policies and perhaps conclude that the most moral, realistic, prudent and even religiously sound position is to continue bargaining for a nuclear freeze, reduction, or abolition but to do so from a position of strength and not of weakness militaristically speaking.

Strength need not become the euphemism for superiority that some would want it to be. The lesser of evils in our circumstances, where there are so few goods that are within reach, is a situation in which terror indeed is balanced so that neither side can afford to take the risk of striking first. As long as that balance exists, Western Europeans have a relative safety from nuclear devastation, which is as much as any person can be guaranteed in this world. In addition, they also have a degree of freedom and prosperity that few persons under Soviet domination enjoy. The prices of peace are always high. The dilemma that faces the Western European Peace Movement is how much to pay for what kind of peace. Those who advocate destabilizing an already instable situation by taking stands that make a moral statement—unilateral freezes or disarmament steps would be the best and most dangerous examples—may be correct in saying that conventional policies of nuclear deterrence are mad. But in a world with as many dark sides as this one, theirs might be even more so. Mistrust spawned the nuclear arms race initially. If mistrust is what makes it so hard to stop such competition, that same factor also ought to make us quiz very hard whether the most deep-seated yearnings to disarm are coming too fast and too trustingly. Trust and mistrust—those realities point to another issue, a broader one standing at the heart of these matters and specifically at the core of the religious motivations behind the Western European Peace Movement.

In God We Trust?

One who testified at the 1981 World Council of Churches hearing in Amsterdam was the distinguished Dutch Catholic theologian, Edward Schillebeeckx. His remarks contain a helpful sample of views that continue to form the most fundamental issue raised by the religious proponents in the Western European Peace Movement. Following up his assertion that "the need for unilateral nuclear disarmament forces itself upon us," Professor Schilebeeckx went on to say:

> If we consider that private citizens cannot exercise any direct influence on the decisions of other countries, but on the other hand do have some influence on the decisions of authorities in their own country, I would, taking everything into account, venture to maintain that the strategic slogan "Free the world of nuclear weapons, and first of all our own country," implies a responsible historical decision, which is closer than any other to the demands of the Gospel. It becomes the social-political content of Christian hope in terms of a historical practice. In this light there are solid grounds on which also the Christian churches, in view of their prophetic task with regard to universal peace as work of global justice, can base *a theologically responsible decision* to back the first risky step of starting with unilateral nuclear disarmament, without any naivete, but not without *the theological hope* against all hope.[15]

Two concepts are of particular interest in this statement, which is rather typical of the religious language that guides the Peace Movement in Western Europe and in the United States as well. They are the ideas of *theological hope* and of *theological responsibility.*

If the meanings of those concepts are unpacked, they include some basic convictions about the nature of reality itself. Prominent among them would be: (1) faith that God exists; (2) conviction that God's power (whether omnipotent or limited) favors what is good, thus falsifying in the long if not the short run the proposition that human might alone makes right; and (3) belief that in contemporary life the policies formulated by the Peace Movement are at least in their general orientation, if not in their precise detail, so consonant with God's will that, if they are pursued, not only is theological responsibility carried out but also there is good reason to hope that they will prevail. Usually words of caution are added to such statements to alert people that smug presumption about the righteousness of a particular set of plans must be avoided, for God's ways are not necessarily those of any one human community. Nor does this outlook suggest that there is some cosmic insurance policy to guarantee that the projects of peacemaking will win out. Schillebeeckx, for one, speaks forthrightly about the risks involved. Yet the outlook described here does affirm that reality ultimately contains a moral component. Power itself is finally governed by a trancendent goodness. Divine Providence, to use an older theological category, is real and cannot be challenged with impunity. The religiously responsible person tries to locate the ways of that Providence, lets his or her life be defined by them as far as possible, and strives to advance those ways by using human energies in their service.

Implicit or explicit, appeals to Divine Providence are nothing new where nuclear controversy is concerned, nor are they to be found only among religious proponents in the peace movements of the West. Versions of appeals to Divine Providence also can be found where the pronuclear policies of the superpowers are concerned. In the United States, for instance, those who advocate greater defense spending are not devoid of the sentiment that God intends to keep on blessing America, but if and only if we are armed to the teeth. And though some would hold that the Soviet Union has moved beyond rigid ideology, no deception could be greater than to think that its strategies have abandoned a Marxist foundation which observes an irreversible historical dialectic at work, moving events along—with the help of military might—to a time when a Communist transformation of the world shall prevail.

Conflicting views of history's providential qualities keep people at odds within a spectrum that banks on some trancendent power or other that has a hand in an essentially moral governance of being itself. What is intriguing about such views, however, is that virtually all of them also emphasize that what happens in any particular historical era does depend largely on human decisions and human strength. It is possible, of course, to extend the emphasis on the human factor so that talk about transcendent elements of power becomes little more than a rhetorical flourish, its main function being to bolster support for policies that are really based solely on calculations about what men and women can and cannot, or will and will not do. It is even possible that such rhetorical flourishes can disappear altogether, a result suggesting that human affairs are precisely that, thus implying that even if human might does not make right, human power is absolutely decisive in determining what forms of right and wrong are going to exist.

However dimly the fact may be understood, formation of public policy—and nowhere more so than in decision-making where nuclear weapons are concerned—hinges upon beliefs concerning the presence or the absence of transcendent moral authority in the universe. To illustrate how pivotal those beliefs may be, one can do little better than to consider some claims made by the German social theorist, Max Weber, in his essay "Politics as a Vocation"

(1919). "Sociologically," wrote Weber, "the state cannot be defined in terms of its ends."[16] Political regimes have had multiple aims historically, but if that fact makes it impossible to define what a state is in terms of objectives, this realization does make it possible to see that one state is like every other in terms of "the specific *means* peculiar to it, as to every political association, namely, the use of physical force."[17] In Weber's terms, then, a state is much more than "a human community . . . within a given territory."[18] It is also "a relation of men dominating men, a relation supported by means of legitimate (i.e., considered to be legitimate) violence."[19] One crucial corollary, Weber goes on to say, is that "the decisive means for politics is violence."[20] However much we might wish it to be otherwise, Weber's succinct appraisals about the nature of the modern state ring true. To the extent that they are true, moreover, they carry some important implications for our understanding of responsibility. Weber himself helps to draw them out.

Whatever its ends may be and however noble they are, the existence of a state depends on its ability to use and to control violence. Political leaders, cautions Weber, lose sight of that reality at everyone's peril, which is to say that political leaders who bank too much on any version of Divine Providence will not be acting responsibly, at least not in terms of their political function, which cannot be divorced from the recognition that political leaders are at once to direct and serve the state. To make his or her state survive and flourish is the political leader's calling as political leader; to do anything that compromises those aims is to betray politics as a vocation.

Weber contrasts this "ethic of responsibility," as he calls it, with what he designates an "ethic of ultimate ends." One ingredient in the latter, he asserts, could be an attitude that says one must do what is right and leave the results to God.[21] If that position has affinity with what Professor Schillebeeckx calls "theological responsibility," Weber would have no quarrel with it on that level alone, because the theological view has a coherence and a consistency that give it integrity. But he would underscore that political responsibility and theological responsibility are never easily matched, if they can be joined at all. For a political leader can ill-afford to risk leaving the results to God in any sense, precisely because violence, like it or not, is so much the warp and woof of politics. The political leader can try to do what is right, but what is right in his or her eyes is bound to be influenced by an awareness of political responsibility that pretty well rules out the advocating of public policies which ultimately rest on the principle "In God We Trust."

Weber's point and mine in drawing this contrast is not to say that one perspective is necessarily better than the other or that one is necessarily true and the other false. It is, however, to affirm that the stands taken on a whole range of nuclear issues do involve religious considerations of the most profound kind. Furthermore, unless people become quite clear with each other about their beliefs on these matters, unless they discern how political priorities are shaped by the presence or absence of convictions about the reality or unreality of versions of Divine Providence, we shall all—not only in Western Europe but everywhere else—be blindly playing with fire that could consume us all.

Some Conclusions about Public Policy

These reflections on the prices of peace began with an excerpt from Reinhold Niebuhr. Constantly tugged and pulled between Christian idealism and political realism, Niebuhr once said of himself: "I persevere in the effort to combine the ethic of Jesus with what might be called Greek caution. . . . I might claim for such a strategy the full authority of the gospel except that it seems to me more likely to avoid dishonesty if one admits that the principle of love is not qualified in the gospel and that it must be qualified in other than the most intimate human associations. When one deals with the affairs of a civilization, one is trying to make the principle of love effective as far as possible, but one cannot escape the conclusion that society as such is brutal, and that the Christian principle may never be more than a leaven in it."[22] Niebuhr's poignant statement provides a framework in which to sum up three of the most important public policy considerations that this study of the Western European Peace Movement suggests.

First, Niebuhr understood how powerfully the human heart can be touched by a moral voice that dares one to study war no more and to take the risks of loving one's enemies. Society is brutal, but it is not simply brutal, and individuals especially can be moved to act on the highest principles of prophetic religion. The Western European Peace Movement—springing as it does from a mixture of yearnings for self-determination both nationally and collectively within Europe, from a mistrust of American determination to defend Western Europe or a conviction that such a defense would destroy that region, from a feeling that ultimately it would be more acceptable to be "Pink, if not Red, than Dead"—would be a political force to contend with in its own right. But when one adds in a religious factor to buttress cries for peace that are predicated on a weakening of the military clout of the West, the power of that movement is escalated considerably just because it can now draw on the ideals of a prophetic stance. The determination that can lurk there may even be so strong that it discounts the fact that its own right to speak and to take its stand is a result of governmental resolve that is trying to keep people from being overshadowed by the USSR. The first public policy consideration, then, is that no one who is politically savvy will underestimate or oversimplify the Western European Peace Movement precisely because it has strong religious underpinnings.

Second, as Niebuhr struggled to find a way of combining Greek caution and the ethic of Jesus, repeatedly he had to probe the very foundations of his thought and existence. Niebuhr's belief in God was steadfast, but he spent a lifetime trying to achieve a responsible understanding of God's relation to history. On that score, apparently, Niebuhr's trust in God was less than complete, or, to put the claim more adequately, Niebuhr's trust in God entailed that human destiny remained very much in the hands of men and women, left to them in such a way that a miscalculation about what people, especially collectively, might do in wasting human life could be nothing less than disastrous. No one needs to conclude that Niebuhr's analysis was correct once and for all, but everyone ought to recognize that convictions about what is ultimate make a vast difference in determining what our practical policies will be. Religion, then, is a matter of public policy. It always has been, and, as long as people exist, it always will be. Nowhere is that fact demonstrated more clearly and more decisively than in reflection about humankind's present capacities for nuclear destruction.

One way to interpret the buildup of nuclear arms is to say that it is a symptom of the fact that we live in the time of "the death of God." At least functionally speaking, nuclear warheads and their ballistic delivery systems make the statement that human beings are all-too-tragically in charge of their own destiny. We might wish it were otherwise, and religious voices claiming it is otherwise are far from silent. No doubt that situation will also remain. Hence things will be more complicated than they might be if everyone concurred that human power in history is what is ultimate, or if everyone agreed that there is an ultimate power transcending human existence and that it is a moral force which will ensure, in some sense, history's redemption. But if such matters are not to be settled, it does not follow that it is unimportant to bring them up. On the contrary, disagreements are rarely more dangerous than when they remain latent, undiscussed, and ill-understood. As a matter of public policy, then, every interested party, but especially those who hold political power and those who actively seek to change it, could do far worse than to meet each other not only to debate specific practical proposals about nuclear arms, but also to probe their beliefs about what is ultimate and their reasons for thinking as they do. Then we might at least grasp better why we are in the dilemmas that confront us, and we might find ways to accommodate each other that have gone undetected because we have failed to look for them.

The brutality of society was one of Niebuhr's persistent themes. If that brutality was enough to ensure that the ethical principle of religion could only be a leaven in human affairs, Niebuhr thought that leaven was still mighty important. It could at least help to keep men and women from doing their worst. Nonetheless, even the leaven would have to be watched so that its power would not waste more than it saved. Here is the challenge both for those within the religious sectors of the Western European Peace Movement and for those who stand—whether for religious or non-religious reasons—outside of that perspective. Clearly the Peace Movement wants peace, but, at the same time, it is also flirting with a neutralism that could well turn out contrary to Western European and American interests. For if the NATO alliance is weakened, the temptations for the Soviets to flex their muscles may become irresistably high. If successful, those Western Europeans who see their peace efforts as a much needed expression of autonomy against the superpowers could find that the results of their efforts reduce autonomy overall by further destablizing an already unstable nuclear world, thus allowing the vise of Soviet authority to close very tightly indeed.

No one has more to gain from Western European neutralism than the Soviet Union. Those who form public policy in the United States and in Western Europe have to face the issue squarely: Is that advantage for the Soviets what the West wants? The answer to that question, however, is not going to be simple or obvious, because of two others that have to be dealt with as well:

First, what intentions govern Soviet policy? Second, what, if anything, should be done to dispell a tendency to think in terms of some version of the "better Red than Dead" option? Where its religious elements are concerned, the Western European Peace Movement is apparently willing to impute essentially benign motives to the Soviets. That issue must be joined, not in a propagandistic way, but in terms of the best inquiry and information available. At least historically, there is ample reason not to look on the Kremlin in a sanguine way. No analysis that is sound will overlook that basic fact. Unless there are well-warranted reasons to think that Soviet ways have fundamentally changed, it seems important that responsible policy-makers seize the initiative in arguing that the best chances for peace really do lie in a preparedness that maintains such a high expense to launch nuclear devices, that neither side can afford the risks of doing so. Such a position need not entail a lack of negotiation or even the impossibility of a reduction of nuclear arms where the Soviets and the Americans are concerned, but, rather, current Western European dispositions that would trade weakness for strength as one of the prices for peace are probably striking a bargain that is no bargain at all, not least because the alternatives are simply not restricted to variants of the "either Red or Dead" dichotomy.

Strength and resolve can secure enough stability in this unstable world to keep democratic freedom alive. The prices for peace of that kind are going to be high, too, but those who make public policy will not be doing their jobs as well as possible if they fail to argue as persuasively as they can that a stability based on strength is still the most trustworthy basis for peace that presently exists. Such a plan need not be non- or anti-religious. No less than others that have unfurled religious banners, this approach can affirm unapologetically that its stance is based on an ethic that takes the wasting of human life as its enemy. A divinely inspired respect for human life can and ought to be the end which its means try to serve, insofar as the realities and possibilities of our life together responsibly permit. Reasonable prices of peace require aiming, as Reinhold Niebuhr said, "at some stable equilibrium between moral adventure and necessary caution." To seek that equilibrium is indeed fundamental for religion and politics in Western Europe, and in every part of the world as well.

NOTES

1. Reinhold Niebuhr, *Leaves from the Notebook of a Tamed Cynic* (San Francisco: Harper & Row, 1980), p. 167.
2. James E. Will, "European Peace and American Churches," *The Christian Century* (March 24, 1982), p. 330.
3. *Ibid.*
4. Ben ter Veer, "The Dutch Say 'No' to Nukes, 'Yes' to a Politics of Peace," *Christianity and Crisis* (January 18, 1982), pp. 388–89.
5. See Marjorie Hope and James Young, "The Renaissance of the European Peace Movement," *The Christian Century* (November 4, 1981), p. 1132.
6. *Ibid.,* p. 1133.
7. See, for example, Bruce Best, "War That Passes All Understanding," *One World,* No. 73 (January–February 1982), pp. 9–11. *One World,* published in Geneva, Switzerland, is a monthly magazine of the World Council of Churches.
8. ter Veer, p. 389.
9. *Ibid.,* p. 390.
10. Paul Kittlaus, "German Protestantism and the Peace Movement," *The Christian Century* (December 23, 1981), p. 1340.
11. *Ibid.,* p. 1341.
12. Robert F. Smylie, "Things That Make for Peace," a special double issue of *Church & Society* (November–December 1980—January–February 1981), Introduction, pp. 3–4.
13. "Give Ear to These Voices," *Christianity and Crisis* (January 18, 1982), pp. 370–71.
14. Michael Novak, "Nuclear Morality," *America* (July 3, 1982), p. 6.
15. Edward Schillebeeckx, "A Time for Prophecy," *Christianity and Crisis* (January 18, 1982), p. 373. The italics are mine.
16. Max Weber, "Politics as a Vocation," in *From Max Weber: Essays in Sociology,* ed. and trans. H. H. Gerth and C. Wright Mills (New York: Oxford University Press, 1976), p. 77.
17. *Ibid.,* p. 78.
18. *Ibid.*
19. *Ibid.*
20. *Ibid.,* p. 121.
21. *Ibid.,* p. 120.
22. Niebuhr, pp. 196–97. The passage was written in 1928.

5

The Many Faces of Islamic Revivalism

EDWARD AZAR AND A. CHUNG-IN MOON

Islam is a very big sea, but which star should one choose to steer by?[1]

"Muslims are coming! Muslims are coming!" Lately such cries have resounded across the Western world. Indeed, together with the Russians, the recent resurgence of Islamic activism seems to be regarded as the largest potential threat to the Western world's interests, order, and stability. From the remote corners of the Saharan Desert across the strategic crescent straddling the crossroads of three continents, and to the southern tier of the Pacific Ocean (Indonesia and Malaysia), the visibility and influence of Islamic activism with a revivalist orientation is growing sharply. Efforts to rediscover Islam's spiritual roots and to reassert its political, economic, and social power in a collective or individual manner have been manifested in various forms of activism which range from successful revolutionary crystalization in Iran, to violent underground resistance in Egypt and Syria, and the unique Afghan armed struggle against the Soviet Occupation Army. Its list of enemies includes a range that runs from corrupt individual Muslims to atheists, capitalists and finally, repressive political rulers who are regarded as not sufficiently God-fearing.

Why is Islam suddenly blossoming in a highly politicized form? As a prominent Orientalist, H. A. R. Gibb, observed quite some time ago, did not Islam erode as a value system and as a political force long ago?[2] To borrow a bit of 1960s modernist jargon, did not Islam wither away like the "shattering of glasses"[3] in the face of a high tide of modernization which swept Muslim societies? Or as optimistically projected, was not Islam doomed to be progressively incorporated into a dialectical synthesis of "a secular humanism-pragmatism" in the deterministic manner?[4] Contrary to all these earlier projections, Islam is far from dying. Perhaps we are even witnessing a vehement return of its spirit rising from the depth of Islam's past glory. In the last several years, Islam has proven beyond a doubt that it is still alive, vigorous, and full of spirit. It moves, transforms, and overturns individuals, societies, and even the world. It provides Muslims with a *modus operandi,* a normative buttress, strategies, an ideology, and higher goals to strive for. Islam has not yet eroded; nor has it "shattered away." Islam is not yet doomed to be incorporated into a secular humanism-pragmatism. Rather, Islam is reasserting its vital functions as an ethical system, a mode of conduct, and most importantly, as a revitalized political power.

Why have earlier theoretical conjectures proven incorrect? What is the nature and structure of the recent resurgence of Islamic activism? How does Islamic revivalism fit into the political spectrum in the contemporary world? What messages do Western audiences receive from these revivalist trends? What impact will this revivalist movement have on the broadly perceived order and stability of the international system? These are the questions to be raised and discussed in this paper. It is our desire and intention that candid discussions of the issue will reduce the cognitive gap between Muslims and non-Muslim Westerners by augmenting the general body of knowledge about Islam.

The Western Perception of Islamic Revivalism: A Critical Overview

For the last several years, we have experienced a series of drastic events in the Islamic part of the world. These include the collapse of the Shah's regime and the emergence of Ayatollah Khomeini (1979), the Mecca Incident in Saudi Arabia (late 1979), the Soviet invasion of Afghanistan and the subsequent Mujahideen resistance (1979–present), and the dramatic assassination of Anwar Sadat in Egypt (1981). These events are sufficient to trigger mass-media enthusiasm and academic interest. The Western mass media has intensively covered the rising tide of Islamic revivalism, and scholars in the Western hemisphere—notably Americans—have now paid greater attention to this new syndrome. As a result, an extensive literature has accumulated on the topic.

The recently burgeoning literature offers five major explanations for Islamic Revivalism.[5] The first interprets the revitalization as a return to the fundamentals of the faith: the original teachings of the Quran and the Sunnah are to be restored, and the society of the early Caliphate revived in all its aspects. Hence, it envisions Islamic

Revivalism as the total reconstruction of the society and polity in the Islamic manner. Ultimately, such a reconstruction takes the form of a transformative political movement.

The second theme or explanation which often appears in the literature is an emphasis on the distorted impacts of modernization or secularization on the Islamic movement. It argues that the galloping, uncoordinated pace of modernization has reaped bitter fruits, one of which is Islamic Revivalism. This theme is an extension of the idea that tension between traditionalism and modernization inevitably emerges in all developing countries and that the rise of Islamic Revivalism is just another manifestation of this ever-present tension.

Another important common theme is the tendency to identify Islamic Revivalism as a militant opposition movement. However, the moderate and legitimizing aspects of this revivalist movement are seldom noted. This may be related to a positive semantic association between the term *Jihad* (Holy War) and the movement. While it is indisputably central to the movement, the term *Jihad* has multiple subtle meanings. When it is discussed in conjunction with Islamic Revivalism, however, it is seen as violent, aggressive, brutal, and oppositional. The worst example is the effort to link nuclear industrial development in some Islamic countries to a so-called "Islamic bomb," which implies an atom bomb.[6]

The fourth important common theme in the literature is an emphasis on what is termed as a regressive return to the past. This is best illustrated by quoting Wilfred C. Smith:

> The fundamental malaise of modern Islam is a sense that something has gone wrong with Islamic history. The fundamental problem of modern Muslims is how to rehabilitate that history; to get it going again in full vigour, so that Islamic society may once again flourish as a divinely guided society should and must.[7]

In other words, most recent analysts who focus on the Islamic movement tend to view the revivalist trend as a product of a cognitive dissonance between Islam's glorious historical past and its presently perceived status. This line of reasoning is preoccupied with the historical nature of the Islamic identity in which the restoration of past glory and idealism constitutes the core of the revivalist movement. Proponents of this idea confine themselves to the idea of Islamic history and tend to overlook other important elements of the current situation.

The last common dimension is an inclination to reject a paradigmatic approach or an aggregate comparative analysis to explain Islamic Revivalism in general. In fact, the only way to understand Islamic Revivalism is through contextual analysis. Neither universal claims nor subsequent application to particulars are acceptable, because, as in the words of Edward Said, "Islam varies from place to place, subject to both history and geography."[8]

The five common themes outlined above can be combined in the following definition of Islamic Revivalism: *a militant and fundamentalist revitalization of core Islamic values in the form of historical regression, occurring as a reactionary protest to the modernization process, which can be explained by particularistic, contextual analysis.* To a very limited extent, this conventional interpretation of Islamic Revivalism is acceptable; it has some validity and predictive power. Yet, we do not fully support this definition to the approach to the problem because it entails a narrow perspective which is fraught with methodological imbalance.

The first noticeable shortcoming is the identification of revivalism with fundamentalism. According to the *Oxford Dictionary,* "revival" is the "act of reviving after decline or discontinuity." Hence the revival of Islam from partial discontinuity and forced decline can have many different forms and dimensions. It may have a fundamentalist character *à la* early wahabbism or the Iranian revival. But Islamic revival need not be exclusively fundamentalist. Modernist-reformist trends may constitute the central part of revivalist movements, as in the cases of Jamal al-Din Afghani, Mohammad Abdu, Mohammad Iqbal, etc. Thus, it is fallacious and unfair to fully equate revivalism with fundamentalism. Rather, today's revivalism is a broader, more comprehensive trend, of which fundamentalism is only one part.

Second, contrary to assertions made by Western scholars and journalists, Islamic revivalism does not necessarily require or connote militant violence, and opposition movements are not the only ones which are inspired by it. Islamic revivalism is wide in its choice of activistic instrumentality. It can be militant, violent, and massively transformative. Yet it may also appear in forms of moderate bargaining, accommodation, and incremental protests. Here again the militancy of revivalism is not the only approach available to current Islamic resurgence movements. The leaders of each movement have a wide array of choices in this regard, and the choice of tactics and instruments is a function of various factors.

These factors include the context in which the movements are located, leadership style, intensity and pervasiveness of repression and injustice, and ruling regimes' responses. Furthermore opposition groups do not have a monopoly on revivalist elements of Islam. These elements are also widely utilized and manipulated by the ruling regimes as effective legitimization tools. Thus it is risky and fallacious to label recent revivalist movements as militant, violent, and exclusively tools of opposition groups.

Third, conventional interpretations of Islamic revivalist movements are far too preoccupied with the role of history and the dichotomy of modernization and traditionalism. It is correct to point to the rapid pace of modernization as the primary cause of Islamic revivalism. It is equally valid to argue that history has become an idealized source of future direction in Muslim societies. However, this approach overlooks the fact that the rate of modernization is less important than its overall direction and outcome. If the direction and outcome of modernization disturb the core values of Islam, create social and political inequalities, and require the victimization of the masses in Muslim societies, they are certainly central to understanding the rise of Islamic revivalist movements. But it is quite fallacious to assert that traditional Islam opposes any and all modernization efforts, or that the Islamic revivalist movement demands an unconditional, blind regression to the past. In Islam, progress that remains within the boundaries of the *Quran* and the *Sunnah* is most valued, and encouraged. This concept of progress inspires Muslims to incorporate modernization creatively and to recapture or advance the declined glory of Islam. The excessive emphasis on history which is so prevalent in the current literature can hinder more than enhance a correct understanding of Islamic revivalism.

Finally, the insistence on understanding each separate revivalist movement within its particular context undermines a systemic conceptualization of this transnational phenomenon. While particulars are important for analysis, the universal characteristics in the rising tide of Islam cannot be ignored. Without a firm grasp of these universal characteristics and attributes, it is impossible to comprehend the particulars or to measure relative distances between different revivalist movements. Without such measurement of relative distances, any projection of the global implications of the movement will be a difficult task. Thus our key methodological assertion is such that we can and must formulate a universal framework through which we can understand numerous particulars in a coherent and systematic manner. It follows that aggregate data analysis is a useful tool for understanding this transnational revivalist phenomenon.

Typologies of Islamic Revivalism: Search for Many Meanings

Explicit in the above critique is the fact that current interpretations of Islamic revivalism are based on a narrow definitional category. Such interpretational orientations help us see only a segment of the wide range of Islamic revivalism, which, in turn, induces us to confuse the nature of the part with that of the whole. Thus, what we propose is to formulate a much broader definitional boundary that can help us analytically to capture diverse variants of the revivalist movement in comparative perspective.

For the sake of simplicity, the definitional structure of Islamic revivalism can be analyzed by examining ideologies, strategies, tactics, and the perceptions of revivalist movements in order to extract goals and means. There is a high degree of homogeneity of congruence of goal structure among revivalist movements, while the means to attain the goals vary from one movement to another. The goal which is most common among revivalist movements is clear-cut: the creation of a social order organized around the notion of the *Muslim Umma*[9] (a community of believers), based on sincerity and good deeds, and where the basic principles of Islam are well preserved and the *Shariah* is fully implemented. The reconstruction and maintenance of the *Dar al-Islam* (the House of Islam),[10] as against the *Dar al-Harb* (the House of War), is the ultimate goal of these movements. Preservation of the *Dar al-Islam* creates conditions for the full satisfaction of the spiritual and material needs of the people, as prescribed in the *Quran* and *Sunnah*.

This common goal of revivalist movements is best understood by looking at the doctrine of *tawhid* (the Oneness of God). The doctrine of *tawhid* refers to the oneness or unity of God, as is clear from the most fundamental tenet of Islam which is, "there is nothing but Allah (God)."[11] It is by this doctrine of *tawhid* that Islam transcends an ordinary Western meaning of religion. The principle of *tawhid* requires that Muslims regard the entire universe as "a unity, instead of dividing it into this world and the hereafter, the physical and metaphysical, substance and meaning, matter and spirit."[12] It follows from this doctrine that Islam is viewed as a total, unified, and comprehensive way of life, such that boundaries between secular sociopolitical realms and religious realms become blurred. The Ummaunity of the *Umma,* and the relations of individuals to it are logically deduced from this principle of *tawhid.* In other words, the notion of *tawhid* and realization of this principle—reconstruction and preservation of Muslim *Umma* as an ideal social order—constitute the core of the goal structure of Islamic revivalism. It is due to this goal structure that the Islamic revivalist is not purely a religious one in the restricted sense of the word "religion," but rather it encompasses all segments of society, the "realm of immanence."

The neat goal structure of the revivalist movement as substantiated by the principle of *tawhid* is subject to many different interpretations, which implies a multitude of means to actualize the goals. Ideally, the unity of God and its extension to society (*Umma*) and to individual believers (*Mu'min*) is spontaneous. In reality, however, it may be characterized by "an incoherent combination, full of division, contradiction and incongruity, possessing conflicting and independent poles, and disparate and disconnected essences, desires, calculations, criteria, aims, and wills."[13] When individuals and societies approach the unity and totality of God, a multitude of interpretations and conceptions of the correct manner in which to strive for the goals is unavoidable. The following three quotations succinctly illustrate such differences shared by three prominent leaders of Islamic revivalist movements:

> The law of Islam is *eternally* applicable, because it is not based on the customs and traditions of any particular people, and it is not for any particular period, but it is based on the same principles of the nature on which man has been created.[14]

> I support religion; I support a reformed, revised Islam, specifically leading to an Islamic renaissance movement . . . The image of Islam must therefore be changed; the socially traditional to be transformed into an ideology; the collection of mystical studies currently being taught replaced by self-conscious faith; the centuries-long decline into a resurgence . . . He would confront the cultural imperialism of the West and, with the force of religion, awaken his own society stupefied with religion. He would thus mobilize society.[15]

> The message of Islam was sent to the world fourteen centuries ago. Does it need reinterpretation? Is it not meant for the whole world and for all time? The answer to both questions is in the affirmative. Even if a message

is true, and in a sense eternal, it is, by the very premises essential to understand it, in accordance with the science, philosophy, psychology, metaphysics and theology of the modern world . . . I wish to understand the Quran as it was understood by the Arabs of the time of the Prophet, only to reinterpret it and apply it to my conditions of life and to believe in it, so far as it appeals to me as a twentieth-century man . . . I am bound to understand and accept the message of Islam as a modern man, and not as one who lived centuries ago.[16]

Common to all three passages is the idea that the revitalization of Islam is a challenge which should be met in the contemporary era. All search for ideal conditions of an orderly and just society based on Islamic precepts. Nonetheless, they differ regarding the ways and means to achieve the goal. Abul ala Maududi, the author of the first quotation, believes that the fundamental tenets of Islam as prescribed in the *Quran* and the *Sunnah* can be understood on their own terms and their entirety. Any recourse to other sources, particularly exogenous ones, will lead to immorality and spiritual harm. There is no need to rely on other sources for references, because Islam is universal, timeless, and encompassing. It provides a necessary and sufficient solution to any type of problem. This is applicable regardless of time and space. Thus, the evolution of society and individuals should take place purely within the framework of Islam as prescribed by the *Quran* and the *Sunnah*. This is very much a fundamentalist approach. The fundamental roots of Islam are strictly adhered to and there is no association with supplementary sources. The same line of reasoning can be seen in the works of Hasan al-Banna, Sayyid Qutb, and Ayatollah Khomeini and their followers.

While the first quotation reflects an orthodox-fundamentalist orientation, the second one (Ali Shariati) displays a slightly different approach to the creation of an ideal Islamic social order. It reveals a strong love for Islam. It sets Islam as an ideal goal, through which society and individuals are to be rescued. But the image of Islam should be changed in such a manner that it becomes progressive, transformative and dynamic. What Ali Shariati had in mind in this quotation is that Islam should be reinterpreted or reformed in order to cope with actual pathological reality. This requires a radical (or, as others accuse, socialistic) reinterpretation of Islamic sources. Of course, this reinterpretation is supposed to be aided by an exogenous ideology. Ali Shariati and his followers argue that Islam has endogenous sources which make radical interpretation possible. But it seems clear that the availability of socialist ideology has induced them to reinterpret the *Quran* and *Sunnah* in their own particular manner. His enemies are Pharoah (the symbol of political oppression), Croesus or Korah (symbol of capital and capitalism), and the Balaam (the symbol of the hypocrisy exercised by intellectuals and priests, i.e., *mullahs* and *ulama*).[17] The destruction and eradication of these three evils are the preconditions for the creation of an ideal society of Muslim *Umma* as dictated by *tawhid.*

The last quotation is from Asaf A. Fyzee, a prominent jurist of Kashimer. It reflects the modernist line of reasoning, in sharp contrast with the other two. His exhortation is clear: Muslims should break away from blind adherence to tradition (i.e., that of the fundamentalist orientation) and allow Islamic values to assimilate modern values coming from the West. From this perspective, Western ways of science, philosophy, and others are not only conducive to understanding Islamic revelations, but also instrumental in the actualization of the goals of Muslims as prescribed in the source of Islam. This line of thought has been well advanced by a number of revivalist leaders like al-Afghani Abduh, and Iqbal. These three persons asserted that many Western scientific and philosophic ideas originally came from Islam. Thus, the rationale behind their advocacy of assimilating the Western civilization is based on the notion that Islam is getting back many of the things that it had given away to the West in the past. In theory and in actual practice, this acceptance of incremental and accommodative changes pervades many varieties of Islamic revivalism.

A brief comparison of these three revivalist thinkers illustrates a relative distance among the various revivalist movements. In fact, the ultimate destinations or goals of these movements are identical, in the sense that they serve to create and maintain an ideal Islamic society. However, there are many different ideas about how to achieve it.[18] As explicit in the above, they could be fundamentalistic, radical, or modernistic. The paths to the goal vary from one group to the next, depending on the leader's interpretation of core Islamic values and the situations under which the revivalist movement is emerging. This diversity of the paths may be well understood by carefully looking at the major structural properties of revivalist movement to change social reality in a preferred direction on the basis of Islamic principles as its proponents perceive and interpret them. As is common to most social reform movements, however, the notion of change involves three major properties, that is, the object, the rate and amount and types of tactical means of change.[19] Thus, the best way to distinguish different variants of revivalist movements is analytically and empirically to locate the differentials in these properties. Since the nature of the goals preferred by them is homogeneous, it is difficult for us to differentiate different revivalist movements with reference to it.

The object of change can be either the individual or society, or both; revivalist movements may aim at changing individuals first through revivalist sentiment and discipline. The line of reasoning related to the choice of the individual as the primary object of reform usually comes either from the idea that societal level change can be achieved only if individuals are previously changed and reformed, or the notion that societal integrity as such is good and virtuous, but individuals, themselves, are contaminated. Or this line of thinking may come from the belief that any attempts to trigger changes on the societal level entail undesirable disorder and instability of the society. Thus it is better to change the society incrementally by beginning with individuals. However, an opposite line of reasoning is also possible. This phenomenon is that individuals are uncontaminated and good, but evil is a social whole instigated by corrupt rulers and elites, as well as the institutions they create. Once an evil-laden social structure is reformed, change (or reform) at the individual level is automatically and spontaneously accomplished. From this perspective then, the immediate object of change should be the sociopolitical structure or social relations, not the individual. One caveat is, however, in order: the dichotomy between individual and society is, of course, artificial, because the ultimate goal of the revivalist movement is to reform both the individual and society, as made clear in the principle of *tawhid.* Yet, the reason behind this dichotomy is such that in the dynamic reality of the revivalist movement, there is a tentative or transitory division between individual and society. That division is instrumental, not premanent, as a way of placing initial emphasis or priority of change. The careful delineation of this priority ordering in the choice of object of change would enable us to examine the nature of each movement more precisely.

The second important property of revivalist movements that can help us elucidate the nature of Islamic revivalism is the rate and amount of change. The rate and amount of change can be measured by the velocity and gravity of change which each revivalist movement pursues. For example, some groups may advocate total and immediate change of society. "Total" means complete change of the individual or society according to the principles of Islam. No exogenous value systems or influences are allowed in the process or in the final stages of reform. "Immediate" means no delay in initiation and implementation of the change. Thus, when a group pursues a total and immediate change, it tends to be very radical. On the other hand, some revivalist movement may search for incremental and partialistic change of society and individuals. In this case, the existing framework of their society is not totally rejected. Nor does it forbid a modest and just incorporation into Islam of exogenous values, particularly values associated with modernization. Thus, gradual and partial reform tends to be accommodative, absorbing the existing reality. The distinction between immediate and total on the one hand, and incremental and partial on the other, is not rigidly drawn. Rather, they are located on the same continuum. The velocity and gravity of change may range from one extreme of what is immediate and total to another extreme of that which is incremental and partial.

The last important dimension is the tactical choice of the means of change. The means of reforming society or individuals varies in revivalist movements. And the range of choice is wide—from affirmative-moderate to negative-militant. Any revivalist movement employing affirmative and moderate means tends to be accommodative and less likely to resort to violent means. The social establishment and the existing status of individuals are taken for granted, and the reform is initiated within the framework of this existing reality. Persuasion, coalition, logrolling, bargaining, and sometimes deception, become the tools for instituting or spreading the voices and ideologies of the revivalist movement. On the other hand, revivalist movements which choose the second tactical course tend to be aggressive. They are highly likely to rely on violent and militant protests and struggles. They wish to negate the existing reality totally and repudiate it by violent means. Organized underground resistance, street demonstrations, harsh application of coercive tools, and even guerilla warfare become salient means of change. Nonetheless, one must remember that a tight and discrete bipolarity between these two types of tactical means does not exist. They are intermingled and movements may swing between the two extreme poles, depending upon the nature of reality unfolding out there.[20]

Figure 5.1 locates various different types of Islamic revivalist movements in the three dimensional coordinates by utilizing the three salient properties of the revivalist trend. It is our assertion that the typologies formulated here include all the existing revivalist movements in one single analytical universe, which in turn enables us to understand the overall trend, direction, diffusion, and intensity of each revivalist movement in a historical and comparative perspective. Let us briefly discuss the eight typologies made here.

Type I: Dimensional Coordinate A: Individualistic Militant Revivalism. Individual militant revivalism can usually be seen in aggressive Muslim minority movements like the Mindanao National Liberation Front (Philippines), Pattani Liberation Movement (Thailand), and some Muslim minority movements in India, China, and the Soviet Union. It focuses on the individual Muslim as an immediate object of reform in order to enhance Islamic identity among Muslims, which eventually can be used to oppose the regimes of the majority. Their ultimate goal is the creation or preservation of a Muslim *Umma,* in which the *Sharia* (as opposed to secular law) becomes available to Muslims, even under the majority rule of another ethnic group. However, their immediate goal is not the reform of Muslims in a fundamentalist manner. They recognize that, inevitably, Muslims will be mixed with the dominant exogenous culture and that they are under the legal and *de facto* influence of the secular social structure. Yet their means of reform are very militant and negative. This is mainly a function of the intensity of the majority regime's repression and the lack of communication with the majority regime. As we shall discuss, this type of revivalism is prevalent in societies where ethnic distinctions coincide with class distinctions, and where Muslims are structurally victimized by the ethnic discrimination. Of course, it must be noted that a movement under this category may go beyond the initial stage of "individualistic" orientation and eventually enter into the stage of collective efforts to preserve its own Islamic community—not only by social reforms from within, but also by social revolutions against the existing majority rule.

Type II: Dimensional Coordinate B: Individualistic Fundamentalist Revivalism. This version of revivalism is unique in many ways. It does not emphasize the social structure as an object of reform; instead, it focuses on individuals. But the reform is directed toward a total repudiation of any secular, heterogeneous elements contained in individuals. Their means, perceptions, and ways of

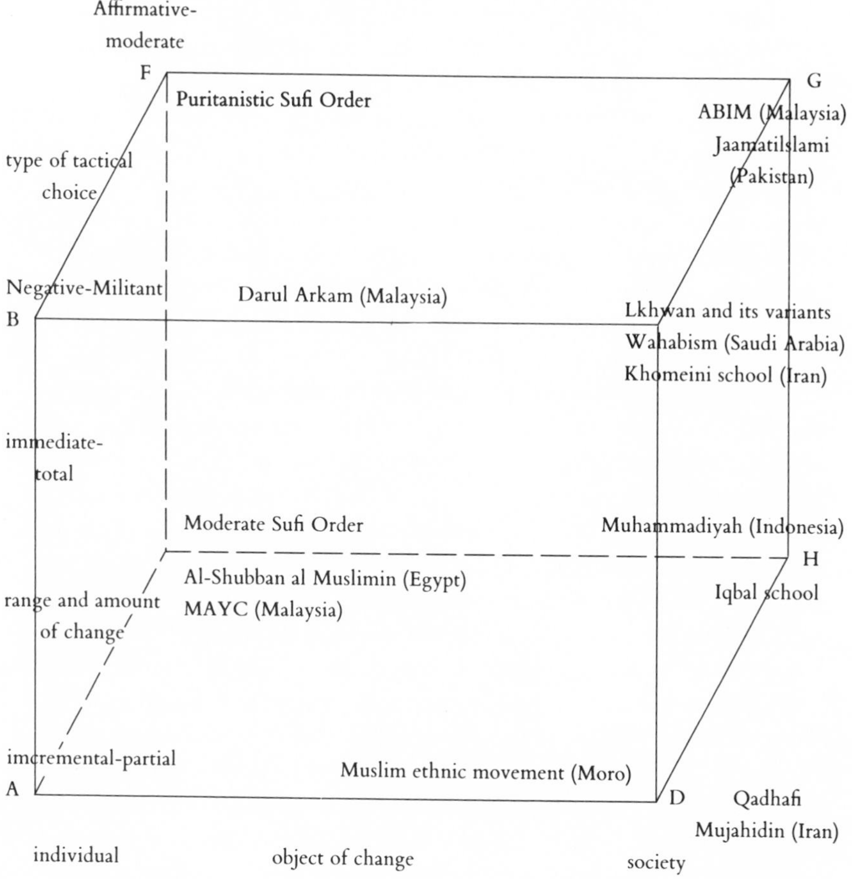

	Dimension Coordinate	*Title* 1
Type I =	A	Individualistic Militant Revivalism
Type II =	B	Individualist Fundamental Revivalism
Type III =	C	Orthodox Fundamental Revivalism
Type IV =	D	Partialistic Radical Revivalism
Type V =	E	Incremental Modernist Revivalism
Type VI =	F	Introvert Fundamentalist Revivalism
Type VII =	G	Incremental Fundamentalist Revivalism
Type VIII =	H	Eclectic Modernist Revivalism

Figure 5.1: Typology of Islamic Revivalism

rejecting the social establishment are militant and negative. The followers of this trend are opposed to a secular reality and try to destroy it militarily. They pursue an extreme version of fundamentalist ideas by reviving the mode of conduct which prevailed in the time of the Prophet and early Caliphates. They are exclusive; they seclude their followers from the rest of the society, and create their own self-reliant micro-*Umma.* Here re-education of Muslims who are believed to have been contaminated by harmful exogenous values constitutes the central part of the movement. This can be seen in the *Tabligh* movements of India and Pakistan,[21] and *Dar al-Arqam*[22] of Malaysia.

Type III: Dimensional Coordinate C: Orthodox Fundamentalist Revivalism.[23] Orthodox Fundamentalism is the most visible and influential trend among Islamic revivalist movements. The best and most successful example is the case of Iran under Ayatollah Khomeini. The followers of *Ikwhan-il-Muslimin,* both new and old,[24] of Abul ala Maududi (Pakistan), and early Wahabbism belong in this category. They argue that both societies and individuals are corrupted deviants which have attempted to introduce innovations *(biba)* to the *Quran.* The reform should take place simultaneously. However, individual reform is impossible unless the social structure and its progeny, the existing corrupt political structure, are dismantled. Hence societal improvement slightly precedes the individual change. The rate and direction of reform in Orthodox Fundamentalist Revivalism is immediate and total. Islamic law is to be universally applicable, regardless of time and space. Exogenous values, and conflictive interpretations, as well as suspicions of the Holy law, are intolerable. The society and the individuals within must be completely changed in accordance with Islamic law. The *Shariah* should be transformed into a *"Theo-democracy."*[25] On the other hand, realization of this ideal social vision generates harsh resistance from the existing regime and classes supporting the regime. This resistance cannot be overcome without the use of equally violent and militant measures, including Muslim mass revolution. In this context, a moderate and accommodative attitude is considered hypocritical and cowardly.[26]

Type IV: Dimensional Coordinate D: Partialistic Radical Revivalism. Muammar Qadhafi's Third Universal theory,[27] Ali Shariati and his followers like the *Mujahidin* in Iran,[28] and the Islamic socialism expounded in the early Nasserist period[29] are all good examples of this trend. For them, the utmost social evii is the prevailing social structure in which the masses suffer from the exploitative behavior of the ruling class—dictatorial political rulers, capitalists, petit bourgeoisie intellectuals and *ulama.* Unless the social structure is dismantled, there is no hope of bringing justice and peace to the masses, which they perceive as the central tenet of Islam. Thus, society becomes the target. But this reform need not necessarily be fundamentalist. A radical interpretation of the fundamental sources of Islam, together with some exogenous sources (particularly Marxist socialist ideas), is even permissible.[30]

In this sense they advocate a partial application of Islamic principles. However, since their ideal vision of society radically differs from the existing one, they are destined to face considerable opposition and repression from the ruling social classes and forces. At this point, they resort to covert or overt militant and violent means of struggle. To a certain extent, Islamic revivalism itself becomes instrumental for social transformation into an ideal state where Islamic principles are combined with exogenous values.

Type V: Dimensional Coordinate E: Incremental Modernist Revivalism. Incremental modernist revivalism is introverted and moderate. Its proponents focus on individuals rather than on the macro societal structure. Less politicized and participatory, they seek to educate Muslims to be good and pious. They want Muslims to be adaptable to changing societal conditions. This goal is reached incrementally, not in a total, violent, and militant fashion. Although this line of revivalism is very individualistic, groups which initiate this kind of movement have emerged. *Al-Shubban al-Muslimin*[31] of Egypt and Malaysian Association of Youth Clubs (MAYC)[32] of Malaysia are good examples. They use Islamic principles to inspire Muslims to become well-adapted to the existing societal establishment and be successful within it. They do not believe that Islamic values clash with modern values. This perception in turn conditions their moderate and affirmative attitude towards reform. This movement is quite often accused of passivity and opportunism by other radical and fundamentalist groups. Meanwhile, most governments in the Islamic countries pursuing the line of modernism or socialism encourage explicitly or implicitly this form of Islamic activism, which enables separation between religion and politics.

Type VI: Dimensional Coordinate F: Introvert Fundamentalist Revivalism and Type VII: Dimensional Coordinate G: Incremental Fundamentalist Revivalism. Introvert fundamentalist revivalism is one of the most powerful trends among recent revivalist movements. The Jamaat-i-Islami, both in Pakistan and Bangladesh,[33] the World Assembly of Muslim Youth (WAMY),[34] Malaysian Muslim Youth Movement (ABIM) and various minor Islamic revivalist groups all over the Islamic world are representative of this line. To a great extent, many are identical with the Orthodox Fundamentalist Revivalist movement in that they advocate total societal and individual reform in complete accordance with Islamic principles. To them, evil has permeated both individual and society. Individual and society should be reborn. However, a difference emerges with respect to instruments for reform. While Orthodox Fundamentalist Revivalists tend to employ militant means in their total negation of the establishment, Incremental Fundamentalist Revivalists take a moderate path in which they do accept the existing social framework to some extent. Of course, even if they accept it, this social reality is subject to incremental change. To effect this, however, they do not withdraw from society. They participate directly or indirectly through political parties, pressure groups, and social movements. They wish to increase their power, social base and leverage in order eventually to repudiate the establishment and to create an ideal Islamic order in the society. This affirmative aspect prevents followers from utilizing militant and violent means of reform. This approach of moderation without altering the fundamentalist goal of reform has attracted a wide range of supporters. Furthermore, this group does not totally forbid *Ijtihad* (independent reasoning). It allows an Islamic interpretation of modern trends, as illustrated by the words of Anwar Ibrahim, head of ABIM:

> Does modernization mean having liquor factories? If so, then we are against modernization. Does modernization mean electronics factories? Then we are for modernization. There is nothing against development in Islam, but such development must have a moral basis. It must be just, not exploitative.

Type VIII: Dimensional Coordinate H: Eclectic Modernist Revivalism. Eclectic modernist revivalism has constituted the mainstream of modern Islamic revivalism since the 19th century. Its original proponents—al-Afghani, Abduh, Rida, and Iqbal—are still influential in shaping the direction of the revitalist movement as a whole. The key theme of this trend is an emphasis on the compatibility of Islam with Western modern civilization. The tide of modernization is not to be feared, but wisely digested and incorporated to the benefit of Muslims. The practical and scientific achievements of the West are not considered satanic evils to be labelled as *bida* and *shirk,* but, rather, a merit to the Muslim *Umma.* For these scholars, the scientific spirit of the West was inspired by various Islamic thinkers, and what Muslim societies have been doing in the process of modernization has been nothing but getting back what was theirs previously, though in a more developed form. It requires reconstruction of society as a whole in addition to individual reconstruction. More specifically, its proponents favor incremental modification of society via introduction of a new modern educational system and other beneficial Western innovations. Explicit here is the advocacy of a partial societal reform through an eclectic synthesis of basic Islamic principles and selective Western modern values. They prefer gradual and moderate societal reform to radical militancy. Gradual and persuasive enlightenment of individuals and society becomes an important tactic to reform society. This moderation can be clearly observed in al Afghani's assertion that there is no sound justification for dismantling the despotic regime, no matter how unjust and dictatorial, because Muslims are perceived as having lost the capacity to create a sound and creative political entity such as a republic.

The partial, affirmative-moderate, and societal reform advocated by Eclectic Modernist Revivalism cannot be achieved without a liberal interpretation of basic Islamic principles. In fact, they have progressively interpreted the *Quran* and *Sunna,* and widened the opening of the gate of *Ijtihad* to accommodate some liberal Western values and scientific achievements. As Muhammad Abduh succinctly prescribed, they attempted to translate *maslaha* into utility, *shura* into parliamentary democracy, and *ijma* into public opinions. In this manner, Eclectic Modernist Revivalism has attempted to keep pace with the growing tide of modernization. Nonetheless, this does not mean that it has deviated from the main orthodox line of reasoning, with respect to the fundamentals of Islam. Its proponents argue that the roots *(usul)* of Islam are untouchable, but the branches *(furu')* are subject to reinterpretation, contrary to dogmas of some *ulama.* Government authorities of many Islamic countries now trying to modernize, while maintaining Islam as a basis of legitimacy, have accepted their ideas in one way or another. At the same time, many Muslim social organizations, like *Muhammadiyah* of Indonesia, have adopted their principles.

The different types of revivalist movements formulated above clearly help us understand the diversity of Islamic revivalism in a comprehensive and comparative framework.[35] Their goals are identical, as epitomized by the doctrine of *tawhid.* In other words, their final goal is the preservation, cohesion and strengthening of the *umma* and that this religious community, by definition, is Islamic, that is, under the rule of the *Quran* and everything this rule entails. All its social institutions are meant to realize the Islamic way of life where Islamic concepts of 'justice', 'equality', 'rights', 'freedom', and 'welfare' and so on can be made operative. Yet their means of achieving these goals are wide-ranging and diverse. If the goal is identical, how have differentials emerged in ways and means?

The eight typologies formulated above are by no means static and fixed. They move around dynamically from one dimensional coordinate to another. Under what conditions does this transformation in the choice of means and ways take place? The next section deals with these two sets of questions in a comparative manner, using an aggregate data base.

The Causal Structure of Islamic Revivalism

Why is Islam reviving? And why do different types of revivalist movements exist? Why does Islamic Revivalism possess a dynamic nature, characterized by changes from one kind of movement to another, rather than a static nature? These important questions must be examined in order to grasp the overall nature of revivalism. Nazih Aybui, an Egyptian sociologist, makes an interesting remark regarding these questions: "If resistance is taking more of an Islamic form in such countries, it is partially because Islam represents one of the most entrenched (and therefore least alien) cultural traits in the society. More practically, however, revolt takes an Islamic expression because quite often there are no other outlets left in society for channeling political demands."[36] Although we disagree with his claim that Islam is used simply as an outlet of last resort, we agree that Islam is the most entrenched cultural trait and that Islamic resistance is a result of the discontent of masses who happen to be Muslims.

We will attempt to show that Islamic Revivalism can be explained by the gap between the ideals shaped by the Islamic socialization process and the reality faced by masses of Muslims. In order to understand this gap, we employ two major concepts of social psychology: those of cognitive dissonance, and those of relative deprivation.[37] Cognitive dissonance refers to the level and degree of incongruence between the internalized images of the socio-economic-political world and the world that actually exists. Relative deprivation describes the discrepancies between the perceived 'ought' and the perceived 'is' of collective value satisfaction. Using these two methodological concepts, we may be able to explain the causal structure of Islamic revivalism cogently.

Islam does not distinguish between immanence and transcendence, church and politics, religion and economics, secularism and divinity, and so on. Islam is a unified way of life. Islam, as a social totality, plays important socioeconomic and political roles in the socialization process of Muslims. It determines their mode of conduct and ethical systems. It shapes their conception of political and economic reality. And it provides a sense of group solidarity.[38] Thus, Islam powerfully contributes to the formation of internalized collective images of the ideal society in the process of socialization. The internalized images of the ideal society are directly or indirectly linked to the basic principles of Islam revealed in the *Quran* and *Sunnah,* and to their concrete crystalization in the period of the Prophet and early Caliphates. The internally socialized images of ideal society include the following dictates:

1. The political community should be fully legitimate by securing the service of God through *shura* (consultation) and the other democratic elements. No repression, dictatorship, or domination is allowed. People are prevented from exploiting each other, the individual freedoms are protected, and law and order prevail. And the *ijma* (consensus) of the *Umma* (community) becomes the very basis by which governance is to be executed. Since sovereignty belongs to God alone by the principle of *tawhid,* all people are equal in the *Shariah,* the law of God. And political leadership is subject to the choice of the *jama'a* (the group), being the *ahl al-'aqd wal-hall* (those with power to bind and to loosen), as representative of whole political community.[39]

2. In the economic realm, social justice and the promotion of public goods are the basis of the Muslim society or *Umma.* By the same principle of *tawhid,* God alone is the owner of all the bounties of the earth, and people share the resources and materials provided by God equally. As a manifestation of God's sovereignty, everyone in the *Umma* is entitled to all those things provided by God,

and all its members have legitimate claims on equal shares in it. It is by this principle that basic human needs should be given priority. Thus, in principle, Islam does not tolerate monopolies, inequitable income and wealth distribution or any type of exploitation of the economically helpless. Islamic institutions, such as *Zakat* (alms-giving), *Sadaqa* (voluntary alms), prohibition of interest *(riba)* and so on, are some good examples of implementing economic justice in the Islamic system. And the leadership of an Islamic system has the obligation to regulate these individual rights and to protect the community from excess. In the ideal Islamic regime, there are no class distinctions or handicaps attached to social status or occupation, and thus complete equality of opportunity for all believers is preserved and guaranteed.[40]

3. In the social, historical, and cultural realms, Islam has pursued independent and glorious ideals and practices of its own. Islam does not permit any form of mass alienation or social atomization, characteristics of modernized society's pathological dimension. It rejects any factors which would reduce mankind to moral degradation or personal frustration. In a true Islamic *Umma,* moral integrity and virtues prevail and individual souls blossom to their fullest. Communal and familial solidarity among Muslims is firm and therefore there is no chance for Muslims to go astray or become alienated. Islam is an autonomous ethical and social system that does not need any exogenous sources to rely on.[41]

In addition, the historical legacy of Islam fortifies Muslims with pride in its glorious past. The light of Islam glowed from Granada to Delhi. Less than a hundred years after the death of Muhammad, his followers had burst out of the Arabian desert to conquer and create an empire whose glories were to shine for a thousand years. They defeated the Byzantines, conquered the Persian empire, and spread the faith through North Africa into Spain, to the Indus River, Malaysia, Indonesia, and the Black tribes of Africa.

To this historical expansion, there is also a cultural pride in past history. While darkness prevailed in Europe, Islamic culture and civilization were the bridges between Hellenistic heritage and Europe's modern renaissance. On top of this, Saladin's victory over the Crusaders, the cultural preservation of Islam even under the Mongol conquest, and the creation of a new Islamic empire under the umbrella of Ottoman rule are all indicative of past glory. Furthermore, the role of Islam in resisting Western imperialists in the late 19th and 20th centuries made a firm impression on the minds of Muslims. Overall, Islam has been a religion of victory and noble pride, rather than one of exodus and cruxification.[42]

In sum, the ideals inherent in Islam have induced or compelled Muslims to cultivate and socialize a collective vision of an ideal society in which a legitimate and consultative polity exists, a just and equitable economic system is set in motion, social harmony and moral integrity prevails, and the past glory of victory and independence is restored. What, however, does the present reality have to offer? Political repression and domination, economic injustice and social atomization, injured pride over past glory, and systematic penetration of the values and economic domination . . . these are the foundations of the current reality. Our conjecture is that the incongruence between the perceived 'ought,' created by the socialized ideals of Islam and the perceived 'is,' manifested in today's reality of collective value satisfaction, is the core force which triggers, shapes, and conditions the direction of Islamic revivalist movements. Since the structure of Islamic ideals are outlined above, the best way to trace and explain the causes of revivalism would be to analyze the present situation which confronts Islamic countries.

What are the present circumstances in Islamic countries? According to an official account of the World Muslim League and the Organization of Islamic Conferences, in all [total] there are forty-four Islamic countries which have gained independence since the Second World War. The present political, economic, and socio-historical conditions in these countries fall quite short of the ideals and visions set by Islam. Despite the recent surge of oil wealth in some of these countries, the overall socio-political-economic conditions are desperate, helpless, chaotic, and fragmentary. Political repression, worsening living conditions, social atomization and withdrawal, and injured historical pride constitute the daily bread in these countries. Within these general conditions, Islamic revivalism easily spreads firm roots. Alienation, poverty, anger, and misery translate into collective cognitive dissonance and deprivation which eventually burst into various forms of Islamic revivalism. Thus, Islamic revivalism is not a purely "religious" phenomenon. It is in this fact that a collective expression of indignant protests over the perceived reality which falls far short of the ideals and visions of Islam that have been so deeply engraved in Muslim minds throughout the socialization process. Thus, in order to describe and explain Islamic revivalism, we must first carefully examine the social, political, and economic roots of this trend.

Political Reality: Emerging Legitimacy Crisis

As noted above, Islam urges the maintenance of a political entity full of virtue, goodness, and justice. In a truly Islamic polity, *shura* (consultation), *ijma* (consensus), and *maslaha* (public interest) prevail in a clearly defined institutional manner. Hence, the authentic nature of Islam preserves individual freedoms, enhances social justice, and promotes communal unity and solidarity. This ideal vision has been mercilessly shattered by the political reality of contemporary Islamic states. The function of *shura* has been replaced by a one-party system, military junta, and ruling family meetings. *Ijma* has degenerated into personal whims and dogmatism of authoritarian military rulers and monarchical leaders. In addition, the notion of *maslaha* has been interpreted as class interests of family or personal interests. In *Table 5.1*, it is clear that among 44 Islamic countries, only a handful resemble the ideal polity envisioned in Islam. Iran, Saudi Arabia, and some Gulf Emirates pursue principles of Islam, retain Islamic legal entity, and maintain to some extent an Islamic form of government. Other than these countries, most Islamic countries fall into secular, authoritarian military, or traditional monarchical regime types.[43] What we are arguing here is that not only does political reality diverge widely from the Islamic ideal, but there are, in addition, actual pathological syndromes associated with the political realities in most Islamic countries.

Pathological syndromes of the current Islamic political reality can be analyzed from many different angles. The first syndrome would be ideological exhaustion of political leadership. With the influx of modern ideologies, political leaders in many Islamic countries have attempted to emulate them. Kemalism, Nasserism, Ba'athism, Destourism, and scientific socialism are indicative of this trend. None, however, were at all successful. Despite an initial triumphant rush, Kemalism failed to both fully eradicate the vestiges of Islam and institute complete secularism in Turkey. Islam in Turkey still remains a strong social force, not only in the political arena, but also among the masses. In Egypt, Nasserist ideology was shattered with military defeat in the later part of the 1960s. And that subjugated Islamic zeal is resurfacing is clear from Sadat's assas-

TABLE 5.1

Regime Type and Level of Legitimacy of Islamic Countries

	Pluralistic or Quasi-Pluralistic Regimes	*Military or Quasi-Military Regimes*	
level of legitimacy	H: none	H: none	
	M: Cameron Gambia Malaysia Senegal	M: Algeria Mali Tunisia	
	L: Lebanon Gabon	L: Afghanistan Bangladesh Egypt Chad Gabon Indonesia Iraq Libya Niger	Pakistan Somalia Syria Tunisia Turkey Upper Volta Yemen A.R. Yemen P.D.B. Mauritania
	Conservative Monarchy Regimes	*Islamic Regimes*	
	H: none	H: none	
	M: Bahrain Kuwait U.A.E.	M: Qatar Saudi Arabia	
	L: Jordan Morocco Oman	L: Iran	

sination. Exogenous liberal and/or radical ideologies have been instrumental in the seizure of political power and the consolidation of political leadership. However, their outcome was failure which created ideological exhaustion and chaotic political order.

This ideological exhaustion has coincided with a series of impending national crises, which, in turn, has led to recognition of the political incompetence of leadership. Now most Islamic countries are facing acute national crises. Spiralling inflation, deepening unemployment, economic inequalities, and delayed results of economic development are the striking features of today's Islamic countries. In addition, anarchic political strife manifested in the form of ethnic conflicts, class conflicts, and regional disputes constitute their overwhelming political reality. Confronting this set of acute national crises, the political leaderhip have been unable to cope with them effectively. The incompetence of political leadership could once have been buttressed by a leader's charismatic ideology. Now given that this ideology has been proven ineffective, another pathological dimension has been added to the dilemma of these countries.

The third dimension of political pathology is a growing inequality in the distribution of political power among social forces. With the inception of authoritarianism in most Islamic countries, the traditional political functions of Islam, that is, the notions of *shura* and *ijma,* have been structurally deprived. The deprivation of the functional mechanism of *shura* connotes systemic exclusion of mass participation. The enforced invalidation of *ijma* has eradicated the once powerful role of a traditional force, the *ulama,* in Islamic society. The consequence of this rearrangement of political power by coercive means has been a sharp asymmetry of power distribution among major social forces. This inequality of political power and the systemic obstruction of demands for participation by the Muslim mass and the traditional forces such as the *ulama* have consolidated an artificial legitimation of political repression.

Ideological exhaustion, leadership incompetence, and growing political repression, all indicative of political pathology in today's Islamic countries, have led to a serious dilemma. The legitimacy base of the ruling regimes in these countries is fast eroding. As Max Weber argues, legitimacy is essential to resolve conflict management, and bring about long term stability and endurability of any ruling regime. Without a legitimacy base, regimes are doomed to die away. The present political reality in Islamic countries is best characterized by lack of legitimacy or chronic legitimacy crisis. The legitimacy crisis becomes imminent with the continuing failure of political elites to establish a legitimate public order within viable political communities. Its immediate symptom is a sporadic or systematic rejection of public authority. This rejection erupts in the form of conflictive individual or collective behavior against authority. It may then be possible to determine the extent of the legitimacy crisis by measuring the intensity and frequency of domestic conflictive and cooperative behaviors in relation to public authority, that is, government. *Table 5.1* again indicates the various levels of legitimacy crisis in Islamic countries. We broke down the level of legitimacy in each country into three planes, that is, *high, medium,* and *low,* with the quantification of conflictive and cooperative behaviors which are stored in *COBDAP.*[44] The startling result is that out of 44 Islamic countries, not a single country displays a high level of stability and legitimacy. And the majority of countries in focus (27) have low levels of stability and legitimacy, implying acute legitimacy crisis. Only 17 countries, most of them wealthy in resources due to oil, display a medium level of stability and legitimacy. Furthermore, military or quasi-military regimes are inclined to coincide with low levels of stablility and legitimacy. On the other hand, most of the countries falling into the categories of pluralist and Islamic regime have much higher levels of stability and legitimacy.

The pathological syndrome of these Islamic countries, as manifested in the form of acute legitimacy crisis, is, in our opinion, a critical cause in the emergence of Islamic revivalism. Once a certain regime has exhausted its ideological credibility, it will inevitably confront a deepening legitimacy crisis, and it seems quite natural that an ideology which is not only powerful enough to replace the old and failed one, but also authentic and peculiar to its own political climate, comes into existence. This constitutes the core of revitalization of the Islamic movement.[45] It is particularly true given the fact that people have been politically socialized by the elevated ideals and visions of Islam. One caveat is in order here, however. This prevalent legitimacy crisis does not necessarily instigate a total fundamentalist reform of society in the Islamic manner. The rate, amount, object, and means of Islamic reform are contingent upon the perceptions of revivalist leaders, and their followers' perceptions of political reality. The direction of the reform movement varies around the eight dimensional coordinates (see Figure 5.1) depending upon the levels of legitimacy and stability.

Economic Reality: Structural Victimization. As was briefly discussed above, visions of the ideal economy for any Islamic society have also been implanted in Muslim minds. On the basis of the Quranic injunctions and the actual historical record of the Prophet and early Caliphate days, Muslims envision an ideal Islamic economic system in terms of prosperity, equality, and the effective provision of basic needs for the members of the community. In Islam, God is conceived to be the ultimate possessor and giver of infinite bounty *(Dhul Fadl il 'Azim)*. It is by this basic attribute of God that economic ideals of prosperity, equality, and the satisfaction of basic needs are followed. God gives Muslims bounty on the earth, not to be left idle, but as a trust to be wisely exploited by people in the lawful manner. Thus, economic development compatible with basic principles of Islam is not only recommendable, but also imperative to initiate and to follow. Yet, the wealth and prosperity achieved through economic development and the exploitation of God's gifts like natural resources are not to be monopolized by a handful of people (Quran 59:7). They are to be equally shared among the members of *Umma* with the calculation of difference in talent, ability, and amount of works paid. No excessive accumulation of wealth is allowed, because by dint of the principle of *tawhid,* all material goods are owned only by God (Quran 31:26; 5:120; 7:128 etc.), and *Umma,* as a collective representation of God's will, is entitled to it for the equitable sharing for the benefits of the community. And this egalitarian distribution pattern of ideal Islamic economic system is to be actualized through effective provision of basic needs for the economically deprived (Quran 51:19; 70:24–25). One central function of the Islamic polity is the regulation of excessive wealth taken by the few and the provision of basic social needs, such as shelter, clothing, food, adequate education, medical protection, and provision of equal economic opportunities. Thus, the ideal economic system of a Muslim *Umma* is characterized by social justice and high productivity with the actualization of humanitarian concerns.[46]

In contradistinction with this ideal image of the Islamic economic system, however, the present economic reality of Islamic countries is better described by economic backwardness, deepening inequality gaps, and deteriorating conditions of life. Following a standard measurement of economic wealth in a given society (i.e., per capita GNP), we have attempted to identify the level of economic performance in these Islamic countries. As *Table 5.2* indicates, per capita GNP on the individual basis ranges from the world's highest, that of the United Arab Emirates ($26,850 as of 1980), to the lowest, that of Chad ($120). However, if we exclude oil-producing Islamic countries ($9,867), the absolute and relative level of economic wealth of Islamic countries is strikingly low. Non-oil Islamic countries' average per capita is $363, meaning lower than the average of developing countries as a whole ($575). Even if per capita GNP of oil-exporting Islamic countries is slightly

TABLE 5.2

Selected Socio-Economic Indicators of Islamic Countries (1980)

Countries	*(Millions) Population*	*Per Capita GNP (Dollars)*	*PQLI*	*Adult Literacy % 1976*	*Average Index of Food Production (1970 = 100)*
Algeria	18.79	1,590		35	75
Bahrain	0.34	4,050*			
Bangladesh	84.64	90	28.5	26	92
Cameroon	8.25	560			110
Chad	4.38	120	21	15	
Comoros	0.40	180*			
Djibouti	0.29	450*			
Gabon	0.55	3,199*			
Gambia	0.58	210*			
Guinea	4.91	280	36	20	86
Guinea-Bissau	0.56	180*			
Indonesia	143.58	370	55.1	62	103
Iran	36.70		58	50	109
Iraq	12.40	2,410	60		86
Jordan	2.90	1,180	67	70	89
Kuwait	1.27	17,100	76.6	60	
Lebanon	2.13		80		86
Libya	3.13	8,170	50	50	113
Malaysia	13.31	1,370	73.4	60	112
Maldives	0.15	140*			
Mali	6.41	140	18	10	88
Mauritania	1.49	320	20	17	75

TABLE 5.2

Selected Socio-Economic Indicators of Islamic Countries (1980) (continued)

Countries	*(Millions) Population*	*Per Capita GNP (Dollars)*	*PQLI*	*Adult Literacy % 1976*	*Average Index of Food Production (1970 = 100)*
Morrocco	18.80	740	42.6	28	83
Niger	5.45	270	18	8	89
Oman	0.87	2,510*			
Pakistan	77.90	260	38.1	24	101
Qatar	0.21	11,370*			
Saudi Arabia	8.06	11,260	33		96
Senegal	5.47	430	19	10	88
Somalia	3.89		39	60	85
Sudan	17.76	370	32.3	20	105
Syria	8.37	1,030	67	58	145
Tunisia	6.37	1,120	66	62	118
Turkey	44.24	1,330	60.4	60	110
Uganda	13.10	290	41.7		90
U.A.E.	0.91	26,850	68		
Upper Volta	6.70	180	4		93
Yemen A.	7.30	420	18	13	95
Yemen P.	1.80	480	20	27	106
Egypt	38.9	480	52.2	44	93

Sources: World Bank, *World Development Report, 1981* (Washington, DC: World Bank, 1982), *World Military and Social Expenditure,* 1981, and the Overseas Development Council, *The United States and World Development Agenda 1982* (New York: Praeger, 1982)
*1977

higher than that of some selected advanced industrial countries, actual economic reality of these countries is devastating, as reflected in the phrases, "rentier economy" or "one crop economy." The overall poverty syndrome and structural weakness encompassing the economic reality of Islamic countries are quite sufficient to incur cognitive dissonance among the Muslim masses, which is directly or indirectly linked to the rise of Islamic revivalism.

Economic problems in Islamic countries do not only consist of the overall size of the economic wealth pie. The distribution of the economic pie has been persistently problematic in Islamic countries. GNP does not fully capture the distributional inequalities, as a group of developmentalists have argued recently.[47] To solve this problem, they developed a new measurement for the levels of economic distribution and satisfaction of basic human needs. This new indicator, the physical quality of life index, is a composite of three sub-indicators: life expectancy, infant mortality, and literacy rate. They reason that a society well-equipped with basic human needs such as shelter, clothing, and food will produce higher life expectancy, and lower infant mortality. At the same time, high literacy rate reflects a better education level, which will eventually provide more economic opportunities and thus more income. Utilizing this physical quality of life index, we have attempted to measure the overall economic equality dimension of these Islamic countries.[48] The surprising result of this measurement is such that overall living conditions, both in terms of economic equality and the satisfaction of basic human needs, are tremendously low in Islamic countries compared with other areas. As is clear in *Table 5.2* and also in *Table 5.3,* Islamic countries have the lowest average physical quality of life index. This is even including oil-exporting Islamic countries. The average, 51.5, is relatively and absolutely low, given the fact that the average in developed countries is 94, in developing countries 57, and in the world as a whole, 66. Another remarkable fact is that while most of oil exporting countries remain in top tier for per capita GNP level, they show very low performance in improving their people's physical quality of life. For example, Saudi Arabia has per capita GNP of $11,260, while its PQLI is merely 33, far short of even developing countries' average. Among 36 Islamic countries for which data are available, only two of them fall into the upper tier (75–100), namely Kuwait and Lebanon. And the majority (22 out of 36) fall into the lower tier (0–49).

TABLE 5.3

Relative Comparison of the Physical Quality of Life Index (1980)

World Average	66
Developed Countries	94
Developing Countries	66
Islamic Countries	51.5
Oil Exporting	57.7
Non-oil Islamic	48.7

The theoretical range of PQLI is 0-100.

Sources: World Bank Development Report 1982, *The U.S. and the Third World Development* (Washington D.C.: Overseas Development Council, 1982)

Note: In calculating the average values, data on Bahrain, Cameroon, Djibouti, Gabon, and Guinea Bissau are omitted due to the unavailability of the data needed.

What is implied here is that Islamic countries are not only suffering from structural poverty and economic backwardness, but they are also experiencing a growing inequality gap and the poor satisfaction of basic human needs in the society. Overall living conditions, as manifested in terms of this physical quality of life index, are especially sensational. The current massive accumulation of oil wealth does not necessarily trickle down to the grass roots. This economic malaise, prevalent in Islamic countries, can be best explained by the notion of "structural victimization."[49] Structural victimization is defined as "the condition of rank inequality and disequalibrium in a system which has emerged as a by-product of the historical development of a specific social system."[50] What this term denotes is that individuals are structurally victimized by the socio-economic-political reality. Indications of this reality are structural political and economic inequality, aggravation of the quality of life, and the structural obstruction of political, economic, and social opportunities. The causal structure of structural victimization is unequal distribution of power and capabilities among the social forces in a given society. At this junction, we may be able to clarify the sources of the present economic malaise in Islamic countries. They are not simply colonial legacies, as political leaders of these countries argue. Nor are they the results of traditional institutional factors embedded in the Islamic value system as Weberians point out. They are, rather, a function of the domestic political power structure and secularizing ideologies adopted by political leaders.

The economic malaise of Islamic countries becomes politicized when the masses are structurally victimized and this is coupled with Islamic revivalism. In other words, the present economic conditions, no matter how aggravated and miserable, may not become the direct catalyst for the emergence and diffusion of Islamic revivalism. It is the domestic and external socioeconomic and political structure that is responsible for the acceleration of this Islamic activism. The feeling of relative deprivation and collective cognitive dissonance comes into existence with the direct or indirect conception of built-in mechanisms of inequality and social injustice, which Islam not only negates, but also prohibits and curses.

Socio-Historical Reality: Pathology of Defeatism

In an ideal Islamic society, political soundness and economic prosperity and justice should be complemented by moral integrity and consolidation of the Islamic historical identity. Islam is conceived to be a religion with a perfect ethical system, a religion of victory and glory. Muslims believe that Islam provides them with the necessary and sufficient conditions for the formation and preservation of moral integrity, which leaves nothing to be borrowed from other exogenous ethical systems. At the same time, Muslims become excited whenever they hear of the battles like that of *Badr,* in which the Prophet fought and won. And they take great pride in Islamic civilization and culture. In addition, they are fascinated by historical episodes which describe the expansion of the Islamic empire and the Muslim defeat of the Crusaders. Islam, as a self-sufficient ethical system and as a source of a glorious past, shapes and locates the present locus of the pathological dilemma of socio-historical reality of Islamic countries.

Contrary to this ideal vision of moral integrity and historical pride, Muslims of Islamic countries today are tainted with moral confusion and injured historical pride. With the massive influx of Western influence, either through colonial legacy or through the massive modernization process, the authentic Islamic value system has been endangered. This derives not from the superiority between the two, but from the social destructiveness accompanied by this influx. Massive urbanization has led to social atomization, alienation, and mental frustrations among the Muslim masses. The immense penetration of Western values with its decadent nature, as revealed in liberalized sexual life styles, pervasive prostitution, and other negative values, through global networks of the mass media, has eroded the authentic and desirable values of Islam. Most importantly, Westernization has entailed a Hobbesian version of egoistic atomized individualism in these societies, which is threatening the Islamic notion of family and *Umma,* so central to the ethical and social system of the Islamic world.

In addition to this Western-inspired moral degradation, Islam is facing another crucial historical crisis: a feeling of defeatism prevails, with respect to exogenous forces. This defeatism has culminated in consecutive military defeats with Israel, and the loss of Jerusalem and the Al-Aqsa mosque.[51] The Soviet invasion of Afghanistan revealed this defeat all too clearly: Islamic countries were helpless, despite their condemnation of the invasion. On a much broader level, this defeatism can be found in the deepening of economic, cultural, military, and political dependency on the West. In other words, even after the attainment of formal independence from the colonizers, these Islamic countries are bound by the power and influence of the dominant actors in the international system, not only in the realm of international politics and military relationships but also in economic and cultural spheres. If it is not the actuality, there has been at least a *common feeling* among the Muslim masses that modernization paths pursued by the Muslim world has meant Westernization and a drifting away from Islamic moral values, and that political leaders of Islamic states have been totally dependent upon foreign forces such as communism and Western capitalism combined with Zionism.[52] In particular, the existence of a subtle form of patron-client linkage between corrupt or authoritarian rulers and dominant international actors (i.e., U.S.A. and Soviet Union) has further aggravated a collective image of self-defeatism among the Muslim masses.

In sum, it has been argued that Islamic revivalism is caused and conditioned by the cognitive dissonance of the Muslim masses between ideal visions of Islamic society and actual performance. This cognitive dissonance syndrome has been salient and pervasive in the Islamic countries in terms of the political legitimacy crisis, economic structural victimization, and socio-historical defeatism. However, it is important to keep in mind the fact that, as there are many different levels of these political, economic, and socio-historical malaises, there are correspondingly different types of revivalism, such as we have elucidated in Figure 5.1. Depending upon the intensity and depth of political, economic, and socio-historical conditions, the rate, direction and means of Islamic revivalism can differ, revolving around those eight dimensional coordinates. The relationship between the causes and the resultant patterns of revivalism is, therefore, multiple rather than single. And, the study of these multiple relationships will be reserved for another time. To be more specific, for example, if the overall performance level in legitimacy, structural victimization, and socio-historical defeatism is high, the direction of Islamic revivalism is likely to move from the militant, social and total transformative efforts (i.e., the CDGH dimension in Figure 5.1) to the moderate, individual and partial dimension (i.e., the ABEF dimension). On the other hand, if the degree of incongruence is large (i.e., performance level is low), the reverse trend is likely to emerge in the revivalist movements.[53]

Political Implications of Islamic Revivalism

So far, we have discussed major causal factors leading to the rise of revivalist phenomenon and the resultant types of revivalist movements. Given the multiplicity of types and causes of the revivalist phenomenon, however, it is quite difficult to delineate a discernible commonality of political implications universally applicable to all the cases. Political ideologies, formation of major political actors, political issue context, and tactical and organizational character of each revivalist movement may not be subject to cogent generalization. This is mainly so because all the political factors listed above are contingent upon dynamic changes in the causal structure and the subsequent patterns of revivalist movements.

For example, a revivalist movement in the line of Eclectic Modernism (Type VIII) is likely to be less politicized with moderate political ideology. Thus, the overall political implication of this line of revivalist movement may be less visible or significant in relation to the existing socio-political mood of a given country. On the other hand, Orthodox Fundamentalist (Type III) and Partialist Radical (Type IV) revivalist movements pose visible and significant political impacts on the existing socio-political structure. In the latter case, political ideologies are much more politicized, formation of political actors sympathetic with, or actually involved is well articulated, and the level of political protests and organizational capability are quite sufficient to threaten the existing regimes.

For all the dynamicity and multiplicity of the revivalist phenomenon, however, it is not impossible to diagnose the present status and project future trends of these revivalist movements in a general and/or comparative sense. A careful examination of the causal variables in the comparative perspective sheds some light on the proper diagnosis and projection of the overall political contents of the revivalist movements. Put differently, a comparative data analysis of legitimacy crisis, structural victimization, and socio-historical defeatism, briefly discussed above, helps us capture the overall direction of the revivalist movements.[54] With this in mind, the following section attempts to discuss the various political implications entailed by recent Islamic revivalist movements, with specific focus on the domestic and international dimension.

Domestic Dimension

In the domestic realm, Islamic revivalism is showing at least the three important political characteristics. These are the pervasiveness of the followers, gradual intensification in the form of political protests, and the dual politicization of revivalist sentiments. First, compared with past historical records, Islamic revivalist sentiment, albeit differences in the types of revivalist ideology, is becoming pervasive among the masses in Islamic countries. Islam no longer remains as a bureaucratic religion left to administrative domain of the court or the ministries of Awqaf and religious affairs, or as petrified traditional religion monopolized by *ulama* and other traditional actors. As *Time* magazine has recently reported, Islam is becoming the religion favored by the youth, women, and the masses themselves.[55] A number of people attending the Friday prayer, observing fasting during the month of Ramadan, and participating in informal religious meetings have rapidly increased. Young women are voluntarily wearing veils in public, and Islamic student organizations have become the dominant student organizations in many parts of Islamic countries. Briefly, the mass level efforts to search for Islamic identity and consciousness have grown spontaneously. This could be a reflection of the overall worsening conditions of causal factors leading to the rise of Islamic revivalism. That is to say, enduring legitimacy crisis, deepening structural victimization, and the accumulation of socio-historical defeatism are responsible for this pervasive nature of Islamic revivalism.

Second, this expanded basis of popular sector mobilization in terms of Islamic revivalism is becoming coupled with a further intensification of the militant nature of revivalism. In other words, there is a growing tendency in various revivalist movements to move from the moderate, individual, and partial transformative dimension (i.e., the ABEF dimension in Figure 5.1), to the militant, social, and total transformative dimension (i.e., CDGH dimension in Figure 5.1). The Iranian revolution, the assassination of Anwar Sadat, the Mecca Incident, growing militancy of Islamic student organizations in Egypt, Algeria, Syria, Malaysia, Turkey, and Indonesia, etc., are good indicators of such a trend. It is important here to keep in mind that these violent and militant movements have gained substantial popular support. The massive popular support for the Iranian Revolution in its initial stage, the surprisingly low level of people's condolence shown on the violent death of Sadat, and the chain effects of the Mecca Incident in other regions of Saudi Arabia and its neighbors indicate that there is a direct relationship between the expanding base of revivalist sentiment among the masses and the high level of intensity and frequency of political violence in the revivalist movements. This tendency in turn implies a high probability of socio-political instability in many Islamic countries. It is particularly so, given the possibility that militant oriented revivalist movements may have strong spillover effects on the followers of other moderate and eclectic revivalist movements. As a matter of fact, this possibility is becoming much more plausible in the sense that the success of the Iranian Revolution has implanted a high aspiration among militant revivalists with specific lessons of the tactics, strategy, organization, and ideology of struggle.[56]

The third important political content of Islamic revivalism is the dual politicization of Islamic revivalist sentiments. While opposition groups, in particular, and the masses, in general, have attempted to delegitimize the incumbent ruling regimes, the ruling regimes, in turn, have recently tried to enhance their legitimacy base and consolidate power by utilizing Islam. At the crossroad of the exhaustion of exogenous ideologies and subsequently weakened legitimacy, it would be quite a natural choice for political elites to mobilize Islam as a counterveiling instrument to the mounting opposition from the various revivalist groups. A telling example would be the case of Pakistan under Zia ul-Haq. Zia has witnessed the consecutive failure of two exogenous ideologies: that of capitalism under Ayub Khan and of socialism under Zulfiqer Bhutto. Thus, Islam was a logical choice for him. Immediately after the seizure of power, he proclaimed the comprehensive introduction of the Islamic system *(Nazim-i-Islami)*, by which the *Sharia* benches are supposed to be established, *hudud* (Islamic punishment of drinking, adultery, theft, and false testimonies) are implemented, and the gradual actualization of the Islamic welfare system is promised.[57] Zia's choice is fundamentalistic and orthodox, to the extent that it has gone beyond original expectations of Islamic opposition groups such as the Jamaat-i-Islami. Nonetheless, there is no sign of reduction of political opposition. Rather, opposition has intensely grown, and the political climate in Pakistan has become more precarious. The reason behind this stalemate is that Zia attempts to realize Islamic goals by violating other essential elements of Islamic political principles, such as consent, consensus, and consultation with Islamic community. Surely military autocratic rule of the present regime will not provide him with the Islamic legitimacy that he is desperate to obtain.

The dual politicization of Islamic revivalism in terms of antagonistic conflict between legitimation and delegitimation is not unique to the case of Pakistan. Immediately following the Mecca Incident, the ruling regime in Saudi Arabia had pursued a tighter implementation of the *Sharia* in all aspects of society. This was not only in response to a specific event, such as the Mecca Incident, but also a part of the overall attempts to re-enhance the weakened political legitimacy of the ruling regime in the process of rapid modernization. However, oppositional sentiments are prevalent among *ulama,* young Muslim fundamentalists, and some traditional actors.[58] Qadhafi's adherence to Islam,[59] Sadat's advocacy of Islam in the eclectic modernist line,[60] Bathist regimes' appeasement policy to Islamic opposition groups in Syria and Iraq,[61] and Mahathir's accommodative approach to Islamic fundamentalists in Malaysia,[62] and so on, are good examples of utilizing Islamic revivalist sentiments to legitimize their regimes and consolidate political power from broader segments of society. For all the political concessions and goodwill gestures on the basis of incremental, eclectic, modernist revivalist sentiments, however, the ruling regimes seem to face continuing political difficulties. Surely, the future pattern of political violence, and hence the dynamics of political change in Islamic countries, are likely conditioned and affected by the levels and degrees of the gaps between these two extreme poles of politicization of Islamic revivalism. And the narrowing of such gaps and the increased coping capability of the ruling regimes may be achieved if, and only if, they are able to solve the current structural pathological problems as manifested in terms of legitimacy crisis, structural victimization, and socio-historical defeatism.

International Dimension

Political impacts of Islamic resurgent movements are not limited to the domestic political arena. Rather it has become a transnational phenomenon with actual and/or potential impacts on the order and stability in the international system. Some salients of its international political implications may be summarized by looking into the four major issue-areas: transnational linkage, international Muslim solidarity, strategic impacts, and anti-Western sentiment. During the last decade, first, one of the most noticeable attributes of Islamic revivalism seems to be a growing network of transnational linkages among various revivalist movements. Revivalism has not been confined to a specific region or countries. It permeates national borders, not only among Muslim majority Islamic countries, but also among Muslim minority countries. The nature of the linkage network, through which revivalist sentiments, ideologies and tactics are spread all over the world, is by no means a systematic nor elaborate one. It is rather random and spontaneous. Yet, its intensity and pervasiveness have been quite impressive. The Iranian Revolution has incurred a series of intense chain effects not only to neighboring Gulf states, but also to Egypt, Morocco, Algeria, and down to Malaysia and Indonesia. The agents of transmission of revivalist messages are not clearly delineable. But they are eventually disseminated to the grass roots level masses of Islamic countries. A more amazing aspect of this transnational linkage is its visible impacts on Muslim minority countries. As a good example we may cite the case of China. Throughout the 1970s and particularly in the early 1980s there has been a series of serious Muslim revolts in the Western provinces of China, particularly Yunan and Xinjiang. These revolts have ended up with quite a number of casualties highlighting the political significance of Muslim minorities in the western provinces of China. The surprising fact is that the rebellions led by Muslim youths were encouraged by the worldwide resurgence of Islamic sentiments, eventually linking defense of Islam with local political autonomy. Since then, the central government of China has shown remarkable appeasement policies to Muslim ethnic groups.[63] This linkage phenomenon is becoming more pervasive, encompassing the Soviet Union,[64] India, Sub-Saharian African countries,[65] and Southeast Asian countries including the case of Mindanao in the Philippines.

As some observers point out, however, this recent global politicization of Islamic revivalism may not generate significant collective power bases of Islamic countries, despite the aforementioned global diffusion and linkage.[66] Diversified pluralism, fragmentation, and political divisiveness may be responsible for the weakened power base of worldwide Islamic community. As a matter of fact, bitter Sunni vs Shi'a division, growing socioeconomic stratification and the overall rank differentials, and a considerable heterogeneity in political ideologies and regime types are the central part of today's reality of the Islamic world. Surely, the basis of unity and solidarity among Islamic countries have eroded in the long historical process and the idea of Pan-Islamism, as proposed and advocated by al-Afghani, *Ikwhans,* and King Faisal, has been overshadowed by pan-Arabism and other variants of local nationalism and socialism.

For all its heterogeneity and fragmentation, however, there was, until the Iran-Iraq war, a growing epicentric structure of international Islamic solidarity and unity. The success of OPEC and OAPEC collective actions generated political, psychological and economic leverages which could lead to further cohesiveness among Islamic countries. The recent politicization of the Organization of Islamic Conferences, systematic utilization of the Islamic Development Bank attached to it, and the ever-increasing bilateral economic assistance between capital-rich Islamic countries and poor ones provided world Islamic community with a strong sense of Islamic identity and solidarity. While the past efforts to spread pan-Islamism ended up with failures mainly due to empty promises and resolutions, this pattern of cooperations and consultations was concrete and practical enough to induce the voluntary feelings of unity and solidarity. Apart from these formal economic and political organizations, there have been equally growing voices from international Islamic missionary groups. The World Muslim League *(Rabitat al-Alam al-Islami),* the central religious organ encompassing all the global Islamic organizations, has played a more efficient and powerful role in coordinating and orchestrating divergent interests and opinions of Muslim organizations. *Dar ul Ifta* of Saudi Arabia, the Islamic Call Society of Libya, and the World Assembly of Muslim Youth supported by the Saudi government have engaged in the global dissemination of revivalist sentiments. They have sent out thousands of *D'ai* (missionary workers) all over the world, particularly developing Islamic and Muslim minority countries, and have been involved in publishing Islamic booklets, organizing international conferences, and supporting Muslim revivalist organizations financially and spiritually. Other than these organizational efforts to promote unity and solidarity on the global plane, the annual gathering of Muslims at Haji,[67] educational activities at the major international Islamic universities, such as al-Medina Islamic university and al-Azhar university have created an intangible international infrastructure of Islamic revivalist movements through which new ideologies are spread, the network of personnel connections is instituted and maintained, and finally a homogenized feeling of unity and solidarity becomes prevalent, particularly among non-governmental actors, which are the major part of revivalist movements.

This growing unity and solidarity can be related to the expanding zone of Islamic influence in the global political scene. As a matter of fact, according to a recent report, the Organization of Islamic Conferences is carefully studying the feasibilty of collective actions among Islamic countries in a much more concerted way.[68] Among others, economic integration scheme, formation of producers' cartel in major primary commodities, and the creation of a systemic body of economic cooperation among Islamic countries are seriously being considered. And although they may end up with symbolic exercises, the resolutions and agreements made at the recent Taif Summit meeting of the Organization of Islamic Conferences have revealed a growing consensus in political agenda among Islamic countries and their commitment to solving impending political problems through collective actions. The OIC's ever increasing influences over the Arab League, Non-Alligned Movement, and various fora of the United Nations have been remarkably visible. One of the underlying forces affecting the degree of unity and solidarity among Muslims and their governments may be a currently prevailing disenchantment and disillusion with the external powers, particularly the two superpowers. In other words, Islamic revivalist movements in a high tide are pressurizing the discard of both capitalist and socialist lines of political ideologies and the search for an Islamic alternative.[69] Even if there is very little chance of doing so in the domestic arena of Islamic countries, there is likely to be a high plausibility of such a choice in their external behaviors.

To be more specific, the upsurge of Islamic revivalist movements and Islamic countries' accommodative attitudes to the demands of oppositional revivalist movements may lead to a strategic consensus among them in such a manner that they refute strategic dependency on the Soviet Union and the United States. This potentiality seems to generate substantial impacts on the broadly perceived order and stability in the present international system. Strategically, the Islamic zone (so called Green Belt) is located along the buffer zone between the West (USA) and the East (USSR), spreading from the Straits of Malacca (Malaysia) to the Indian Ocean, Persian Gulf, and to the sensitive part of the Mediterranean Sea. Given the present status of power vacuum with the collapse of the Baghdad Pact, any changes in this sensitive zone of superpower rivalry may affect the existing balance of power system significantly by shaping the different patterns of strategic calculations by the United States and the Soviet Union.

The last important implication of recent Islamic revivalism is its tendency to negate the West, particularly the United States. Disenchantment with the West is not a new syndrome among Islamic countries. It has been a historical pattern originated by a strong common feeling of the past historical reality manifested in terms of bitter memory of the Crusades, colonial experiences, and the persistent cultural penetration. But recent recurrence of such feelings can be differentiated from the former in the sense that the latter has a much more specific target, that of the United States. In fact, the central part of revivalist hostility has been intense and violent anti-American sentiment. The scenes generated by the Iranian hostage crisis, popular attacks on American embassies in Libya and Pakistan, and most recently, the mass boycott movements of American goods in Malaysia well illustrate such sentiments prevalent in many Islamic countries.[70] This phenomenon can be interpreted as an inevitable consequence of American foreign policy behaviors. The inseparable connection between the United States and Israel, and the loss of Jerusalem and al-Aqsa mosque, the U.S.'s explicit and implicit alliance with oppressive and exploitive regimes of the Islamic world in particular, and of the Third World in general, and the nature of mass-culture stemming from the U.S. are directly or indirectly responsible for this anti-American sentiment. Of course, this is an unavoidable cost to be paid for the maintenance of hegemonic power in the international system. Nonetheless, the cost is likely to be prohibitively high in the future.

Concluding Remarks

The primary objective of this study has been to identify different types of Islamic revivalism, to trace its causal structure among them and to measure political impacts derived by revivalist movements. Our findings (or assertions) are such that: (1) Islamic revivalism cannot be confined to one type, i.e., Militant, Fundamentalist, and Orthodox revivalism type. Depending upon the object, rate and amount, and types of tactical means chosen, Islamic revivalism can be classified into at least eight different types. (2) The causal structure of Islamic revivalism cannot be attributed to one sole factor, such as the failure of modernization, an historical factor, or political incompetence of ruling regimes. It is, rather, a function of three clusters of causal variables, that is, the level of political legitimacy crisis, the extent of structural victimization, and the depth of socio-historical defeatism. (3) The types of revivalist movements are mainly determined by the relative distance between Islamic ideals socialized in the minds of Muslims and the actual reality of these three causal factors. And (4), political impacts of Islamic revivalism can be characterized by growing politization of Islam, affecting order and stability of the existing political systems, both internally and externally. The research efforts rendered in this paper are the initial part of an ongoing massive comparative research enterprise. The next step to be followed includes the elaboration of analytical schemes, generation of rich hypotheses, and the empirical testing of such hypotheses on the basis of additional aggregate data.

NOTES

We have benefited from the comments of Cesar A. Majul and the editorial and research assistances of Erica Andes, Kate Shnayerson and Hedayatollah Tahbaz.

1. Mohammed Heikal, *Iran: The Untold Story, An Insider's Account of America's Iranian Adventure and Its Consequences for the Future* (New York: Pantheon Books, 1981), p. 129.
2. H. A. R. Gibb, *Mohammedanism* (New York: Oxford University Press, 1962), pp. 190–192.
3. M. Halpern, *The Politics of Social Change in the Middle East and North Africa* (Princeton: Princeton University Press, 1963), Chapter 7.
4. Donald Smith, *Religion and Political Development* (Boston: Little, Brown and Co., 1970), p. 244.

5. For exemplary works in this line of reasoning, refer to the following books: Mohamed Ayoob, *The Politics of Islamic Reassertion* (New York, St. Martin Press, 1981); Hillal A. Dessouki (ed), *Islamic Resurgence in the Arab World* (New York: Praeger, 1982); J. Esposito (ed), *Islam and Development* (Syracuse, N.Y.: Syracuse University Press, 1980); M. Curtis (ed), *Religion and Politics in the Middle East* (Boulder, Co.: Westview, 1981); Yvonne Y. Haddad (ed), *Contemporary Islam and the Challenge of History* (Albany, N.Y.: CUNY Press, 1982); P. Stoddard, D. Cuthell, and M. Sullivan (eds), *Change and the Muslim World* (Syracuse, N.Y.: Syracuse University Press, 1981).
6. The Western media and some scholars have linked the nuclearization efforts of Pakistan, Iraq, and Libya to the formation of militant Islamic power in the international system. To put it differently, they tend to perceive the nuclearization of some Islamic countries in terms of potential sources of nuclear terrorism backed by militant Islamic revivalism.
7. Wilfred C. Smith, *Islam in Modern History* (Princeton: Princeton University Press, 1957), p. 18.
8. Quoted from interview with Edward Said, in *Time:* "Special Report on World Islam" (April 16, 1979), p. 54. Also refer to his *Orientalism* (New York: Vintage Books, 1979).
9. The word *Umma* is derived from the Arabic etymological root meaning "mother or source," by which it comes to have more expanded meaning of Islamic community or the organic family of Muslims. *Umma* should be differentiated from *millet* (a non-religious community living in the larger Islamic community), *asabiyya* (kinship groups), *qawm* (ethno-linguistic peoplehood), and *watan* (territorial notion of nation-state). *Umma* is a broader concept that transcends national borders, political boundaries, and racial-ethnic distinctions. The foundation of *Umma* is the principle that designates submission to the will of God, obedience to His law and commitment to His cause. For a good discussion of this concept, refer to Michael Hudson, *Arab Politics* (New Haven, Ct: Yale University Press, 1977), pp. 34–38; Ziya Gokalp, *The Principle of Turkism* (Heiden E and Brill, 1968), Chapter 1.
10. *Dar al-Islam* refers to a domain in which Islamic jurisdiction is applied. While *Umma* is a communal notion, *Dar al-Islam* is a legalistic concept supplementing the former.
11. For the concept of *tawhid,* consult Muhammad Abduh, *Risalat al–Tawhid (Theology of Unity),* trans. Ishaq Musa'ad and Kenneth Cragg (London: Unwin, 1966), pp. 29–40.
12. Ali Shariati, *On the Sociology of Islam* (Berkeley: Mizan Press, 1979), p. 82ff.
13. *Ibid.*, p. 82.
14. Abul Ala Maududi, *Understanding toward Islam* (Beirut: The Holy Quran Press, 1977), p. 210. Ital. is ours.
15. Ali Shariati, "Bazgasht bi Khistan" (Return to the Self), as found in *Islam in Transition*, ed. J. Donohue and J. Esposito, (New York: Oxford University Press, 1982), pp. 305–7.

16. Asaf A. A. Fyzee, *A Modern Approach to Islam* (Bombay: Asia Publication House, 1962), p. 98, as found in Donohue and Esposito, *Ibid,* p. 190.
17. Ali Shariati, *Hajj* (Houston, Tx: Free Islamic Press, 1978), pp. 101–102.
18. For recent good discussions on different types of Islamic revivalist movements, refer to Charles Butterworth, "Prudence vs. Legitimacy," in Dessouki, *Islamic Resurgence,* pp. 84–114. His article deals with philosophical origin of revivalist movements with specific focus on modern and contemporary Islamic thinkers. From the political perspective, R. S. Humphreys, "Islam and Political Values in Saudi Arabia, Egypt, and Syria," in *Middle East Journal,* 33:1 (Winter, 1979). Also John O. Voll's *Islam: Continuity and Change in the Modern World* (Boulder, Co: Westview, 1982), provides us with broad comparative historical perspective on Islamic revivalism.
19. In identifying these three structural properties, we are indebted to Saad Eddin Ibrahim's "Anatomy of Egypt's Militant Islamic Groups: Methodological Note and Preliminary Findings," in *International Journal of Middle Eastern Studies* 2:4 (1980) pp. 423–453.
20. The flexibility allowing different interpretations of the object, rate and amount, and means of change does not come from our analytical arbitrariness. It is mainly due to the possibility of interpreting the *Quran* and *Hadith* in different ways by different scholars. The following excerpts from the *Quran* and *Hadith* do, for example, show such a possibility. "Call unto the way of thy Lord with wisdom and fair exhortion, and reason with them in the better way. Lo! thy Lord is best aware of him who strayeth from His way, and He is the Best Aware of those who go aright." (*The Quran* XVI, 125) This verse explicates the virtue of persuasion. Yet, another verse reveals quite a different tone and voice: "Fight in the way of Allah against those who fight against you, but begin not hostilities. Lo! Allah loveth not aggressors./And slay them whereever ye find them, and drive them out of the places whence they drove you out, for persecution is worse than slaughter" (*The Quran* II, 190–191). The translation of the Quranic verses is from Muhammad M. Pickthall's. And one sound *Hadith* also illustrates the multiple possibilities in choosing the means of change. "Whosoever of you sees an evil action, let him change it with his hand; and if he is not able to do so, then with his tongue; and if he is not able to do so, then with his heart—and that is the weakest of faith." Quoted from An-Nawawi's *Forty Hadith* (Damascus: Holy Quran Publishing House, 1977), p. 110. Trans. E. Ibrahim and D. Johnson-Davies.
21. The *Tabligh* (Revival) movement was started in Delhi around 1945. Its aim is to produce good Muslims, born again Muslims. A good Muslim must give an hour a day, or one day a week, or three days a month, or four weeks a year, or four months in a lifetime to personal missionary work *(muballigh),* mainly house-to-house visits. If finances allow it, overseas missionary work is also recommended resembling that of the Mormons. Its organizational structure is very much diffused along mosques. For all this diffused organizational structure, five million Muslims gathering on annual assembly in Tongi, a small town near Dacca, reveals its potential power and influence. This movement is gaining a high popularity in West Asian and South East Asian countries. G. Jensen, *Economist* (September 4, 1982), p. 42.

22. *Dar al-Arqam* (House of Arqam) was founded by Ustaz Ashaari in 1971 in Malaysia. Its members have adapted a communal style of life in a small village just outside Kuala Lumpur, where every possible attempt is made to follow the traditions of the prophet Muhammad and to avoid Western influences. Television, movies, and other Western-influenced innovations are strictly prohibited. This movement is limited to a Malay community, and is a combination of social withdrawal and economic self-reliance, negating the existing social structure. For a concise discussion of this movement, refer to Judith Nagata, "The New Fundamentalism: Islam in Contemporary Malaysia," in *Asian Thought and Society,* 5:14 (September 1980).

23. Orthodox fundamentalism and orthodox fundamentalist revivalism is differentiated in this paper. This distinction is based on the assertion that orthodox fundamentalism is a static and somewhat completed form, while revivalism is that of becoming. For example, Saudi Arabia and some other Gulf states following Wahabi orientation may be regarded as orthodox fundamentalism, in which fundamentalist ideas are institutionalized in terms of legal entity.

24. 'Old' *Ikwhan-il-Muslimin* (Muslim Brotherhood) refers to the early movement founded by Hassan al-Banna and his immediate followers in Egypt. And 'new' Muslim Brotherhood movement includes various offshoots from the old one, such as the Islamic Liberation Party, *al-Takfir wal-Hijra,* and other militant Islamic groups in Egypt, and other variants of the Brotherhood movement in Syria, Sudan, and the Gulf states. For a good distinction, refer to Abd al-Monein Said Aly and Manfred W. Wenner, "Modern Islamic Reform Movements: The Muslim Brotherhood in Contemporary Egypt," in *Middle East Journal,* 36:3 (Summer 1982), pp. 336–361. Also refer to Saad E. Ibrahim, *Anatomy of Islamic Groups.*

25. This term is used by A. A. Maududi, "Political Theory of Islam," in Khurshid Ahmad, ed., *Islam: Its Meaning and Messages* (London: Islamic Council of Europe, 1976), pp. 147–170.

26. The militant nature of orthodox fundamentalist revivalism is well epitomized in the words of Maududi: "Islam is a revolutionary ideology *(Fikrah inqilabiyyah)* and a revolutionary practice, which aims at totally destroying the social order of the world and rebuilding it from scratch." Requoted in Evan Lerman, "Maududi's Concept of Islam," *Middle Eastern Studies,* 17:4 (Oct. 1982), p. 500. Also R. Khomeini's *Islamic Government* (Arlington, Va: National Technical Information Service, 1979) is a good source for the understanding of this version of revivalism.

27. There is an ongoing debate on the authenticity of Islamic ideology in the political practice by Libyan leader Muammar Qadhafi. For all his own claims that his Third Universal Theory is based exclusively on Islam, a careful reading of his three volumes of Green Books and his actual political practices, such as the official downgrading of the *Sunna,* indicate that his so-called theory is very much influenced by other exogenous sources, such as Marxism. For a good discussion of this aspect, refer to Ann Mayer, "Islamic Resurgence or New Prophethood?: The Role of Islam in Qadhafi's Ideology," in Dessouki, *Islamic Resurgence,* Chap. 10.

28. Shariati was highly critical of what he called Safavid Islam, the religious and political views of the established *ulama* and ayatollahs. Against this, he wished to actualize Alavid Islam, Islam in its state of original purity. However, his way of interpreting Islam is said to be greatly influenced by Marxism, existentialism, and phenomenology. The Mujahidin shares with Shariati in the sense that both negate the monopoly of power and knowledge by mullahs and ayatollahs.

29. For a political justification of the idea of Islamic socialism under the Nasser regime, refer to Mahmad Shaltut, "Socialism and Islam," as found in Kemal H. Karpat, *Political and Social Thought in the Contemporary Middle East* (New York: Praeger, 1982), pp. 108–116.

30. There can be a difference of opinions on this matter. Many scholars tend to classify Qadhafi, Shariati, and the Mujahidin as proponents of fundamentalism—a total reform of society and the individual in the Islamic principles. In our opinion, however, they differ from an orthodox line. They want the reform of society with the reorientation of Muslims into the direction of class consciousness and radicalization. For them, ideal Muslims are not those of the traditional orthodox, but those of the highly mobilized and committed to the reform of society with new exogenous ideas in mind.

31. *Al-Shubban al-Muslimin* literally means Muslim Youth. It was established in 1927 in emulation of the Western institution known as YMCA. The founders, headed by a retired army general, Salih Harb, meant it to be a non-political social athletic organization. Saad Ibrahim, *Anatomy of Islamic Groups.*

32. MAYC (Malaysian Association of Youth Clubs) is a social, rather than a religious organization. However, it has missionary wings under it, and plays some influential roles in shaping revivalist sentiment in the Malaysian society. And it performs a function of buffering *vis à vis* fundamentalist demands from other Islamic militant groups.

33. The Jamaat-i-Islami (Islamic Party) used to be one movement under the leadership of Abu ala Maududi, and now functions separately in the two countries, Pakistan and Bangladesh. Although it was initiated by Maududi and follows ideologies formulated by Maududi it has become very much accommodative and incrementalistic in its approach to reform society. And the Jamaat in both Pakistan and Bangladesh is as political as it is allowed to be. In this sense, it has become a political pressure group, rather than a revolutionary movement, contrary to the original intention of Maududi.

34. The World Assembly of Muslim Youth, headquartered in Riyadh, is an international Muslim youth organization supported by Saudi Arabian government, particularly by the Ministry of Higher Education, and partially by the Organization of Islamic Conferences.

35. In classifying the typology of Islamic revivalism, an additional factor, other than the three aforementioned, may be considered. That is the type of agent of change. Surely, the types of actors involved in the initiation and implementation of revivalist movements are important in understanding the nature of movements. It is because the nature of revivalism can be sharply different, depending upon who initiates the movement (e.g., *ulama* groups, ruling polit-

ical elites, or mass or alienated intellectuals and students). However, we decided not to choose this actor criterion as a determining factor of the types of revivalism. The rationale behind this decision is mainly due to the fact that a clear analytical distinction among these actors is not possible in reality. They are divided among themselves, depending upon the issue context and the overall nature of environment.

36. Nazih N. M. Ayubi, "Political Revival of Islam: The Case of Egypt," *International Journal of Middle East Studies,* 12 (1980), p. 487.

37. For these social-psychological notions, refer to Ted Gurr, *Why Men Rebel* (Princeton: Princeton University Press, 1970); and R. Clark, Jr., *Development and Instability: Political Change in the Non-Western World* (Hinsdale, Ill.: Dryden Press, 1974).

38. For a good discussion of political values in Islam, refer to R. S. Humphreys, "Islam and Political Values in Saudi Arabia, Egypt, and Syria," *Middle East Journal.*

39. Regarding this matter, consult the following Quranic injunctions: "Blessed be He in whose hands is dominion, and He over all things has power" (Sura 67:1); "O you who believe! Obey God, and obey the Messengers (of God) and those charged with authority among you. If you differ in anything among yourselves, refer it to God and His Messenger, if you do believe in God and the Last Day. That is best, and most suitable for final determination" (Sura 4:59). Also on the evolution of political thought in Islam, refer to Hamid Enayat, *Modern Islamic Political Thought* (Houston, TX: University of Texas Press, 1982).

40. On the matters of economic justice, refer to the following two excerpts from the *Quran:* "O you who believe! Stand firmly for justice, as witnesses to fair dealings, and let not the hatred of others to you make you swerve to wrong and depart from justice. Be just: that is most close to piety, and mind God for God is well-acquainted with all that you do" (Sura 5:9); "And the Firmament has He raised high, and He has set up the Balance (of Justice) in order that you may not transgress (due) balance. So establish weight with justice and fall not short in the balance" (Sura 55:7–9). For a comprehensive understanding of economic aspects of Islam, refer to Kharshid Ahmad, ed., *Studies in Islamic Economics* (Leicester: The Islamic Foundation, 1980), and to J. Cummings, H. Askari, and A. Mustafa, "Islam and Modern Economic Change," in Esposito, ed., *Islam and Development,* pp. 25–48.

41. H. Abdalati, *Islam in Focus,* pp. 123–125.

42. For a good introduction to the cultural and historical legacy of Islam, consult Abul Hassan Ali Nadwi, *Islam and the World* (Beirut: the Holy Quran Publication House, 1977); M. Lombard, *The Golden Age of Islam* (New York: American Elsevir Publishing Co., 1975).

43. There are many ways of classifying regime typology. In this study, we focus on major political actors in power as a determinant of regime type, rather than on the nature of legal entity or organizational and ideological structure of the state. Thus, by pluralist regime is meant the existence of the multiplicity of interest groups and political parties. Military or quasi–military intervention

either on the institutional basis or on personal basis. And in differentiating conservative monarchy from Islamic regime, political influences of religious actors and the resultant pattern of legal entity are taken into account.

44. In measuring the level of legitimacy, we have set out an hypothesis that the higher the level of behavioral violence, the less the level of political stability and legitimacy. Here the level of behavioral violence is determined by measuring domestic interaction events data of Islamic countries which are stored in Azar's Conflict and Peace Data Bank (COPDAB). Domestic interaction events are categorized into cooperative events of which scale values spread from 1 to 5, and into conflictive events of which scale values spread from 11 to 15. In measuring a country's level of behavioral violence, then, the average weight of both conflictive and cooperative scale values in each Islamic country for the last 15 years has been calculated. And if the average weight is less than 5, the level of legitimacy is considered to be *high,* less than 10 to be *medium,* and more than 11 to be *low* in legitimacy level. (COPDAB's scale ranges from 1 to 15, scale value 1 being complete absence of domestic violence, and 15 being revolution or civil war.) For more detailed methodological aspect, refer to Edward Azar, *Manual on COPDAB* (College Park, Md: The Center for International Development, University of Maryland, 1982).

45. In a similar vein, for example, Michael Hudson argues that the activistic nature of popular, fundamentalistic Islamic political movements has been shaped by the conjunction of the three major factors: influx of secular, Western rationalistic ideas, decline of influence of the Islamic actors, and the failure of liberal Islamic reformers to accommodate the ideals of modernization. Refer to his article, "Islam and Political Development," in Esposito, ed., *Islam and Development.*

46. The Association of Muslim Social Scientists, *Islam and Development* (Plainfield, Indiana: AMSS, 1977). Also Khruhid Ahmad, "Islam and Economic Development," in K. Ahmad, ed., *Studies in Islamic Economics.*

47. This argument has been advanced by the proponents of the Basic Needs Strategy. The International Labour Organization, the World Bank, the Overseas Development Council, and the Bariloche Foundation have been strong advocates for this strategy.

48. We borrowed the definition of the physical quality of life index from that formulated by the Overseas Development Council. For this, refer to various issues of *The United States and World Development* annually published by the Council.

49. Edward Azar, "Peace Amidst Development: A Conceptual Agenda for Conflict and Peace Research," *International Interaction* 6:2 (1979).

50. *Ibid.,* p. 129.

51. On the linkage between military defeatism and the rise of popular Islamic movements, refer to Nazih Ayubi, *Political Revival;* and to S. E. Ibrahim, *Anatomy of Islamic Groups.*

52. The designation of capitalism, communism and Zionism as the ultimate enemies of Islam has been the most common theme of Islamic revivalist movements regardless of types and national origin.

53. Using the three clusters of causal factors as independent variables and the eight different types of revivalist movements as dependent variables, we may be able to generate many interesting hypotheses to be tested. For the sake of brevity, however, an in-depth study of multiple relationships between the causal factors and the types of movement will be reserved for future research agenda.

54. We are in the process of collecting massive comparative aggregate data on these three variables on the longitudinal time series base encompassing all the Islamic countries and some important Muslim minority countries such as India, China, and the Soviet Union.

55. "Special Report on the World of Islam," *Time* (April 16, 1979).

56. The success of the Iranian Revolution has greatly affected militant Islamic revivalist movements in Egypt, Malaysia, Algeria, and some Gulf States including Saudi Arabia. The most important thing regarding this matter is the fact that Islamic cause and actors could be successful in overthrowing the existing political regimes. Thus, symbolic as well as practical implications derived from the case of the Iranian Revolution can be evaluated as being substantial.

57. Mohammad Zia ul-Haq, *Introduction of the Islamic System in Pakistan* (Islamabad: Government of Pakistan, 1979).

58. It has been said that a growing number of students at the Mecca Sharia College of the King Abdul Aziz University and at al-Medina Islamic University have shown a feeling of disenchantment with the conservative and accommodative line of Sheikh Abdul Aziz Bin Baz, the ultimate authority in Islamic matters in the Kingdom. And it is also reported that there have been quite a substantial number of sympathizers with the rebels of the Mecca Incident.

59. Ann Mayer, "Islamic Resurgence" in Dessouki, *Islamic Resurgence.*

60. Saad Eddin Ibrahim, *Anatomy of Islamic Groups.* Also refer to Daniel Crecelius, "The Course of Secularization in Modern Egypt," in Esposito, ed., *Islam and Development,* pp. 49–70.

61. For example, in a recent debate on the constitutional role of Sharia in the Syrian state system, the Syrian government has given concessions to Islamic groups by retreating from its initial insistence on the secular, Baathism-based nature of the new constitution. Iraq also has pursued an appeasement policy to Shia opposition groups centered around the Shia holy cities of Najaf and Kerbela. Consult R. A. Hinnebusch, "The Islamic Movement in Syria," in Ali Dessouki, ed., *Islamic Resurgence,* Chap. 7. Also M. Hudson, "Islam and Political Development," in Esposito, ed., *Islam and Development.*

62. Mahathir has been successful in co-opting Anwar Ibrahim, president of ABIM, the most fundamentalist opposition group, into a part of his regime. It was known that Ibrahim's participation in the ruling regime was made possible as a result of Mahathir's consent that religious matters remain the domain of Ibrahim. In fact, Ibrahim was appointed as deputy minister in charge of religious affairs in the prime minister's office and the recent development in Malaysia indicates that Mahathir government pursues very accommodative policies on the demands of the fundamentalist groups.

63. Lillian C. Harris, "China's Islamic Connection," a paper presented to annual convention of Association for Asian Studies, (March 1981) Toronto; Raphael Israeli, "The Muslim Minority in Traditional China," *Asian and African Studies* 10:2 (1975).

64. G. Jukes, "The Soviet Union," in Ayubi, ed., *The Politics of Islamic*, Chap. 13. A. Bennigsen, "Official Islam and Sufi Brotherhood in the Soviet Union Today," in A. Cudsi and A. Dessouki, eds., *Islam and Power in the Contemporary Muslim World* (Baltimore: Johns Hopkins University Press, 1981).

65. Sulayman S. Nyang, "Sub-Saharan Africa: Islamic Interpretation," in Stoddard, Cuthell, and Sullivan, eds., *Changes and the Muslim World,* pp. 145–150.

66. This point was asserted by Faud Ajami, *Arab Predicament* (New York: Cambridge University Press, 1981).

67. For a good description of the socio-political aspect of *Hajj,* refer to David Long, *The Hajj Today* (Albany, NY: State University of New York Press, 1979).

68. Organization of Islamic Conference, *Areas of Economic Cooperation Among Islamic Countries* (Ankara: Statistical, Economic and Social Research and Training Center for Islamic Countries, 1980).

69. According to a recent report, Iraqi prisoners of war detained in Iran are forced to recite the following phrase every day: "*La Sharqiun La Gharbiun Jumhurial Islamiun* (Neither West, not East, but Islamic Republic)." This episode can be interpreted as an effort to search for Islamic alternative.

70. As a result of the Israeli invasion of Lebanon, the Malaysian Muslim Youth Movement, in cooperation with student organizations, waged a nationwide boycott movement of American goods, with the accusation that the United States, by its constant support of Israel, was responsible for the Lebanese tragedy.

6

The Impact of Religion on Contemporary Politics: The Case of Iran

FARHANG MEHR

In the last three decades, Islam has emerged as a political force in many countries, including Iran. It has been a driving power behind revolution, assassinations, seizure of holy places and terrorism.

Although the Islamic governments, in earnest or for political expediency, claim adherence to Islamic principles, their interpretation of Islamic laws *(Shari'a),* their attitudes towards modernization, and their views on the role of Muslim clergy *(ulama),* differ. The repeated assertion by overzealous Muslims that there is only one Islam, is more rhetoric than real. Islam is as divided as Christianity, Buddhism and other great religions. In addition to the traditional division of Islam between two major sects of Sunni and Shi'a, militant Muslims distinguish between the Established Islam, Islam al-Rasmi, or Islam of the establishment; and the populist Islam, Islam al-Sha'bi, or the pure Islam professed by the ordinary Muslims. The ruling classes use Islam as a legitimizer, trying to both ward off the attacks by the militant forces and retain their positions of power. In contrast, the dissidents try to falsify the ruling classes' claim to Islam.

Militant Muslims are as much opposed to Saudi's ruling house or to General Zia's Islamic state as they were to the Shah of Iran or Anwar Sadat of Egypt. The Saudis have always considered themselves defenders of the traditional Islam. Yet the militant group of al-Salafi, who are considered the populist counterpart of Wahabis, would not spare them. In the fall of 1979, al-Salafi occupied the mosque in Mecca and caused tremendous trouble for the Saudi Government. Al-Salafi is a Sunni sect and, as such, have no appreciation for Khomeini's Shi'a. Yet Khomeini's regime was first to praise and approve of their action—not out of love of al-Salafi, but hatred of Saudi's monarchy. To militant Muslims, Sunni and Shi'a alike, Khomeini's Islamic Republic of Iran, at least at its inception, represented a populist Islamic government.

Militant Islam is a movement of protest for real or perceived grievances against the established regimes and foreign domination. It is a movement against political oppression, economic injustice, social inequality and, above all, foreign domination. With all its tactics, including terrorism, militant Islam is an expression of fear and frustration, anger and revenge against some real or perceived enemies. Yet, these targets constitute the only common factors to various militant muslim groups—without them, their end-goals, strategies and tactical approaches collide. The strife between militant Shi'as and militant Sunnis in Lebanon is not over Islam, but supremacy and group survival. Therefore, a realistic appraisal of the current impact of religion on the official policy and governmental structure of each country can only be made in its historical context: the record of the colonial rule in that country, indigenous conditions, cultural background, and people's real and perceived grievances. History explains why a particular people have adopted certain tactics in attaining drastic and immediate changes at individual and collective levels. Contemporary settings identify those forces which make for political and social changes. A balanced assessment of the relative importance of those forces helps some realistic projection into the future.

On these premises, the case of Iran should be viewed as an indigenous event, rather than an offshoot of a worldwide political tide. Terrorism and cell-like organizational structures, tape-recorded doctrinal appeals, demonstrations and social protests, temporary tactical alliances, and other methods are employed by secular, religious rightists and leftists alike, and these approaches do not make them offshoots of a worldwide religious movement. Rather, they may be classified as various manifestations of the worldwide protest. Attention in particular should be paid to the political movements for liberation from an autocratic rule or a foreign dominance. Foreign dominance and interferences have left bitter memories in the indigenously Muslim-populated countries. An intelligent prognosis of the future course of events in Iran requires careful evaluation of the extent to which post-revolutionary Islamic regime has infused religiosity in the Iranian polity. The study should also take into account the credibility of clergies and the religious laymen who rule the country, bearing in mind that change is an organic process.

The 1979 Iranian revolution evolved from Islam and the assumptions of the worldwide leadership of militant Muslim movements. While the intensity and rapidity of the Iranian revolution remain enigmatic, its cause, nature and ideology are unfolding themselves. The revolution of Iran, which seemed at its outset to be merely a negative outcome of uncoordinated modernization, has now emerged as a positive force whose objective is to revert the country to the fundamentals of Islam, to revitalize Islamic values, and to reconstruct the Iranian society in accordance with the Islamic precepts. It asserts to be a positive movement, aimed at restoring the past Islamic glory, and liberating the nation from foreign dominance and economic exploitation. So far, however, it has proven to be regressive, looking back nostalgically to the early Islamic society of the seventh century.

Undoubtedly, Islam played a significant role in realization of the 1979 revolution. As evidenced by the events, populist Islam has had a great impact on the governance and public policy of post-revolutionary Iran. It has become a vantage for the clergy that is continuing. The present study is presented in three parts: (1) The historical role of religion in Iranian political upheavals during the last century; (2) The impact of religion on domestic and international public policy in the Islamic Republic of Iran; and (3) Projection into the future role of the clergy in Iranian politics.

The Historical Role of Religion and Other Forces in Political and Social Changes in Iran During the Last Century

Emergence of Shia'ism as an Effective Politican Tool. The forces of religion, nationalism, liberalism, monarchism and foreign influences have all played a role in the 1979 Iranian shake-up. Economic dislocation, political repression, displacement and loss of identity, excesses of the security police, corruption, waste and other disruptive socioeconomic factors were the inevitable outcome of interaction of the various forces which may be considered the immediate cause behind the revolution.

In the texture of Iranian history, religion, nationalism and monarchism are interwoven. This came about when Artaxerxes I, the son of a Zoroastrian priest, founded the Sassanid Empire in 226 A.D. He proclaimed Zoroastrianism the official creed of the state. Thenceforth, the monarch became protector of the land, propagator of the faith, and the symbol of nationalism. During four hundred years of conflict between Iran and Rome, Zoroastrianism served as a "nationalizer theology" and proved a considerable force for preservation of the nation's solidarity.[1] The unity of state and church continued in a different context after the Arab invasion of Iran in 651 A.D. Under Islamic principles, nationalism was eliminated in the interest of loyalty to Islam. The country was placed under the Khaliph's rule and the concept of the nation was replaced by that of *Umma* (believers in Islam). It was in 1502 A.D., under Safavids, that nationalism and religion again intermingled and Shi'aism became the formal creed of Iran. For four centuries the combined forces of nationalism and Shi'aism preserved Iran's independence against Ottoman expansionism. Ottoman emperors had assumed the authority of Khaliphs and, as such, demanded the loyalty of all Muslims.[2]

Since 1502, Shi'aism in Iran gradually became hierarchical, influencing and working with the government, but remaining independent of it, both structurally and financially. Since then, Shi'a *ulama* (clergy) have enjoyed a particularly privileged position. Collection of sizeable taxes under the titles of Khoms and Zakat, management of substantial revenue from Vaghfs, and endowed lands gave them leverage to meddle in politics.

The Shi'a *ulama* having gained supremacy after seven centuries of subordination to Sunnis, were determined to use their authority in full. Their exercise of power at times clashed with that of the monarch. In such confrontation, *ulama* argued that the legitimacy of the king's power related to the Divine Will; and in the absence of the Twelfth Imam, Divine Will was represented by the *ulama*. As a corollary, they required the kings to have their coronations consecrated by them. The Safavid kings acceded to that demand, and this practice has persisted into our time. Thus, during Safavids, Shi'aism, in addition to being a "nationalizer," became a "legitimizer" theology.

In Zoroastrian Iran, too, the king bore the mark of divinity. The difference was that Sassanid kings, themselves, represented Providence on earth; whereas in Islamic Iran, this was represented by the *ulama*. With the short-lived dynasties in Islamic era, the legitimacy of kingship often depended on personal power and strength of character, rather than on the clergy's authority. This explains the frequency of the phenomenon of autocratic rulers in the country.

'Inheritance of privilege' was an Iranian institution that found expression in 'hereditary Imamat,' running in Ali's descent. Claiming to be Sayyids, descendants of the prophet through his daughter, the Safavid kings encouraged Shi'a clergy to travel and settle down throughout the country. Their purpose was propagation of faith, primarily to fortify national solidarity against Ottoman. This enhanced the mullahs' prestige and influence with the masses. Illiterate people in the rural and urban areas turned to the mullahs for almost all their social and economic ills. Gradually, the clergy established their hold among the people and assumed exclusive jurisdiction over judiciary and education—rights they have since been claiming and jealously guarding.

The predominance of Shi'a clergy continued until the time of the Constitutional Revolution in the year 1907, when the liberal intellectuals moved to curtail *ulama* authority. They partly succeeded. The process of secularization was set into motion, and was continued during the Pahlavi regime. Since the establishment of the Islamic Republic in the year 1979, the process has been reversed. All that was achieved during the past 72 years in the direction of separation of state and mosque was destroyed.

Religion in Relation to Other Forces. In the last hundred years, on at least four occasions, the *ulama,* by themselves or jointly with other groups, assumed the leadership of the opposition against the established government. The significance of the role played by the clergy on each occasion indicated the relative importance of religion, compared with other forces in the Iranian political arena.

The first occasion was in 1891, when Ayatollah Shirazi effectively challenged Nasser al-Din Shah Qajar. The Shah had granted tobacco concession to a British entrepreneur.[3] Ayatollah Shirazi condemned the grant and boycotted all transactions in, and consumption of, tobacco in Iran. The Shah was compelled to cancel the concession. In that movement, bazaris and modernists under the banner of nationalism and in obeisance to Ayatollah Shirazi's Fatwe, joined forces with the *ulama* and operated under their leadership.

The second occasion was that of the constitutional movement of 1905–1909. It was started by the liberal intellectuals in protest against the autocratic rule of the Shah. Liberalization of the political system, establishment of a representative government and total resistance to foreign influence constituted their main demands.[4] Modernization of the country on the Western pattern, social justice, and equality of the people before the law, irrespective of sex, ethnic origin and faith, and eradication of corruption, extravagance and inefficiency in the government machinery appeared as top priorities in their programs. To them, Westernization was synonymous with scientific progress. Some of the intellectuals went so far as to advocate changing the Arabic alphabet into Latin as a device to facilitate universal literacy programs. Abandonment of the Arabic script was also meant to serve the purpose of severance of their cultural relation from a phenomenon they considered a cause of their backwardness. Those demands were in line with those done twenty years later in Turkey, under the leadership of Kemal Ata-Turk.

However, the intellectuals soon realized that their movement would be doomed to failure if they could not enlist popular support. To achieve this they had to have the clergy actively on their side—which required modification of their socio-political manifestoes. They started expressing their ideals in Islamic terms, thus following the example of Jamal al-Din Assadabadi. The plan worked. Popular support was rallied and a national movement emerged. The Shah was compelled to issue a Royal Proclamation, consenting to the establishment of *Majlis* (parliament), and formation of a representative government.

The first round of the contest was won by the liberals. The constitution contained no reference to Islam. The movement was secular. The national poets openly assailed the practice of Islamic veil for women, criticized fanaticism and superstition, and ridiculed the greedy mullas. Soon dichotomy in the allied ranks surfaced. The cleavage between the secular intelligentsia, with liberal beliefs, on the one hand, and the orthodox clergy, with fundamentalist precepts, on the other hand, was about to endanger the success of the movement. The clergy spread the slogan: "We want Mashru'ah (meaning the rule of Shari'a) and not Mashruteh (meaning the rule of constitution)." A few months later, in an act of compromise, the liberals consented to the adoption of the "Supplement to the Constitution." In that document, significant concessions were made to the clergy. Those included recognition of Twelve Shi'a as the state religion, conferring veto-right on a five-man committee of *ulamas* in all matters relating to legislation and reserving the judiciary for the clergy. Furthermore it was inserted in the Supplement that the Shah should profess "Islam of the Ja'fary Twelve Imam sect," and propagate the true doctines of that faith.[5] The five men were to be chosen from among *ulama,* versed in Islamic law and jurisprudence. They were to scrutinize the legislation passed by people's representatives in Parliament, and reject those which in their view contravened the Islamic law. Thus, in the second round, the *ulama* emerged victorious, although the provision regarding scrutinization of legislation by the five-man committee never implemented.

While the clergy and the liberals were still counting their wins, the Russians and British were at work with intrigues and plots, interfering in domestic affairs of Iran. The Russians urged the Shah to abolish the constitution and continue his despotic rule.[6] The British supported the constitutionalists and invited them to stand firm. After several years of fierce struggle, the constitutionalists triumphed.

The emergence of Britain, after the first World War, as the unrivaled power in the region, enabled that country to put into action its long-awaited plans. With their secret dealings with the Russians, Qajar kings had forfeited the confidence of the British. They were also resented by Iranians due to their "promiscuousness" in private and public life. Despite their previous support for the constitutional monarchy, the British now preferred a strong leader and a stable government for Iran. Having suffered lingering insecurity, unceasing political disturbances, and distasteful personal rivalries among the national leaders, the impatient Iranians were disillusioned with democracy. They were ready to forego their political rights and yield to the authoritative rule of an autocratic government. The natural choice was Reza Pahlavi, a strong army officer with national prestige. A *coup d'ētat* was staged and four years later, Reza Pahlavi assumed kingship. Between the 1921 *coup d'ētat* and Reza Pahlavi's ascent to the throne in 1925, some Western-educated Iranian liberals and intellectuals worked for the replacement of monarchy with republic. They wanted to imitate Ata-Turk. Ironically, the Shi'a clergy at that time opposed the republic as being an anti-Islamic institution.[7] Although Shi'a, they were alarmed at the abolition of Khalifat by Ata-Turk.

Reza Shah undertook a rigorous centralization and an intense modernization program. He crushed all separatist movements, curtailed the power of the clergy, and wiped out individual and group resistance to his programs. He secularized education and judiciary, forbade women to wear chador and veil (Islamic dress), and replaced Sharia's criminal rules with those of the Napolean code. Unlike Ata-Turk, Reza Shah did not strike at the source of the power of the clergy: *ulama* continued to collect religious taxes and Vagf's revenues, and thus have the financial means of fostering opposition to the regime.

Anglo-Russian occupation of Iran in 1940 destroyed all that had been achieved by Reza Shah and forced him into exile. Separationist groups, resurgent tribes and foreign–fostered political parties reappeared on the scene. Having experienced sixteen years of an authoritarian government, Iranians were now mentally ready to re-experience a constitutionally representative government. The call was for democracy. Political parties, trade unions, social groups and religious associations grew overnight. Free press mushroomed and indiscriminate criticism of the past became order of the day. *Ulama* resumed their political activities. This political scene persisted until the political crisis at the time of Mossadegh in 1951–53.

During the 1951–53 uprising, the driving force was clearly nationalism. The movement was triggered by the liberal intellectuals in protest of half a century's exploitation of Iranian oil by the British owned Anglo-Iranian oil company. The movement was fueled by the Russians through the instrumentality of Iran's communist Tudeh party. With the Anglo-American backing five years earlier, Russians had been denied access to the oilfields in Northern Iran and this was the time for the Russian response. Once again the clergy joined with the liberals, this time under the secular leadership of Mossadegh.

Mossadegh was an experienced liberal politician with a brilliant record of struggle against autocracy and foreign interference. During the occupation of Iran, Mossadegh emerged as a prominent figure. After his successful maneuvering in parliament against the granting of oil concessions to Russia, he initiated the Act for Nationalization of the oil industry in Iran.

Mossadegh came to be regarded as the embodiment of loftiest national aspirations. His immaculate integrity, passionate patriotism and uncompromising stand against foreign pressure had gained Mossadegh nationwide credibility. He had become an incontestable national leader.

Mossadegh's national movement, with tacit backing of some foreign elements, nationalized the oil industry, but failed to market Iran's oil in the face of Britain's intrigues. Economic conditions worsened. A rift developed between the Shah and Mossadegh. Apparently fearful of the coalition of liberals and the communists, the clergy, with British instigation, broke away from Mossadegh and aligned themselves with the Shah.

The part played by clergy in alliance with the monarchists, and the covert support of the American CIA and British Intelligent Service in overthrow of Mossadegh, is common knowledge today.[8] In the struggle for nationalization of oil, the role of the clergy was definitely secondary to that of the liberals and the Western-educated intellectuals.

Ten years elapsed before Mohammed Reza Shah could consolidate his power, though Mossadegh's ghost never left him in peace. In 1963 the Shah launched his "White Revolution" program. It was a big stride on the road to modernization of the country and secularization of the state. Its main components were land reform, nationalization of forests and pasture lands, sale of government factories, workers' profit-sharing plans, electoral reform and women's suffrage. It also provided for the formation of a literacy corps, manned with the university and secondary school graduates, to be engaged in combatting illiteracy in the rural areas.[9]

Three items in that reform program particularly antagonized the clergy. The first was land reform. It deprived *ulama* and Shi'a establishments of their traditional revenues, and thus, of an important leverage in their social and political operations. Women's suffrage and the ensuing reform of the family law was the second. They considered it a flagrant deviation from Koranic law. The Family Protection Law of 1967 had largely modified the Koranic principle of non-judiciary and unilateral divorce by the husband, and had curtailed the practice of polygamy. It had also replaced the authority of the religious courts, in matters of personal law, with that of the secular courts. Worst of all, it allowed non-Muslims to sit on the judiciary bench. The extension of the military conscription to women was the third issue. It provided for the military training of the women alongside men in the same campus. This was unacceptable to the clergy. These were hard blows to the clergy's power position in the society. The first denunciation of the Shah by Khomeini came in 1963 after the announcement of the reform program.[10] Strangely enough, since the Iran-Iraq war, the Islamic Republic has reintroduced conscription for women as an Islamic duty.

Despite the great importance ascribed in retrospect to the 1963 Khomeini-led riot as a preamble to the 1978 revolution, the truth is that the economic growth and social prosperity that ensued from the Shah's bold and imaginative economic development projects after 1963, pushed that incident into oblivion. Repeated reminder of that event, during and after the revolution, by Khomeini and his followers, was a device to give a greater legitimacy to Khomeini's leadership of the revolution and also a justification for his vindictive policies.

A study of day-to-day accounts of the 1978–79 revolution reveal that the first effective challenge to the Shah's regime came from the guerrilla activists of the Fedaiyan and Majahedin–Khalgh in the late 1960s. Non-violent protests by Mossadegh's followers had never ceased. The first open letter of protest in the year 1977 came from the former politicians of the banned National Front of Dr. Mossadegh. They demanded political liberalization, respect for human rights, observance of the constitution and an end to corruption. Similar appeals were made by associations of lawyers, writers, journalists, judges and other groups. The first anti-government demonstration was organized by the university students, National Front, Liberation Movement and leftist groups. It was only in January 1978, after a clash in the city of Qum between the mullahs and the security police, that the mullahs became visible in political demonstrations. This, however, should not imply that the clergy had not been covertly active before that.[11]

During the Shah's reign, mosques provided shelter for the opposition, secular or religious. Ali Shariati, a free religious thinker, Mehdi Bazargan, the leader of the Liberation Movement, and Ayatollah Taleghani, a left-of-center religious leader made the best use of pulpit. Their political messages were communicated in the course of religious lectures. This, too, gave the *ulama* a preemptive claim to the revolution.

The final victory for the clergy, vis-à-vis other opposition groups, came in the fall of 1978, when the secular opposition to the Shah, the leaders of the National Front and Liberation movement, went to Paris to meet with Khomeini. After the meeting they eulogized Khomeini as a wise and courageous leader, tacitly approving his tactical policies. This accorded Khomeini enormous credibility, as well as legitimacy as the leader of revolution. The purpose of the secular leaders was to capitalize on the religious sentiments of the masses against the Shah. They were also deceived by Khomeini's promise to retire to Qum after removal of the Shah. This was confirmed by Bazargan, the first prime minister of Islamic Republic, in his weekly nationwide televised address. Bazargan, who had been frustrated by Khomeini's ceaseless and unwarranted interference in the running of the government, complained to the nation that when he and Khomeini first met in Paris, Khomeini promised that after the downfall of the Shah, he would go to Qum and resume his religious functions at the theological institute, leaving the affairs of government to the politicians. Bazargan asserted that the conversation had been taped and was available for verification.

This incidence reveals that even people like Bazargan had not read Khomeini's treatise on Velayat-e-Faghih, in which he had unambiguously stated that: (1) the Islamic government is based on the religious authority; (2) the government on earth, in the absence of the Twelfth Imam, rests with the *ulama;* and (3) the leadership should be in the hands of one or several Faghihs (just and pious clergies versed in Islamic jurisprudence). Khomeini had always advocated the Divine Reign of the clergy, but, before the revolution, few people knew about it.

Khomeini's force of character, obstinacy, personal charisma, and militant ideology definitely contributed to his success. Other factors, such as tactical errors of the Shah and leaders of secular opposition to the Shah, accidents of history, external forces and socio-economic conditions also had significant share in this national syndrome.

Khomeini's shrewd and skillful maneuvering, prior to, during, and after the revolution helped him to isolate his rivals and consolidate his own position. Two months after the revolution, the first confrontation between Khomeini's Hezbullah and Mojahedin–Khalgh occurred. Ayatollah Taleghani's son, a former member of Mojahedin group, was arrested by the fundamentalist revolutionary Guard (Hezbullah). Ayatollah Taleghani denounced the arrest as arbitrary and labelled it a return to dictatorship. It was an obvious reference to Khomeini. Taleghani demanded immediate release of his son and threatened to retire forever from politics. After three days of uncertainty and suspense, Taleghani consented to visit Khomeini in Qum. The meeting took place on camera. After that, Taleghani appeared on television and reaffirmed his unconditional support for Khomeini. Sometime later, Taleghani joined Khomeini in deploring Forghan, a religious anti–Khomeini group. Taleghani died suddenly after a visit to his house by the Soviet ambassador, which lasted until after midnight. The meeting was said to have been amicable.

Khomeini and the fundamentalists shrewdly managed to neutralize Bazargan, leaders of the National Front and moderate ayatollahs like Shari'atmadari. Shari'atmadari was later placed under house arrest. These religious and national figures were wholly intimidated by Hezbullah. They did not even venture to voice their opposition to Khomeini's violent crackdowns on Sunni Kurds, Turkamans and Arabic speaking minority in Khuzistan. Khomeini also had Khaghani, the spiritual leader of the Sunni Muslims in Khuzistan, exiled to Qum, the seat of Shi'aism in Iran.[12]

Another factor favorable to Khomeini was the presence in Iran of supportive foreign elements during the initial stage of the revolution. They preferred to see a strong religious leader, rather than a weak liberal or a pro-communist individual, replace the Shah. Moreover, Khomeini's exotic appearance before mass media had already earned him wide recognition. Once in power, nothing short of an absolute control would satisfy this aged and stubborn man. His ambitions spelled out in his book on Velayat-e-Faghih are prophetic. Throughout this time, he has remained faithful to his precepts. His many tactical lies may be explained by the Shi'a principle of Taghieh (lying in the interest of religion and the final victory). Khomeini's merciless treatment of his veteran supporters, bears evidence to his thirst for power and complete lack of compassion. Ghotbzadeh was executed, Bani Sadr fled to exile, Vazdi was totally isolated and Bazargan was continuously threatened and battered by Hazbullah.

This brief review shows that in all Iranian political upheavals in the last century, the force of religion has been distinctly present. In the case of opposition to the Tobacco Monopoly of 1891, leadership was in the hands of the clergy. In the Constitutional Revolution of 1907, the liberals were the forerunners with a joint secular-religious midway; however, in the end, the secularism won. During the 1950s movement following the nationalization of oil, the religious leadership was secondary to the national/liberal leadership of Mossadegh. In the 1979 Islamic Revolution, groups with different political ideologies and economic policies coalesced, with one common goal: to overthrow the Shah. After the success of the revolution, they could not agree on a joint policy. Confrontation, split and inside rivalries abounded, from which Khomeini emerged an autocratic leader, and Shi'a fundamentalism triumphed.

Another observation is historical evidence of the frequent resignation of Iranian people to autocracy. This has not been for lack of the desire for freedom. It has been an unfortunate result of Iran's invasion by Arab, Turks and Mongols, short-lived dynasties, miscalculations by the national leaders and absence of salutary alternatives. In the course of the 1979 uprising, many activists thought that, without the use of the tool of religion, the removal of the Shah would be delayed. They were completely unaware of the political and managerial abilities of the theocrats. Moreover, the liberals are less disciplined and decisive than theocrats, communists and other groups that favor one party system. It is regrettable that in the last century, the fruits of the revolution have always been seized by anti-liberal groups.

The Significance of Non-Religious Forces. Notwithstanding the tendency to view the 1978–79 Iranian revolution as part of the worldwide Islamic militancy, it was an indigenous phenomenon conditioned by its historical and contemporary settings. Shi'a fundamentalism was not designed to prevail after the revolution. Nationalism, liberalism and socialism had claims to the revolution that were as strong as those of the fundamentalists.

The force of national consciousness in Muslim countries is largely overshadowed by the fear created by militant Islam, escalation of cold-blooded and indiscriminate killings, and the widespread terrorism. It is often forgotten that the movements that rapidly terminated colonialism in many Afro-Asian countries between 1947–67 were nationalistic. It would be wrong to think that, in the absence of militant Islam, the Shah of Iran would not have been toppled, Anwar Sadat of Egypt would not have been assassinated, and the Russian invasion of Afghanistan would have passed unresisted. These events are as much ascribable to nationalism as to religious militancy. It is nationalism that is currently expressing itself in religiosity.

Religion has become a channel for expression of real or perceived grievances by oppressed people. Militant Sikhism in India, militant Buddhists in South Asia, and militant Christians in Central America are illustrations in point. They want to free themselves from the real or perceived yoke of foreign rule. Jamal al-Din Assadabadi (Afghan), one of the early leaders of the Islamic movement, envisaged the emergence of independent and strong Islamic nations (countries) through adherence to Islamic principles. This was a paradox since Islam recognized only *umma,* and not nations. Assadabadi's aim could not have been achieved through secular accommodation of religious principles. Militant Islam has become a vehicle for political aspirations. It is a resurgence of nationalism and anti-colonialism. It is a positive exhibition of xenophobia. Terrorism is not an inherent feature of militant Islam. Nor is martyrdom peculiar to Shi'aism. The crusaders precipitated martyrdom, the Japanese practice of hari-kiri is an act of martyrdom. Following Imam Hossein's example, martyrdom is admittedly more pronounced with fundamentalist Shi'as. Nevertheless, overestimation of the religious feature of Shi'a Fundamentalism has given it a grotesque vitality beyond all proportion that may prove fatal in future, as will a false self-confidence to the militants. A predominantly religious interpretation of the Iranian revolution would be misleading. Uncoordinated modernization, political suppression, corruption and associated socioeconomic evils had their shares in the shake-up. These make the Iranian syndrome an indigenous malaise, rather than a branch of a worldwide political tide.

Among the socioeconomic factors, political repression, corruption and social injustice stand out. Reza Shah's reforms had several backlash effects. Destruction of the traditional social structure, political repression and a greater social and geographical mobility were among them.[13] The structure of Iranian society was, before Reza Shah, corporate.[14] It consisted of tribes and village groups in rural areas, and of small merchant associations and craft guilds in town. The clergy operated across the nation. Through these corporate groups, the people could voice their individual, social and political desires and grievances, express their sense of social purpose and participate in the civic affairs. In his vigorous attempts for centralization and modernization, Reza Shah suppressed tribal and local autonomy, dissolved the political groups, neutralized craftsmen and merchants and weakened the clerical centers of influence.

During the fifteen years after Reza Shah's abdication, Mohammed Reza resumed his father's modernization and secularization plans at an ever-increasing speed. The economy boomed, health and education improved, living standards rose, women's status ameliorated and Iran prided herself for remarkable achievements.[15] Nevertheless, Mohammed Reza Shah failed to create a solid political structure, and provide for the integration of the newly-emerged social classes in the system. The over-centralization of the government reduced the real and much desired participation of the people in the political process and policy making. With one-man rule, favoritism, discrimination and corruption escalated. The absence of an independent judiciary further frustrated the people.

The Shah, in an ostensibly honest belief that pressure-groups and self-interested individuals hampered his modernization plans, concentrated all powers within himself and a handful of his trusted men. His belief was based on the experience of the first thirteen years of his reign. As a result, all genuine political parties, professional groups, merchant and craftsmen guilds, and traditional corporate bodies were nullified. The Westernized middle class, who had benefitted from the socioeconomic changes in the country, and on whom the Shah so much relied, turned against him at the time of crisis. Those who had received higher education in the Western institutions and were acquainted with the Western democracy, could not endorse the Shah's autocratic rule. Even a small number who remained loyal to the Shah until the end, had associated themselves with the Shah's one-party system only in a passive way. The lack of political support for the Shah became abundantly clear during the revolution.

The Shah's distrust of organized political groups was deep-rooted in him. Apprehensive of the influence of the "Iran Nowin Party," he, in 1975, without any notice (even to his prime minister who was secretary-general of the party), dissolved it. On the same occasion, he also banned two other political parties, both loyal to him. Iran Nowin had been formed 12 years earlier, with the Shah's blessing, and had received the title of 'Guardians of the White Revolution.' The decision to dissolve the Iran Nowin party and introduce a one-party system, apparently had been made at the suggestion of the Minister of Interior. The Interior Minister was not a party member. Iran Nowin had been charged by the Ministry officials with having meddled with the votes in a close race with the Mardom party, the main opposition party. Although authentic political party regimes had been put in obeyance since 1963, the Iran Nowin party, exercised semi-democratic practices within the party and could conceivably have formed a nucleus for the future political infrastructure, so badly needed in Iran.

The last straw was corruption, waste and squandering of the oil revenue that reached their peak in the process of celebration of the 2,500 anniversary of Iranian monarchy. From early 1970, tacit and gradual collaboration was in the making between the intellectuals, liberals and leftist Muslims against the Shah. Ali Shariati, a religio-political intellectual, who had concentrated all his scholarly ability on extracting the revolutionary messages of Islam, started preaching in mosques and universities, on the virtues of revolt against injustice and spoke of dreams of a classless society. He was indeed reinterpreting Marxist principles in Islamic terms. He employed Islam as a 'liberator theology.' This was palatable to the Muslim youth, underprivileged and intelligentsia. Shariati soon emerged as a prominent Islamic ideological theoretician. Since the revolution, Mojahedin-Khalgh have declared themselves the ideological followers of Shariati.

After the 1974 oil boom, the pattern of economic growth became haphazard. The immediate result was a massive imbalance of income among various sectors of the society. The gap between rich and poor widened. Widespread corruption in upper layers of the society, public and private, including members of the royal family, was taken by the general public as license for depravity. The condoning of corruption, more than corruption itself, raised public disgust and fury. High military and civil officials were charged and arrested for corruption, and with the Shah's oral approval, released a few months later. Some of them were even reassigned to higher government positions. The Shah treated the treasury as his personal purse, and the people as his personal servants. Had it not been for the corruption during the revolution, the Shah could have presented the people with an excellent record of economic development and social achievements during his reign, and won the day.

Despite their handsome financial gains, thanks to the Shah's economic programs, traditional bazaris joined the revolution soon after it started. Certain radical changes had alerted them. Construction of commercial centers, banks and sophisticated industrial and financial institutions on the Western pattern, were taken as a threat to their vested interests. The profits of the money-lending bazaris, who charged exorbitant sums under the name of Islamic commission, not interest, were greatly diminished by the establishment of commercial banks giving loans at quoted rates of interests. Destruction of the traditional hole-in-the–wall bazaar in the vicinity of Imam Reza's shrine in Mashhed provided the mullas with additional pretext to challenge the religiosity of the Shah. The Westernized shopping center that was constructed in that place during the time of Shah is now a source of pride to all devout Muslims.

The newly prospered Westernized businessmen were aligned with the Shah until Fall of 1979, when the government waged a war against speculators. The method of investigation and bringing charges against the merchants tended to resemble communist patterns of behavior during the Russian Revolution and Chinese Cultural Revolution. This presented another flaring example of uncoordinated policies under the old regime. It created an immense sense of insecurity in the business circle. Some of the rich businessmen who had amassed their riches during the time of the Shah, extended financial help to the revolutionaries, in the hope of subsequently rescuing their own wealth.

During the breakdown of the economic structure in 1976–78, the alliance of the bazaris and the clergy strengthened. This was not so much for the restoration of the traditional way of life, but for the failure of the government to make the system function adequately. It was not modernization *per se,* that angered the people, but the manner in which it had been carried out.

In the post-1974 oil boom, economic dislocation increased. The impact of inflation on the lower classes—workers, urban migrants and farmers—was great. Despite allocation of collossal subsidies for food and other necessities, from the explosive oil revenue, the living standards of the people in terms of real purchasing power was rapidly declining. The government, in its efforts to crush the soaring price of land and reduce the spiralling rent in towns, brought the transaction on land and construction industry to a complete standstill, causing widespread unemployment. Speculators in land joined the ranks of opposition. Dislocation of a large number of young people escalated public agitation. The urban population doubled in a decade. The poor and unemployed, who had flocked into the cities, played a decisive role in the 1979 revolution. The tightening of credits by the government, in an attempt to harness inflation, compelled the agricultural banks and institutions to lower the ceiling of cash advancement to the newly enfranchised landowners.

At the same time people who were facing financial hardship resented the Shah's financial assistance for crackdown on insurgents in Oman, North Yemen and Zaire. This provided additional reasons for discontent. People had no praise for Iran's assumption of the gendarme role in the Persian Gulf. They also disapproved Iran's financial aid to Egypt and Pakistan, and argued that charity starts at home. These cases were quoted by the opposition as a proof of the Shah's blind submission to his American masters. This squandering of national resources abroad was compared with economic failures during the last three years at home. In the fifth five-year plan, the government had targeted the construction of one million housing units and was unable to reach one tenth of it. Unloading of the ships had been halted at ports due to bottlenecks. Considerable demurrage had to be paid. The discharged goods had remained in open air for months and had decayed or been partly stolen. Successive delinquency by the government in the fulfillment of its duties and promises had led to a complete mistrust and cynicism. All this was happening in the face of the Shah's rhetorics that Iran was approaching the gates of a great civilization. The Shah's inflated promises had unduly raised people's expectations and were producing backlashes. Government officials were unable to provide convincing explanations for such failures. All had been caught in an oppressive public machinery.[16]

Popular discontent had started, only to be fanned by secular and clerical opposition. Deficient road repairs, an inefficient communications system, lack of health facilities in the rural areas, want of sewage systems, shortage of some food items, insufficient skilled workers and technicians, surplus of unskilled labors and secondary school graduates, inadequacy of economic plannings and inadequate managerial personnel provided visible evidence and plausible grounds to attack the Shah, who for years had allowed himself to be presented as the sole arbiter of Iran's development plans.

A scene of insecurity prevailed. That in itself was a sufficient factor to rally people around the Shah's opponents.

The united opposition to the Shah consisted of the following primary groups: (1) The remnants of old political groups weakened or outlawed by the Shah, (Mossadegh's National Front and the Communist Tudeh Party); (2) The newly politicized individuals, (intellectuals including returnees from Western universities, who held liberal or leftist views and were obstinately opposed to foreign interference, and students in the Iranian institutes of higher education many of whom, without the free education introduced under the Shah, would not have been able to afford a higher education); (3) The unemployed and economically dislocated (urban migrants, the new proletariat sprouting in major cities, the unemployed secondary school graduates); (4) the opportunists and newly disenchanted well-to-do persons (Westernized businessmen, some high-positioned civil servants, the opportunists across the nations including some past ministers, rich industrialists and businessmen); (5) The clergy; and (6) The newly formed militant political parties (Mujaheddin, Fedaiyan guerrilla groups, etc.).

The most consequential factor in the swift breakdown of the monarchy was the Shah's indecisiveness in the last year of his reign. Whatever its reason, he continuously played into the hands of the opposition. His decision to intern his most loyal men, to make continuous concessions to his foes at wrong moments and to display weakness in confrontation with crisis, precipitated his downfall.

Finally it is important to emphasize again that, although the socioeconomic factors expedited the process of revolution, it was not modernization *per se,* its extent and speed, that caused the revolution. It was the manner in which it was conducted and the errors committed by the regime that led to the catastrophe.

Religion and Foreign Intervention. To assume the 1979 revolution was free from all foreign intervention would be naive; to assert that it was all planned, programmed and implemented by one or several foreign powers[17] would be speculation. The popular belief that Shi'a clergy are British political tools is a remnant of the past, when Britain was the unrivaled power in the region.

The performance of the British Broadcasting Corporation during the revolution aroused suspicion of a collusion with the revolutionaries, particularly with religious leaders. Undoubtedly the external services of the B.B.C. are monitored by the British Foreign Office,[18] and undeniably, from the time Khomeini landed in Paris, until the time he left Tehran, he was "the object of saturation reportage by B.B.C. correspondents."[19] The inference is that the B.B.C., with the knowledge and approval of the British Foreign Office, disseminated regularly and intensively the latest Khomeini's directives for strikes and demonstrations to the people of Iran. For all practical purposes, B.B.C. was provocative and destructive to the regime. Most Iranians construed this attitude as a clear indication that the British government and her allies were determined to remove the Shah.

The B.B.C. explanation was that they broadcasted the news received from their correspondents and other reliable sources. The fact that all the news about, and instructions by, Khomeini were instantly communicated by his men via telephone network to all cities in Iran, they argued, falsified the contention that the B.B.C. was instigating the revolution. This explanation neither satisfied the Shah, nor changed the belief of the people. The fact remains that the B.B.C., whatever its intentions, expedited the spread of the news, and, above all, lent credibility, which greatly helped the revolutionaries. Its broadcasts and commentaries aroused riots and animated demonstrations.

For an evaluation of the role of B.B.C. in the success of the revolution, the test question is: would the process of revolution have slowed down if the B.B.C. had toned down its news or commentaries? The answer would be in the affirmative.

Despite a statement by Andrew Young, then U.S. ambassador to the United Nations, that France and its mass media greatly contributed to the success of the revolution, in reality, this was not correct. The facts revealed since the revolution indicate that the French government was ready to deny Khomeini entry into France and refuse an extension of stay permit, if the Shah had so desired.[20]

The books and articles published by prominent Americans involved in the Iranian crisis of 1979, including those by President Carter and Ambassador Sullivan, reveal that the American Administration at that time was misinformed,[21] often badly advised,[22] and consequently their policy, if any, was based on a miscalculation,[23] and at the most, it was mismanaged. Some factions in the State Department preferred that the Shah go, and other factions in the Administration wanted him to stay. The messages of American support of the Shah from President Carter or Brezinski always came at the wrong time, in the wrong context, and further weakened the Shah. There was no need for overt support. The conclusion is that, even if the United States did not contribute by design to the downfall of the Shah, it did so by accident. If nothing else, the United States allowed the Shah to be toppled, and, particularly towards the end, encouraged the Shah's downfall. The Shah's indecisiveness and his vacillation in the last months of his reign were, to a great extent, a reflection of American indecisiveness and lack of a coherent policy.[24]

When the trends of events started to move irreversibly against the Shah, the Western allies decided to join Khomeini's bandwagon. After the four nations' heads of state met in Guadeloupe and reviewed Iran's case, the United States decided to contact Khomeini and the liberal leaders to make provision for the rescue of her threatened position in Iran. Likewise, France started to draw on the protection and amenities she had extended to Khomeini and his entourage during their stay in France.

There was no overt, and no evidence of covert, intervention by the Soviet Union in the 1979 revolution. They had no contact with *ulama* either. This does not mean that other communist countries did not help the revolutionaries. It has been revealed that Fedaiyans and Mojahedin guerrillas, as well as many members of Khomeini's Hezbullah, were trained in the PLO training camps in Lebanon, under East German and Cuban instructors.[25]

Khomeini had close relations with PLO chief Yasser Arafat, Syrian president Hafez Assad and the Libyan leader Muammar Khadafi. After the establishment of the Iranian Islamic Republic, all three were invited by Khomeini to visit Iran.[26] Syrian involvement included supply of passports to Khomeini's men, like Ghotbzadeh, sheltering of the Iranian dissidents, and procurement of funds and arms for the revolutionaries from sources like Khadafi. PLO men actually participated alongside with Fedaiyan and Majahedin in anti-Shah demonstrations in Tehran and attacks against military establishments to the day of takeover. Certain evidence also points to their participation in the Black Friday massacre.

The Shah, in his interviews in exile, and in his book "Answer to History," has charged three major oil companies with conspiracy against himself. In the absence of proof, it is difficult to relate any particular oil company to the revolution unless special interests can be identified. The Shah masterminded the price increase in December 1973, but the companies gained from it. The move for nationalization of oil in OPEC countries was the natural sequence to the oil embargo, following the Arab-Israeli war and the U.S.A. support for Israel. The Shah was not its author.

In his foreign policy, the Shah tried to balance his ever increasing reliance on the U.S. and Western Europe, with expansion of trade and industrial cooperation with the Soviet Union and Eastern Europe. He showed greater affinity to the Arab countries and the Islamic world, while maintaining close relations with Israel. He also cultivated relations with China. There is again no evidence to indicate that these subtle changes in foreign relations had any bearing on the revolution. However, the fact is that the more he attended to foreign relations, the area which greatly interested him and on which he was extremely well-informed, the less time he spent on domestic problems, of which he proved to be ignorant. Perhaps he would have made a better foreign secretary than a leader.

The impact of foreign intervention, direct or indirect, on the revolution should neither be exaggerated nor minimized. A post-mortem examination of the last days of monarchy reveals orchestrated efforts, from inside and outside, to bring the uprising to fruition.

Revolution as a Game of Struggle for Power. Looking for the unknowns is the scholars' privilege. In this pursuit, sometimes the obvious escapes attention. Search for the ideology and the contributing socioeconomic factors is a fascinating intellectual exercise. Yet revolution is, like many other individual and collective activities, a game (play). It is the game of a struggle for power. In a game (play), the players' skill, and not the ideology, determines the result. The aim of the contestants is to win and the immediate factor for success is skill. Accidental factors, luck and misfortune, have their share in the outcome of the game. Coaching efficiency, spectator support, and domestic or foreign financing are secondary matters. The intangible objective or ideology differs even within the contestants. Some have the drive for fame, some for financial gain, some for the emotional pleasure, and others for a handful of other reasons. Too much concentration on ideology and search for causes would distort the realities. Furthermore, play (game) "lies outside the antithesis of wisdom and folly, and, equally outside those of truth and falsehood, good and evil."[27]

The Iranian revolution was a game. It was struggle for power. Each group worked for a 'win,' with its own ideology. The contestants were the Shah on one side and the alliance of his opponents on the other side. The component groups in opposition had one objective in common: to win the contest and strip the Shah of his title, honors, power and functions. In political terms, they had formed an alliance to overthrow the Shah. They did not have a unified ideology. Their ideology ranged from constitutional monarchy to republic, Islamic fundamentalism to moderate Islam, socialism and communism. The fact that, since the success of the revolution, all political parties have, on more than one occasion, changed or modified their political stand on a number of issues, proves that the immediate aim for the opposition, before and after the revolution, was the assumption of power and not ideology. Had it not been for many tactical mistakes of the Shah and his domestic and foreign advisors, the revolution would have, if at all, taken a different course. Shi'a fundamentalism would not have emerged so powerful, and terrorism would not have reached its present monstrosity.

An overall view of the components of the revolution does not indicate a predominately fundamentalist nature. The pre-revolution emergence of Marxist-Islam, and the post-revolution short-lived Majahedin-fundamentalist alliance, show that Islam has often been adopted as a political vehicle rather than an ideology. It is good to recall that in the 1940s Ayattolah Taleghani was a Tudeh Party candidate for Parliament. He became an admirer of Islam dialectics formulated by the theorist Shari'ati after Marxist dialectics. His main aim was the establishment of a socialist economy. Like Jamal-al-Din Assadabadi, Teleghani and Shari'ati had come to the conclusion that religion could be used as an effective tool to achieve socio-economic aims. These examples also indicate how Islam may be modified with the demands of political expediency.

The Shah opposition game was played at an international level. In the subsequent games of struggle for power played at the national level between the component groups of the opposition front, the teams of liberal Muslims under Bazargan, traditionally moderate Muslims under Shari'atmadari, subversive leftist Muslims like Mujahedin and the communist Tudeh party lost their games. Hezbullah emerged champions. As history has shown, no champion can retain his title forever. Because of full identification of Shi'a fundamentalism with Hezbullah, Shi'aism runs the risk of going down with Hezbullah, when the time comes.

Had the Shah not chosen, whether by his own judgement or under Carter's pressure as is widely assumed, that most inappropriate time at the end of 1976 for launching his liberalizing program, the Iranian monarchy might not have been lost. Had he not made several tactical blunders in the course of the play, he or his son might still be on the throne. The play of Iranian Revolution needs more scrutiny.

The Impact of Islam on Contemporary Politics in Iran

Ayatollah Khomeini's catchword is Islam. He says he works for Islam and nothing else. Retorting to critics of his government's economic policies, Khomeini has reaffirmed that the aim of revolutionary Islam is the protection and promotion of religion, and not the economic development of the country or social welfare of the people. He has a nostalgia for the early Islamic society at the time of Prophet and his immediate successors, the Kholafay-e-Rashedin. What he overlooks is that the establishment of the early Muslim society owed much to raid and plundering of the defeated tribes and countries. Spoliation was the common economic practice of Muslims in the initial stages. Contrary to Khomeini's claim, what was not practiced at that time was ascetism. Martyrdom, another

Khomeini catchword, has a different history. It was a virtue from Islam's inception. Those who lost their lives in Ghasvehs, the prophet's wars, and those who died in *Jihad*, Holy Wars, would have their rewards in heaven. In Shi'aism this was reaffirmed by Imam Hossein's example. Khomeini's first objective was Islamization of Iranian life and polity. Next he hopes to export his revolution to other Muslim countries. Therefore Islamic considerations are heavily infused in Iranian public policy, both in internal and international arenas. The 1979 constitution of the Islamic Republic of Iran is, as stated in its preamble, "the expressor of the cultural, social, political and economic institutions of Iranian society, (and) is based upon Islamic principles which reflect the true aspiration of the Islamic community."[28]

In the next section, Islamization and polity in Iran will be discussed under the separate rubrics of internal policy and international relations.

The Impact of Islam on Internal Policy.

Institution of Veleyat-e-Faghih and Absolute Dominance of the Clergy. This institution is of far-reaching consequences. It lies at the very foundation of the Islamic Republic of Iran. It was the issue that widened the gap between Khomeini and Shari'atmadari. Prominent *Mujiahids* (religious leaders), including Ayatollah Taleghani, were against it.

Regarding Velayet-e-Faghin, two schools of thought exist in Shi'aism. One school, to which Khomeini and Hezbullah belong, maintains that the spiritual and secular leadership should rest with one individual, who must look after the interests of faith. This was the tradition of the prophet and the four pious Khalifs. The other school believes that the religious leaders should attend Shari's and religious affairs, leaving the governance of the secular affairs to men of politics. They do not favor rule by clergy. In support of this view, the prophet is cited to have said that "after his death there will be caliphs for thirty years and then sovereigns."[29] The practice in Iran has been for the Shah to appoint a most superior scholar to the office of Shaik–ul-Islam and to give him absolute charge of the religious affairs.

In the 1979 Constitution, the unity of the highest religious and secular offices is recognized. Velayat-e-Faghih represents that office. Velayat-e-Faghih can veto the legislation, judiciary decisions and executive ordinances. In practice, the institution stands above the law. In Article 2 of the Constitution, the phrase "positive leadership and its sensitive role in the continuity of the Islamic Republic" is skillfully added to Imamat, and in the context of five essentials of Shi'aism: monotheism, Divine Revelation, Resurrection, justice and Imamat. "Positive leadership" is defined in the context of occulation of the twelfth Imam in Article 5. It says that "during the time when the Twelfth Imam is in occulation, the leadership of the affairs, legislative, executive and judiciary, lies with a just and pious theologian-jurist, al-Faghih, who is courageous, vigorous, well-informed and keen." It suffices that people know and accept him as leader. No plebiscite is needed. As Nayeb-e–Imam, he will represent the absent Twelfth Imam. To secure this lofty position for Khomeini, at a time when other great Ayatollahs claimed precedence over him, Article 107 stipulated that Khomeini be the theologian-jurist, al-Faghih, who, by virtue of his distinguished religious Marja' (authority), has been recognized by the people as the leader. He, the great Ayatollah Imam Khomeini (the title given to him in the constitution), has the sanctimonious command." Thus, Khomeini became Nayeb-e-Imam for lifetime. He enjoys the highest legislative, executive and judiciary power in the country, and is answerable to God alone.

Evidently the institution of Velayat-e-Faghih is at variance with the principle of sovereignty of the people. Nor does it agree with the principle of separation of power. Contrary statements in the Constitution should be taken as lip-services for publicity purposes.[30] Velayat-e-Faghih is not a figurehead; he rules.

What will happen to Velayat-e-Faghih after Khomeini? The Constitution provides for that eventuality. The responsibility for electing The Faghih or Faghihs lies with the Guardianship Council. The Council after careful consideration, elects the most highly qualified and virtuous of the living Muslim jurists (Faghihs), as Nayeb-e-Imam. Should the Council find several jurists equal in rank and competence, it would appoint three or five of them to act collectively in the Council of Leadership in the capacity of Nayeb-e-Imam.[31] The process is generally in accord with the tradition of early Islam. Abu Bakr who already controlled the affairs of the community and enjoyed a great influence among the masses was appointed Imam by *Ijma'* (consensus) of *Umma;* Omar was nominated by Abu Bakr; Uthman and Ali by the *Shura* (Council or consultation) of the leaders of the community.[32]

In addition to the veto right granted to him in all matters, Velayat-e-Faghih has several judiciary and military rights that makes him the absolute suzerain of the country. As the supreme judiciary authority, Velayat-e-Faghih appoints the highest judiciary of the country and six members of the Guardianship Council. He has the right to nullify the decisions of the judiciary at his pleasure.

In the area of military and defense, Velayat-e-Faghih exercises the authority enjoyed by the highest executive official in other countries, president or prime minister. He is the commander-in-chief of the armed forces. In that capacity he appoints and dismisses the chief of the joint staff, the chief commander of the Guardian Corps of the Islamic Revolution and the members of the National Defense Council. The Defense Council consists of five ex-officio members and two advisors all appointed by the Leader. Declaration of war and peace are entrusted to him. That is why no person other than Khomeini can decide on the continuation or termination of war with Iraq.

No leader in a Western democracy enjoys such extensive power as Velayat-e-Faghih in the Iranian Islamic Republic.

Guardianship Council. Next to Velayat-e-Faghih in the exercise of an overriding authority, particularly in legislative matters, is the Guardianship Council. It consists of twelve expert theologian-jurists, six of whom are appointed directly by Velayat-e-Faghih and six by the Assembly from among the qualified Muslim jurists proposed by the High Council of Judiciary.[33] Their term of office is six years. In the first term after three years, half of each group of six will be replaced by drawing of lots.

The main functions of the Guardianship Council are the following: (1) To ensure that laws enacted by the Assembly do not contravene the Islamic precepts as well as the constitutional principles; (2) To interpret the constitutional principles whenever the need arises; (3) To examine the competence of those who have been nominated to stand for presidency; and (4) To supervise all the general elections and referendums including those of president and Islamic Assembly.

The Council's power to scrutinize the acts of parliament is not new in Iran. The Supplementary Constitution of 1907 specified that "at all times there shall be constituted body of at least five devout Islamic theologians *(Mujtahis Jame al-Shrayet),* who shall at the same time be conversant with the exigencies of their age."[34] In this respect, the Constitution of 1907 was more democratic than that of 1979. The former provided for the Assembly to elect five individuals out of twenty qualified Muslim high jurists proposed by the most learned jurisprudents in the country. The law, however, did not lay down the manner in which the twenty individuals were to be nominated. Under the old regime this legal provision was never implemented.

The Source of Sovereignty. In an Islamic state, the sovereignty belongs to God. The prophet and Imams exercised the Divine Power.[35] In the absence of the Twelfth Imam in Shi'a society, that power would be exercised by Nayeb-e-Imam. Hence people's sovereignty, as defined by the European philosophers of the eighteenth century, cannot have any application in Islam. In Islam, man is God's slave and, by definition, slave has no right against his master.

The basic difference between the 1907 and 1979 Constitutions lies in their conception of the sovereignty and the source of law. In the 1907 Constitution, both "Islam" and "the will of the People" were recognized as the sources of sovereignty and law. Principle 26 of the 1907 Constitution laid down that "the powers of state are derived from the Nation." At the same time, it provided that no act of Parliament would become law if it contravened Islamic principles. Also, the kingship was a Divine benefaction bestowed upon the Shah by the Will of the People. It recognized Islam, according to the Jafari doctrine of Twelve Imam, as the state religion. The Shah of Iran had to profess and propagate that faith.[36] Hence, the compromise between religious and secular was the thread running through the constitution.

In the 1979 constitution, the predominance is with Islam. The will of the people was relevant to the extent that they expressed their desire for the establishment of an Islamic society. Beyond that, it is the Islamic law, and not the will of people, that prevails. The constitution of the Islamic Republic of Iran states that "the government does not arise from the notion of class position, social contract or supremacy of an individual or group, but it is the crystalization of political ideals of the people of the *same religion.*"[37] The key point here is that it is 'the same religion,' and not culture, history, customs, aspirations or other factors, that binds people together as a nation. Indeed, Khomeini has on several occasions denounced the nationality concept as pre–Islamic and Imperialist. As a result, in the Islamic Republic of Iran, the powers of state originate in Islamic precepts and not in the will of nation. The precepts of Islam are incorporated in Koran and *Sunna* (tradition), and except for the different interpretations, they can easily be ascertained. The will of the

'Islamic community' is a debatable issue among various Muslim sects. Sunnis believe in the populist consensus of *Umma*, and Shi'a in the consensus of *ulama* (theologian-jurists). The official religion of Iran being Islam of the Jafari Twelve Imam sect, the consensus will be that of the Muslim theologian-jurists and not of the *Umma* as a whole. This further widens the gap between democracy and Shi'a.

"The Islamic government is the government of the Divine Law," writes Khomeini, and the "power of legislation is confined to God."[38] The same view is expressed by the leading Islamic political philosopher, Maududi, in these words. "God has retained the right of legislation to himself."[39]

Based on the continuous religious leadership and the command of sanctity of the Imam and Velayat-e-Faghih, democracy can hardly flourish in Islamic Iran. The country is ruled by theologians. Legitimacy of this system is, they argue, based on Koran and tradition. Koran says "Give the administration to the clergy who know and can safeguard that which God allows, *halal,* and prohibit that which God forbids, *harams.* Tradition shows that Islamic societies have been ruled by theologians. In Islam, mosque and state are not separate, and religious and civil leadership are inseparable. Also the principle of separation of power and distinction between legislative, executive and judiciary is foreign to Islam. The Islamic Iran is ruled by the clergy in all areas and is supported by religiously-minded intellectuals with a parochial attitude towards world politics.

The Rights of Religious Minorities. "Iranian Zoroastrians, Jews and Christians are the only recognized minority religious groups."[40] This is in accord with the tenets of Koran and Sunna. It recognizes only those religions that are monotheistic and believe in Divine Revelation and Resurrection. The Islamic label for them is Zimmi. In the Islamic Society of *Umma*, Zimmis had to pay poll-tax in order to enjoy freedom to practice their own religion and to live as secondclass citizens. Strictly speaking, non-believers in those three precepts, if living in Dar-ul-Salam, should either accept Islam "or be put to death."[41]

Persecution of Bahais, who believe in the foresaid three principles, is for other reasons. Bahais accept Zoroastrianism, Judaism, Christianity and Islam as revealed religions. By such acceptance, they accept Islam before embracing Bahaism. They also believe their prophet, Bahaullah, is the Mahdi promised by Mohammad.

Muslims assert Mohammad was the seal of prophets. Acceptance of revelation as a continuous process, and with Mahdi having reappeared, Muslims would have to accept Bahaism. In particular there will be no legitimacy for Velayat-e-Faghih. Islamic society is a closed society: everybody can join in, but nobody should leave. Those who betray Islam by leaving the *Umma*, are exposed to death penalty. The atrocities committed against Bahais are appalling.

Within the domain of Koranic principles, the constitution declares that persecution of beliefs and ideologies is forbidden and no one may be penalized for the mere *possession* of a certain set of beliefs. Possession implies holding an ideology, short of practicing or propagating it.

The Islamic Assembly. The word coined for Parliament in the 1907 Constitution was Majless-e Shuray-e Melli, or the Consultative National Assembly. The name implied that it was an Assembly in which the people's representatives assembled and, after consultation with one another, enacted laws for the nation. The 1979 Constitution has changed the name to Majless-e Shuray-e Islami, indicating that the Assembly enacts laws for the Islamic society. This reflects Khomeini's aspiration for the export of revolution to other Muslim societies. Furthermore it was an attempt to minimize the significance of nationality as against Islam.

Regarding legislative jurisdiction of the Assembly, Khomeini writes: "Islam replaces the legislative body by a planning council."[42] The only legislator is God, who has revealed his Law in Koran. Koran is as much a canon of faith, rituals and ethics, as it is the source of civil and criminal law. It also regulated social and economic affairs of the Islamic society and the relations between the *Umma* (Islamic community) and the nonIslamic people.

The Islamic Assembly may enact laws within the limits of its jurisdiction specified in the constitution. This includes three main areas: economics, foreign relations[43] and inquiry into affairs of the country, particularly the conduct of the executive.[44] Scrutiny and approval of the budget,[45] conformation of loans, international treaties, and contracts are specifically reserved for the Assembly.

Ironically the Islamic Republic follows the same procedure for candidacy in the Assembly as was used by the Shah in his one-party system. In each constituency, from among the candidates, the clergy chooses a limited number (for each vacancy, three or five) as eligible candidates to stand for election. The people may vote only for one of them and not the others whose names do not appear on the clergy's list. Such a system can hardly be described as a representative parliamentary system. In the Islamic regime of Iran the government conducts the affairs in accordance with the rules outlined in Koran and Sunna, as interpreted and expounded by the Velayat-e-Faghih, the clergy in the council, as well as by the individual clergies in executive or judiciary. As the result, more often, unpredictability and chaos prevail.

Judiciary: Exclusion of Laws Alien to the Islamic Law. The area in which the impact of Islam is more extensively felt is the judiciary. From the start, the Islamic Republic set its mind on re-Islamization of the judiciary as regards both substantive and procedural laws.

Following the abolition of capitulation treaties, and in a move to assure foreigners of the adequacy of Administration of Justice in Iran, Reza Shah in 1928 caused the Parliament to place a liberal construction on the Principle 27(2) of the 1907 constitution. This allowed the establishment of secular courts alongside Shari'a courts and the introduction of French procedural system into the Iranian law. It also cleared the way for replacement of Islamic criminal law by French criminal code. The modified version of principle 27(2) reads: "the judicial power, whose function is to determine the right, it reserved to the religious courts in matters relating to Shari'a (Islamic law), and to the judiciary in secular law."[46] This amounted to the legal recognition of two systems of courts and two systems of laws. The application of religious law and jurisdiction of the religious courts were restricted to personal law and family matters. Criminal cases and civil disputes other than family matters were placed under the jurisdiction of the secular courts which applied the secular laws. The jurisdiction of Shari'a courts was further reduced by the change in the family law, restriction of polygamy and unilateral divorce and uplift of status of women under Mohammed Reza Shah.

In Article 2 of the 1979 Constitution, "the continual practice of qualified theologian-jurists based upon Koran and Sunna of the prophet and Imams" is proclaimed a matter of faith.[47] The function of the judiciary is "to guard the right of people upon the way of the Islamic movement."[48] It is based upon "Islamic justice" and "precise religious precepts."[49]

The Islamic government of Iran is rigorously applying the Koranic criminal code, based on retaliation. It has deemed the modern concepts of reformation and rehabilitation of the perpetrators as ineffective. Punishment is used as a deterrent. In the administration of justice, the distinction between civil and criminal courts has disappeared. So is the two degree adjudication. Summary trial without right of appeal is reintroduced. The Islamic rules of evidence are vigilantly applied. The evidence of two women equals that of one man, and evidence of a Zimmi is not entertained against that of a Muslim. In most cases, including political charges, the professional services of an attorney are denied the defendant.

In the sphere of substantive law, lapidation, scourging, and amputation of the limbs are enforced. The Constitution of 1979 requires judges "to refrain from the execution of any government decree, which should prove contrary to Islamic laws and precepts."[50] This right can be exercised by any judge or small and inferior court. This, in many cases, has resulted in contradictory judgments. In Shiraz in 1982, a clergy without any assigned jurisdiction in that city, and without reading the files and records of the inmates, changed the prison sentences of several inmates, previously issued by a Shiraz court of competent jurisdiction, to death sentences and had them executed on the spot. The competent judge who had issued the original prison sentence complained to Khomeini, but it was of no avail. Consequently he resigned. That is not an isolated case. The result has been legal insecurity in the country.

The cruel and crude Islamic punishments have gained momentum in recent years. Flogging of young girls in public, and stoning of adulterous women to death have become common practice. In his treatise on Velayat-e-Faghih, Khomeini writes: "Punishing an alcohol drinker with eighty whip lashes in public is justified, because most of the social calamities such as traffic accidents, suicides and drug addictions take place in the moments of drunkenness." Similarly he argues that, "the stoning of an unmarried adulteress is the most effective method of preventing fornication, abomination and corruption in a great and vast nation."[51] The Iranian press reported sometime ago that, in Kerman, a pregnant woman charged with adultery had been stoned to death.

A full-fledged Islamization of the judiciary is in process. It has been reported that some politicized female students, charged with the membership of Mojahedin-Khalgh, were sentenced to death. Discovering afterwards that they were virgin, the girls were given as concubines to some revolutionary guards a few hours before the execution sentence. Thus, the relevant Islamic rule forbidding the execution of unmarried females was observed.

Human Rights and Islamic Government of Iran. Khomeini has no qualm of conscience in rejecting the Western concept of human rights. Human rights were defined by the eighteenth century political philosophers, and since have been incorporated in the American and French declarations of Human Rights and subsequently in the charter of the United Nations. Undoubtedly such concepts are foreign to Islam. Equality exists among Muslims and not among non-Muslims. Zimmis (Christians, Jews and Zoroastrians) are treated as second-class citizens. They may not be assigned to the judiciary and to the high executive positions. The testimony of a Zimmi may not be admitted against a Muslim because a Zimmi is unjust *(fasigh)*.[52] A Zimmi may not marry a Muslim woman. Such a marriage is void and the man punishable. The reverse is admissible. Zimmis must pay poll-tax[53] and be held in contempt.[54] For all practical purposes, they are treated as inferior citizens. Arab pagans, atheists, agnostics and apostates should choose between Islam and sword.[55] The Islamic government of Iran calls Bahais, apostates, and Mojahedins, Revisionist *(Monafegh)*, and puts them to death. The inferior position of women to men, in Islam, is common knowledge. In the Koran the authority of husband over wife is likened to that of governor over citizens. An honest women remains obedient to her husband. If the woman turns disobedient and rebukes the husband, the husband has the right to chastise her.[56] In describing the power of man over his wife, Koran says: "your wives are your tillage."[57] A girl's inheritance is half that of a boy. The inequality between man and woman in marriage and divorce is well-known and need not be mentioned here. Some Muslims, in defense of such injustice, argue that polygamy is allowed only if the man can do justice to all women, and that is humanly impossible. The cynic may ask: would polyandry be allowed under similar conditions?

Iranian law has now reinstituted polygamy and unilateral divorce by husband. In a recent Friday prayer, the Speaker of Parliament, Rafsanjani, and the President of the Republic, Khomeini, urged men to marry several wives. This is necessitated, they declared, by the death of many men in the war. They emphasized that those men lost their lives for Islam and it is an Islamic duty of other Muslims to protect the family of the martyrs by marrying their widows.

Reintroduction of those primitive laws should not be surprising. Koranic rules may not be modified or put into abeyance; they must be observed and obeyed forever. On this, Khomeini writes: "What was permissible by Mohammed is permissible today until the day of resurrection, and what was forbidden by him is forbidden to the day of resurrection. . . . The belief that Islam came for a limited period of time and for a certain place violated the essentials of Islam."[58]

Since its foundation, the Islamic Republic of Iran has been one of the four top violators of the human rights in the Amnesty International's annual report. Amnesty International has frequently criticized Iran for not allowing contact with prisoners and for persecution of minorities.

Economy and Islam. It is stated in the preamble to the 1979 Constitution that, "In Islam the economy is a means intended to be a part of the work of improvement and the means cannot become the end."[59] It goes on to criticize both the capitalist and socialist economic systems in these words: "unlike other economic systems where the objective is concentration of wealth and profit-seeking (capitalists), and in materialistic-oriented societies (socialist), where economics is itself the objective and therefore in the stage of growth, economics become an element of destruction, corruption and deprivation"[60] (the added words in brackets are mine).

Public sector constitutes the main sector of economy. It extends across industry, trade, transport, service and mass media. It covers major industries, large mines, dams and irrigation networks, energy plants and industry; foreign trade, banking and insurance; shipping, railway and aviation; post and telegraph; radio and television. These must be nationalized. One of the first economic measures of the Islamic government was nationalization of banks and insurance companies.

In the economic sphere, the second rank is given to production and distribution cooperatives, which are to be set up in both the urban and rural areas. The law emphasizes that these cooperative companies should be established according to Islamic criteria. This is a legal device to allow the incorporation, in the Islamic legal system of the Republic, without it bearing the stamp of socialism. The private sector gets the residuary of the country's economy. The Islamic character of such an economic system is debatable.

Another important impact of religion on economy has been the abolition of usury, though the nationalized banks continue to pay interest to depositors under some Islamic legal jargons. The change is only a matter of legal terminology and not of substance. Payment of commission or profit-participation serves the same purpose. Government credits to private sector still carries a high punitive interest rate, as it was under the Shah. Thus the change is more hypocritical than real.

Iran's drive for self-sufficiency in production has failed, due to an incoherent economic policy, the sinking of the oil price and shortage of qualified personnel and managerial skills. Excluding oil revenue, the annual drop in Iran's national income had been continuous since the revolution.

Social Status of Women. The present Islamic regime of Iran is obsessed with putting women back in chador and veil (Islamic dress). The female revolutionary guards enforce the dress code and the punishment for the first time violation of the rules is 74 lashes. Additional physical and mental pains inflicted on the violators of the dress code include shaving of parts uncovered by scarf or chador, removing cosmetics from the face with a razor blade, cutting the nails and the displaced long hair. Violators of the law may also be assigned to correction centers for one week. Women are required to wear, in public, clothing that reveals no more than their hands and faces. Men are advised to dress modestly and avoid wearing tight blue jeans or shirts with Western images or slogans. At the universities, in the classrooms, in the mosques and in all public places, males and females should be segregated.

The government has closed down boutiques and is persecuting those engaged in selling decadent clothing.

International Policy. The impact of Islam on international policy of the present regime of Iran may conveniently be discussed under the following headings: Relations with Muslim Nations; Relations with Non-Muslim Nations of the Free World; Jerusalem and Israel; Relations with the Communist Countries.

Relations with Other Muslim Countries. Khomeini adheres to the principle of brotherhood of *Umma* (Muslim people) and seeks unity of all Muslims. He loathes nationalism and denounces it as a pre-Islamic concept. His aspirations for the formation of one Islamic community is inspired by the Koranic division of people into two camps: believers (Muslims) and disbelievers (non-Muslims). Koran also divides the world into two parts: *Daral-Islam* (the Zone and home of Muslims and peace) and *Daral-Harb* (the zone of war and non-Muslims).

During the last fifty years, several Muslim leaders have tried to unify the nations of the indigenously Muslim countries. They used different methods. The intended unity was not claimed to be so much for the restoration of Islam's greatness, but for the purpose of fighting Israel and Imperialism. The most forceful of such leaders was Nasser of Egypt who used pan-Islamism as a device for unity amongst the Arab states. He also had an eye on the oil revenue of Saudi and other oil exporting Arab states. He wanted the money to be used for development of all Arab countries and to fight against Israel. To achieve his dream, Nasser relinquished the glorious history of Egypt associated with that land and changed that name of the country to United Arab Republic. Khomeini, perhaps, is the first who from the start operated under the banner of Islam to the exclusion of ethnic or national affinities. He founded the Islamic Republic of Iran and immediately set upon himself the task of exporting his revolution to other Muslim lands.

In the preamble to the 1979 Constitution, the Islamic Republic of Iran is praised for having built "the model society with Islamic norms, principles and missions which reflects the beliefs of the movements and conditions and values of Islam."[61] It then declares that "the Constitution will prepare the ground internally and externally for the continuation of the revolution."[62] Finally, in reference to other Islamic countries, it states that Islamic government of Iran, "particularly (prepares the ground) for establishment of *relations with* other Islamic and *populist movements* as it tries to prepare the way for the advent of a unified world community."[63] The key word here is 'populist movements' or Islam al-Sha'bi. This constitutes the basic general policy of Khomeini's movement. They do not seek unity with the Islam al-Rasmi. Exportation of the Iranian type of Shi'a fundamentalism is a distinctive feature of Iran's international policy. Khomeini, in his book on Islamic government, writes: "colonialism has partitioned our homeland and has turned the Muslims into separate nations. . . . The only means that we possess to unite the Muslim nation, to liberate its lands from the grip of the colonialists, and to topple the agent governments of colonialism, is to seek to establish our Islamic government."[64] Khomeini maintains that nationalism is un-Islamic and that "Islam came to eliminate national fanaticism."[65] He believes that unification of *Umma* is possible only through a victorious Islamic revolution.

Khomeini's Hezbullah is actively pursuing that objective in Lebanon. Iran has been involved in international hijacking, hostage-taking and terrorism. Khomeini is praised by militant groups and his portraits adorn their offices. Had it not been for the Iran-Iraq war, Khomeini would have enjoyed much greater support in the Arab Emirates. Although it was Saddam Hussein who invaded

Iran in 1980, Khomeini's obstinacy in continuing this repulsive war has damaged his reputation among Arabs. The continuation of the war may be explained in historical, ethnic religious and personal terms, but cannot be justified on Islamic precepts.

The alliance of Khomeini's Islamic regime with Hafez Assad's secular government is additional proof that, despite all Islamic rhetoric, political expediency may be the final determinant in international relations. In 1981, Heydan, the spokesman for Ba'ath Party of Syria, publicly said that Syria's support for the Iranian revolution was not for religious reasons, but for political expediencies. While he intimated that Islam can be used as a means of terminating the historical Iran-Arab hostility, he pointed out that Syria's view of the role of religion does not correspond to that of Iran's revolutionary Islam. Ba'ath Party of Syria, like its counterpart in Iraq, have tried for twenty years to keep the religion and politics apart, to modernize their countries and to stop clergy interference in governmental affairs.

In the international arena, Iran is very much isolated from Arab countries. Except for Syria and Libya, Iran is isolated in OPEC and in Islamic conferences. Khomeini continues to retain contact and to finance militant Muslim groups, Shi'a or Sunni, in all countries. The Sunni fundamentalist group of Tawheed in Tripoli is one of them. The group is led by Shaikh Saeed Sheban, a close ally of Iran. In the complexities of Lebanese politics, the militant group of Tawheed receives help from both Khomeini and Yasser Arafat, and is harnessed by Hafez Assad. Syria and Iran despise Arafat. All this shows that in the case of a conflict between ideology and the short run play element, the latter prevails.

Relations with non-Muslim Countries. The Islamic Republic of Iran is irrevocably committed to the policy of non-alignment. This is inserted in the constitution so that no government may deviate from it.[66] The Islamic Republic maintains mutual peaceful relationship with non-belligerent nations. It is also committed to defending the rights of all Muslims and to supporting any rightful struggle of deprived peoples against the oppressing classes anywhere in the world.

The 1979 Constitution forbids the giving of a military base in the country to any foreign state even if they are committed to peaceful purposes.[67]

Khomeini's relation with non-Muslim countries is generally framed on an intensive resentment of Western culture. He financially attacks Westernization. He profoundly distrusts the West. "Annihilation of Islam, domination and control of the Islamic land is the sole objective of Westerners," writes Khomeini. He sees the Christian missionaries, the orientalists, and the information media all cooperating with their governments in this plot. He considers the importation of foreign laws and constitutional democracies into Muslim countries as a camouflage and deception by the Westerners to exploit the natural resources of the Islamic people. Otherwise, according to Khomeini, there is no room for any improvement in the comprehensive system of Islamic government. He denounces the West as a source of decadence and muddled values. Khomeini firmly believes that the Shah's dependence on the West, particularly on the United States, has been responsible for the failure of Iran's political system. He has the conviction that both capitalism and communism are responsible for maldistribution of wealth and widespread poverty in the world. He considers moral and cultural decadence as the source of all social ills. Only in Islam, does Khomeini find an alternative ideology for the recovery and complete justice.

Khomeini does not believe in peaceful coexistence, on an equal basis, of even great religions. He advocated subordination of the Zimmis. The late Beheshti, one of the closest followers of Khomeini, had suggested reintroduction of *jazyeh* (poll-tax) for Zimmis in Iran.

Relations with Israel and the Case of Jerusalem. Khomeini believes in a Judeo-Christian conspiracy to destroy the Muslim world. To him, the power of Zionism is satanic, and the United States, by supporting Israel in all its actions, becomes the great Satan (this is the name used by Khomeini for the U.S.).

Khomeini views the Jews as the arch-enemies of Islam. At the inception of Islam, they "initiated a counter-activity by slandering and distorting its reputation,"[68] and now, by occupying the Palestine, the land of Islam, make millions of Muslim homeless. Jews, although people of the Book, are "acting as enemies" and Jihad against Zionists is a religious duty.

Since 1914, when the last Sultan (*khalif*) of Turkey called on Muslims to join the war on the side of Germany, Turkey's ally, there has not been any universal ordinance for *Jihad.* Yet Khomeini has made several calls for *Jihad* against Israel, none of which has been taken up seriously. Nevertheless, destruction of Israel is on his agenda. Iran's covert arms deals with Israel have damaged Khomeini's image as Israel's sworn enemy. As a counterstep, Iran dispatched a garrison of Persian volunteers to Lebanon to fight Israelis, a measure with which the Syrians were not very happy. In his treatise on Islamic government, Khomeini states "the laws governing *Jihad* and defense of the Muslims, secures their independence and dignity. . . . Had Muslims adhered to the meaning of the Koranic verse on *Jihad* and had they been ready to fight under all circumstances, it would not have been possible for a handful of Jews to occupy our land and damage and burn our al-Asqa mosque without being faced with any resistance."[69]

In the 1979 Constitution, it is stated that the Islamic Republic Army and the Revolutionary Guards Corp will be responsible not only for defending the borders of the country, but also for the mission stated in the holy book of Koran, of holy war in the way of God and fighting to expand the rule of God's law in the world.[70] Khomeini's Hezbullah in Lebanon are discharging that mission.

Compared with the Palestinian issue, the Israeli control of Jerusalem is a more infuriating case for Muslims in Iran. Jerusalem is as important to the Muslims as it is to the Jews. Khomeini does not stand for a regime of free access to all holy places by all. He wants the sovereignty of Islam over the city. Khomeini has entered the day of occupation of Jerusalem in Persian calender as the day of Ghods. That is a reminder to Muslims of their religious duty to liberate Jerusalem.

Relations with the Soviet Union and Communist Countries. Khomeini is as hostile to communism as he is to Western democracy and capitalism. Yet, for the first three years, he allowed the Marxist groups to operate. This was a political exigency; he could not have fought on two fronts: Americans and Russians. The Soviet Union was happy to see American policies in Iran discredited. The anti-American slogans and curtailment of American interests in Iran pleased the Soviet Union, which was taken aback by the revolution. This, however, did not last long. The reason was twofold: The continuance of the Soviet sale of arms to Iraq and ideological penetration into army and schools through the Iran Tudeh party; and, Iran's relation with the Soviet Union deteriorated in 1982. The government banned the activities of the Tudeh party and seized their leaders. They were shown on television admitting to espionage for the Soviet Union. One of the most prominent theoreticians of the Tudeh party, in a sequence of television programs, compared communism with Islam and concluded that only Islam can bring happiness and success to Muslims of the world.

While, for reasons of practical politics, the Islamic Republic does not want to lose Soviet support in the event of another confrontation with the U.S., Iran is determined to fight communism as an ideology and prevent its permeation in the Iranian younger generations. As a result, the country is following the Shah's policy of maintaining good relations with the Soviet and other communist states, while striking at communism as a political philosophy. As for the populace, a socialist economy is appealing. Shariati tried hard to prove that economic justice in Islam is as essential as the spiritual aspects of the faith. He showed that many socialist (Marxist) economic principles correspond to those in Islam. The term "Marxist Muslims" was coined for such mixed ideological beliefs. The Marxist atheism, however, does not appeal to the profoundly spiritual masses of Iran. In his recent television talks, Ehsan Tabari, a lifetime theoretician of the communist Tudeh party, who was jailed by Khomeini, has tried to bring home to his listeners that Islamic socioeconomic justice is superior to its Marxist counterpart.

The general trend in Iran's foreign policy is to increase relations with the outside world and bring Iran out of isolation. This requires pragmatism, which is incompatible with the basic Islamic policies spelled out in the constitution. Interference of the clergy, with their parochial attitude, in the foreign policy of Iran is another impediment in Iran's attaining its objective.

Projection of the Future Role of the Clergy in the Politics of Iran

The two questions raised in connection with future politics of Iran are the following: (1) Will the present regime survive after Khomeini? and (2) Is a return to secularism feasible?

Viability of Khomeini's Regime. The viability of Khomeini's regime depends on: (1) the answer it will provide for the military, economic, social and political problems created by the Islamic regime, and for the unfulfilled promises made before and during the revolution; and, (2) on the credibility of the clergy.

Politically, the regime had managed to infuse Islamic principles into the governmental and societal fabric. Theocratic despotism has been established. The nature of Khomeini's Islamic republic has proved to be anti-national, anti-democratic, anti–modernization, anti-Westernization, anti-secularization and reactionary. It is militant and brutal. It stands for a rapid and total reconstruction of the society in accordance with the Shi'a principles. The change should be effected at any cost. For Khomeini, the means are not as important as the end. The dominance of Hezbullah in every aspect of the Iranian national life, subordination of all institutions to clerical authority, encroachment of the individual political and social liberties, and trespass of private properties have generated more fear and resentment than in the Shah's regime.

The anti-nationalistic attitude of the Islamic regime is offensive to the sentiments of a large segment of Iranians who are imbued with strong nationalism. The government has almost completely deleted the pre-Islamic history of Iran from the school textbooks. The twelve centuries of pre-Islamic history of Iran: Medes, Achaeminians, Parthians and Sassanides are explained in fewer than ten pages. Article 17 of the Constitution reads: "The official beginning of the history of the country starts with the migration of the Prophet of Islam. Both the solar and lunar calendars are valid, but the date to be used by the government is solar. The official weekly holiday is Friday."[71] The Iranian names of the cities, streets, oil-wells, ships and public places have been changed into Islamic names. At the initial stages, the Islamic government suggested Persian language be gradually changed into Arabic. Article 16 of the Constitution states: "The language of Koran is Arabic as well as being the language of the Islamic sciences and teachings; and, as the Persian language is completely mixed with that, Arabic language must be taught in all classes and in all fields after the elementary school until the end of the intermediate school.[72]

Khomeini criticized the Shah for his autocratic rule, for the creation of the one-party system, for elimination of individual liberties and for corruption. Nevertheless, he has systematically nullified all political parties that allied with him for the overthrow of the Shah; reestablished a de facto single party system; and assigned all effective government jobs to the clerics of his own party. His secret security police (SAVAMA) have proved more ruthless, repressive and torturous than the Shah's secret police (SAVAK). Khomeini, through mass media, invites and encourages children and parents to spy on one another. On one occasion, Iran's Radio and Television eulogized a mother who had spied on her son. The son, who was a member of Mojahedin, was arrested and executed.[73]

In order to be admitted into the institutions of higher education, the students must be scholastically qualified and Islamically competent. The religious competence is ascertained through interviewing the neighbors, the student's companions and the district mullas. The candidate's bedroom and wardrobe may be inspected without prior notice. Finding of an un-Islamic dress, a music record or a forbidden book will forever disqualify the person for admission to the institutions of higher education. "We do not want a non-Muslim professional," is the slogan.

The accumulation of power in the hands of *ulama* has led to extraordinary corruption, both in the upper layers of the dominant group and in its rank and file. The involvement of one of Khomeini's closest relatives in the opium traffic in Germany is only one example.[74] Prominent mullahs have been caught receiving bribes in illicit arm deals, in smuggling precious stones and in stealing museum articles.[75]

Economically, the regime has failed to adduce any positive policy, and there is no indication of its capacity to produce one. The nationalization of the major industries, banks and insurance companies at the initial stage of the revolution has produced economic failures.

Inflation has skyrocketed since the change of the regime. Unemployment has exceeded 40%. Inconsistency and continuous change in economic policies have added to the insecurity of the bazaris. Most food items have been rationed and the government has been unable to meet the demands made on it. The economic collusion of clergy and the civil servants, so far has led to the emergence of a new rich class of mullahs.

Khomeini's anti-Westernization policies and constant denunciation of the West have exasperated a large number of youths who have been educated abroad and are accustomed to, if not impressed by, certain features of the western life. The seculars, the Westernized, the liberals and a large number of women deplore the reactionary policies of the Islamic regime, including the ban on music and arts, and the closure of social clubs.[76] People are living different lives at home and in public. At home they are Westernized in dress, liberal in eating and drinking habits, and modern in listening to music and watching videotapes. In public they are Islamized in attire, and pretend to observe the rules concerning halal and haram. This dualist attitude to life has led to the development of a double personality in individuals, particularly in the youth. Those who previously purchased liquor and wine in the shops, are now producing them at home. Opium consumption is on the increase.

The closing of the universities and institutions of higher education for two years, which had never occurred during the time of the Shah, antagonized many high school graduates and their parents. The youth's time was wasted and their dreams belied. The shortage of professionals, particularly physicians and dentists, has already alarmed the regime. A large number of medical doctors have migrated to America and Europe since the revolution, and regime attempts to have them return home have failed.

Iran was dragged into the war by Saddam's invasion of Iran in September 1979. It is a war between two Muslim countries. After realizing that the invasion was a strategic blunder, Iraq declared its preference to see the war end. The Arab countries were ready to pay compensation to Iran on Iraq's behalf. Khomeini rejected the offer. He made the peacetalk conditional upon resignation of Saddam and termination of the Ba'thist regime in Iraq. The mid-1982 counterinvasion of Iraq territory by Iran was also a disastrous mistake. The employment of "human wave" strategy, the enlisting of teenagers in the army by Iran, the brutal bombing of Iranian cities, and the use of chemical weapons by Iraq have caused great human loss and casualties to Iran. Khomeini's negative response to the peace efforts made by international and Islamic organizations has further isolated Iran and widened the gap in the Muslim world. The radical states of Syria, Libya and, to a lesser extent, Algeria, support Iran. The conservative Muslim states of Saudi Arabia, Sudan, Egypt, Jordan, Kuwait, United Arab Emirates and, to a lesser degree, Qatar, assist Iraq. On the first day of Saddam's invasion of Iran, Khomeini said that the invasion was inspired by God and that God will eliminate Saddam for having attacked the Islamic Republic of Iran. But Saddam is still ruling Iraq after years of war! This has damaged Khomeini's claim to Divine power.

Khomeini is a stubborn person. His personal animosity towards Saddam and his inability to give a convincing explanation to the Iranians as to why Saddam has not yet been destroyed, are two major impediments in any peace effort. While Khomeini is alive, the Iran-Iraq war will continue, unless Saddam is removed by assassination of a *coup d'etat.* That event would undoubtedly strengthen Khomeini's position in export of his revolution, which would be a great plus to the regional stability.

To the intelligentsia, Khomeini's push for a supernatural Islamic government sounds a utopian fantasy. Iran's resort to terrorism and its collaboration with terrorist groups in the region, and its subversive activities in the Persian Gulf Emirates have unified the conservative Muslim countries against Iran. With a closer watch on activities of the Iranian agents in the Gulf, the risk of subversion for the time being is reduced. Nevertheless, Iran's subversive activities in Bahrein in 1981, and in Beirut during the recent years are part of its external policy.

So far, Khomeini's regime has failed to provide satisfactory answers to the economic, social and political problems created or inherited by his regime; and the likelihood for finding solutions without a complete change of its policies is remote. The present leaders of the Islamic regime of Iran do not seem to have the capacity or insight to overcome these difficulties and pave the way for economic development and an increase in the people's welfare.

Feasibility of a Return to Secularism. In Khomeini's lifetime, no essential change in policy is expected. The drive for Islamization of internal institutions will continue, the war with Iraq will not end and Khomeini's support for world militant groups including terrorism will persist.

What will happen after Khomeini? Three possibilities exist: (1) change of leader with no change in policy; (2) change of policy with the change of leadership; and (3) change of regime.

Change of leader without change of policy presupposes the existence of a successor to assume the same role and exert the same political and moral authority as Khomeini. Nobody in the ruling class commands that authority or anywhere near it. In the absence of complete endorsement of the present policies by the ruling clergy, a change in policy seems inevitable. At present a large number of Khomeini's colleagues want peace with Iraq but fearing Khomeini they do not voice their opposition. The ruling clergy have also been divided on the limits of private ownership and the role of private sector in trade. Each time such differences have surfaced, Khomeini has intervened and resolved the issue. No other member of the ruling elite seems capable of discharging that function in the future. A compromise would be a change of policy.

Rule of force has legitimacy in Iran. At present any opposition to Khomeini is crushed by the fanatical and well-paid revolutionary Guards, committees and Hezbullah. The ruling class, out of conviction, respect, fear or combination of all, show blind obedience to Khomeini. This cannot happen with his successor.

In terms of change of policy with change in leadership, most likely after Khomeini's death a struggle for power will take place among the ruling clergy. In such chaotic situations, presentation of new policies by contesting clerics for the position of al-Faghih would be a matter of gaining votes and winning the game of struggle for power. This is what happened in Egypt after Nasser and in China after Mao Tse-tung.

Prolongation of war, fall in the oil price, escalation of budget deficit, increase in the claims on the government by martyrs' families and revolutionary guards, political repression and economic mismanagement pose potential threats to the future of the Islamic regime. The clergy has to solve these problems in order to remain in control. That requires a change of policy. Should a rapprochement between Hafez Assad and Saddam be brought about, Iran may find herself even more isolated in the Muslim world. The Soviet Union cannot become a reliable ally, unless Iran shows greater tolerance to the Iranian communists. In 1980, at the start of the Iran-Iraq war, the Soviet Union called back from the Persian Gulf a ship carrying arms for Iraq and remained impartial until Iran's crack-down on the Tudeh party. The U.S.S.R. then started shipment of arms to Iraq. Iran cannot remain a power in the region without amelioration of her relations with the U.S. and the Western democracies.

A change of regime is foreseeable, with the rapid erosion in credibility of the present ruling class in Iran.

Historically, Iranians favored Shi'a *ulama* because of their resistance to the Sunni Arabs. Shi'aism provided a good basis for "revitalization of nationalism," which was semi-dormant after the Arab invasion. The liberating function of Shi'a is a new phenomenon. That function is not peculiar to Shi'aism. Nor is militancy. Militant Christians in Central America, militant Buddhists in South Asia, militant Sikhs in India all are struggling against a real or perceived injustice by the ruling class, dominant ethnic groups or foreign-agent governments. The political use of religion is gaining momentum everywhere. Disillusionment with secularism, capitalism and communism is another reason for resort to religion. The religiously-oriented dissident groups use militancy, terrorism and other devices for attaining their objectives. Obsession with, and overreaction to, the religiosity of such movements by Westerners are self-defeating.

Besides the challenge of nationalism, the theocratic regime of Iran faces a challenge from the intellectuals and two generations of Westernized young people. A return to the original simplicities of seventh-century Islam does not satisfy their sophisticated expectations. How can any regime in Iran prevent people from listening to broadcasts from foreign stations propagating Western ideas, music and art?

Another aspect of the revolution often overlooked by the analysts is the exposure of the clergy to criticism and challenge—a new phenomenon in Shi'a world. For the first time since the establishment of Shi'a as the state religion in the early sixteenth century, the clergy has become structured hierarchically and directly involved in the administration of the government. Before that, they had managed to remain independent. Thus, they were in a position both to influence and criticize the governments without being blamed for governments' failures. There was also a common belief that *ulama*, particularly the seyyeds, Descendants of Ali, had a special spiritual power, commensurate with their clerical position in the hierarchy. As such they had become irreproachable.

In the Iranian Islamic government, the position of the clergy has substantially changed. In the people's eyes, the Shi'a establishment is now identical with the government. Consequently the clergy are directly blamed for the inefficiencies, irregularities, corruption, favoritism and other inevitable evils in the administration of the state. The Islamic government of Iran is conducting a large part of its activities through the clergy and via the mosques. The administration of food and fuel rationing, the electoral operations, the management of the revolutionary committee and a handful of other important functions are carried out in mosques. This has marred the spiritual image of the clergy. The clergy is exposed to criticism and reproach. Today they are as much challenged and threatened as the Shah's officers during the last days of his reign. The challenge is made not only by intelligentsia and liberals, but also by the man in the street. There is a serious shrinkage in popular support for the clergy.

Notwithstanding the present government's endeavors to supplant the Iranian nationalism with Islam fanaticism, the latter has been maligned and attenuated by Khomeini's reactionary demeanor, vituperative language and outrageously inhuman treatment of his political opponents. In reverse, nationalism is strengthened through people's sense of grievance and resistance to the ruling class. The Iraq invasion of Iran also fortified nationalism. People came to realize that the arsenal stockpiled by the Shah, and the military trained in his time had saved the country. Even pro-Khomeini Iranians acknowledged that much infrastructural work had been done in the old regime.

In any comparison between the Islamic movement in Iran and in other Muslim countries, it should be kept in mind that Iranian nationalism, with several thousand years of history, independence and sovereignty behind it, is much more deeply rooted than the Arab nationalism in the newly formed Islamic states of Asia or Africa. When Khomeini invited the abandonment of the national festivities, the people reacted pointedly by celebrating them more elaborately and ostentatiously. The 1979 revolution was a political resurgence against dictatorship and social injustices. It was not, in essence, the result of tension between religiosity and secularism, Islam fundamentalism and Westernization, traditionalism and modernization. Khomeini hijacked the revolution.[77] Khomeini is unaware of the life beyond his residential village. Islamic regime of Iran is bound to come to a fierce head-on collision with Westernized and moderate Muslims, who, like Ali Shari'ati, advocate the use of Western science, philosophy, art and scientific methodology for a better understanding of the Islamic way of life. Khomeini wants people to remain ignorant of the conditions of life in the West, while Shari'ati wanted them to learn and compare the two, using their own judgments. That was also the attitude of the enlightened Iranian religious leaders of the past such as Jamal al-Din Assadabadi, whose writings were a source of inspiration for men who drafted the Iranian Constitution of 1907.

In this writer's opinion, the Islamic regime of Iran will not be able to survive Khomeini unless it makes an earnest attempt to meet the demands of modernity. This requires reinterpretation, reform or modification of some Islamic norms in order to meet the exigencies of our time. So long as the regime remains intransigent and continues to oppose incorporation of modern values in Islam, a change of regime seems a historical necessity. This may first start as a change of policy associated with the change of leadership and then move to a change of regime.

Khomeini represents an ideology based on the ideals and visions of Islam, as interpreted by him. Once it is discredited, his regime will lose its legitimacy. The question then is: In what direction will the regime go? With the rapid changes in internal and international scenes, prediction is impossible. An educated guess is the best that can be offered.

The change of regime must originate in Iran. Starting from the extreme left, the Tudeh Communist Party does not seem to stand any chance at this time. After 1983, it has become defunct. Communism, as a political ideology, has been discredited, and the Soviets are viewed as Imperialist and exploiters, as are the Western capitalist nations. With the family scandal of its leader, and obtaining financial support from Iraq, Mojahedin-Khalgh has lost its appeal. They committed the blunder of uniting with Iraq which invaded Iran. The emergence of personality cult in the movement has been another weak point for the party. The leadership of the party is much criticized for terrorist activities in Iran, which has resulted in the death of several thousand young men and women. The idea of going to a right of the center, republican regime based on Western models and a Constitutional Monarchy is gaining ground.

With the fall of the clergy, theocratic rule will end. Reestablishment of secularism, if not as early as intellectuals expect, will not be as late as the clergy hopes, assuming that return to a secular government be feasible.

Will it be an autocracy of democracy? The writer's belief is that democracy is not incompatible with the present political awareness, socioeconomic conditions and general aspirations of the people of Iran. However in the dynamic politics of our age, the situation may change and the Iranian dream for democracy may not materialize in the foreseeable future.

NOTES

1. *The Cambridge History of Iran,* vol. 4 (Cambridge: Cambridge University Press, 1975), p. 316.
2. *Ibid.,* vol. 3, p. 427.
3. Edward G. Brown, *The Persian Revolution of 1905–1909* (London: University Press, 1910), pp. 31 ff.
4. *Ibid.,* pp. 120–122.
5. Principles 1, 2, 27(2) and 58, Supplementary Constitution of October 1907, Trans. Mussa Sabi (Tehran, 1974).

6. Firuz Kazemzadeh, *Russian and Britain in Persia, 1864–1914* (New Haven: Yale University Press, 1968), p. 522.
7. Ahmad Kasravi, *Enghlabe-e-Mashrootiyat Iran* (Tehran, 1937), p. 211.
8. David Wise and Thomas B. Ross, *The Invisible Government* (New York: Random House, 1974), pp. 106–112.
9. Mohammed Reza Pahlavi, *Mission for My Country* (London, 1961), p. 173.
10. Mohammed Reza Pahlavi, *Answer to History* (New York: Stein & Day, 1980), p. 66.
11. John D. Stempel, *Inside the Iranian Revolution* (Bloomington: Indiana University Press, 1981), pp. 82 ff.
12. *Ibid.,* p. 204.
13. Ann K. S. Lambton, *Islamic Society in Persia* (London: School of Oriental and African Studies, 1954), pp. 16 ff.
14. *Ibid.,* p. 30.
15. Fred Holliday, *Iran, Dictatorship and Development* (Harmondsworth, Middlesex: Penguin Books, 1979), pp. 15 ff., 285 ff.; also Stempel, *Inside Iranian Revolution*, p. 8.
16. Amin Saikal, *The Rise and Fall of the Shah* (Princeton: Princeton University Press, 1980); Robert Gramham, *Iran: The Illusion of the Power* (London: Croom Helm, 1978).
17. See Dreyfus, *Hostage to Khomeini* (New York, 1980).
18. In connection with broadcasts for Afghanistan, which is equally true for Iran, see Hansard, *Parliamentary debates, House of Lords,* 412:172, Thursday, July 24, 1880, p. 506.
19. Michael Ledeen & William Lewis, *Debacle: The American Failure in Iran* (First Village Book edition, 1982), p. 149.
20. *Ibid.,* p. 150.
21. *Ibid.,* p. 124.
22. Jimmy Carter, *Keeping Faith: Memories of a President* (New York: Bantam Books, 1982), pp. 431–572.
23. *Ibid.,* p. 473.
24. William H. Sullivan, *Mission to Iran* (New York: W. W. Norton & Co., 1981), p. 56; Stempel, *Inside the Iranian Revolution,* p. 119.
25. Michael Ledeen and William Lewis, *Debacle,* p. 110.
26. *Ibid.,* p. 117.
27. J. Huizinga, *Homo Ludens: A Study of the Play Element in Culture* (1958), p. 4.
28. The Constitution of the Islamic Republic of Iran, official translation by Islamic Propagation Organization, Tehran, Preamble, p. 5.
29. Fadlullah Bin Ruzbihan Isfahani, *Suluk-ul-Muluk: Muslim Conduct of State,* trans. and annot. Muhhamad Aslam (Islamated: University of Islamabad Press, 1974), p. 54.

30. Cf. Article 47, Constitution, 1979.
31. Article 107 of 1979 Constitution.
32. Fadlullah Bin Ruzbihan Isfahani, *Suluk-ul-Muluk,* pp. 52–53.
33. Article 91 of 1979 Constitution.
34. Principle 2, Supplementary Constitution, 1907.
35. Ruhullah Khomeini, *Velayat-e-Faghih or al-Hukumat al–Islamiyah* (1974). Selections of the book translated and incorporated in Tareq Y. Ismael, *Iraq-Iran Conflict,* (Syracuse: Syracuse University Press, 1982), p. 102.
36. Principle 1, Constitution, 1907.
37. The Method of Government of Islam, preamble, Constitution, 1979, p. 11.
38. R. Khomeini, *Velayat,* p. 118.
39. Abul A'la Maududi, *A Political Theory of Islam,* ed. Khurshid Ahmad, (Lahore, 1960), pp. 17 ff.
40. Article 13, Constitution, 1979.
41. Fadlullah Bin Ruzbihan Isfahani, *Suluk-ul-Muluk,* p. 506.
42. R. Khomeini, *Velayat,* p. 118.
43. Article 77, Constitution, 1979.
44. Article 76, Constitution, 1979.
45. Article 52, Constitution, 1979.
46. Interpretation of Principle 27(2) of 1907 Constitution by Majlis.
47. Preamble to Constitution, 1979, p. 19.
48. *Ibid.,* p. 15.
49. *Ibid.*
50. *Hedaya or Guide: A Commentary on the Muslim Laws,* trans. Charles Hamilton (2nd ed. Standish Grove Grandy, London, 1870), p. 178. Lapidation consists in carrying the convict to a barren place and placing him or her in the ground, ready to be stoned to death by bystanders; also Article 170 of the Constitution, 1979.
51. Khomeini, *Velayat,* pp. 104–105. Some Muslim reformists defend the harsh Islamic punishment on the ground that they are subject to conditions which are almost impossible to fulfill.
52. *Hedaya,* op. cit., p. 362.
53. Koran, Chapter of Repentance, Stanza 29.
54. Tritton, A. S., *The Caliphs and the Non-Muslim Subjects* (1930; reprint London, 1970), p. 227.
55. Koran, Chap. 66, "Prohibition," Stanza 9; and Chap. 9, "Repentance," Stanza 123; also Fadlullah Bin Ruzbihan Isfahani, *Suluk-ul-Muluk,* p. 506.
56. Koran, Chapter of Women, Stanza 34.
57. Koran, Chapter of the Cow, Stanza 46.
58. Khomeini, *Velayat,* p. 110.

59. Preamble, Constitution, 1949, p. 13.
60. *Ibid.*, p. 10.
61. Khomeini, *Velayat,* p. 145.
62. Preamble, Constitution, 1979, p. 11.
63. Article 11, Constitution, 1979.
64. Khomeini, *Velayat,* p. 115.
65. *Ibid.*, pp. 1–7.
66. Article 152, Constitution, 1979.
67. Article 146, Constitution, 1979.
68. Khomeini, *Velayat,* p. 101.
69. *Ibid.*, p. 113.
70. Preamble to the Constitution, 1979, p. 15; Articles 143, 144 and 150.
71. Article 17, Constitution, 1979.
72. Article 16, Constitution, 1979.
73. International Iran Times, 20:40. Friday, Dec. 1980.
74. Sadegh Tabatabai, *New York Times,* Feb. 20, 1983.
75. Royal Jewels, Keyhan, Dec. 14, 1982.
76. J. H. Hanson, *Militant Islam* (New York: Harper & Row, 1979), p. 192.
77. William H. Sullivan, *Mission to Iran,* p. 200.

7

Hinduism and Islam: Their Antagonistic Interaction on the Indian Subcontinent

ARVIND SHARMA

Chronologically the proper period to commence a study of the antagonistic interaction between Hinduism and Islam in modern times is the eighteenth century, when the British began to establish themselves in India militarily, and thereby settled on a course which was to culminate in the establishment of British paramountcy over the entire subcontinent. But just as the modern phase of Hindu-Muslim interaction flows out of the eighteenth century, previous phases of Hindu-Muslim interaction flow into it. From this point of view it is important to bear in mind that the British Raj in India put an end to Islamic ascendancy in India.[1] This is the central historical fact with which one must start when dealing with Hindu-Muslim interaction. There are, however, certain aspects of the Islamic ascendancy in India which must be borne in mind if the antagonistic interaction between Hinduism and Islam in the modern period is to be fully understood.

The Islamic conquest of India took place by stages. The first stage was marked by an abortive attempt on the part of the Arabs to occupy Sindh in the eighth century A.D. The second stage was marked by the invasion of the Turko-Afghans in the eleventh century, which led to establishment of a Muslim dynasty in Delhi in the early years of the thirteenth century. The third stage is marked by the Mongol invasion of 1526 A.D. The Mongols had by now been converted to Islam, so, in effect, the fight between the last dynasty of the so-called Delhi Sultanate and the Moghul invader, Babur, was a fight between two Muslim powers for the domination of northern India. A fourth stage is represented by the penetration of Muslim power in southern India. The climactic event in this case was the defeat of the Hindu Vijayanagar empire by a confederacy of five Muslim states. A fifth stage is represented by the Afghan invasion in 1761 which defeated a Hindu confederacy near Delhi.

From this quick survey it becomes clear that, while Islamic ascendancy in India was established over the Hindus in general, the struggle for power did not preclude one Muslim dynasty fighting against another Muslim dynasty. Moreover, there was always some Hindu kingdom around to challenge Islamic domination of India and, in fact, a Hindu military resurgence in India in the eighteenth century under the Marathas virtually put an end to effective Muslim rule till they themselves were defeated by the British. It should also be noted that geographically, northern and central India, rather than peninsular India, was the theatre of the armed conflict between the Hindus and the Muslims. In these conflicts it was not unusual for Hindu or Muslim kings to form alliances on political, rather than religious, lines.

The overall significance of the fact that Hinduism and Islam had interacted over a prolonged period of some five hundred years,[2] and that in the course of this interaction had evolved various patterns—some not merely antagonistic either—is important from at least two points of view. Firstly, it meant that there was no one set pattern for Hindu–Muslim relation, but rather, several models before these two communities to choose from when the question of a redefinition of the relationship arose in modern times. This perhaps accounts for the various twists and turns in the relationships between the two communities. Secondly, in few other parts of the world has Islam had such a long history of existing in a pluralistic environment. This gave, and gives, a peculiar flavor to the situation of the Muslims on the Indian subcontinent. Negatively, one could say that the presence of Hinduism and Islam in India represents the greatest failure of the other tradition. Hinduism absorbed all previous invaders with their different religious beliefs within its ample (some would say promiscuous) bosom. But it could not absorb Islam. Similarly, with a few exceptions, Islam was also religiously successful in converting its subjects wherever it became politically dominant. But in India it was only partially successful in this respect. Positively, one could argue, as pointed out earlier, that nowhere has Islam had such a prolonged experience of religious pluralism as in India; nor has Hinduism had to coexist with such a radical option to its own life-style for so long.

Let us now examine the actual pattern of interaction between Hinduism and Islam in the modern period.

This actual pattern of interaction between Hinduism and Islam cannot be discussed without reference to the rise of nationalism in India in response to British rule. This nationalism itself can be subdivided, for analytical convenience, into political nationalism and religious nationalism—and the latter again for convenience into Hindu nationalism and Muslim nationalism.

A few crucial facts, however, need to be kept in mind before one embarks on a schematized discussion of the various aspects of nationalism outlined above. In the opinion of most scholars, the emergence of nationalism in India was associated with the rise of the educated middle class resulting from the spread of Western education. When the British first introduced Western education in India, the Hindu response to it, shaped by such figures as Rammohun Roy, was enthusiastic. The Muslims, being the losing group in Bengal where such education was first vigorously introduced, held back for cultural and emotional reasons. The mutiny against the British in 1857–1858 did not help matters either. In a nutshell, while the Hindus had reconciled themselves to British rule early in the nineteenth century, the Muslims began to do so, under the leadership of men like Sir Sayyid Ahmad Khan, only in the last quarter of that century. Thus Muslim education along Westernized lines lagged behind the Hindu by more than half a century and fed Muslim fears that, in the event of the departure of the British, they would fall under the domination of the Hindus.[3] The need for a separate homeland for Indian Muslims was in part based on this fear. It must be added, however, that this represented the view of the so-called Aligarh School and that a more traditional Deoband School was opposed to the division of India on the ground that "Muslims may be in danger in a united India but Islam will be in danger in Pakistan," the orthodoxy of many of whose supporters was suspect.

The first formal forum where the stirrings of political nationalism found their expression was the Indian National Congress, founded in Bombay in December 1885. This political movement, which had now found an institutional expression, may be seen as passing through five distinct, though connected, phases from the point of view of our concerns.[4]

The first phase may be said to extend from 1885–1905. During this phase the Indian National Congress basically represented democratic liberalism, and the movement of religious nationalism, if anything, was somewhat opposed to it.

The second phase may be said to extend from 1905–1920. During this phase "the Congress nationalist movement was frankly Hindu and revivalist."

The third phase may be said to extend from 1920–1940, when the Congress represented the "resistance of India as a whole to alien domination" and "the political purpose of the Congress and its general outlook in regard to the future of India was entirely non-sectarian."

The fourth phase may be seen as extending from 1940–1947, during which the two major religious components of Indian nationalism—the Hindu and the Muslim—jointly or singly led to the political bifurcation of the country.

The fifth phase, the post-Independence phase, may be seen as extending from 1948 to the present day.

The period also witnessed the successful achievement of the major goal of political nationalism, namely, political independence.

First Phase

There are at least three pieces of evidence which show that political nationalism, as expressed through the Indian National Congress from 1885–1905, was largely independent of religious nationalism. The first of these is the fact that, during this period, there was a renaissance of Hinduism, which was inspired by *reaction against Western influences,* while the members of the Congress, at this time, "represented a Western and liberal point of view and were great admirers of the British." The renaissance of Hinduism referred to above is an allusion to the fact that during this period "three distinct religious movements sprang up: viz. the Arya Samaj in North India, which was founded by Dayanand Saraswati in 1875, the Ramakrishna Mission in Bengal, which was started in 1897 by the disciples of Ramakrishna Paramhamsa under the leadership of Swami Vivekananda, and the Theosophical Society in South India."

The second piece of evidence which shows the relative independence of the political nationalism, as expressed through the Indian National Congress, from the religious, while at the same time illustrating how thin was the line which separated them, is the fact that when in 1887 "a Hindu delegate wished to move a resolution in favor of prohibition of cow-killing, which the Muslims would have opposed tooth and nail . . . it had to be laid down that no resolution should be moved, and no subject discussed, to which there was unanimous or nearly unanimous objection on the part of either the Hindu or Muslim delegates." Thirdly, it may be noted that Muslim nationalism, as represented by Sir Sayyid Ahmad Khan, opposed the Congress movement as a Hindu one.

It is obvious, then, that at this stage in the evolution of political nationalism, it was kept more or less insulated from religious nationalism and to a certain extent was suspect in the eyes of Hindu and Muslim nationalists. Not only did the Muslim community by and large take "no part in the movement, but resolved to abstain from political agitation, under the leadership of Sir Sayyid Ahmad Khan, who founded an anti-Congress association." The "Congress also failed to obtain support from the great body of Hindu conservative opinion."

Second Phase

The situation changed dramatically with the Partition of Bengal in 1905. The agitation against the Partition of Bengal both extended the popular base of political nationalism and also gave to it a Hindu character. An interesting account of both these developments as manifesting themselves in the life of an Indian can be found in Chapter 3 of the autobiography of "the brilliant, if sometimes eccentric," Bengali scholar Nirad Chaudhuri. More generally, the political significance of the agitation against the Partition of Bengal lay in the fact that ultimately "the issue, until then successfully veiled and now openly raised, was not whether Bengal should be one unpartitioned province or two partitioned provinces under British rule, but whether British rule itself was to endure in Bengal or, for that matter, anywhere in India." Moreover, the agitation against the British also acquired an economic dimension through the boycott of British goods under the slogan of *Swadeshi.* It also led to the "growth of a radical section in the Congress" and increase in terrorist activity against the British. The agitation against the Partition of Bengal resulted in a "general state of serious unrest," not just in Bengal, but even in the Punjab and Madras.

In order to popularize the agitation, the leaders of the agitation appealed to Hindu symbols and sentiments. Thus, even Surendranath Banerjee "urged that a religious turn be given to the movement by means of ceremonies in honor of Kali and Sakti, and meetings held in temples and vows to boycott British goods taken in the name of Kali did much to popularize the cause."

It was mentioned earlier that one consequence of this agitation was a strengthening of the radical wing within the Congress. The Congress, when it met in 1906, "for the first time in its history, laid down as its goal 'the system of government obtaining in the self-governing British colonies', which the President summed up in one word, 'Swarāj'." The chief spokesmen of this new spirit were B. G. Tilak, B. C. Pal and Lajpat Rai, who belonged to the so-called "extremist" section. It clashed with the "moderates" represented by S. N. Banerjee, P. S. Mehta and B. G. Gokhale in 1907 at Surat and stayed out of the Congress for nine years, uniting with them in 1916 at Lucknow.

It was shown earlier how Surendranath Banerjee, a "moderate," advocated the use of religious sentiment and symbolism to serve political ends. This applies with more force to the extremist leaders Balgangadhar Tilak, B. C. Pal and Lala Lajpat Rai—the so-called BAL-PAL-LAL triumvirate.

Third Phase

The next major phase is represented by the emergence of Mahatma Gandhi as the leader of the Congress. By the end of the second decade of the century, several factors had contributed to the growth of political nationalism, "two of which deserve special mention, viz. the atrocities in the Punjab and the Khilafat agitation." In 1919 the Government introduced a set of repressive measures known as the Rowlatt Acts to suppress political nationalism and this resulted in what is known as the Amritsar massacre, in which the army fired on an unarmed crowd. "The casualties were officially estimated at 379 killed and over 200 wounded. This was followed by the proclamation of martial law, severe punitive measures, and humiliating orders. Order was restored in the Punjab but a scar was drawn across Indo-British relations deeper than any which had been inflicted since the Mutiny. Racial feeling was intense." While on the one hand opposition to the British intensified, the movement against the British also became unified. The Muslims resented the part played by the British in the dismemberment of the Turkish Empire, and a movement against the British was organized by the Ali brothers. Mahatma Gandhi and the Congress supported this movement wholeheartedly, which resulted in "unprecedented fraternisation between the Hindus and the Muslims."

Thus, by 1920, Mahatma Gandhi had emerged as the leader of the Congress. The crucial issue henceforth was to be whether political nationalism in India was strong enough to dislodge the British and broad enough to absorb religious nationalism—which found expression during this period in the activities of the Hindu Mahasabha among the Hindus and the All-India Muslim League among the Muslims. With the benefit of hindsight, K. M. Panikkar has remarked that "The period of cooperation with the Muslim League and the interlude of the Khilafat agitation should not blind us to the fact that the strength of the Congress lay primarily in the Hindu revival and in an integral nationalism based on the Hindu masses."

It is a much debated point in modern Indian history whether the Hindu coloration of political nationalism is to be blamed for the alienation of the Muslims or the divide-and-rule tactics of the British or perhaps both. It cannot be gainsaid, however, that by 1940 the Muslims of India felt sufficiently alienated to demand an independent Muslim state in the event of a British withdrawal. The turning point in the Muslim attitude is said to be the Congress decision in 1937 not to form a Coalition ministry with the Muslim League after sweeping the polls in elections held under the Government of India Act of 1935, under which a measure of self-government was introduced in India. If, however, this assertion is substantially true, then it is of capital significance in the history of the interaction between political and religious nationalism. For, here, we have a case where a *political* decision may have had religious implications of the first magnitude. The above-mentioned political decision, if it was the proximate cause for the formation of Pakistan, ultimately not only intensified the religious ferment in India but may have led to a religious crisis—resulting in the convulsions which accounted for and then followed the formation of Pakistan. What has been referred to above as the "second phase," also seems to present an example of a similar development. If the Partition of Bengal, a political or administrative act, did much to inflame feelings against the British and laid the foundations of the Hindu-Muslim divide in Indian politics, then there we once again have an illustration of a decision taken in the political arena producing reactions both in the areas of political as well as religious nationalism. The influence of religion on politics is often pointed out, but the influences of politics on religion, it seems, may have been equally consequential in the context of modern India.

Fourth Phase

Thus the fourth phase of the interaction between political and religious nationalism witnessed the centripetal forces of political nationalism being overcome by the centrifugal forces of religious nationalism seeking political expression. Already, by 1930, the signs of the parting of ways between Indian and Muslim nationalism were beginning to surface, and by 1947, Pakistan had become a reality. It has been said that "Sayyid Ahmad Khan gave Indian Islam a sense of separate existence; Iqbal a sense of separate destiny" and that "The ideology of Iqbal, the visions of Rahmat Ali, and the fears of Muslims . . . were united by the practical genius of Jinnah to bind Muslims together as never before during the British period and lead *(sic)* to effect an act of political creation."

One interesting aspect of the interaction between political and religious nationalism is the fact that the spokesmen of both Hinduism and Islam held different views regarding the relationship between the two, apart from the fact that some of them, especially those on the Islamic side, also held different views about them at different stages of their life. Thus the "Ali brothers swung round from the preaching of Hindu fraternalism to the championship of Muslim rights." Iqbal became convinced of the futility of Hindu-Muslim unity towards the end of his life, and Mr. Jinnah, who later propounded the theory that Hindus and Muslims represent two separate nations, "had once vehemently protested against the view that India was not a nation."

Fifth Phase

Just as the fourth phase was marked by the division of India into India and Pakistan, the fifth phase was marked by the division of Pakistan itself into Pakistan and Bangladesh. In the fourth phase, political nationalism on the Indian subcontinent was overwhelmed by religious nationalism, more specifically Muslim nationalism, seeking political expression. In the fifth phase, religious nationalism within Pakistan was outgunned by political nationalism, more specifically Bengali nationalism.

The events leading up to the emergence of Bangladesh in 1971 illustrate this point. Pakistan originally consisted of two wings—a western wing and an eastern wing. The two wings were separated by a thousand miles of Indian territory and what united them was the fact that both were Muslim. Gradually, however, the eastern wing, as a result of politico-economic decisions taken by the government in West Pakistan began to feel increasingly discriminated against both economically and politically. The break came in 1971 when the eastern wing, with Indian military backing, declared itself an independent country, after the western wing refused to hand over power to the predominantly Bengali political party which had secured a clear majority in the elections. Once again a political decision had impacted on religion: the Muslim population of the Indian subcontinent had been trifurcated.[5]

These developments, and the current situation, may now be analyzed from various aspects. It is hoped that these reflections will be diverse without being incoherent, and broadbased without being scattershot.

One may begin with a few reflections on the formation of Pakistan and then supplement them with further reflections on the formation of Bangladesh. The following aspects of the situation are worth remarking in this respect. (1) The division of India and Pakistan had the demographic effect of bringing 95% of the world's Hindus (who constitute 82.5% of India's population) under a single central government. Despite this, India is a secular not a Hindu state, though the country of Nepal next door to it is in fact a Hindu state. The long-run effect of this political consolidation of the Hindu community needs to be watched. This consolidation of the Hindu community was also accompanied by the division of the Muslim community, for a sizable number of Muslims continued to live in India. (2) For those Muslims who continue to live in India, the question of functioning in a non-Muslim state has to be faced. It has been said that the issue, from the Indian point of view, is one of making Indian Muslims into Muslim Indians. The status of those Muslims who continued to live in India after the partition of the country (who were also called nationalist Muslims) in some respects may be compared to that of exilic Jews as opposed to Zionist Jews, though the analogy may not be pushed too far. The point to be considered is that the exilic mode of existence, with which many Jews even seem to feel at home, is something to which the Muslims are relatively unaccustomed. One might compare here the forced diaspora of the Jews after the Roman occupation, with the voluntary migration of the Prophet from Mecca to Medina. This *Hijrah* represents a classic Muslim response to living in an environment hostile to Islam—namely, to pack up and leave. Ironically, although it was the states of Punjab and Bengal which were subdivided, the demand for Pakistan was mainly supported by Muslims living in the Indian state of Uttar Pradesh. These Muslims, therefore, responded in terms of the *Hijrah* model and migrated to Punjab or East Bengal. (3) On the question of the formation of Pakistan the question inevitably arises: was it inevitable? In this respect it is an interesting point that Pakistan was formed in the liberal phase of modern Hinduism, as represented by Gandhi and Radhakrishnan as distinguished from its more conservative phase under men like Tilak. It is also interesting that Mahatma Gandhi, derided in Pakistan for opposing partition, was killed in India for being regarded as pro-Muslim! It is possible that a great opportunity for Hindu-Muslim raprochement was lost under Gandhi—who more than once asked the British to hand over power to Mr. Jinnah, the head of the Muslim League, the main Muslim body demanding Pakistan, and leave. A further curiosity lies in the fact that the leaders of both the Indian National Congress and the Muslim League were lawyers—and lawyers typically strike a deal, which, however, they failed to in this case.[6]

The subdivision of Pakistan itself into Pakistan and Bangladesh suggests some points. (1) It has been argued that while conversion to Islam in northwestern India was both religious and cultural, it was religious rather than cultural in Bengal, where the converts retained specially the use of their native language Bengali. This difference may in part account for the break between the two wings of Pakistan. (2) The case for democracy in the context of Indian Islam seems to present special problems. It was the prospect of the introduction of democracy in India and the fear of being outvoted which led in part to the formation of Pakistan. But it was the prospect of its introduction in Pakistan itself which led to the break-up of that country. It may be that Islam in India has acquired a "dominant minority syndrome" as a psychological residue of its historical experience and that the Muslims of northwest India are the particular legatees of this syndrome. When the dominant minority status was threatened in India they opted for Pakistan; when it was threatened in Pakistan itself by a Bengali majority they opted for West Pakistan. On the question of "minorities" and "majorities," psychology can be as important as statistics. It has been suggested, for instance, that as a result of being subject to prolonged foreign rule, the Hindus, though a majority, have the psychology of a minority which may have prevented them from making crucial concessions to the Muslims to prevent partition.

The formation of Bangladesh also revives a very significant debate. One of the basic arguments of those Muslims who opposed the formation of Pakistan was that Islam as a religion has not succeeded in uniting its followers politically. The formation of Bangladesh seemed to confirm this conclusion with regard to India. It also further subdivided the Muslims of the Indian subcontinent into those living in Pakistan, those living in India (who ironically outnumber those living in Pakistan) and those living in Bangladesh. Thus the political factor has assumed an increased importance in this situation.

What are the policy implications of the foregoing discussion of antagonistic interaction between the Hindus and the Muslims? One may begin by considering what might be called total solutions: that the whole subcontinent becomes Muslim or all of India is reconverted to Hinduism. Apart from their implausibility, it is not at all clear that a Muslim or Hindu India will be a united India. Islam has not been particularly effective in uniting its adherents politically, nor has Hinduism for that matter. Hence the problem of conflict on the subcontinent would not automatically be resolved if its religious dimension were removed.

Turning to the narrower issue of the current situation religiously, it was pointed out how Islam in India has had the longest experience of existing in a pluralistic society and how Hinduism has entered a somewhat universalistic phase. These are hopeful signs; the dangers are that Islam in a pluralistic context may tend towards revivalism and Hinduism, never so politically united as now, may become aggressive. At this point, however, a fundamental consideration may be introduced. Although the general drift of the discussion has been in terms of the influence of religion on politics, in modern India, political decisions have profoundly affected religion, as was pointed out earlier. The partition of Bengal in 1905, for instance, prefigured the partition of India in 1947. In other words, policy as politically formed and implemented can be very consequential and even decisive. Thus, the actual political policies being followed by the governments of India and Pakistan are going to be of prime significance in determining the degree to which the interaction between Hinduism and Islam is going to be antagonistic.

What policies then should a country like the U.S.A. follow towards India and Pakistan in the light of this discussion? In such decision-making, one central fact must be kept in mind in relation to India—that Pakistan *had* seceded from India, so that there is the unarticulated but latent Indian hope of in some way at least reducing Pakistan's strength, although any thought of annexing it can only be dismissed as wishful thinking. However, the less danger Pakistan poses to India, the more likely it is going to be psychologically acceptable. On the other hand, as India had assisted in the break-up of Pakistan, any increase in the military power of India fuels Pakistan's fears that India is out to get it. Therefore, in the current situation, the best policy for a country like the U.S.A. to follow is to be—and appear—even-handed in its dealings with India and Pakistan.

The Russian move into Afghanistan is not without its significance for the antagonistic interaction between Islam and Hinduism. Here, once again, the political is intertwined with the religious. India's close relations with the U.S.S.R., and Pakistan's friendlier attitude towards the U.S.A. would indicate an exacerbation of the relationship. However, the traditional route of invasion into the subcontinent has been through Afghanistan, so that the Russian move really poses a threat to both India and Pakistan in the long run. From a more religious point of view the whole issue of the relationship of Islam and Hinduism to Marxism and Communism, and how the differences in their attitudes in this respect might affect the interaction between them, remains to be explored.

The preceding discussion of Hindu-Muslim antagonism has gained a certain relevance after the recent upsurge in Hindu-Sikh antagonism in India, as highlighted by the action of the Indian army against the militants in the Golden Temple, and the subsequent assassination of Mrs. Indira Gandhi. The growth of Hindu-Sikh separatism provides points of both convergence and divergence when compared with the growth of Hindu-Muslim differences. The basic parallel is provided by the fact that this separatism also has its roots in the political climate of British India and the policies pursued by the British government. The common interest of the Hindus and the Sikhs in opposing separatist Muslim aspirations, however, especially in the Punjab, kept potential Hindu-Sikh differences in the background.

These surfaced after the achievement of Indian independence. Interestingly, just as the political success of the Indian National Congress in 1937 gave a fillip to Muslim separatism, it was the political success of the Indira Congress in the state elections in the Punjab in May 1980 which acted as a catalyst for Sikh separatism. However, unlike the case of Bangladesh where the electoral verdict was not respected by the government of Pakistan, the Indian government allowed the Akali Dal—the political party of the Sikhs—to assume power in the state in September 1985, after it secured a majority. The main threat to it is posed not by the Congress which is supporting it, but by the Sikh extremists.

There is another major difference. Irrespective of the truth or otherwise of Western implication in the crisis, there is no third political force *in situ* to complicate matters, as was the case with the British presence in the context of Hindu-Muslim antagonism. In every other part of India, separatist movements have abandoned their separatism upon gaining political power and have been functioning successfully within the political framework provided by the Indian constitution. This is instantiated by political developments in Tamilnadu, Nagaland and now Mizoram. Whether the Sikhs will confirm or challenge this trend remains to be seen.

NOTES

1. S. M. Ikram, *Muslim Civilization in India*, ed., Ainslie T. Embree (New York: Columbia University Press, 1964), concluding chapters.
2. Percival Spear, ed., *The Oxford History of India* (Oxford: Clarendon Press, 1958), pp. 799–780.
3. Hafeez Malik, *Moslem Nationalism in India and Pakistan* (Washington, D.C.: Public Affairs Press, 1963), pp. 192–197, 206–212.
4. This section of the paper relies heavily on Chap. 2, Pt. 2 of Hal W. French and Arvind Sharma, *Religious Ferment in Modern India* (New York: St. Martin's Press, 1981).
5. See W. Norman Brown, *The United States and India, Pakistan, Bangladesh* (Cambridge, Massachusetts: Harvard University Press, 1972), Chap. 11.
6. I am indebted to Sheila McDonough for this observation.

8

The Impact of Religion on Politics in Contemporary Israel

MICHAEL BERENBAUM

In no region of the world is the relationship between religion and politics more pronounced and probed than in the Middle East. The rise of militant Islam, the fanaticism—and willingness to accept martyrdom—of Ayatolah Khomeini and his followers, the rivalry between Shi'ite and Suni Moslems, the struggle between Moslems and Christians in Lebanon, the Arab-Jewish wars of the past sixty years, and the tensions between observant and secular Jews in Israel have all focused attention on the problem. Yet most treatments of social and political developments in contemporary Israel have been shallow at best in their consideration of the complex interaction of religion and politics endemic to the region. When social analysts have considered the problem of religion and politics in Israel, they have generally selected for study the role of state-supported religion and its clerical functions, or the process by which traditional Judaism—itself the product of diaspora and powerlessness—has been transformed in the context of the modern state.

Even the most sensitive of observers have often limited themselves to the dynamic of religious parties and the compromises with tradition compelled by statehood.[1] Such issues are certainly interesting and important; it is compelling, for example, to investigate the changes in a religious framework (formed when Jews had neither the possibility nor the obligations of statehood) required to accommodate the Jewish people in a Jewish state responsible for all services—the army, industry, police, transportation, judiciary, etc. However, the most critical religious development in contemporary Israeli politics—namely, the shift from clerical demands for religious observance to ideological predominance in the state—has gone largely unreported. Religious parties have intensified their agenda, pushing not only Orthodox demands for religious conformity by other segments of Israeli society, but staking out a claim for a more fundamental legitimacy.

Ironically, while social living patterns, educational structures and even army services for religious Jews have become more ghettoized, religious politics has moved ideologically out of the ghetto. The rise of Likud, the growth of nationalism, the militancy of religious messianism (Gush Emunim), and the weakening of Israel's Labor party are an outgrowth of demographic, political, social, and economic realities, yet purely religious factors are also involved.[2] Underlying religious values affect the complex of power and search for national goals that shape the contemporary Israeli political horizon.

The Lure and Failure of Emancipation

Classical Zionism originated in reaction to harsh events. Political Zionism actually had two births: the first in 1881 with Leo Pinsker's book *Auto Emancipation* (yet at that time the movement was stillborn), and the second with the emergence of the concrete political program of Theodore Herzl and the Zionist movement he shaped. Pinsker's book was little known, but most powerful. Indeed, years later when Herzl finally read Pinsker's work, he indicated that had he known of its existence, he would never have written *The Jewish State.* Pinsker's writings were the product of his disappointment with the process of emancipation, driven home to him so brutally by the pogroms of 1881, when the Jews of Czarist Russia faced death, conversion, or emigration. In response to the violence, two processes that were to reshape contemporary Jewish history began—massive immigration to the United States and a more ideological and limited immigration to Palestine.

Herzl's Zionist writings were also the product of his disappointment with history.[3] The Dreyfus trial convinced Herzl that emancipation could not solve the Jewish problem. European anti-Semitism was too pervasive. As exceptional Jews, Pinsker and Herzl were both pariahs, standing outside of their own community yet also alienated from Gentile society. History had revealed to them the impossibility of their situation and the futility of a purely personal solution to the "Jewish problem." Both men proposed a political alternative that was to form the core of Zionist ideology.

The Zionist vision was fourfold. It sought the normalization of Jewish people, independence, an end to vulnerability, and the ingathering of exiled Jews scattered throughout the diaspora. While for other Zionist thinkers this vision was merely a prelude to spiritual or religious revolution (Ahad Haam or Rav Kook), for Pinsker and Herzl—as with Baruch Spinoza centuries earlier—a political solution itself was the goal.

The Politics of Normalization

Normalization has been a goal of many Jews since the very beginning of the Emancipation. Originally, it expressed itself in the desire for citizenship and an end to legal discrimination. The quest for normalization began as a movement of elite Jews whose contacts with the gentile world were increasing. And it soon developed an intellectual infrastructure to legitimate its claims and to foster its agenda. The movement of *Wissenschaft des Judentums,* the Science of Judaism, was another manifestation of the desire for normalcy. The Wissenschaft movement attempted to understand Jewish existence without resorting to the supernatural or the extraordinary. Ordinary categories of social, scientific, humanistic, and historical inquiry were applied to the study of Jews and Jewish tradition. Jewish religious leadership—conservative by nature and design—was suspicious of the goals of Wissenschaft. They regarded normalization as a renunciation of the particular and unique role of the Jewish people. Even those religious thinkers who sought to limit the social stigma of Jewish differences were reluctant to abandon an explicitly supernatural vocation for the Jewish people. Only Mordecai Kaplan in early twentieth century America was willing to relinquish the concept of chosenness and see Jewish life within its natural dimensions.[4]

Yet, however much Jews sought normalcy, their status in Europe—described by Hannah Arendt and others as "between pariah and parvenu"—denied them the possibility of the normal situation they ardently desired. Unique to Zionism was the possibility of achieving normalization, not of the status of an individual Jew, but of Jewish existence.

Herzl's dream was that the Jewish state would become a state like any other state, a Switzerland of the Middle East—clean, efficient, well-organized, without significant controversy (in short, boring). For some of his contemporaries and the early Zionists, normalcy required the inversion of Jewish economic status, a return of Jews to the working classes of farmers and factory workers, shepherds and bus drivers, along with the more traditional Jewish roles of middlemen, teacher, scholar, banker and small entrepreneurs. Even the early newspapers of Tel Aviv celebrated the return of the Jewish people to normalcy by taking particular pride in the arrest of the first Jewish criminal and prostitute in the early pre-state period. It was the conviction of Herzl and the political zionists that normalization of Jewish life could only be achieved by the resumption of Jewish political life and the eventual acquisition of sovereignty and power—a state and an army.

At that time, the Zionist platform was a minority position among the Jewish people; denied by many segments of Orthodoxy (which rightly regarded Zionism as an agent of secularization), by Reform Jewry (which was uncomfortable with any assertion of Jewish nationalism and peoplehood), and by those seeking a personal solution to the Jewish problem either within Europe or America (for whom the plan was unnecessary). Only the most extreme manifestation of Jewish abnormality, as expressed in Nazism, later convinced the vast majority of Jews that, not only was normalcy desirable, but Zionism was the only way to achieve it.

Jacob Neusner has written brilliantly of the aftermath of the second destruction of the Temple in the year 70 C.E., when Jews lost their political independence and the capacity for self-defense, yet retained spiritual independence and self-government.[5] Under these conditions, Jewish life was dependent on the consent of the sovereign and the good will of others who maintained a near monopoly on the instruments of power. The great German Jewish theologian of the early twentieth century, Franz Rosenzweig, turned this regrettable reality into a celebrative theology. For Rosenzweig, the task of the Jew was to gaze at eternity, untouched by the vicissitudes of history and uncorrupted by the exercise of power.[6] In effect, for Rosenzweig, Judaism was the goal and Christianity the way. Christianity's task was to convert the world to belief in one God through its coersive political power. It was permitted compromise and corruption. Although Rosenzweig enjoyed a distinguished following within pre-war Germany and post-war America, his teachings have been overwhelmingly rejected by the Jewish people who, in the aftermath of the Holocaust, moved toward political independence and chose to enter power history.

After World War I, European Jewish leadership had argued for the protection of Jewish rights as part of a guarantee for minority rights in majority cultures. Not so after the Holocaust. From the Biltmore conference of 1943 onward, Jews enthusiastically supported the call for Jewish independence. They wanted to end their reliance on the benevolence of humankind or the compassion of world leaders.

The Decision to Enter History

For Herzl, Jewish independence was a matter of will. David Ben-Gurion would often say, "I don't care what the nations (goyim) think, what concerns me is how the Jews act." Echoes of this position resound in former Prime Minister Menachem Begin's defiance of America and oft proclaimed and exaggerated annoyance at Israel's presumed status as a "banana republic." Sovereignty and power were not only needed to achieve normalcy for the Jewish people, they were also expected to end its dependence on the nations of the world, and permit it the freedom for non-apologetic self-expression.

Similarly, the quest for power was motivated by a desire to end Jewish vulnerability. A sovereign Jewish state could guarantee its own security and would transform the image of the Jew both at home and abroad. Israel was to stand as the guarantor of Jewish safety throughout the world. Jews could now assume a new posture as fighters and farmers—assertive rather than submissive—unbowed by the weight of centuries of oppression and impotence.[7] If normalization was the strategy to end anti-Semitism—a tactic suggested by both Freud and Herzl—then independence was a prerequisite for developing sufficient power to end Jewish vulnerability. The stories that Israelis often tell at state occasions celebrating their independence or commemorating the Holocaust are instructive, for they represent not only a break with tradition, but a reassertion of human initiative in Jewish history.

A New Self-Consciousness

For example, in the traditional rendition of the Passover story, God is regarded as the principal actor within Jewish history. The name of Moses does not even appear in the Passover story "for God—not an angel nor a messenger"—is the agent of redemption. In the traditional celebration of Hanukkah and Purim, the two holidays that celebrate Jewish political and diplomatic victories over oppression, God is given principal credit for the victory. By contrast, former Prime Minister Yitzhak Rabin recalled at his final Holocaust commemoration while in office that Jewish resistance in the Warsaw Ghetto was essentially unarmed. Jewish fighters were forced to match their naked strength against the power of the Nazi army. Armed more by courage than by weapons, Rabin said, they resisted until their deaths. Rabin declared: "Now that we have a Jewish state, Jewish fighters need not proceed unarmed. They can now defend themselves and protect their families—their wives, their mothers, and their children. The traditional Haggadah reads: "In every generation they rise against us to destroy us and the Holy One, Blessed be He, saves us from their hands." Israeli self-consciousness now proclaims, however, that the Jewish people shall themselves have the means of self-defense against those who would seek to destroy them. This transformation in consciousness was reflected most clearly in bumper stickers that appeared just after the 1967 Six Day War. "Israel trust in TZHAL" (The Israel Defense Forces), they declared, substituting the army for the Psalmist's call, "Israel trust in the Lord."

According to the original Zionist vision, the emergence of the state was to bring an end to Jewish vulnerability, not only within Israel, but throughout the diaspora, since those who would oppress Jews would soon learn that Jewish blood could not be shed without consequence. Undoubtedly, the founding of Israel and its successful defense against destruction in 1948, 1967, and 1973 added immeasurably to Jewish pride and to the hold of the state upon the Jewish people. In addition, for nearly three decades there was a direct correlation between the growth of the state as a viable national entity and the decline of anti-Semitism.[8]

Ingathering of the Exiles

The fourth of the Zionist dreams was the ingathering of the exiles. Jews were to migrate from the four corners of the earth in return to their ancestral homeland while the remaining diaspora, faced with assimilation and persecution, would wither away. Diaspora community would progressively weaken, both culturally and religiously, as productive centers of Jewish life. Israel was to become the heart of Jewish life, contributing to the welfare of the diaspora and eventually witnessing its extinction. The creativity of an assertive, non-apologetic Jewish culture, in touch with the many traditions of the Jewish people and at home with its language, was to eclipse the creativity of diaspora community by the quality of its creations, their authenticity and cultural integrity.

The fourfold vision dominated the pre-state years of the Zionist movement and the initial decades following the establishment of the state.

Ironically while Zionism succeeded beyond its wildest imagination, its ideological underpinnings have been severely challenged by the events of the past decade. On the one hand, no one could have imagined at the time of Herzl that, within half a century, a Jewish state would become a reality, that it would possess the ability to defend itself, that it would absorb more than two million Jews, that it would become a regional power, and develop an advanced technological infrastructure capable of making deserts flourish and of exporting agricultural produce from an extremely rough and parched terrain. On the other hand, many of the events of the past decade have shown the inadequacies of the fourfold vision, the failure of which has generated religious and nationalistic myths in an effort to fill the void.

The Chronic Abnormality of Jewish Existence

Labor Zionism was conceptually ill-prepared for the persistent abnormality of Jewish existence in Israel. For the past thirty-eight years, Israel has been denied even the prerequisite of normal national existence, i.e., recognition by its neighbors. Egypt, the first of its neighbors to offer the possibility of normalization, received the entire Sinai Peninsula with its oil fields in return—an almost unprecedented concession for the promise of normalization. Egypt's leader, Anwar Sadat, was immediately treated as a pariah among his fellow Arabs and he eventually paid with his life for the gesture of recognition. His successor has been most cautious in reaching out to Israel.

Nowhere is the surrealistic abnormality of Jewish existence more apparent than at the United Nations, which has passed resolution after resolution condemning Israel, including the infamous motion equating Zionism with racism—despite the fact that Jews are a multiracial people who permit conversion and who daringly rescued Black Ethiopian Jews. Soviet block nations and the Arab world have transformed the United Nations into what Senator Daniel P. Moynihan, Ambassador Jeanne Kirkpatrick, and Michael Novak have termed an international forum for anti-Semitism. Even the predominance of the Israel issue in the Security Council and the General Assembly—where no other issues threatening world peace receive as much attention, including the Soviet invasion of Afghanistan and the Iran-Iraq war—has but further emphasized the abnormality of contemporary Israeli existence.

Nor is Israel, alone, the location where Jews retain abnormal status. In the Soviet Union, Jews are persecuted for their religious identity. (In fact, Soviet Jews play a structurally similar role in the Soviet Union to the one that they assumed under Christianity; i.e., they deny that the Messiah has come. By pressing to emigrate they testify to the fact that Soviet society is not the secular "kingdom of God on earth.") Even the Western world has not treated Jews normally. The statement of Prime Minister Raymound Barre in the aftermath of the 1980 attack on Rue Copernic may be instructive in this regard. Barre said: "It is unfortunate that the terrorists wanted to kill Jews on their way to the synagogue; it is regrettable that innocent Frenchmen were killed instead." Barre contrasted the word "Jew" and the word "Frenchmen" in a country which first granted the Jewish people rights of citizenship in 1789. The word "Jew" was also juxtaposed with the word "innocent," a contrast that was to mark former Austrian Chancellor Bruno Kreisky's response to another attack on a Vienna synagogue only 13 months later. Kreisky said: "It is the implacable attitude of the Israelis toward the Palestinians that is to blame for these excesses." It made sense for Kreisky to hold Viennese Jewish worshippers responsible for the behavior of Israelis in Judea, Samaria and the Gaza District, some four thousand miles away. It was psychologically credible for the Chancellor to blame the victim for the attack.

Even American Jewry, whose achievements in the American climate of normalcy have been celebrated by Charles Silberman,[9] has had uncomfortable moments in the past several years when either domestic or international issues challenged their tranquility. The oil crisis, American arms sales to Arabs countries friendly to the United States but hostile to Israel, the war in Lebanon, the Bitburg controversy, and the Pollard affair are examples of American Jewish discomfort, even within a climate of tolerance and pluralism without precedent in Jewish history. Stephen Rosenfeld has written persuasively of the role of anti-Semitism in American foreign policy, an article, still relevant today, that was prompted by the 1981 AWACs sale to Saudi Arabia and the attack on ethnicity in American foreign policy by Senator Charles Mathias.[10]

Only two segments of the Israeli population were prepared to confront the chronic abnormality of Jewish life: the nationalists and the religious. The former consider anti-Semitism endemic to gentile society. The latter believe that the religious mission of the Jews as God's people will naturally provoke anti-Semitism. At Sinai, they teach, *sinah,* hatred, was also introduced to the world.

Classical political Zionism and its Labor party descendants, which aimed to transform the Jewish condition in order to end Jewish abnormality, was ill-prepared for its failure. The movement could not understand why Israel was not treated as a "normal" state. Indeed the hope of normalcy persists even today. Whether it takes the form of the Sadat peace initiative or the participation of other Arab countries in negotiations, any movement toward recognition rekindles the dream of normalcy and weakens the power of nationalistic and religious sentiments within Israel. Ironically, however, it was a nationalistic/religious coalition that signed the peace treaty with Sadat, even though they continued to expect deception.[11]

Independence

The Zionist dream of normalization was coupled with a hope for independence. Israel proclaimed its independence at a time when colonial rule was beginning to wane in Asia and Africa. In 1948, Israel was committed to neutrality and self-reliance; it was unwilling to take sides in the major power conflicts dividing East and West, and determined to defend itself in a hostile world. Although Israel's power was limited, a sanguine use of that power was the best guarantee of independence. Within twenty-five years, Israel achieved regional dominance and survived three wars, fending off attacks in all directions. Yet precisely at the height of its power, the Jewish state found itself again dependent upon the good will of a gentile leader for its basic survival. At a critical moment of the Yom Kippur War, Israel was in desperate need of an American airlift in order to resupply troops dangerously short of ammunition and basic supplies. For forty-eight hours the fate of Israel was in the hands of Richard Nixon (whose commitment to Israel was not matched by his love for Jews) and his principal advisors—the first Secretary of State "of Jewish origin," and a Secretary of Defense, who, although of Jewish ancestry, was a practicing Christian. This shock to Israel's self-esteem can not be overestimated.[12] Radical dependence was a blow to Israel's ideological self-esteem. And the impact of this dependence has only grown with the years as the proud, strong and defiant Israeli slowly confronted this linkage with the long history of Jewish dependence.

Ironically, Jews achieved their independence precisely as the world was moving toward interdependence. The key to Israel's survival, its relationship with the United States and the West, lies in the interdependence that marks the geopolitical and defense relationships of the last fifteen years of the twentieth century. American friends of Israel sought to recognize this changing reality by pressing for a new understanding of the Israel-American relationship. In the 1980 presidential campaign, Jewish supporters of all three candidates pressed the nominees to speak of Israel as a strategic asset in the Middle East and as the only dependable democratic ally in the region. After some rough starts, including the ill-fated Memorandum of Understanding and the ups and down of Menachem Begin's tenure as Prime Minister, the "strategic alliance" has gained strength and gives a concrete expression to the interdependent relationship. A geopolitical and strategic facade for the American-Israel relationship has supplemented, perhaps even supplanted, a cultural and moral perspective that was the basis of previous American commitments. The language of international relations has changed. The perception of Israel as an ally has major policy implications, and limits the duration and intensity of crises between Israel and America.

The stormy tenure of Begin as prime minister may shed light on the essential dream of Jewish independence. When the Reagan administration suspended the Memorandum of Understanding in response to the extension of Israeli rule to the Golan Heights, Begin responded with a long tirade addressed to U.S. Ambassador Samuel Lewis. Among other things, Begin said that Israel could not be treated as a banana republic by the U.S., and that the Jewish people have survived 3,700 years without the M.O.U. and would survive another 3,700 without it. Throughout the diatribe, Begin defiantly, if not arrogantly, reasserted Israeli independence in relationship to Israel's only dependable ally in the world precisely at the moment when Begin and his supporters were hoping that Israel could be perceived as an ally in an interdependent—not dependent—relationship to the U.S.

Suffice it to say that the dream of independence was dealt a harsh blow by the Yom Kippur War, and by a recognition of the complex interdependence of Israel and the United States geopolitically, strategically, economically, and politically. Nevertheless, Israel resents its interdependent circumstances and fears dependency, especially on American aid and political support.

A dialectical politics results. Israeli politicans who can resist American pressure or who react defiantly to American statements and policies are rewarded with broad popular support; yet if they are perceived as damaging the relationship substantively, their behavior is regarded with suspicion and testiness. The U.S.-Israel relationship may be strained but not broken. To prove its independence, Israel can never easily acquiesce to an America request.

Vulnerability

It was hoped that Zionism would bring an end to Jewish vulnerability by giving Jews sufficient power to defend themselves. By achieving the normal status of a country, anti-Semitism and other conditions that endanger Jews would be reduced. However, for the past thirty-eight years, Israel faced implacable Arab adversaries unwilling to recognize its existence. For more than half a century, ever since the Hebron riots in 1929, Jewish-Arab coexistence in Palestine has been marked by strife and open warfare.[13] Prior to 1982, after each of the wars, Israel emerged stronger than before, more secure and less able to be destroyed, yet the feeling of vulnerability persisted.

The 1981 raid on the reactor in Bagdad may have illustrated the real dilemma confronting the Zionist dream of an end to vulnerability. Vulnerability may swiftly become the fundamental condition of all nations as irresponsible regimes or terrorist groups gain control of nuclear technology. By bombing the Bagdad reactor, Israel sought to rid itself of nuclear vulnerability for a decade, by which time the possession by non-major powers of a nuclear option may well be a worldwide problem requiring an international solution. Yet it is not only nuclear vulnerability and the persistence of Arab antagonism that has dealt the Zionist dream a mortal blow; rather, as events of the last war so aptly illustrate, sovereign Jewish existence in Israel has the ability not only to dampen international anti-Semitism, but to arouse it as well. European anti-Semitism is gaining wide attention and although surveys indicate that anti-Semitism is on the decline in America, Jews are generally convinced that it is on the upswing.[14]

The politicalization of Jewish existence caused by Israel and economic dislocation can fuel the hatred of Jews. Statements by Black power advocates against Jews in the late 1960s, the United Nations Resolution equating Zionism and racism, and the image of Israel in the media throughout the War in Lebanon have brought to an end the period following the Holocaust when the expression of anti-Semitism, even if deeply felt, was restrained. In short, Israel has not eliminated Jewish vulnerability; it has altered the context in which vulnerability can be combated. This change is all-important, but it falls short of the original dream.

The Exiles Do Not Feel in Exile

Finally, Zionism envisioned the return of the Jews to the land of Israel and the gradual withering of the diaspora. Since 1948, more than two million Jews have come to Israel to find their home. The Jewish population has increased more than fivefold, from 650,000 in 1948 to 3.5 million today. Nevertheless, the diaspora has not disintegrated. American Jewry has produced a new generation of scholars, teachers, and rabbis to staff its diverse institutions. American Jewry is proud and self-affirming, and there is little evidence to indicate that the tide of assimilation is insurmountable, the safety of American Jewry so precarious, or the attraction of Israel so great that American Jewry will emigrate en masse.

Secondly, more than 500,000 and perhaps as many as 700,000 Israelis, or almost 20% of the Jewish population of Israel, have left the country, preferring to settle in diaspora communities despite the social stigma of *yeridah* ("descent" from Israel). Zionism underestimated the persistence of the diaspora. It did not account for the fact that Israel stands at the periphery of Western culture and that its sons and daughters who aspire for greater cultural stimulation may be forced to make their way westward—at least for a time, if not permanently. While central to Jewish culture and standing on its own considerable achievement, Israel remains marginal to world culture.[15]

All immigration movements follow a general push/pull pattern. For large scale immigration to take place, there must be a push from the native country or a pull to another country that the immigrant finds attractive. In the absence of a push from the West, the pull of Israel attracts the best and the worst of American Jews, i.e., those who because of their intense Jewish idealism feel attracted to life in

Israel, or those who do not find themselves at home in a pluralistic American milieu. And the "pull" of America, its economic, cultural, and intellectual excitement, proves irresistible to many Israelis, at least for a sustained time.

Furthermore, Israel is also interdependent on a strong and vibrant American Jewish community that can argue forcefully and behave politically to enhance American support for Israel. Ideology aside, Israel would be ill-served by a withering of the American diaspora even if all American Jews went to Israel.

An Ideological Crisis

Only two segments of Israeli society were prepared for the ideological crisis in the Zionist movement: the nationalists and the religious. The nationalists sensed that anti-Semitism was less a response to the behavior of the Jew, and more a problem endemic to gentile society. They were prepared for an enduring struggle. Their answer to vulnerability was power; their reaction to dependence, defiance. With Menachem Begin as their leader, they were rooted in Jewish tradition and comfortable with its language and symbols, upon which they were able to draw just as the secular Zionist symbolic world was beginning to lose its power and meaning.

For example, the concept of the *land* of Israel has had a long and important place in Jewish tradition. For an exiled people, land was a symbol of past glory and future solace. Religious commandments were dependent upon the land; holidays and festivals were observed differently within the land than outside of it. In comparison, the concept of the Jewish state and questions of sovereignty, power, and rule have a limited role in Jewish tradition and within the emotional matrix of its symbolism. Yet throughout the pre-state years, Jewish sovereignty and statehood were the goal, the dream of the Jewish population in Palestine. During the first years of the state, *mamlachtiyut* (statism) became an operative political policy pursued relentlessly by Ben-Gurion and the forces he controlled. For the generation coming to maturity after the state was born, a Jewish state was accepted as a normal, natural reality worthy of support, allegiance, and respect, but incapable—except in times of crises and war—of bestowing a sense of meaning and purpose. The land of Israel, on the other hand, echoed the yearnings of centuries and proclaimed a challenge for tomorrow.

Even now, Israel is deeply divided over the question of Zionism's most fundamental value. At stake is whether Zionism is the return of the Jewish people to its land—and hence the land must be retained even if populated by Arabs resistant to Israeli rule; or if Zionism is the reestablishment of a sovereign Jewish state—and hence the state must be preserved by the voluntary sacrifice of land and the deliberate choice not to exercise the historic right of the Jewish people to the land.[16]

The nationalist position has remained relatively consistent over the past three decades. Perhaps the single most dramatic change occurred with the Camp David agreement returning Sinai for the promise of normalcy and peace with Israel's most powerful neighbor. The religious position has changed more radically, most especially after the Yom Kippur War. This shift, coupled with the demographic and economic forces, led to the decline of Labor's hold on the Israeli electorate that eventually toppled Labor's 29 year rule.

The religious segment of Israeli society was prepared for the persistent abnormality of Jewish life and for tenacious anti-Semitism. They could move beyond as an ideology because religious ideologists never accepted the state as the goal of the Zionist movement. For a very small minority of religious Jews, the Zionist movement is an heretical agent of secularization usurping God's prerogative to restore the Jewish people to their homeland according to His plan. For others, the state is a purely secular entity, a state like any other state. No religious significance is attached to it whatsoever. This is the position of Agudat Israel and of Professor Yishayahu Leibowitz, an eccentric but influential Israeli scientist and rabbi, who is most critical of religious parties in Israel.[17] It is preferable, Agudat argues, for Jews to be governed by Jewish rather than Gentile rulers. A state controlled by Jews creates some religious difficulties with regard to Jewish law that must be ameliorated, but otherwise the state is of no religious interest.

A third, intensely Zionistic, position is reflected in the words of the prayer for the state authorized by the Chief Rabbinate of Israel. The state is referred to as the "dawn of redemption," and this attitude toward the state is characteristic of many religious Zionists. They differ on the implications of the "dawn" and the meaning of redemption. According to Rav Kook, the elder,[18] the state was a mere prelude to the building of a sacred Jewish society, the precondition for a revolution but not the revolution itself. Rav Kook's vision permitted religious Jews to compromise with secular Zionists. It maintained both the integrity of a religious position and the excitement of an ideological revolution, for it viewed the state as a necessary but not sufficient pre-condition for the religious revolution. Kook's concept of Zionism as the dawn of deliverance allowed for the participation of a religious minority within the secular Zionist movement.

Both throughout the pre-state period and in pre-1973 years of statehood, the religious parties (whether Zionist or avowedly clerical) had limited goals. They sought to maximize the religious observance of the state, to minimize the desecration of traditional religious practices, and to enhance state support for religious institutions (which in turn increased the political patronage the parties could dispense.) Religious parties reserved the right to exercise an ideological claim upon the greater society, but did not pursue it with vigor outside of the clerical and occasionally the juridical domain. They were in a defensive position defending the status quo ante against an ascendent secularism. This changed in 1973 with the shock of the Yom Kippur War.

Messianic Politics

Yonina Talmon has argued that messianic movements are never the product of catastrophe alone.[19] They are born of an imbalance between expectation and reality, of the disappointments that follow a period of sustained hope. For the Jews, the experience of the past half century has produced quite a buffeting. Jews have endured the epitome of inhumanity as victims of governmentally sponsored and systematically structured mass death in the Holocaust; they have also witnessed the flourishing of hope with the rebirth of the Jewish people in their ancestral land but three years after the destruction. The history of the state was also characterized by cycles of despair and hope—war and armistice, then war and triumph crowned by the return to Jerusalem. The impact of 1967 was startling. The victory created a new reality and a bold, optimistic reaction. The reunification of Jerusalem touched something most profound in the soul of the nation and sparked a reaffirmation of the Jewish past.

For religious Zionists, the 1967 war meant the return of Jewish sovereignty to the ancestral lands, Jewish rule over Jerusalem, and a sense that the state as the dawn of redemption had completed its most significant task. Even the failure of the Arabs to make peace in the aftermath of the war failed to dampen the spirit of the country. Therefore, the 1973 Yom Kippur War came as a profound shock. The war signified a return to vulnerability after a period of invincibility. The realization that Jews were again dependent upon the good-will of Gentile leaders for their very survival provided little comfort. The indecisiveness of the victory that was permitted Israel meant that the country would face harsh choices in an atmosphere of loneliness and isolation that replicated the fate of diaspora Jewish communities. Even the presence of Henry Kissinger seemed to herald the return of the *shtadlan,* the intercessor between Jews and the Gentile rulers. Above all, the price that Israel paid for its victory was overwhelming. Some 3,000 Israelis were killed, which in terms of the percentage of the national population would be the equivalent of 225,000 Americans—and in three short weeks. In the aftermath of the war, a new messianic religious movement gained credibility. Gush Emunim [the block of believers] was formed in 1974.

Gush Emunim's attraction for religious Jews and its power as Zionist ideology grew out of a sociological, as well as a religious, reality. In Israel there are two parallel—separate but equal—educational systems, a religious educational apparatus and a secular school system. (Ultra-Orthodox Jews maintain yet a third separate system less deferential to the state.) Almost without exception, Orthodox Jews attend religious schools and they have a separate youth movement that offers many extracurricular activities, including field trips and camping. Orthodox Jews may also fulfill their army service in separate units designed to allow them sufficient time to study sacred texts and national service. They are taught by a faculty that shares a common world view, and, as in the Jesuit training of an earlier time, until religious school system students are in their early twenties, they need not encounter secular youngsters with a cognitively dissonant world view.[20] Thus much of Israel's Orthodox youth are raised in a self-segregated environment designed to preserve and sustain their religious world-view. Even neighborhoods have become segregated according to religious practice so that the atmosphere of the Sabbath pervades the street, as well as the home and the synagogue.

After the 1973 war religious Zionists moved in a rather different direction. Perhaps the most interesting theological exposition of the religious Zionist position was presented by Rabbi Yehudah

Amital, the head of Yeshivat Har Etzion, a talmudic academy set in the Judean desert in the rebuilt Etzion block destroyed by the Jordanians in the 1948 war. Amital's *Hamaalot Memaamakim,* Ascent from the Depths,[21] is a slim, powerful collection of address on the meaning of war. It was compiled but a year after the 1973 war. Lurking in the background of Amital's thoughts (and Israeli reality) is the Holocaust, which by its magnitude and scope presents a challenge even to the most devout Jews. How is one to account for such a catastrophe? In a sense the Holocaust can only be accepted religiously as a prelude to redemption, as the birth pangs of the Messiah. Unlike other Orthodox thinkers such as Rabbi Joseph B. Soloveichik,[22] who sees Israel as a consoling yet quiet manifestation of divine presence, Amital viewed Israel messianically. His immediate dilemma was to account for the Yom Kippur War.

From the 1967 War, Amital argued, we learned that war can serve a redemptive purpose since—without any desire on Israel's part for the war, and following a specific request to King Hussein that Jordan stay out of the war—the Jewish people were restored to the city of Jerusalem and all the sacred sites. Although the Yom Kippur War at first appears to be an anti-redemptive manifestation of history, the opposite may be the case insofar as the Israeli victory was greater than in 1967.

The choice of Yom Kippur as the day to begin the war, Amital reasoned, was an implied attack on Jews and Judaism, an assault by Islam against the God of Israel, yet Western nations were the real losers of the war. The false Western God—the idol of technology—was clearly addicted to oil and cheap supplies of energy. Amital argued that Israel's massive victory against powerful armies and overwhelming odds was a great act of divine salvation. The purpose of the war, Amital told his disciples, was to mold and purify the Jewish people into a more solid and spiritually pure unit able to withstand the pressure of the Messiah's footsteps. Amital called for the reintensification of efforts, a deepening of commitment and an effort equal to the Messianic stakes.

It is interesting that Amital was politically astute in his assessment of the West, yet stubborn in his refusal to see the war politically as stemming from real grievances and fought for military/diplomatic purposes. He returns to the language of a pre-secularized warfare, a languge sanctioned by tradition and yet one which classical Zionism sought to overturn. He has further immunized his disciples and their fellow travelers from responding to political pressure, viewing all such compromises as a retreat from a divinely mandated task. Furthermore, he was non-apologetic with respect to Israel's position, and unwilling to consider the world in demystified geopolitical terms.

One should not overestimate the strength of this ideological perspective. It is certainly a minority position within the Orthodox community, which itself is a minority position among Israelis. Nevertheless, one dare not overlook its attractiveness or explicative value. Secular Zionism cannot deal with the continuing enmity of the Arabs toward the Jewish people, with the scope and vehemence of opposition to Israel, and with the persistence of anti-Semitism within the world community. The goal of an independent state has been reached. Patriotism and statism is not an all-encompassing world view capable of bestowing a sense of purpose and meaning, especially as the imperfections of an Israeli state are experienced in daily life and exposed by a free press.

Furthermore, Amital's thought intensified—perhaps beyond recognition—values common to the entire society. Secular Zionists also believe that Israel is the dawn of redemption and religious Zionists see Israel in Messianic terms, yet for both the idea is less than dominant and not necessarily understood as the basis for serious politics. Secular Zionism hopes for a revolution within the Jewish people and radical changes in the Jewish situation. Its solution was political and state centered. Amital's aspirations were the same, but his means are religious and his solution to the conflict were messianic.

Amital's position is even more interesting because he moderated his views after the war in Lebanon. Given the militant patriotism of the *hesder* Yeshiva students (those who combined national service with Yeshiva study), they volunteered for the elite units of the IDF, often replacing Labor Zionism's elite, the kibbutzniks. Under the circumstances, the Yeshiva students were on the frontline for the war in Lebanon and suffered extremely high casualties. Death became a reality for these students—and their teachers. Amital's response was bold. He told his students the Jewish responsibility to the land of Israel must be balanced by the commitment to the Torah of Israel and the people of Israel. If the former is emphasized to the exclusion of other commitments, then the future of Israel is misconstructed. Only the future will determine the scope and depth of his change of perspective. Nevertheless, while the war in Lebanon may have exacerbated and hardened many positions, it moderated at least one. He was immediately ostracized by former political allies.

With the weakening of the secularist-oriented Labor party and the collapse of the civil religion of Zionism,[23] ultra-Orthodox Jews also became increasingly militant and self-confident, demanding greater concessions and support from government, pressing their political and social agenda, and reaching out to further isolate their homes and children from Israeli society. They have in part succeeded with their agenda and their success has created a backlash. Ultra-Orthodox Jews increasingly live in a social situation that segregates them from other Orthodox Jews, and not only from secularists. They too have become militant, seeking to preserve the unique character of their life-style, to extend the boundaries of their community, and to insulate themselves from external Israeli society. Recent bus shelter burnings and the extreme reaction of hostile secularists by burning a synagogue may be a mere prelude of trouble to come.

With the weakening of classical Zionist ideology, the revolutionary zeal that characterized the founding generation of Israel has been captured by the religious community. The larger society can only view this development with a combination of admiration and fear. The radical vision has itself transformed the role of the religious parties and it has emboldened their demands. Ironically, though, as a political development, it has weakened the traditional religious parties since Gush followers often prefer more avowedly and less compromising nationalist parties to their own. One result of this shift was the election of Meir Kahane.

Kahane, the American-born ultra rightist rabbi, was elected to the Knesset in 1984 after two unsuccessful tries. Recently deprived of his right to sit in the Knesset, Kahane politics are ultranationalistic. He advocates the gradual expulsion of the Arabs from the land of Israel, first in return for generous compensation and later by force if necessary. He unites the religious zeal for a revolutionary change in the behavior and observances of Jews, with the nationalists' devout commitment to the land. Yet unlike the mainstream of both political camps, he offers no allegiance to democracy—at least not a democracy that encompasses Jews and Arabs.

In a sense, Kahane is the ultimate assimilationist. He advocates that Jews treat Arabs the way that Jews were historically treated by Christians and Moslems when they were in a minority. He thus tacitly acknowledges Nietzsche's critique of Judaism as the religion of the powerless. Kahane is also unable to distinguish between the task of a leader of a minority group agitating for rights and recognition by a dominant culture (which will surely tame the more outrageous of the minority's demands), and the responsibility of a majority people, sovereign in their own land. Kahane is fond of saying that only he is willing to follow the logical implications of the nationalist and religious positions to the end—and there is merit to his self-perception.

The divisions we witness in Israel are but a surface manifestation of a much deeper struggle as to the essentials of the Zionist revolution in Jewish life. Is the fundamental value of Zionism a return to the *land* of Israel, the flourishing of the *state* of Israel, or the triumph of the *religion* of Israel? Each ideological belief generates its own politics, and every manifestation of Arab zeal and internal strife among Jews fortifies one or another of these positions.

The extremism of Kahane's views, the lure of messianism, and the militancy of the ultra-Orthodox position have reinvigorated mainstream state-oriented Zionist ideologists. For values that were regarded as commonplace before such as democracy, pluralism, civility, and tolerance cannot be assumed under current condition. They must struggle for primacy in the clash of political and civic values.

The accomplishments of secular Zionism are great; they are far more than could have been imagined at the beginning of the century, yet fall short of its original aspirations. Arab enmity toward Israel and the *Kulturkamf* among the Jews has deepened the struggle, changed the stakes, and transformed the nation! It has also given rise to the possibility of apocalyptic politics.

NOTES

1. S. Z. Abramov's *Perpetual Dilemma* (Rutherford: Fairleigh Dickinson University Press, 1976) is the best treatment of religion in Israel. Unfortunately, Abramov, the former deputy speaker of Israel's parliament, completed his work prior to the declericalization of the religious parties, and their emergence as a force in mainstream politics.
2. See Howard R. Penniman, ed., *Israel at the Polls: The Knesset Elections of 1977* (Washington: American Enterprise Institute, 1979) for an excellent discussion of the changes in the Israeli electorate.

3. See Amos Elon, *Herzl* (New York: Holt, Reinhart and Winston, 1975); and Alex Bein, *Theodore Herzl* (New York: Atheneum, 1970); as well as Arthur Herzberg, *The Zionist Idea* (New York: Atheneum, 1969).
4. Mordecai Kaplan, *Judaism as a Civilization* (New York: The MacMillan Company, 1935) reissued by the Jewish Publication Society in 1982 in honor of Professor Kaplan's 100th birthday.
5. Jacob Neusner, *From Politics to Piety* (Englewood Cliffs: Prentice Hall, 1973).
6. Franz Rosenzweig and Eugen Rosenstock-Huessy, *Judaism Despite Christianity* (University of Alabama Press, 1969). See my discussion of Rosenzweig in "Franz Rosenzweig and Martin Buber Reconsidered," *Response* 10:4 (Winter 1976–77).
7. Even the early Israeli treatments of the Holocaust were designed to recover the heroic posture of the ghetto fighters and resistance warriors. Israelis were uncomfortable with the history of the Jew as victim. See Yehudah Bauer, *The Emergence from Powerlessness* (Toronto: The University of Toronto Press, 1979); and *The Holocaust in Historical Perspective* (Seattle: The University of Washington Press, 1978), pp. 30–50.
8. Earl Raab, "Anti-Semitism, 1982 as a Fact and a Commodity," paper in draft form.
9. Charles Silberman, *A Certain People: American Jews and Their Lives Today* (New York: Summit Books, 1985).
10. Stephen Rosenfeld, "Dateline Washington: Anti-Semitism in U.S. Foreign Policy," *Foreign Affairs* (Summer, 1982).
11. Paul Eidelberg, *Sadat's Strategy* (Dollard Des Ormeaus, Quebec: Dawn, 1979).
12. Amia Lieblich, *Tin Soldiers on a Jerusalem Beach* (New York: Pantheon Books, 1978).
13. Netanel Lorch, *One Long War: Arab Versus Jew Since 1920* (New York: Herzl Press, 1976).
14. See Raab, "Anti-Semitism."
15. I am grateful to Amiram Gonen, a professor of Social Geography and Dean of the Students at the Hebrew University for these insights.
16. Uriel Tal, "The Land and the State of Israel in Israeli Religious Life," in *The Rabbinical Assemble Proceedings 1976* (New York: The Rabbinical Assembly, 1977).
17. Yishayahu Leibowitz, *Judaism, the Jewish People and the State of Israel* [in Hebrew] (Tel Aviv: Schocken Books, 1975).
18. Even Rav Kook's famous analogy, equating the building of Israel by the pioneering generation with the construction of the Holy of Holies in the ancient Temple, considers Zionism as a prelude to the religious revolution and merely defers the *Kulturkamf* until all immediate tasks have been completed. His son and disciple understood the contradictions in his father's thought and refused to defer the crisis much longer. See Zvi Yaron, *The Teachings of Rav Kook* [in Hebrew] (Jerusalem: The World Zionist Organization, 1974).

19. Yonina Talmon, "The Pursuit of the Millennium: The Relations between Religion and Social Change," in Norman Birnbaum and Gertrud Lenzer, ed., *Sociology and Religion* (Englewood Cliffs: Prentice Hall, 1969), pp. 238–254.
20. S. Z. Abramov, *Perpetual Dilemma,* pp. 224–264.
21. Yehudah Amital, *Ascent from the Depths* [in Hebrew] (Jerusalem: Alon Shevut, 1974).
22. J. B. Soloveichik, *In Aloneness, In Togetherness* [in Hebrew] ed. with an introduction by Pichas A. Pelli (Jerusalem: Orot, 1976), pp. 331–400.
23. Charles Liebmann and Eliezer Don-Yehiya, *Civil Religion in Israel: Traditional Judaism and Political Culture in the Jewish State* (Berkeley: The University of California Press, 1983).

9

The Impact of Religion on Politics in Contemporary Africa

WELLINGTON W. NYANGONI

The final communique of the Pan-African Conference of Third World Theologians, held at the Ghana Institute of Management and Public Administration (G.I.M.P.A.), Green Hill, Accra, Ghana, from December 17 to 23, 1977, captured the sentiments and current thinking of many Africans when it declared:

> We believe that African Theology must be understood in the context of African life and culture and the creative attempt of African peoples to shape a new future that is different from the colonial past and the neocolonial present. The African situation requires a new theological methodology that is different from the approaches of the dominant theologies of the West. African theology must reject, therefore, the prefabricated ideas of North Atlantic Theology by defining itself according to the struggles of the people in their resistance against the structures of domination. Our task as theologians is to create a theology that arises from and is accountable to African people.[1]

African theologians view the role of religion as that of liberating mankind from social, psychological, economic, and political oppression. Recognizing that Africa has suffered from the ills of slavery, colonialism, imperialism, and neocolonialism, these African religious leaders commit themselves to resisting these oppressive structures, and liberating Africa from the European domination of the past. Their goal is to work toward the overall social, political, and economic development of Africa.

In this study I take the position that African traditional religions, Islam and Christianity, all play constructive developmental and liberational roles. I also subscribe to the view that religion should be considered an instrument for furthering and harmonizing African social, political, and economic interests. In addition to being knowledgeable about the existing political and economic sytems which continue to exploit the African majority, I suggest that African theologians join hands with politicians who call for economic democracy in order to eliminate poverty, disease, hunger, and political oppression.

African Traditional Religion

Traditional African religions have permeated the fabric of African life. In African societies before the advent of Islam and Christianity, religions were intrinsically integrated into the total well-being of the African within his cosmos. Religious permeation and integration into all social institutions (economic, political, educational, and family) were so complete that it was impossible to isolate any one from the others. We speak of African traditional religions in the plural because each African ethnic group has its own religious system. Yet, regardless of their differences, African traditional religions have some of the following common elements:

- Belief in one Supreme Deity who controls the universe and is involved in the daily activities of man's life on earth.
- Belief in lesser divinities (of varying importance in different African regional areas), including some who represent attributes or functions of the Supreme Being (for example, Shango, the Yoruba god of thunder).
- Belief in spirits or "animism" in the sense of recognizing and accepting the existence of non-material forces or entities which might periodically be domiciled in trees, rocks, shrubs, animals, underground, or in water.
- Belief in ancestors—veneration for the forefathers, including offerings of food and drink to the dead at graveyards, under trees and special shrines. Ancestors are not worshiped.
- Practice of medicine and psychology. Efforts are made to control supernatural resources for personal ends, for example, making effigies of enemies, and/or employing practical materials—e.g., medicinal herbs—to help others. Both have religious and ritualistic aspects and lean perhaps more closely to psychology than religion.

To ignore these African traditional religious beliefs, attitudes, and practices is likely to lead to a gross misunderstanding of African behavior and world view. Religion is the strongest element in the traditional background and exerts probably the greatest influence on perceptions of social, economic, educational, and political institutions.

Little has been known or studied by Westerners about traditional religions of Africa and their complex cosmological systems. What has been written or reported, mostly by missionaries, colonial administrators, anthropologists, and popular writers, has too often been confusing and derogatory, with misinformed emphasis on terms such as "ancestor worship," "pagan," "simple," "unstructured," "primitive," "animism," and "witch doctor." Only recently have theologians in Africa, Latin America, Western Europe, and North America, begun scholarly study and comparisons of African religions with other major global religions.

The study of African religions is further compounded by the following factors:

- Africa has approximately one thousand different languages.
- African traditional religions are numerous and diverse.
- African societies are characterized by different social and cultural structures.
- Deliberate attempts were made by the colonial powers to weaken and destroy the political and social anchors of the foundation of African traditional religions.
- Islam and Christianity have been aggressive, disruptive, and penetrative influences on African religions, sometimes with the support of the colonial power.

Prior to the advent of Islam and Christianity, African religions were both political and spiritually integrative factors in African life. African traditional religions were intrinsically integrated into the various African politics. Political leaders were also religious leaders. The role of African kings, emperors, army generals, village elders, and heads of households also incorporated religious functions. In addition, African traditional religions are agencies for harmonizing the complex generational interests. Their function is spiritually to unite the dead (ancestors), the living, and those yet to be born.

Religion became the basis for success, peace, war, and national identity. The impact of religion on pre-Islamic and European colonialism in Africa was overwhelmingly noticeable. During the eras of Islamic and European colonial expansion in Africa, African religious leaders fought nationalist wars against foreign invaders. Traditional religious leaders and spirit mediums spearheaded the struggle against colonialism. After colonization, a majority of traditional African religious leaders maintained their animosity towards the European colonial and capitalist ruling class. Throughout Africa, Western-educated elites who were to lead the struggle for decolonization constantly sought support and legitimacy from African spirit mediums and religious leaders. During the post-independence era, new heads of African sovereign states have, in the quest for national integration, appealed to traditional leaders for support of their governmental policies.

Islam

Islam is both a religion and a way of life for about fifty percent of the entire population of the African states. Over ninety percent of the African Muslims (also spelled "Moslems") are in Nigeria, Egypt, Morocco, Algeria, Libya, Mauritania, Senegal, Guinea, Kenya, Ethiopia, Mali, Chad, Niger, Somalia, Tanzania, Sudan, and Djibouti. Smaller concentrations of Muslims are in Uganda, the Gambia, Cameroon, Malawi, Ghana, Upper Volta, and the Central African Republic.

In Arabic, the word "Islam" means submission, in the sense of submission to the will of God. Islam originated in Medina (in present day Saudi Arabia), at the beginning of the seventh century, and began to spread to North Africa, North Eastern Africa, and eventually West Africa after the death of its founder, the Prophet Muhammed, in 632 A.D. Central to its teachings and followers are the "Five Pillars of Islam:"

1. *Shahada,* or the declaration that "there is only one God, and Muhammed is the prophet."
2. *Salat,* or praying five times a day while facing Mecca.
3. Observance of *Ramadan,* or a month of fasting each year according to the Muslim calendar.
4. Performing the *Hajj,* or going on a pilgrimage to Mecca at least once in one's lifetime (if it is at all possible to do so).
5. *Zakat,* giving alms for charity to the poor, orphaned, handicapped, and widows.

Five hundred years after the death of Muhammed, Islam had penetrated more than half of the African continent and some of its islands. Islamic academic centers were found in Africa, and throughout the rest of the Muslim world. Islamic scholars and jurists who interpreted the Koran (*Qur'an*) and the *hadith* (books compiled on the prophet's practice, life style, and theology) served as the foundation of each Islamic community, be it a cluster of nomadic settlements or a state with millions of people. Contributing immensely to the spread of Islam in Africa were the mystic brotherhoods, in which a holy man *(shaik)* served as a chief interpreter for his community of followers.

Although Islam was firmly implanted throughout North Africa, West Africa, Central Africa, and East Africa at the inception of the colonial era, the first forty years of the twentieth century was a period of dramatic expansion of Islam in Africa. Expansion was due partly to the recognition of Islam, and its use in the colonial administration of the Europeans in Africa. The rapid expansion of Islam can also be explained as a reaction to European attempts to compel Africans to adopt a Christianity which some Africans viewed as integrally linked to the oppressive colonial political systems. More importantly, Africans generally viewed Islam as a modernizing influence and an ideology that was not linked to the European colonial world order. Among conservative African Muslim communities, Islam was regarded as a counterweight to, and a bulwark against, rapid social change brought about by Westernization. On the whole, Muslim leaders were strong advocates of decolonization and national self-determination.

Christianity

About ten percent of the African population is made up of Christians. In spite of its small following, interestingly, Christianity has a dominating political, economic, social, educational, and cultural influence in many African States, especially those south of the Sahara. In this region, most of the new African elites were educated in Christian schools, and in Western Europe, Canada, and the United States. Easter and Christmas are celebrated as national holidays in forty African states. Christianity was introduced early into Africa: In Ethiopia, it was the official religion from 332 A.D. to 1974. In Egypt, the Christian Coptic Church was founded in the sixth century. It was also introduced by missionaries from Europe (as early as the fifteenth century) and America (including freed and returned African slaves). Finally, Christianity has been propagated through the ministry of independent African churches in the nineteenth and twentieth centuries.

While recognizing the important contributions that Christianity in Africa has made to the establishment of Western educational systems and social and health institutions; the development of agricultural, technological, and architectural programs; and the support for humanitarian causes, including antislavery activities and decolonization; the Christian church as an institution was nevertheless linked to colonialism. Therefore, Christianity was regarded by radical African nationalists as an agent of Western capitalism and imperialism. Culturally, the church equated Christianity with Westernization and was accused of being insensitive to African traditional cultural values. In an article entitled "Whither African Theology," Bishop Desmond Tutu of the Republic of South Africa wrote:

> The missionaries were bringing the lights of the Gospel to the dark continent. These poor native pagans had to be clothed in Western clothes so that they could speak to the White man's God, the only God, who was obviously unable to recognize them unless they were decently clad. These poor creatures must be made to sing the White man's hymns hopelessly and badly translated, they had to worship in the White man's unemotional and individualistic way . . . [2]

With the attainment of independence by almost all African states and changes in the leadership of Christian churches throughout Africa, African Christian theology is now incorporating some elements of traditional African religions. Christian churches are now at the forefront of the struggle against racism, segregation, and colonialism. These churches are also promoting national self-determination, egalitarianism, and the application of human rights to all people regardless of race, sex, national origin, ethnicity, political and religious beliefs.

The Social Context

Present day African theologians, religious leaders, some political elites, and numerous social activists are aware that Africa is the least developed continent with the largest reservoir of exploited labor and resources, as well as the largest number of refugees (six million). Illiteracy is high in a majority of African states, governments restrict some of the fundamental freedoms and civic rights of their citizens. Christian churches and other religious movements are not indifferent to all these conditions and the ensuing problems faced by the poor and the exploited.

Aware of the consequences of a social order fashioned economically, politically, and ideologically to benefit multi-national corporations and a few elites, religious communities, along with social activists and other concerned people, have begun to make their voices heard throughout Africa and beyond.There is a call for an examination of the social, political, and economic order. Some of these voices are calling for a radical transformation of the present system within the context of a revolutionary struggle. This call for change stresses that all citizens should participate in the governance of the state. In such a society, private ownership of the means of production, distribution, and exchange will be eliminated because it enables a few to expropriate the fruits of labor performed by the workers and peasants and creates class divisions which lead to social inequalities. Those in support of this restructured society believe that such changes will be accompanied by similar changes in the reigns of political power that will ensure the liberty of all Africans.

For the last three decades, a growing number of African Muslims and Christians have participated in revolutionary struggles for African political and economic liberation. Through active participation, they have learned the full context of the exploitation of the African people. Involvement and commitment by Muslims and Christians are major factors in the prevailing life of these communities in African states.

Christian involvement in the liberation process varies significantly in depth and from one African country to another. There are also variances in Christian involvement in the liberation process within and between white-dominated settler societies of Southern Africa and non-settler states in Western Africa. Liberation was initially expressed in groping language that progressively moved forward by trial and error. At times, the dialogue of liberation was bogged down in political quagmires; at other times, it was sidetracked into confusion by political repressions. In general, there is agreement on the importance of liberation theology in Africa, in spite of the differences which may exist within and between Christian, Muslim, and traditional African religions.

Wellington W. Nyangoni

Liberation Theology

Today, about forty percent of the world's Christians live in Africa, the Caribbean, Latin America, and some parts of Asia. In these areas, socialism is blended with Christianity in seeking to raise the standard of living of the peasants, workers, and the unemployed urban dwellers. In these countries, liberation theologians are calling for the eradication of past conditions of political oppression and poverty.

Among prominent writers on liberation theology are Juan Luis Segundo of Uruguay, Jose Miguez Bonino of Argentina (*Christians and Marxists: The Mutual Challenge to Revolution*), Hugo Assmann of Brazil (*A Theology for a Nomad Church*), Alfredo Fierro of Spain (*The Militant Gospel*), and Friar Leonardo Boff of Brazil (*Jesus Christ Liberator*). Most of these theologians in Latin America and Africa were trained in Europe; a few of them are European or North American missionaries.[3]

Liberation theology in Africa and Latin America is different from other brands of theology with which it is occasionally linked and even mistakenly identified. It differs from European and North American theology not only in its analysis of reality, based on more radical and all-embracing options, but also in its way of theologizing. According to Rosino Ghellini, "Liberation theology in Africa does not attempt to offer any Christian justification of positions already adopted; it, however, does purport to be a Christian ideology of revolution."[4] Liberation theology is a process of reflection which starts out from an historical praxis. It views faith from the standpoint of this historical praxis and the way that faith is actually lived in a commitment to liberation.[5] Consequently, the themes of liberation theology are the major themes of all theology, but its emphasis, its way of approaching them, are different.[6]

In his seminal work, "A Theology of Liberation," Father Gustavo Gutierrez, noted that "among more alert groups today, what we have called a new awareness of Latin American reality is making headway. They believe that there can be authentic development for Latin America and Africa only if there is liberation from the domination exercised by the great capitalist countries, especially by the most powerful, the United States of America."[7] Liberation theology is, thus, a method of defining Christian faith in the political context of underdevelopment in Africa, Latin America, and the Caribbean in a partisan spirit committed to social, political, and economic action. This method is not unique for attempting to apply Christian faith to social action. Liberation theology is no less concerned about the working class of Africa and the rest of the world than Pope Leo XIII, whose encyclical underlined Catholicism's responsibility to the poverty-stricken masses. While it has incorporated some aspects of the Marxist ideas into its dogma, liberation theology cannot be universally defined as Marxist.

Liberation theologians argue that Third World countries have been disproportionately dependent on external economic activities and decisions, and that the inequalities between the rich and the poor (with an unusually small middle class) are analogous to Karl Marx's class struggle between the proletariat and bourgeoisie. In his book, *Christians and Marxists,* Methodist theologian Jose Bonino quotes Fidel Castro who questions whether "the theologians are becoming Communists and the Communists are becoming theologians?"[8] While elsewhere in the world Marxism as an intellectual current seems to be stalemated, in Africa and Latin America, Marxism and the church may need each other. Eric Hobsbawm, a leading Marxist historian at the University of London, explains in a 1978 article that

> . . . the churches are now left free to move left, for neither the right nor the state can any longer protect them against erosion. Some Christians may thus hope to retain, or more doubtfully, regain the support of the masses believed to be identified with the left. It is a surprising development. Conversely, parties of the Marxist left, seeking to widen their support, are more inclined to abandon their traditional identification with active opposition to religion.[9]

Some African and Latin American theologians argue that truth lies in revolutionary praxis. According to Father Segundo, the choice of socialism against capitalism is in support of freedom for the peasants, the workers, the unemployed, and the handicapped. He further argues that human life in society constitutes the highest real value to mankind. Liberation theologians place themselves firmly on the side of human rights, economic development, and the defense of religious liberties in Africa, Latin America, and the rest of the world.

When theologians say that liberation theology does not purport to be a Christian ideology of revolution, they do not mean to suggest that it ignores the process of revolution:

On the contrary, its starting point is its insertion in that process to become more self-critical, and hence more comprehensive and radical. This is done by framing the political commitment to liberation within the context of Christ's gratuitous gift of total liberation.

Christ's liberation is not restricted to political liberation, but it occurs in historical happenings and liberative political actions. We cannot bypass these mediating factors. By the same token, however, political liberation is not some form of religious messianism. It has its own laws and its own proper autonomy; it presupposes very specific social analyses and well defined political options. But when we view human history as one in which Christ's liberation is at work, we enlarge the whole perspective and give full depth and meaning to what is involved in political commitment.

The theology of liberation is a theology of salvation in the light of the concrete historical and political conditions of the present day. These mediating factors of present-day history and politics, appraised and valued in their own right, change the way we ponder and live the mystery hidden from eternity and now revealed; the mystery of our heavenly Father's love, of human brotherhood, and of salvation. It is that which the term "liberation" seeks to render present.[10]

It is difficult to understand liberation theology, whether in the apartheid Republic of South Africa, in Latin America, or in other parts of the Third World, unless we understand that it evolved within the context of a new political consciousness. Its origins are inseparably intertwined with human oppression, suffering, exploitation, discrimination, segregation, and powerlessness. Elaborating on the theme of anguish in reference to the genesis of liberation theology in the African diaspora, Bishop Desmond Tutu of South Africa states that

All liberation theology stems from trying to make sense of human suffering when those who suffer are the victims of organized oppression and exploitation, when they are emasculated and treated as less than what they are: redeemed by the one savior Jesus Christ and sanctified by the Holy Paraclete. This is the genesis of all liberation theology and so also of black theology, which is a theology of liberation in Africa. Black theology has occurred mainly in Southern Africa, where blacks have had their noses rubbed in dust by white racism, depersonalizing them to the extent that they have—blasphemy of blasphemies—come to doubt the reality of their own personhood and humanity. They have often come to believe that the denigration of their humanity by those who oppress them is the truth about themselves.[11]

In Southern African countries, Black theology as a theology of liberation, regards itself as an overall ideology which is antithetical to racism, imperialism, colonialism, fascism, and neocolonialism. African church leaders, Black politicians, nationalist revolutionaries, and socialists have joined hands in Southern Africa, Zimbabwe, Angola, Mozambique, Botswana, Namibia, Zambia, and Tanzania, in the struggle for decolonization and the attainment of majority rule based on democratic principles and "one man one vote." The call of the leadership of churches for all concerned Christians in Southern Africa to join the struggle to eliminate racial oppression has brought the church and state closer to each other in Zimbabwe, Zambia, Botswana, Swaziland, Zaire, and Lesotho. It is the teachings of liberation theology that brought the Black churches to their antagonistic relations with the colonial governments of Rhodesia, Angola, Mozambique, and the Republic of South Africa. Throughout Southern Africa, Black theology or liberation theology has become part of the Black consciousness movement, which is concerned with ecumenicalism and the "evangelical aim of awaking in blacks a sense of their intrinsic worth as children of God."[12]

The new consciousness which gave rise to the development of a liberation theology in South Africa, Namibia, and Zimbabwe, was inspired by its North American counterpart which, according to Bishop Tutu,

> . . . existed for so long implicitly in the Negro spirituals that gave heart to black slaves in the heavy days of their bondage and which became more articulate and explicit during the civil rights campaign. It was inspired too by the knowledge that so much of Africa had thrown off the shackles of colonialism. Liberation theology takes very seriously the sociopolitical dimensions of reality as those which, to a large extent, determine the quality not only of secular but also of religious life. Liberation theology dismissed the dichotomy of the secular and the sacred as thoroughly unincarnational and irreligious.[13]

Liberation theology in Southern Africa politicizes African workers, the unemployed, and peasants to fight for self-esteem, human dignity, and political liberation. Through African consciousness, the hopes and beliefs of Africans to exist like other free peoples of the world are reinforced. According to Allan Boesak, a noted South African theologian:

> Through black consciousness black people discover that they are children of God and that they have the rights to exist in His world. Black people discover that they are part of history, and they share this history with God, which means that they are responsible to act as human persons. The sit-

uation in South Africa did not happen just accidentally. It did not just come about. The situation was created by people. It is a system that is still maintained by people through various methods. Black consciousness says to black people that they are human, that they are children of God. Black consciousness gives black people a clear realization of the situation in South Africa and of their human "beingness." When black people see clearly that they are black and are children of God, then they can be proud.[14]

Black liberation theology is a situational theology in the sense that it operates within a defined social, cultural, economic, and political milieu. All theology has always been situational because it operates in some form of a context. To this extent, it is theologically and sociologically naive to say that what is good for the situation in France, as ascertained by French theologians, is also good for the situation in Ireland or South Africa. Each theological concept develops within a particular context. People's theological thinking, that is, the way that they read the Gospel, and the way they comprehend and interpret it, is influenced by their cultural, racial, and historical background and the type of political and economic systems in which they are reared and educated.

In South Africa, there are clear lines of demarcation between how Africans and whites have lived and continue to live in the white settler societies of Rhodesia (Zimbabwe) and South Africa. Political, social, and economic privileges are given according to the racial origins of people and the color of their skins. In the Republic of South Africa, whites have all the social, political, and economic privileges accorded to power and high status. Africans have no political, economic, and legal rights in the Republic of South Africa.

In the rest of Africa, liberation theologians have joined with social activists and government leaders who are advocating political and economic egalitarianism of the poverty-stricken and disenfranchised African masses. Liberation theologians are calling for redistribution of national resources and a change in the ownership of the means of production, distribution, and exchange by the state on behalf of all the citizens (of African states). Foreign multinational corporations that have invested heavily in African states are now being asked to reinvest their profits into the economies of politically independent African states. It is hoped that such reinvested money will alleviate some of the economic and social problems faced by the poor and exploited citizens.

Church and Politics in Africa

Colonial Period. During the colonial period, European missionaries sought the political and military protection of the white administrators of the European colonial governments. Cooperation between white Christian missionaries and colonial government administrators was close. Many European missionaries often eagerly reported the nationalistic activities of anti-colonial activists. Like their European colonial bureaucrats, the European missionaries were extremely prejudiced against Africans and believed in white supremacy. Although these missionaries espoused belief in God and the teachings of Christianity, they shared the racist views propounded by such eighteenth century European thinkers as Voltaire, Rousseau, and Hume.[15]

Eighteenth century European attempts to classify and grade human races were damaging to the reputation of Africans, but the efforts to explain the origin of race were more serious still. The traditional and orthodox view was that of Christian revelation: God created man, a single pair, at a finite time in the not-very-distant past. Scientific versions of this belief in a single creation came to be known as "monogenesis." If the basic tenets of monogenesis were accepted, all the biologist had to do was explain the origin of later variations among Adam's descendants.

> There were many suggestions. Moreau de Maupertuis believed the original creation included the creation of all the racial varieties to emerge later in time. They were latent in the original female egg and the original male sperm given to Adam and Eve, though Adam and Eve were themselves of the white race. When Negro variants appeared, the "normal" part of mankind drove them off into Africa, a less desirable part of the world. Once there, they continued to breed true Negro form and color, though it was still possible that they might one day change back into their original European race.[16]

Of course not all European missionaries and colonial administrators believed in the theories of white supremacy, but a significant segment of them sympathized with the polygenetic theories of the eighteenth century. Other than allowing for the possibility that human beings may have originated from different ancestries, polygenetic beliefs tended to accept the notion that some races descended from "pre-Adamite" ancestors. The attractiveness of polygenesis among the Europeans was due, to a great degree, to the implications that God had created man in "His own image." There was a general belief that the appropriate image was that of the white man, and that non-whites were degenerations of that white image. Although, contrary to biblical beliefs and assertions, polygenesis

> . . . held that each race was a separate creation, distinct from the children of Adam and permanently so. Although polygenesis was a minority position in eighteenth century Europe, it has probably been the most common explanation of race throughout human history. Several European suggestions to this effect had appeared from time to time, in spite of the open contradiction of the Bible. One of the most widely read was Isaac La Peyere's Pre-Adamite published in 1655, which held that Adam and Eve had been the last of a series of special creations, and some of the living non-Europeans were descended from the earlier pre-Adamites.[17]

European colonial administrators and missionaries shared similar cultural, historical, and racial backgrounds. They supported each other politically. In most cases, the missionaries identified their political survival with that of the occupying political power. Both had great disdain and disrespect for African cultures and civilizations.

Most Africans perceived Christianity (unlike Islam in the Colonial era) as part of the ruling colonial power structure. This perception was particularly applicable to the top leaders of the Christian church throughout Africa. The alliance of the church with oppressive colonial governments, capitalists, and imperialists contributed to the general erosion of confidence and trust of the 'godly' mission of the white missionaries. When African states became independent, the African clergy and nationalists wanted the old European Christian church leadership to be replaced with Africans who were sensitive to the social, political, and developmental problems confronting their new states.

Independence and Post Independence

The euphoria of independence brought hopes of prosperity in political, agricultural, educational, and economic endeavors. Africans foresaw themselves controlling their governments, economies, bureaucracies, military institutions, churches, and destinies. Many had hoped that independence would bring a sudden transformation of their societies. Yet, in many ways, independence failed to ameliorate conditions:

> . . . mass poverty continued, appalling housing and primitive sanitation in towns remained, unemployment increased. A gulf grew sometimes between the people and the European-American educated elite who became the Political Establishment; new indigenous rulers tended to become bureaucrats and sometimes dictators. Corruption poisoned the regimes, ministers became rich and lived in mansions which rivalled those of the previous European masters. . . . Power by dominant political cliques was strengthened, one-party states were decreed, sometimes reflecting national unity, sometimes exploiting it, opposition leaders were imprisoned; governments were overthrown by army coups, sometimes radical, sometimes reactionary and supported in the background by American and Western (and we may add Eastern) agencies.[18]

For millions of African peasants, workers, the urban unemployed, some of the clergy, and a few Westernized elites, independence had not brought the anticipated economic prosperity, political stability, increased health care services, additional roads, schools, and peace. While African leaders appeared to be in complete political and economic control, it became quite evident soon after independence, that they were not. According to Dr. Kwame Nkrumah, the first president of the Republic of Ghana, "the essence of neo-colonialism is that the State which is subject to it is, in theory, independent and has all the outward trappings of international sovereignty. In reality, its economic system and thus its political policy is directed from outside."[19] The achievement of independence did not end European control of African economies, health systems, educational systems, and the church administration. As foreign investments patterned and structured on the former colonial relations began to increase after independence, so did the might of neocolonialism.

In response to the elusiveness of development, and the inappropriateness of established modes of analysis, students of Africa have begun to adopt a new approach to the understanding of African politics. This new paradigm is more critical and controversial than the old orthodoxy. The origins of the new paradigm lie in radical European scholarship rather than in American behavioral sciences. It has also incorporated the center-periphery model of Scandinavian scholars and the dependency theory of Latin American intellectuals. It is consistent with the mode of analysis that deals with global as well as local relations, and with the interrelations of international and internal inequalities.

Most African social scientists and liberation theologians subscribe to the view that the world economy is dominated by the capitalist mode of production and is characterized by a vertical international division of labor. Historically, this vertical international division of labor emerged as a consequence of the expansion of the European mercantilist-capitalist system, at unequal levels of economic and military strength from the sixteenth century onward. The militarily weaker societies of Asia, Latin America, and Africa (the "periphery") became both figuratively and often literally the hewers of wood and drawers of water for the militarily stronger societies of Europe, and later North America and Japan ("center"). Thus, African economies are dependent on Western European and North American countries, which in turn exploit this relationship.

According to some African and Latin American social scientists and theologians, the dependency perspective assumes that the development of a national or regional unit can only be comprehended in connection with its historical insertion into the worldwide political-economic system which merged with the wave of European colonization in Latin America, the Caribbean, Africa, and Asia. This global system is thought to be characterized by the unequal but combined development of its different components. As Osvaldo Sunkel and Pedro Paz put it:

> Both underdevelopment and development are aspects of the same phenomenon, both are historically simultaneous, both are linked functionally and, therefore, interact and condition each other mutually. This results . . . in the division of the world between industrial, advanced or "central" countries, and the underdeveloped, backward or "peripheral" countries . . . [20]

The center, viewed as capable of dynamic development responsive to internal needs, is the chief beneficiary of the global links. On the other hand, the periphery, viewed as having a reflex type of development, is both constrained by its incorporation into the global system, and its adaptation to the requirements of the expansion of the center.

Theotonio dos Santos defines dependency as a "situation in which a certain number of countries have their economy conditioned by the development and expansion of another . . . placing the dependent countries in a backward position exploited by the dominant countries."[21] This process of dependency can be understood only by reference to its historical dimension, and by focusing on the total network of social relations as they evolve in different contexts over time. For this reason, dependence is characterized as structural, historical and totalizing or an "integral analysis of development."[22]

The questions that arose in the 1960s are still being asked: How can Africa attain its true economic and political independence? To what degree should foreign multinational corporations and their national governments be involved in Africa? Can Africa develop without foreign aid? Some African political and religious leaders have taken the position that without outside economic and technological aid, the new African states would never reach the same levels of development as the industrialized states. Others have disagreed and held the view that rapid economic development in Africa can take place if African states have complete control of the ownership of the means of production, distribution, and exchange. While not ruling out some measure of the free enterprise system, many theologians and scholars are calling for African states to rely more on themselves, their resources, and skills for their own development.

The churches have a position on these two approaches to African development. A majority of the Christian and Muslim leaders have condemned imperialism and neocolonialism and now support policies that advocate economic independence for African states. At the 1976 United Nations Conference on Trade and Development (UNCTAD IV) held in Nairobi, the World Council of Churches called upon their supporters to lobby their governments to support and implement the recommendations outlined in the charter of the New International Economic Order (NIEO).

Although numerous church leaders, leaders of traditional African religions, and leading Muslim *ulama* (theologians) or *imams* have generally supported government policies, we must still ask 1) What role, if any, does the church play in contemporary African states? and 2) Should churches support the ideological views of politicians? In response to these questions, it is important to note that in Africa, most church leaders believe that the church has a political role to play. Yet, recognizing that the church has political interests in contemporary African societies does not in any way minimize theological differences over which governmental policies and ideologies the churches should accept or reject. The following represent some of the major theological positions taken by African theologians:

- The message was expressed in terms that gave the impression that what really mattered was eternal life and, therefore, what really counted most was to lead a life that prepared us for eternal life. In other words, the world provided the background against which we must work out our salvation in fear and trembling and with patience to endure the problems encountered. By ignoring this world and its activities, the church indirectly blessed the operative social, economic, and political structures.
- The doctrine of divine providence reconciled people to the world. Whatever suffering existed had been permitted by God as part of a pre-ordained design to prepare us for blissful future salvation. We should be satisfied with our lot and not be angry with what is inflicted on us. No revolution was recommended.
- The Christian doctrine of original sin made Christians believe that depraved human nature would always breed injustice in society. It is only individuals who may be converted by the grace of God; we cannot look to human society for justice. Although this is a distortion of the Gospel, African Christians by and large have not related preaching the Gospel with the establishment of justice.
- The notion of divine lordship was extended to legitimate hierarchical secular and ecclesiastical systems on the pattern of the master-servant relationship.
- The Christian message has advocated, and continues to advocate, the ideals of unity and peace separated from the demands of justice. This overlooks the inequities that exist between people and communities. The church thus tends to protect the most powerful and to encourage the submission of the powerless.[23]

Young African theologians and religious leaders are now speaking out publicly against the above interpretations of the Christian teachings that tend to encourage support for the status quo. These young theologians are now calling on Africans to actively work for the solution of the formidable social, economic, medical, and political problems that confront African states. The church, they argue, should be actively involved in liberating the powerless from oppression and economic exploitation.

Other positions articulated by African liberation theologists include the following:

- God is always present in us as an enabler, as a transforming agent, appointing us to be transformers of human life. Turning to God does not mean that we must forget the struggle against injustice. Christian preaching must provide the incentive for constructing a better human existence on earth, no matter how temporary this earthly existence.
- Divine providence is God's redemptive will for all humanity and is manifested in movements and situations that contribute to the positive redemption of humanity. Attempts to bring redemption to humanity will have to work through the structures of society—those in existence or new ones.
- The doctrine of original sin means that the salvation promised by Christ and proclaimed by the church has social implications, as revealed in the redemption of history from the power of darkness. Where sin abounds there divine grace abounds even more to enable us to act differently in spite of ourselves. The doctrine of original sin must not, therefore, cripple humankind's desire for justice.
- The acceptance of the lordship of God should not be used as justification for any system that encourages one-man rule either in political or ecclesiastical government.

  Rather, that affirmation must mean that God in Christ has overcome sin and death and rules all: monarchs as well as subject, president as well as laborer. It should mean God is Lord because of the divine victory in Jesus Christ and, therefore, there should be victory for all mankind.
- The only unity that must be proclaimed and advocated is that in accord with God's will of justice. It requires the conversion of all, even to the point of restitution for the underprivileged and oppressed.[24]

Some clergy in contemporary African societies are now in apparent general agreement that the presence of churches in post independent African states must be felt in the daily administration of these countries. Churches should involve themselves with all aspects of social, medical, educational, agricultural, technological, economic, and political welfare in African states. This implies support for, or criticism of, government policies. The church, like the government of any African state, seeks to create:

> . . . a strong and progressive society in which no one will have anxiety about the basic means of life, about work, food and shelter; where poverty and illiteracy no longer exist and disease is brought under control; and where our educational facilities provide all the children with the best possible opportunities for the development of their potentialities.[25]

Although the church and state share similar concerns on social, economic, and political progress, conflict over ideological differences has erupted in many African states where Marxism has been proclaimed, including Ghana (during the time Nkrumah was president), Angola, Mozambique, Ethiopia, Congo Brazzaville, Madagascar, Guinea Bissau, and the Republic of Guinea. When the presidents of these countries began to implement their ideological programs which de-emphasized religion, both Christian and Muslim leaders reacted negatively. In countries where Islam is the predominant religion, such as Egypt, Algeria, and Morocco, conflicts have arisen between fundamentalist Muslims and the state.

Numerous conflicts between church and state have emerged when the religious leaders request African governments to restructure their policies to address the following needs of the poor, rather than those of the minority of rich elites: the construction and improvement of medical facilities to benefit peasants rather than those located in rich urban centers; additional facilities for primary, secondary, technical, and agricultural schools in the rural areas; low income housing for rural and slum populations rather than continued construction of deluxe modern apartments and residential mansions for the rich.

A further issue of friction between church and state periodically arises over church-operated educational schools, hospitals, and agricultural projects which accept government aid. A problem arises over whether or not the government subsidies to these church-owned institutions entitle the government to interfere in the administration of these institutions. Some African governments, for example, have assumed the right to take over the administration of all schools in their states.

Throughout Africa, African governments have been hostile to fundamentalist Christian and Islamic movements that are perceived as extreme. In Zambia and Malawi, followers of the Alice Lenchina Movement and the Watch Tower Movement were arrested and jailed when they started to discourage Zambians and Malawians from voting in elections. Some fundamentalist movements such as the Islamic Brotherhoods, the Lenchina Movement, and the

Northern Nigerian Islamic extremist religious movement of Alhajj Mohammadu Marwu, have instructed their followers to disobey orders from secular rulers. Recognizing the disruptive implications of such policies, African government in Malawi, Zambia, Ghana, Nigeria, and Egypt have punished the leaders of these radical Christian and Islamic fundamentalist movements.

Without minimizing the conflicts that have existed between the church and state, African theologians see their roles as working and cooperating with African governments to improve the spiritual, moral, social, and economic welfare of the African people. African theologians view themselves as agents for social, cultural, political, and economic liberation. This is why at a conference of Third World Theologians held in Dar es Salaam, Tanzania, in 1976, the following sentiments were upheld:

> Theology is not neutral. In a sense all theology is committed, conditioned notably by the social-cultural context in which it is developed. The Christian theological task in our countries is to be self-critical of the theologians' conditioning by the value system of their achievements.[26]

African theologians in post-independent Africa see their role as an ally of the poor and the politically oppressed. They see their mission on earth as being essentially different from that of theologians from Europe, United States of America, and Canada. According to Sergio Torres,

> European theology, from the Reformation to the theology of hope on the Protestant side, and from the Council of Trent to Vatican II on the Catholic side, has been a response to certain concrete historical situations. I say a response to certain situations, because the churches and theology were very much linked to the dominant class of Europe and did not speak on behalf of the poor and the oppressed. The theologians did not denounce slavery; they did not speak out against exploitation of the working class by the bourgeoisie during the Industrial Revolution, and they were accomplices in the international system of exploitation under colonialism, neocolonialism, and imperialism.[27]

With few exceptions, European and North American theologians of pre-independence African era, did not address the situation of the poor:

> On this point, Catholics and Protestants were the same. Thus, European theology, with a few exceptions, played an important role of ideological legitimization of an economic mode of production that has caused many injustices both in Europe as well as abroad in the Third World.[28]

The themes of the theological discussion about God, Jesus Christ, and salvation were abstract concepts divorced from the historical Jesus who identified with the poor of his time. If the dominant European and North American white theologians did not speak on behalf of the poor and the oppressed class, neither did they speak on behalf of the non-Europeans.

> Whether Rome, Wittenberg, or Geneva prevailed, whether justification before God occurred through works or through faith . . . for the red, the yellow, and the black, all this was irrelevant. It did not change their conditions. For the white confessors of the faith, regardless of their particular Christian line, the people of colour were all destined for bondage; "oneness in Christ" might pertain to heaven, but certainly not to this earth.[29]

African theologians in independent African states make it their business to speak for the poor and the oppressed class. In support of its activist role, the Final Communique of the Pan-African Conference of Third World Theologians declared:

> Despite the colonial experience of depersonalization and cultural invasion, the African cultures have kept their vitality. This vitality is expressed in the revival of African language, dances, music, and literature and in Africa's contribution to human sciences and to the human experience. This cultural vitality is the support of the African people in their struggle for complete liberation and for the construction of a human society. Nevertheless, we must recognize the persistence of the domination that resulted from colonialism. This domination also exists in the churches. The organizational model imported from the West is still proposed and accepted. The life of our churches has been dominated by a theology developed with a methodology, a worldview, and a conception of humanity using Western categories.[30]

African theologians want the churches to be actively involved with African social, cultural, economic, and political wellbeing. In addition to emphasizing the cultural aspects of African development, the African churches now see themselves as catalysts for political and economic development.

Africa and the Universal Man

The African continent has not produced a major religion such as Islam and Christianity that has received worldwide acceptance. Nor has history placed it in the forefront of proselytizing any creed among populations outside its own continent. On the contrary,

Africa, of the last two centuries has been preeminently a continent crisscrossed by European missionaries. With the past two centuries, Christianity has found its greatest number of voluntary emissaries among private agents within the African continent. European Christian nations exported not only businessmen and colonial administrators to Africa, but also peddlers of Catholicism and Protestantism.

Centuries before the advent of Christianity, the Muslims had vigorously disseminated their religious views in many regions of the African continent. Islamic ideas influenced the evolution and expansion of some kingdoms and empires in North Africa, West Africa, East Africa, and North Central Africa. Commerce, trade, politics, and war prompted unceasing contacts between North Africa and West Africa; between East Africa, North Africa, and the Middle East. Islamic cultural influences also spread throughout Mali, Songhai, Hausa, and East African city states.

What Africa has, then, is a variety of indigenous African religions, coexisting in juxtaposition to or interacting with Islam and European Christianity. This is the tripartite soul of Africa which the veteran Pan-Africanist, the late President of the Republic of Ghana, Dr. Kwame Nkrumah, proclaimed in the book, *Consciencism.*[31] Dr. Nkrumah viewed Africa's cultural experience as consisting of three parts: the aspect comprising indigenous traditional cultural life; the segment dominated by the Islamic cultural tradition; and the segment that is comprised of the Western European cultural tradition in Africa. Dr. Nkrumah wanted a new thesis or synthesis to lend coherence to the tripartite soul of the African:

> With true independence regained, however, a new harmony needs to be forged, a harmony that will allow the combined presence of traditional Africa, Islamic Africa and Euro-Christian Africa, so that this presence is in tune with the original humanist principles underlying African society. Our society is not the old society, but a new society enlarged by Islamic and Euro-Christian influences. A new emergent ideology is therefore required, an ideology which can solidify in a philosophical statement, but at the same time an ideology which will not abandon the original humanist principles of Africa.[32]

Dr. Nkrumah suggested a new synthesis of these three elements to develop what he termed "Philosophical Consciencism:"[33]

> . . . the theoretical basis for an ideology whose aim shall be to contain the African experience of Islamic and Euro-Christian presence as well as the

experience of traditional African society, and, by gestation, employ them for the harmonious growth and development of that society.[34]

The success of Philosophical Consciencism in Africa would depend largely upon the attitudes of these three elements toward each other. In addition, Philosophical Consciencism would have to be a catalyst in the realization of the Pan-African dream of African unity.

While recognizing that there are problems that must be confronted in uniting different African political systems, it must be noted that the marriage between religion and politics in Africa has been consummated. According to the December 1977 Communique of the Pan-African Conference of Third World Theologians:

> In post independence Africa and in Southern Africa, theology confronts new challenges, hopes, and opportunities. The vigor of the traditional African religions and cultures and the renewal of the churches, thanks principally to a return to the Scriptures, present us with the resources for our tasks.
>
> Our belief in Jesus Christ Liberator, convinces us that there is a noble future for our countries, if the processes of nation-building are geared to providing the urgent basic needs of all instead of the privileges of a few. We are confident that the creative vitality of our traditional religions and cultures can provide the inspiration for a free and just form of community organization and national development.[35]

Today, most African theologians believe that they have a role to play in the attainment of human rights and economic justice in Africa and beyond. They believe that it is non-Christian to ignore political and economic injustices that are being perpetrated against Africans. In addition, they also state that one of their responsibilities deals with liberating Africans from cultural captivity. Most African theologians view their role in liberation as being international:

> Because oppression is found not only in culture but also in political and economic structures and the dominant mass media, African theology must also be *liberation* theology. The focus on liberation in African theology connects it with other Third World theologies. Like black theologians in North America, we cannot ignore racism as a distortion of the human person. Like Latin American and Asian theologians, we see the need to be liberated from socioeconomic exploitation. A related but different form of oppression is often found in the roles set aside for women in the churches. There is the oppression of Africans by white colonialism, but there is also the oppression of blacks by blacks. We stand against oppression in any form because the Gospel of Jesus Christ demands our participation in the

struggle to free people from all forms of dehumanization. African theology concerns itself with bringing about the solidarity of Africans with black Americans, Asians, and Latin Americans who are also struggling for the realization of human communities in which the men and women of our time become the architects of their own destiny.[36]

Religion has now permeated the foundations of all African political systems. Christians who are heads of states and governments control political power in the Ivory Coast, Senegal, Liberia, Sierra-Leone, Ghana, Togo, Benin, Gabon, Zaire, Angola, Zambia, Zimbabwe, Botswana, Lesotho, Mozambique, Tanzania, Burundi, Rwanda, Uganda, Kenya, Malawi, Mauritius, and the Seychelles. Muslims who are heads of state are also in *de facto* and *de jure* control in Morocco, Tunisia, Libya, Egypt, Somalia, Chad, Sudan, Algeria, Mauritania, Nigeria, Mali, Djibouti, the Gambia, and the Arab Democratic Republic of the Sahara.

Summary

The impact of religion is felt on all aspects of contemporary African political systems. African traditional religions, Christianity, and Islam are also involved in liberational and spiritual roles that have increased the awareness and participation of the citizenry in issues of national interest.

In addition to evangelization, religious leaders turn to problems of economic development, food production, national integration, human rights violations, and national self-determination in South Africa, Namibia, and the Arab Democratic Republic of the Sahara. The help solve these problems, African religious leaders and theologians have adopted liberation theology. Liberation is based on three assumptions which shape economic, political and social realities in Africa: (1) that the majority of Africans live in a state of underdevelopment and dependence; (2) that this condition is "sinful" and unacceptable; hence, (3) it is the duty of people of conscience, and of the churches in their pastoral activities, to commit themselves to the amelioration of this state of affairs.

Although the churches and mosques usually work cooperatively with African governments, differences have often arisen over conflicting religious and political views. For example, in Zambia, Malawi, Ghana, Ethiopia, Egypt, Nigeria, Algeria, South Africa, Guinea (Conakry), and Sudan, religious leaders have been arrested on several occasions when their activities were in conflict with the dominant national ideology. Conflict has also arisen over the question of what control, if any, the government should exercise over religious schools and hospitals.

In general, there is agreement and cooperation between the churches/mosques and African governments on African social, economic, and political interests. African religious leaders and theologians are calling for an end to European and North American economic exploitation of Africa, Western support for apartheid in South Africa, and racism against and segregation of Africans throughout Western Europe and North America. Religious leaders and theologians, along with African politicians, call on Western European countries and Japan to adopt the declaration on the New International Economic Order, and to support an immediate end to apartheid and the attainment of African majority rule in South Africa and Namibia.

NOTES

1. The Final Communique, Pan-African Conference of Third World Theologians, Ghana Institute of Management and Public Administration. Green Hill, Accra, Ghana (December 17–23, 1977), p. 1 (mimeographed).
2. Luke Fashole, Richard Gray, Adrian Hastings and Godwin Tasie, eds., *Christianity in Independent Africa* (Bloomington: University of Indiana Press, 1978), p. 364.
3. Rosino Gibellini, ed., *Frontiers of Theology* (Maryknoll, New York: Orbis Books, 1979), p. 19.
4. *Ibid.,* p. 22.
5. Gibellini, *Frontiers,* p. 22.
6. Petros Mwaki, *Liberation Theology* (Ibadan: Omu Press, 1982), p. 50.
7. Theology is an *actus secundus,* a second step of critical reflection which follows after the praxis of faith. This view of theology was one of the first insights glimpsed by liberation theology. See G. Gutierrez, *La pastoral en la Iglesia latinoamericana, analisis teologico* (Montevidea: MIEC-JECI, 1968), idem, "Notes on a Theology of Liberation;" *idem, A Theology of Liberation,* p. 11.
8. Petros Mwaki, *Liberation Theology* (Ibadan: Omu Press, 1982), p. 62.
9. *Ibid.,* p. 129.
10. *Ibid.,* p. 23.

11. Bishop Desmond Tutu, "The Theology of Liberation in Africa," in *African Theology Enroute* ed. Kofi Appiah-Kubi and Sergio Torres (Maryknoll, New York: Orbis Books, 1979), p. 163.
12. *Ibid.*
13. *Ibid.*, p. 164.
14. Allan Boesak, "Liberation Theology in South Africa," in *African Theology Enroute* ed. Kofi Appiah-Kubi and Sergio Torres (Maryknoll, New York: Orbis Books, 1979), p. 166.
15. Ali A. Mazrui, *World Culture and the Black Experience* (Seattle and London: University of Washington Press, 1974), p. 11.
16. *Ibid.* Also refer to David Hume, "Of National Character," in the *Philosophical Works of David Hume,* 4 vol. (London, 1938), 3.252.
17. Philip Curtin, *The Image of Africa: British Ideas and Action, 1780–1850* (London: Macmillan Press, 1965), p. 41.
18. Fenner Brockway, *The Colonial Revolution* (London: Hart-Davis, MacGibbon, 1973), pp. 155–156.
19. Kwame Nkrumah, *Neocolonialism: The Last Stage of Imperialism* (New York: International Publishers Company, 1965), p. ix.
20. Osvaldo Sunkel and Pedro Paz, *El subdesarrollo Latinoamericano y lateoria del desarrollo* (Mexico City, 1970), p. 6.
21. Theotonio dos Santos, *La crisis del desarrollo y las relaciones de dependencia en America Latina* (Mexico City, 1970), p. 180. See also his *Dependencia y cambio social* (Santiago, 1970) and *Socialismo o Fascismo: el nuevo caracter de la dependencia y el dilema latinoamericano* (Buenos Aires, 1972).
22. Sunkel and Paz, *El subdesarrollo Latinoamericano,* p. 39.
23. Kodwo E. Ankrah, "Church and Politics in Africa," in *African Theology Enroute* ed. Kofi Appiah-Kubi and Sergio Torres (Maryknoll, New York: Orbis Books, 1979), p. 157.
24. *Ibid.*, p. 158.
25. *Ghana Seven Year Plan for National Reconstruction,* 1963/1964–1969/1970, Ghana Government, Accra. Office of the Planning Commission, p. v.
26. Sergio Torres and Virginia Fabella, M. M., eds., *The Emergent Gospel: Theology from the Underside of History* (Maryknoll, New York: Orbis Books, 1977), p. 270.
27. Kofi Appiah-Kubi and Sergio Torres, *African Theology Enroute* (Maryknoll, New York: Orbis Books, 1979), p. 4.
28. *Ibid.*
29. Helmut Gollwitzer, "Why Black Theology," *Union Seminary Quarterly Review,* No. 31 (Fall 1975), p. 41.
30. *Final Communique of the Pan-African Conference of Third World Theologians* held at the Ghana Institute of Management and Public Administration (G.I.M.P.A.), Green Hill, Accra, Ghana (December 17 to 23, 1977), p. 2.
31. Kwame Nkrumah, *Consciencism* (London: Heinemann, 1964), p. 8.

32. *Ibid.*, p. 70.
33. *Ibid.*
34. *Ibid.*
35. Final Communique: Pan-African Conference of Third World Theologians held at the Ghana Institute of Management and Public Administration (G.I.M.P.A.), Greenhill, Accra, Ghana (December 17 to 23, 1977).
36. David A. Gweshe, "African Theologians and the Quest for National Liberation," *Religious Insight*, 1:7 (July 1979).

10

Religion as Legitimator and Liberator: A Worm's Eye View of Religion and Contemporary Politics

WILLIAM R. JONES

I propose to examine the role, status, and value of religion in contemporary politics from the vantage point of those labeled variously as the oppressed, the wretched of the earth,[1] the underclass.[2] These are the groups that occupy the lowest rung of the *economic, social and political* (abbreviated as esp) ladder; these are the groups that view the parade of history from that place where the "trickle down" reaches its final destination; this is the population whose economic, social and political situation restricts it to what could be termed a "worm's eye" view of reality.

The proverbial bird's eye view is familiar to all and requires no elucidation. It is necessary, however, to explain why a worm has been chosen to symbolize the underclass and unpack some of the important nuances associated with the contrasting images of the worm and the bird.

A worm's eye view rivets our attention on the important differences between the esp perceptions, goals, and strategies of the upper and the underclass and, in a more general vein, examines the linkage between one's esp *context* and the *content* of her/his politics and moral code.

Based on this understanding, there is a singular reason why the worm is the preferred symbol for the oppressed, rather than the snake or some other creature that views reality from the ground up instead of from the sky down.

The worm symbolizes the essence of defenselessness against a more powerful, wide-ranging and far-seeing predator. Looking at the issue in terms of esp categories, the enormous armaments of the bird, its beak, superior size and speed all represent the death-dealing surplus of power and spacious access to life-enhancing resources of the elite in the society—objective advantages that equip it for its role as exploiter of the oppressed. From the vantage point of the worm and its gross deficit of power and resources, it appears, sadly, that not only the early bird gets the worm, but the late bird as well. Only in death, when the body returns to the earth from whence it came, does the worm have its day in the sun. Further, the oppressed are also aware of the time-honored legitimation for the gross inequalities of power and privilege that characterize the respective statuses of the elites and the masses; these inequalities are justified by invoking the heavens, the abode of the creator and ruler of the universe, and, not accidently—as the worm interprets it—the playground of the bird.

If one looks at the religious factor in public policymaking from a worm's eye perspective, we are forced to examine the phenomenon called *liberation theology,* the most recent and self-conscious effort by the oppressed to wed religion and politics. A product of the Third—but what Hoyt Fuller contends should be called the First[3]—World, liberation theology seeks to articulate the world view of the oppressed and to advance its esp agenda. We have already witnessed its critical impact in Latin America, and within our own borders, it is a generating force in black, feminist and native American esp movements.

Using primarily the Afro-American expression of liberation theology, I want to analyze its religio-political motifs in a manner that will decipher its inner logic and yield something akin to a background briefing of a movement that policymakers and reporters are bound to encounter in their day-to-day operations. In this way, I hope to illuminate some of the hidden corners about which effective policymakers and judicious statepersons must be aware—if they are to avoid being boxed into them. A further concern in all of this is to highlight the impact that liberation theology is likely to have on current efforts to forge the esp consensus that many see as the *sine qua non* for a viable community. I conclude that the influence of liberation theology, in the long run, is fundamentally salutary; its spirit and ideals are similar to the espoused goals of the revolution that spawned our own nation, the last "great hope" of humankind. In the short run, however, liberation theology will exacerbate the difficulties of establishing a common accord on fundamental matters of esp principle and practice, but these difficulties must be seen as part of the deconstruction that is necessary for reconstructing a more just and humane society.

Religion and Politics: the Not So Odd Couple

The first insight from liberation theology to be considered is also part of the rationale for this joint effort. Implicit in our topic is the belief that religion is an influential, if not indispensable personage in the drama of politics—past, present and future. Sometimes as actor, frequently as agent, on other occasions as producer, repeatedly as director, and habitually as playwright, the impact of religion on politics is unobscure. Whether on center stage as star performer, or off-stage in the wings, religion's involvement in politics is such that any understanding of the esp realm that omits the religious factor can only be regarded as "sound and fury, signifying nothing."

Having said this, let me hasten to add another dimension that is not readily apparent from the title of our effort. Though the title accents the impact of religion on the political arena, liberation theology affirms a dialectical relation between these ongoing expressions of human culture. Politics, directly and indirectly, molds religion and vice versa.

Liberation theology is a most attractive model to illustrate the interplay of religion and politics, the central theme of this volume. Its unique value lies in the fact that it explicitly fuses the religious and the esp spheres of action, all the while goading its opponents and critics to acknowledge the same linkage in their systems. This point can best be clarified by examining an article from *The Plain Truth:* "Humanity Won't End in a Nuclear Holocaust." In response to the suspicion of Dr. Helen Caldicott, President of Physicians for Social Responsibility, that nuclear warfare might annihilate humanity, an editorial writer for *The Plain Truth* counters: "God will intervene and forcibly stop man at the last possible moment from destroying himself. The Bible reveals [it is further argued] that man will use nuclear weapons before God steps in to save man from total nuclear destruction."[4]

Let us reflect, for a moment, on the implications of this opinion for the policymaker. Given this scenario, it appears that: (1) limited nuclear warfare is inevitable; thus efforts, such as the nuclear freeze movement, are doomed to failure. (2) The plot that pictures human annihilation as the by-product of nuclear warfare is blatantly inaccurate. (3) Ontologically speaking, there exists a cosmic lifeguard who will negate those human actions and choices that, in a different universe, would lead to self-destruction. (4) Should we add, finally, that advocates of a nuclear freeze are ultimately opposing the Lord of the universe?

Since this illustration may foster a misunderstanding of my intent, let me clarify my purpose. My concern is not to castigate *The Plain Truth*'s position; nor is it to ridicule esp policies where sacred texts and divine revelation constitute spiritual Ouija boards for clues to the future of the human race and policies to direct us from here to there. I continue to harbor the gravest reservations about these approaches to public policymaking—primarily because they hide the actual authority that is invoked, an authority that is more subjective than is suggested by appeals to the word of God[5] and sacred texts. But I am not concerned here to advance these criticisms. Instead, my purpose is to illuminate some of the unstated messages that this article conveys about the interplay of religion and politics that policymakers too often ignore.

It has not gone unnoticed that esp policies inevitably point back to what Alvin Gouldner terms "background assumptions," that is, a logically prior level of *faith* affirmations about human nature, the nature and working of the universe, and wo/man's place and power within it, etc. Matters that appear to be solely political or economic in nature and thereby assumed to deal purely with practical matters are in fact linked to deeper religious, moral and philosophical affirmations of faith that are informed by very specific understandings about the nature and destiny of the human species. It is this unconscious world view, this hidden and usually unconfessed metaphysics that structures our consciousness about life and colors, in turn, our policy values and decisions. I would also emphasize that this unconscious world view is involved in the most prosaic esp decisions, and it is present regardless of which position one adopts on a given issue.

Several corollaries follow from this understanding. (1) We are forced to admit that esp policies are not ends in themselves; they are blueprints to erect the good society, to establish the common good and *summum bonum* for humanity. (2) When individuals and groups disagree on policy matters, the root of the conflict is usually this level of background assumptions. (3) We determine the merit of esp policies and their outcome by judging the accuracy and adequacy of their metaphysical/religious underpinnings. The method of liberation theology relocates the esp debate at this level of background assumptions.

However, this level of background assumptions is seldom identified as a religious dimension of the debate, and this can be traced primarily to the tendency to operate on a dictionary definition of religion that reduces it to theism. Once this understanding of religion is accepted as the norm, cognitive and value systems that do not explicitly advance a belief in or worship of the Transcendent would not warrant the label, "religious." A different approach that interprets religion in terms of its function would provide a more accurate description of the phenomenon as well as a more adequate basis for decision making. From the functional understanding of religion, whatever is advanced as ultimate for human well-being—be it a political system, such as communism or capitalism, a specific lifestyle, e.g., vegetarianism, jogging; a philosophical perspective, e.g., humanism or atheism—must be interpreted as religious. Given this understanding, the method of liberation theology recommends that we scrutinize the manifestations of oppression—be they sexism, racism, ageism, anti-semitism or classism—as the expression of a religious concern.

What is at stake here for the practitioners of public decisionmaking should be illuminated. From a worm's eye perspective, this level of thought and commitment should be made visible for each citizen's inspection and assessment. Further, though the policymaker may aspire to be a neutral participant with regard to the religious question, the concrete decisions that she or he makes—especially in the normal state of affairs where competing commitments are at stake—means that she or he is inadvertently enhancing or undermining a particular religious perspective.

The Context and Purpose of Liberation Theology

Liberation theology highlights two radically different linkages between the religious and the political order, between the pulpit and the parliament. Religion as *legitimator* and religion as *liberator* will designate these disparate roles of religion for our discussion.[6] If one accents the legitimator role of religion, religion functions as the unflinching bulwark for the existing social order. Religion, within this framework, operates as the sacred foundation and sanctifier for the status quo. By contrast, when religion assumes the role of liberator, it is committed to modifying radically the prevailing esp configurations. Accordingly, it is subversive relative to the present social order.

To clarify these contrasting functions of religion and their respective impact upon the political realm, it is necessary to comprehend (1) the context of liberation theology, (2) its purpose, and (3) its understanding of oppression.

Liberation theology surfaces both as a diagnosis of and prescription for a context of gross esp inequalities that endure from generation to generation. Robert McAfee Brown has accurately pictured this context as a world where:

> Twenty percent of the people control eighty percent of the world's resources, where two-thirds of the human family goes to bed hungry every night, in which the economic disparities between the rich nations and the poor nations are mammoth, in which there is a clear and ugly equation that goes: rich = white; poor = non-white. . . . There is a further equation that goes: affluent white nations = northern hemisphere, poor non-white nations = southern hemisphere. . . . The context is a history in which the powerful rich minority has been increasing its power and riches . . . and a history in which, with very few exceptions, the church has been on the side of power and wealth.[7]

With this understanding of the context of liberation theology as background, its purpose and method can now be delineated. Speaking politically, the *raison d'être* of liberation theology, whatever its geographical location may be, is to ameliorate these gross inequalities and imbalances; in sum, to eradicate esp oppression. Its primary purpose, speaking religiously, is to demonstrate that putting an end to oppression is a moral, spiritual, Christian and biblical imperative. What this means both for the political and religious spheres becomes clearer once we understand the inner logic and operation of the oppression that liberation theology is committed to overthrow, as well as its battle plan.

Liberation theology adopts a virus-vaccine—or more precisely, a toxin-anti-toxin—strategy to abolish oppression. The toxin-anti-toxin strategy is a two phase model. In Phase One, attention is focused on isolating the infectious agent and acquiring as much knowledge as we can about its biological composition and processes. The objective in Phase Two is to develop a specific antibody or anti-toxin that can neutralize or destroy the noxious agent. Obviously, if our findings in Phase One are inaccurate, Phase Two will be a hit-and-miss operation. Translated into the categories of our discussion, oppression is the toxin for which liberation theology is formulated as the effective anti-toxin. Accordingly, it is particularly important to decipher the inner logic and operation of oppression to comprehend the content of liberation theology and its strategies of social change.

The Anatomy of ESP Oppression

For our purposes, oppression can be reduced, structurally, to the following features:

1. As a form of esp exploitation, oppression is most accurately interpreted as a pervasive institutional system designed to maintain a specific group at the top of the esp ladder, with the *accoutrement* of power, privileges and access to the society's resources that this status provides.
2. Oppression can be analyzed from two distinct perspectives, both of which are critical for the inner logic of liberation theology. On the one hand, an institutional analysis is indispensable; this reduces to an investigation of its esp structures. On the other hand, one can examine oppression in terms of the belief system that is its anchoring principle. Liberation theology develops a specific anti-toxin for each of these facets of oppression.
3. Oppression comprises both objective and subjective elements. Its objective components can be condensed to pervasive esp inequalities. But there is nothing that forces one, automatically and as a matter of course, to appraise these inequalities as negative, as something to be eradicated. Precisely because of this ongoing possibility of opposed evaluations of inequalities in power and privilege, liberation theology differentiates between the pre-enlightened and post-enlightened oppressed. The latter interprets the objective situation of inequality as negative and hostile to her/his highest good, whereas the former does not. The crucial difference between these two groups is not traceable, as most people believe, to a marked difference in the objective conditions of their oppression; namely that the post-enlightened oppressed encounter the more severe oppression. Rather, the difference lies in the subjective realm, with the dissimilar belief and value grid used by each to grade these objective inequalities. We will have more to say about this below;

suffice it to say at this point that if power is assigned a negative value, as detrimental for one's highest good, then most assuredly, the person with a deficit of power would believe that s/he is already in the preferred esp situation. Likewise, if the ascetic life is elevated to ultimacy, those with a paucity of material goods and societal privileges would hardly interpret this lack as something that requires correction.

4. Oppression affirms a two-category system; it divides the human family into at least two distinct groups.
5. These groups are arranged in a hierarchy of superiors and inferiors, e.g., in-group, out-group; rich, poor; master, slave; male, female; black, white, etc.
6. This hierarchical arrangement is correlated with a gross imbalance of power, resources and privileges. The alleged superior group possesses the unobscure surplus and the alleged inferior group, the grossly disproportionate deficit.
7. The alleged superior group will also have the *most* of whatever the society defines as the *best* and the *least* of the *worst.* In stark contrast, the alleged inferior group will have the *least* of the *best* and the *most* of the *worst.*
8. This hierarchical division and the esp inequalities it expresses are institutionalized. The primary institutions are constructed to maintain an unequal distribution of power, resources, and privileges; this is their inner design and their actual product.
9. The last two components of oppression to be discussed demand special attention, for they bring us to the heart of our discussion: the religio-political connection. The *two category system, hierarchically arranged, the gross imbalance of power/privilege, and the institutional expression of these are all alleged to be grounded in ultimate reality—nature or supernature (god).* The point to be emphasized here is the controlling role of religion to legitimate both the objective and subjective elements of oppression, and especially, the institutional framework of esp oppression. This means ultimately, as the next section will show, that, from a worm's eye perspective, the role of religion as legitimator must be called into question in order for religion to function as liberator.

10. The oppressed are oppressed, in fundamental part, because of the beliefs, values and attitudes they hold. They adopt, or more accurately, are indoctrinated and socialized to accept a belief and value system that motivates them to conform to the social order, embrace its esp inequalities as good or inevitable, thus stifling their desire to attack the foundation of these disparities in privileges and power. Put in other words, the oppressor must persuade the oppressed to act in a way that preserves and conserves what is already present, to refuse to take corrective action where basic cultural patterns and institutional structures are involved. In sum, the inner logic of oppression requires an attitude of *quietism* and a philosophy of *anti-powerism for the oppressed.*

Oppression and Quietism

How is this accomplished? An early review of *The Autobiography of Jane Eyre* gives us the recipe for generating quietism.

> Altogether *Jane Eyre* . . . is preeminently an anti-Christian proposition. There is throughout it a murmuring against the comforts of the rich and against the privations of the poor, which as far as each individual is concerned is a murmuring against God's appointment.[8]

This review reveals that oppression maintains itself by claiming that its fundamental structures and values are the product of and in conformity with the structures of reality itself, and it is here that the role of religion as legitimator becomes visible. By invoking the supernatural/divine order—one could as well appeal to the natural order—as the foundation for the institutions of oppression, we accomplish several things essential to its maintenance. We immediately establish a suprahuman foundation that, by virtue of its alleged ultimacy and power, compels our acceptance, obedience—in short, our conformity. If it is believed that the social and political order expresses God's will and purpose, corrective action to alter the configurations of power and privilege is unthinkable. Human power could never hope to win against God's omnipotence; "our arms too short to box with God."

But even if we have the power to change our esp position, corrective action would still be inappropriate. Whatever status we have is the status that God intends for us to have; what is, is what ought to be. A similar conclusion would follow from the belief that esp inequalities are the consequence of divine punishment.

Peter Berger has accurately isolated a general and historical function of religion that is picked up by liberation theology.

> The historically crucial part of religion in the process of legitimation is explicable in terms of the unique capacity of religion to "locate" human phenomenon within a cosmic frame of reference. . . . If one imagines oneself as a fully aware founder of a society . . . how can the future of the institutional order be so interpreted as to hide, as much as possible, its constructed character. Let the people forget that this order was established by men and continues to be dependent upon the consent of men. . . . Let them believe that, in acting out the institutional programs that have been imposed upon them, they are but realizing the deepest aspirations of their own being and putting themselves in harmony with the fundamental order of the universe. In sum, set up religious legitimations.[9]

Given this understanding, it should be clear why liberation theology must challenge the role of religion as legitimator to execute its assigned task of religion as liberator.

The claim that core beliefs and values of the religious tradition are essential props for oppression has been and continues to be a principal feature of the Afro-American variety of liberation theology. Benjamin Mays' criticism of "the compensatory ideas" in Afro-American Christianity is a classic statement of liberation theology's position.

> The Negro's social philosophy and his idea of God go hand in hand. [Certain theological ideas] enable Negroes to endure hardship, suffer pain, and withstand maladjustment, but . . . do not necessarily motivate them to strive to eliminate the source of the evils they suffer.
>
> Since this world is considered a place of temporary abode, many of the Negro masses have been inclined to do little or nothing to improve their status here; they have been encouraged to rely on a *just* God to make amends in Heaven for all the wrongs they have suffered on earth. In reality, the idea has persisted that hard times are indicative of the fact that the Negro is God's chosen vessel and that God is disciplining him for the express purpose of bringing him out victoriously and triumphantly in the end. The idea has also persisted that "the harder the cross, the brighter the crown." Believing this about God, the Negro . . . has stood back and suffered much without bitterness, without striking back, and without trying aggressively to realize to the full his needs in the world.[10]

Because the liberation theologian is committed to exterminate esp oppression, s/he must follow certain guidelines for theological construction. Those tyrannical beliefs and attitudes, such as quietism, that smother the impulse toward liberation must be systematically isolated and neutralized. This requires a "rotten apple in the basket" approach in the sense that nothing, at the outset, can be assumed to be non-oppressive. Once the virus of oppression is detected, the entire tradition must be quarantined and each part forced to certify that its oppressive features have been immunized.

It is instructive to consider another area of religion where liberation theology has applied the "rotten apple in the basket" method and uncovered other uses of religion to legitimate esp oppression. What was uncovered can best be illustrated by comparing the liturgical calendars of Judaism and Afro-American Christianity.

The most cursory examination of the Jewish liturgy reveals a dimension that is curiously absent from the Afro-American liturgy: the religious celebration of esp liberation. (This absence, however, is not baffling if one understands the mechanism of oppression.) One is struck by the way the Jewish calendar revolves around events that commemorate their release from bondage, the defeat of despots practicing cultural genocide, etc. Passover, Purim and Hanukkah immediately come to mind. Nor is the theme of esp liberation absent from the rest of the liturgical calendar. Many interpreters, for instance, extract this theme as well from the Sabbath observance.

With this picture of the liturgical content of one oppressed minority as a guide, turn to the liturgical calendar of the Black church and identify comparable celebrations of esp liberation. You will search in vain; there are none! Nor has the Black church paid tribute to its own heroes and heroines as other ethnic communities have done, e.g., St. Patrick's Day. Where is the liturgical celebration of Malcolm X, Soujourner Truth, or Nat Turner? Nor is the tribute paid to Martin Luther King, Jr., an honor given only to a handful in our national pantheon, an exception to this observation. The celebration of this Black hero did not begin as a liturgical event in the Black church that subsequently moved outside its sanctuary. Nor should it be overlooked that the radical wing of Black thought and action, e.g., Nat Turner, is still unhonored in the Black church.

Oppression and Anti-Powerism

Religion, according to liberation theology, has been invoked in another substantial way to instill an attitude of conformity in the underclass. Part of the mechanism of oppression is to motivate the oppressed to adopt a philosophy of anti-powerism, whereas the oppressor lives by the opposite philosophy of powerism. The consequence of all of this is to keep the gross imbalance of power, privilege and resources intact in the oppressor's favor. Let us clarify the distinction between these antithetical philosophies.

Anti-powerism and powerism represent contrasting beliefs and attitudes about the role, status, and value of power in human affairs. Anti-powerism regards power as essentially negative or evil. The essence of this position is best expressed in Jacob Burkhardt's description: "Now power in its very nature is evil; no matter who wields it. It is not stability but lust, and *ipso facto* insatiable. Therefore, it is unhappy in itself and doomed to make others unhappy."[11]

Based on this view, anti-powerism regards ethics and power as incompatible. In addition, those who advocate anti-powerism conclude that we have a moral situation only when we push power outside or to the periphery of the ethical domain. Making power central, according to this view, leads to ethical nihilism, for it means affirming the principle, might makes right. In sum, anti-powerism would even see the quest for coequal power not in neutral, but negative terms.

By contrast, the position of powerism affirms power as a central and indispensable religious category. Power becomes a controlling concept for interpreting not only the basic categories of religion, but morality as well. Advocates of this position ultimately advance power as the preeminent interpretive framework for all aspects of human affairs as well as the natural and supernatural order. Power, from this perspective, is neutral, neither inherently evil nor good; its quality depends upon who wields it and for what purpose.

Disciples of powerism would consider the following an appropriate description. "In any encounter of man with man, power is active; every encounter, whether friendly or hostile, whether benevolent or indifferent, is in some way, a struggle of power with power."[12] Or the equally comprehensive scope of power that is affirmed by Romano Guardini. "Every act, every condition, indeed, even the simple fact of existing is directly or indirectly linked to the conscious exercise of power."

Since the critical variable in oppression is a gross imbalance of power, the underclass can be kept "in its place" to the degree that it adopts the inner logic of anti-powerism. If anti-powerism is right in its characterization of power, then the oppressed, "in their place," are, indeed, in the *best* place. To persuade the oppressed to move from a situation of a gross inequality to coequality of power they must subjectively define a deficit of power as negative and detrimental to one's well-being. Obviously, this mentality will not surface if anti-powerism is the operative philosophy.

Black liberation theologians detect the abundant scent of anti-powerism in familiar corners of the Afro-American sanctuary. It is seen in the white elevation of those black heroes who advocate anti-powerism over those in the camp of powerism: Martin Luther King, Jr. over Malcolm X; George Forman over the black athletes who gave the "black power" sign at the Olympics; and perhaps the most familiar case, Booker T. Washington over W. E. B. DuBois. Washington's statement still remains a classical description of anti-powerism.

> The opportunity to exercise free political rights will not come to the black in any large degree through outside or artificial forcing, but will be given to the Negro by the Southern white people themselves, and they will protect the Negro in the exercise of these rights.[13]

Anti-powerism also seems to be a prominent ingredient in those theological maneuvers that accent the model of Jesus as the suffering servant, that advance a "turn the other cheek" and a "pie-in-the-sky" mentality as preeminent patterns for black social ethics. Indeed, if one recognizes that suffering, in the final analysis, is reducible to an inequality of power, and that accordingly, oppression must be viewed as a variety of negative suffering, then any theological affirmation that makes suffering neutral, or even worse, an essential ingredient of human salvation, undergirds, at the same time, the belief system for esp exploitation.

Based on this interpretation of religion as legitimator of anti–powerism, liberation theologians have joined hands to rehabilitate the category of power. The following citation is representative of this development.

> To become what one must demands the presence, the building up of power. All men need the power to become. Indeed, the Greek word for power *(bia)* and life *(bios)* reflect the essential interrelationship of power and life. Power is basic to life. Without power, life cannot become what it must be.
>
> In religious terms, a God of power, of majesty and might, who has made man to be in His own image and likeness, must will that His creation reflect in the immediacy of life His power, His majesty and His might. . . .

The earliest Christian creed addressed itself to the issue of power. It simply spoke of Jesus as Lord. In the cultural context [this] was an affirmation and commitment of Jesus as the divine embodiment and expression of power. Power as God's breath was infused into the life of man. . . . All that God's power touches is said to be sacred. To be sacred means to reflect the power . . . of God.[14]

Liberation Theology and the Logic of Ethnicity

In recent years the concept of an ethnic approach to a discipline has evolved. This approach isolates a given cultural, racial, religious or national grouping, and accents its particular history, culture and agenda, etc., as indispensable for the content and method of the various disciplines. The *raison d'être* in all of this is to establish the ethnic community as a coequal center of authority and value. The controlling categories in this design are particularity, contextualism and cultural pluralism. Liberation theology can appropriately be interpreted as a representative of this development.

My purpose in this section is to examine the connection between the inner logic of ethnicity and that of liberation theology. Our focus will be the Afro-American variety of this movement.

From the perspective of liberation theology, the mission and function of Black religion has been expertly captured in two statements—one from W. E. B. DuBois many decades ago and the other from Lerone Bennett, Jr., the dean of Afro-American historians. DuBois argued:

> We Negroes form and long will form a perfectly definite group, not entirely segregated and isolated from our surroundings, but differentiated to such a degree that we have largely a life and thought of our own. . . . This fact in itself has its meaning, its worth and its values. . . . And it is this fact that black religion has got to take into account and make its major problem.[15]

In more recent times, Lerone Bennett, Jr. has advanced a parallel admonition:

> The overriding need for the moment is for us to think with our own eyes. We cannot see now because our eyes are clouded by the concepts of [the oppressor]. We cannot think now because we have no intellectual instruments save those which were designed expressly to keep us from seeing. It is necessary for us to develop a new frame of reference which transcends the limits of the oppressor's concepts. [The oppressor's] concepts have succeeded in making black people feel inferior. [The oppressor's] concepts

have created the conditions that make it easy to dominate a people. The initial step towards liberation is to abandon the partial frame of reference of our oppressor and to create new concepts which release our reality.[16]

Liberation theology seeks to translate the DuBois-Bennett prescription into concrete programs for the different areas of the life of the black community, especially the social, political, and cultural areas.

To reduce the misinterpretations that are usually spawned by this part of liberation theology's agenda, let us reduce the DuBois-Bennett prescription to a set of propositions. These will summarize the understanding of religion and theology that liberation theology affirms.

An ethnic approach to theology is both legitimate and necessary because all theologies are particular. We can agree that the intent of theology is universal, i.e., to provide a description of reality that is not simply the idiosyncratic viewpoint of the theologian or her/his community. Yet the basic particularity of theology cannot be ignored.

A simple illustration of this point should be persuasive. If I send you on a scavenger hunt and ask you to bring back F-L-O-W-E-R, you will fail. You can bring me back the word, "flower," but any flower you bring back will be a concrete flower—a rose, a dandelion, an orchid, etc. Likewise with theology, you will discover only particular theologies—Jewish, Christian, American, the theology of X, a theology that enhances oppression, a theology that enhances liberation, etc. It would appear that the only way to escape this conclusion is to endorse the exaggerated realism of the *universale ante rem* position, a position, that, one might add, is not the trademark of opponents of particularity.

Liberation theology insists that to accent particularity in this fashion does not reduce theology to "blackology" or some equally problematic ideology. Nor does it demand the claim that theology does no more than mirror the subjective view of a particular interest group at a specific historical juncture. Rather, it is to affirm commonly warranted principles such as the following: every affirmation is also a negation; each concrete expression of a cultural reality posits specific questions and answers and therby effectively excludes the opposite answers; no single tradition has demonstrated that it exhausts the totality of human knowledge. Finally, it is to demand from those who question the preeminence of particularity that they present to us the alleged universal that does not require supplementation or modification in light of opposing points of view.

Several principles follow from the particularity of theology that we must now examine in sequence. The category of particularity leads to the affirmation of authentic pluralism. Because of the confusion that clouds this term, let us examine its inner meaning and logic by comparing and contrasting it with other models of ethnic relations, assimilation and integration. An anecdote from Moms Mabley provides the key for differentiating between these three models of social interaction. In her inimitable fashion, Moms describes a scene in a lunchroom in Mississippi that had just been desegregated. An elderly black lady sat down at a convenient table and asked to see the menu. After scanning it from cover to cover, she asked the waitress: "Do you have chitterlings?" The waitress responded, "No." The elderly black lady asked: "Do you have collard greens?" Again the response was "no." She inquired about several other items that are staples on any "soul food" menu, but every time the response was "no." Finally, the elderly black lady said indignantly: "You ain't ready for integration."

What she was saying was that the restaurant, at least at the menu level, was still operating on an assimilationist model. That is, a one-category model or a single theme is advanced as the norm or the ideal and everything else is forced to conform to it. It will become clear that, in contrast to both integration and pluralism, assimilation establishes a hierarchy of superior and inferior.

By contrast, integration is a two-category model. At least two things are regarded as coequal and cosignificant; neither is superior to the other. Accordingly, both must be included to obtain the ideal situation. Beyond the affirmation of the coequality of its constituent elements, integration, however, adds another dimension: it blends or combines the coequal items such that the product is different from the individual characteristics of the original components.

Cultural pluralism differs from both assimilation and integration. Like integration, it affirms a multi-category model, and at least two things are regarded as coequal and cosignificant. But here the similarity ends. Rather than blending the items as integration does, pluralism asserts that each should retain its distinctive character, its individuality, its uniqueness. The end result of pluralism—if we use a culinary metaphor—is a cultural smorgasbord.

If these distinctions are accurate, then we must say that liberation theology is committed to cultural pluralism at this phase of its evolution. Its inner logic does not eliminate the integrationist model, but it does insist that the merger of black and non-black perspectives can authentically occur only after the black perspective has been appropriately articulated. In sum, the comprehensive articulation of cultural perspectives that the logic of pluralism dictates must precede the merger phase, that is, integration.

Given this understanding, the failure of a particular community to express and advance its own cultural perspective is, in fact, a form of self-dehumanization. Blacks mastermind their own cultural genocide if they fail to demand coequal authority for their vision of reality. They say, in effect, that it is not necessary for them "to do their thing" because the existing theologies have already captured the quintessence of truth and any Black input is now redundant.

To address other misunderstandings about the heightened ethnicity associated with liberation theology, we must make it clear that cultural pluralism is not an argument for black racism, nor is it a call for racial separatism. What cultural pluralism affirms has been appropriately expressed, for instance, by Michael Novak and Oscar Wilde. Novak perceptively argues: "To be faithful to our own personal vision is not to deny the truth in others' vision."[17]

In a similar vein, Oscar Wilde expresses the precise difference between authentic pluralism and a despotic, assimilationist doctrine. "A red rose," he insists, "is not selfish because it wants to be a red rose. But it would be horribly selfish if it wanted all other flowers in the garden to be red and roses." In summary, cultural pluralism is an attempt to establish the coequality of different cultural perspectives—not the superiority of a single one. Given this sense, it is a threat only to those who seek to maintain a social pattern that is already riddled with esp inequalities, all the while preaching a unity and harmony that requires the enforcement of a single and particular cultural perspective that has yet to document its superiority.

Implications for Politics and Policymaking

We have attempted to describe the inner logic of liberation theology and identify its major motifs. These descriptions will now be used to hypothesize about its destiny and its impact upon the politics of the future.

There is a growing concern of which Alfred de Grazia's perception is representative: namely, that we have reached a crisis in terms of community integration.

> The modern age . . . requires a host of new techniques and beliefs if it is to achieve the necessary minimum of integration. Often its subgroups are so unrelated, separate, and mutually hostile that politics operate solely by means of contemporary compromises, expedients and stopgaps, while group conflicts are emphasized and total community sentiment means little. . . . Nothing less than a wholesale transformation of individual viewpoints can . . . bring them into accord on fundamental issues. They would have to agree on matters most important to political behavior—on what constitutes legitimacy, on basic religious matters, on the extent to which individuals should be competitive or cooperative, on the use or nonuse of violence and propaganda, on the main opportunities an individual should be allowed in his lifetime. . . . These items of agreement would form the consensus of the political community.[18]

This perception of the minimal consensus that a stable political organization requires was advanced by de Grazia more than two decades ago. It is helpful to assess the impact of liberation theology in light of this norm. It would appear that on each of the items identified here, the immediate effect of liberation theology is disruptive. The predominant theme of liberation theology is the announcement of the demise of the old authorities and the call for a radical restructuring of the social order in a manner that substantially redistributes esp power, resources and privileges. And if this were not sufficient to frustrate a developing "accord on fundamental issues," its sanction of counterviolence,[19] interpreted by its critics as the rejection of the nonuse of violence, will further sabotage the residual vestiges of potential consensus formation.

Beyond this, its accent on cultural pluralism and ethnic particularity appears to fragment the already disjointed community into even more pervasive and strident rivalries.

The greater devastation, however, will likely impact what de Grazia terms, "accord on what constitutes legitimacy." The liberationist critique of religion as legitimator produces several consequences, each of which undermines a religious foundation for political legitimacy. The liberationist dichotomy between religion as liberator and religion as legitimator is obviously a distinction between "authentic" and "inauthentic" religions. This categorization, as well, raises questions about the moral stature of religion because of its central role in oppression. This, in turn, exaggerates religion's crisis of credibility and plausibility. Moreover, liberation theology's self-identification as authentic religion forces a situation where the citizen is forced to choose, thereby snipping away religion's unique authority to legitimate social institutions by endowing them with a supra-human and ontologically grounded status. All of this is by way of saying that liberation theology substantially enlarges the secularization process and its attendant impact for political legitimation.

The destabilizing impact upon religion will affect equally the esp sphere. The social and political structures, formerly legitimated by the religious authorities now under attack, will demand a new source of legitimation. Recent developments in Latin America suggest that what was accomplished earlier by the cross and the bible now requires the cannon and the bullet, that is, legitimation based on the naked power of one's superior armaments. Have we not come full circle—back to the worm confronting the bird?

The gross inequalities that we have associated with the objective component of oppression can no longer draw upon the ample resources of an earlier religious attitude that assigned salvific merit to esp sufferings. Here, too, the conflict is likely to be enlarged.

In spite of this litany of the subversive and divisive potential of liberation theology, I am still persuaded that its impact in the long run will be salutary. I reach this conclusion because I see the inequalities that call forth the liberationist ideal as the ultimate cause of societal unrest and divisiveness. What R. H. Tawney has perceived as the consequence of economic inequality for community building is, I would suggest, the key to understanding what undermines community consensus.

> What a community requires, as the word itself suggests, is a common culture. . . . But a common culture cannot be created merely by desiring it. It must rest upon practical foundations of social organizations. . . . It involves, in short, a large measure of economic equality—not necessarily in the sense of an identical level of pecuniary incomes but of equality of environment, of access to education and the means of civilization, of security and independence, and of the social consideration which equality in these matters usually carries with it.[20]

In sum, liberation theology, I contend, has correctly identified inequality, not diversity, as the root of the problem.

I am also salutary about liberation theology's impact for social consensus, because each of its potential destructive accents can be interpreted as clearing away a Humpty Dumpty foundation in order to build a consensus on a more substantial foundation. Its debunking task and its demystification process express the necessary spirit of justified iconoclasm that keeps the human soul from unrelenting idolatry. However, the nagging question that a survey of liberation theology leaves unanswered for me is: are mystifications a necessary ingredient for a viable society? Must the light of truth be turned away from certain regions so that the community can survive intact?

Though today a still small voice, there should be little doubt that liberation theology is emerging as a prominent and inescapable ingredient in the politics of the sanctuary and the politics of the state house. Whether it is saint or sinner, savior or subversive must await the future verdict of history. But until that verdict is announced, liberation theology refuses to be ignored by those in the palaces of power; it represents too many, too long voiceless and too long powerless in the unfolding human drama.

NOTES

1. Franz Fanon, *The Wretched of the Earth* (New York: Grove Press, 1968).
2. Ken Auletta, *The Underclass* (New York: Random House, 1982).
3. Hoyt Fuller (now deceased), entitled the journal that he published on minorities, *The First World.*
4. Michael A. Snyder, "Humanity Won't End In a Nuclear Holocaust," *The Plain Truth* (August, 1982), p. 19.
5. Many have correctly observed that when we hear the word of God, it is always some human who claims to be speaking for God.
6. It would be an error to conclude that these disparate roles of religion are mutually exclusive. In point of fact, both should be regarded as subvarieties of religious legitimation. The one justifies the status quo by appealing to the transcendent, the other sanctions radical social change by invoking a different understanding of the divine will and purpose.
7. Robert McAfee Brown, *Is Faith Obsolete?* (Philadelphia: The Westminister Press, 1974), pp. 120–21.
8. M. A. Stoddard, *Quarterly Review* (December, 1848), pp. 173–74. Cited in W. K. C. Guthrie, *The Sophists* (New York: Cambridge University Press, 1971), p. 6.

9. Peter Berger, *The Sacred Canopy* (New York: Doubleday, 1967), p. 33.
10. Benjamin Mays, *The Negro's God* (New York: Antheneum, 1968), pp. 23–25.
11. Jacob Burkhardt, *Force and Freedom* (Boston: Beacon Press, 1943), p. 184.
12. Paul Tillich, *Love, Power and Justice* (New York: Oxford, 1954), p. 87.
13. Booker T. Washington, *Up from Slavery* (New York: Airmont Publishing Co., 1967), p. 133.
14. Nathan Wright, *Black Power and Urban Unrest* (New York: Hawthorn Books, 1967), p. 65.
15. W. E. B. Dubois, *The ABC of Color* (New York: International Publishers, 1969), p. 37.
16. Lerone Bennett, Jr., *Confrontation: Black and White* (Baltimore: Penguin, 1965), p. 198.
17. Michael Novak, "Exploration and Responses," *Journal of Ecumenical Studies* 10 (1973), p. 139.
18. Alfred de Grazia, *Politics and Government* (New York: Collier Books, 1962), p. 127.
19. Critics of liberation theology overlook this important qualification. The issue to be adjudicated is the legitimacy of *counter*violence, for the contention of the oppressed is that oppression was initiated by the violence of the oppressor. Moreover violence has been utilized throughout to maintain the oppressor in power. In all of this, the oppressed are the victim of the oppressor's violence. Thus, the question of questions, from a worm's eye view, is what amount of force/violence can the oppressed legitimately use against a prior violence directed against them.
20. R. H. Tawney, *Equality* (New York: Capricorn Books, 1961), pp. 31–32.

11

The Impact of the Eastern European Churches Upon Their Own Societies

PAUL MOJZES

Had Marxist forecasts, which were made at the time of the Communist revolutions or takeovers in regard to the impact of the churches or religion, been on target, one could have stated that this impact of the churches on society in the 1980s would be nil or so negligent that a paper would not need to be written. But they were wrong about the "withering away of religion," to borrow a Marxian phrase. And so, likewise wrong were those opponents of Marxism who gloomily made the same predictions when they witnessed the massive Communist onslaught upon the churches, which caused much suffering and destruction. The reality of the Eastern European religious situation is very different from what most people could have expected, and it is much more nuanced and variable than most casual observers and less careful students of the scene are capable of discerning.

Due to different historical circumstances, traditions, church polities and politics, Communist party strengths or weaknesses in application of Marxist precepts to religion and society, there is today an almost bewildering variety of ways in which the impact of the churches is being felt in the Soviet Union, Poland, East Germany, Czechoslovakia, Hungary, Romania, Yugoslavia, Bulgaria, and Albania.

The Communist revolution or takeover brought the greatest challenge to organized religion since Christianity became legally recognized under Constantine the Great, early in the fourth century. There were other great upheavals since that time, starting with the brief restoration of "paganism" under Julian, a cousin of Constantine the Great, emperor from 361–363.[1] Among them, one should mention the great and often violent rivalry between Christians and Jews, between Eastern Orthodox and Roman Catholics, and later in the 16th century between Catholics and Protestants, and the Mongol and Turkish Muslim dominations which caused incalculable upheavals in the Christian communities of Russia and the Balkans. But prior to the time of the Bolshevik revolution in 1917 and the immediate post World War II period when the rest of Eastern Europe became socialist, the religious institutions, particularly the large established churches, had a privileged status in the community and frequently exercised a dominant role in society. Among Christians, this pattern is called the Constantinian model of church-state relations, in which the privileged church supports the social arrangement which, in turn, guarantees it a favored treatment.

It is easy to oversimplify the Constantinian model and present a situation where a particular church exerts such an influence that it factually runs the society and seeks for itself a monopoly situation at the expense of other potentially rival religions. It is already discernible in this oversimplified pattern that not all churches and religious institutions found themselves in the favored, Constantinian pattern. Jews, for instance, never got into such a favored situation and were lucky occasionally to find various degrees of tolerance. The same was true of the Protestant "sectarians," i.e., the so-called "Free Churches" (e.g. Baptists, Methodists, Mennonites, Pentecostals, and Adventists) who sometimes experienced severe repressions by the established state churches. The pattern itself is not fully reliable because it is obvious that during certain historical periods the state exercised a paramount influence over the church, as for instance during the time of Peter the Great and his successors in Russia, who sought to reduce the Russian Orthodox Church to a convenient department of state and strictly controlled church activities. Without succumbing to the temptation to provide a nuanced and detailed picture, it shall suffice to say that many religious institutions enjoyed a status that granted them a great deal of power, influence, and prestige in society. In fact, the relationship between church and society tended to be so close that in many places there was a nearly total identification of ethnicity with religious affiliation. Thus Bulgarians, Romanians, Serbians, Macedonians, Montenegrins, Russians, and at times Ukrainians and White Russians were automatically Orthodox by birth: Croatians, Slovenes, Poles, and for all practical purposes the majority of the Hungarians, Czechs, and Slovaks were Roman Catholic; while East Germans were Protestants. Only in Hungary and among the Czechs and Slovaks were there also Protestants and some Orthodox who were not alienated from their ethnicity by belonging to a different religious tradition. Among Albanians, there were Orthodox, Catholic and Muslims. It is hard for a person outside the region to appreciate this extremely close identification of church with the nation, an identification which to this day plays a very significant role and accounts for a significant part of the impact that many churches still continue to have. As one of the central, persistent factors of religious influence in Eastern Europe, it must not be neglected in any analysis.

When the Communists came into power they generally attempted to implement a Leninist formula, only partially inspired by Marx, of legally separating the state and the schools from religion (the American model of separation of church and state had little influence in Eastern Europe prior to the Communist rule), allowing limited legal existence to nearly all religious communities. From the perspective of the Communist Party, religion was a reactionary reflection of former class societies which stands in the way of progress and must be combated into oblivion by all available means, subject only to avoidance of the boomerang effect, which only causes further fanaticization of religious persons. Since the Communist Party exercises, in Marxist parlance, "*the* leading role" in the state, these two theoretically different approaches coalesced in reality into a single practice of massive state intervention in religious matters seeking to restrict and ultimately abolish institutional religion. The implementation of the overarching policies oscillated, depending on the resiliency of the religious communities and the needs of the state. For instance, Stalin needed the support of the Russian Orthodox Church during the Nazi offensive, so he relaxed some pressures and gave permission for the partial rebuilding of the ecclesiastical hierarchy. Or the churches' aid might be sought in implementation of certain agricultural policies to induce the population to work harder.

The Communist Party tacitly concedes that the Church has influence among certain groups of the population where the Party's influence is small. This is done in exchange for certain privileges to the Church.

New Models for the Churches

It is understood by both the Party and the churches that the ultimate aim of the Communist Party is a society in which no organized religion will exist or exert any influence. Here, no Eastern

European Communist Party has seen fit to adopt the modifications introduced by the Italian Communist Party giving fuller recognition to the progressive impact of religious groups. This radically new position of the church has been described by Bohdan Cywinski, who coined the phrase "the Julian Church"[2] as he attempted to describe the role of the church in the fully *etatized,* secularized society. Cywinski wrote,

> the Julian is exactly the opposite to the Constantinian situation. Instead of cooperating, the secular and ecclesiastic authorities are in conflict. The Church is put in a position in which she has no option but to be in opposition. She is devoid of political power but is recognized by society as its principal moral authority. This provides her with a new source of strength . . . the Julian is not a Church which on its own volition gave up the participation in power. To the contrary, she is rancorous and bitter that she was excluded from participation in it.[3]

This Julian role is, as described by Cywinski, most distinctly applicable to the Roman Catholic Church in Poland, which among the Eastern European churches has the greatest degree of popular support in its own country. It applies to many other churches to a lesser degree.

Other Eastern European thinkers, who likewise dwelled on the obvious, i.e., the disappearance of the Constantinian model, have promoted other models for the churches. The theologians of the Church of the Czech Brethren, taking their lead from Joseph Hromádka, their leading theologian, said the church should welcome the new socialist order and become a "pilgrim church," representing the role of the crucified Christ, eschewing political power, but seeking to transform and help those who are radical transformers of exploitive and unjust class societies.

The Hungarian Protestants coined the phrases "the servant church" and "theology of service" which are consonant with the model of the Church of the Czech Brethren, stressing service to society. Many of their theologians see the demolition of the Constantinian model as a distinct blessing for the church, an opportunity to get back to the real task of the church, namely not to rule but to serve. The early apostolic church is deemed worth emulating.

The Eastern Orthodox Churches, deeply steeped in liturgical (sacramental) tradition, have embraced neither of these models. Their main concern is to continue to offer the salvific mysteries to their people with the conviction that God shall not allow the church to perish. Empires come and empires go, some friendly, some antagonistic, but the Church of Christ will last eternally. Their policy of acquiescence bothers many a Western activist, but it stems from long experience that survival demands flexibility, silence in the political arena, and a dogged determination to provide worship opportunities and preserve the canonical structures of the Church.

Still another model is being embraced by many "sectarians," those belonging to the small religious communities. Dominated by an apocalyptic theology, their perception is that this world is quickly approaching its end, and the power of evil is making its last convulsive efforts to dominate this world. Soon, however, it will be crushed forever by God's glorious victory in which all the faithful will be saved eternally, while those opposing God's reign will be damned. Their emphasis is on personal salvation with little or no interest in making public impact. Yet they often gain adherents, mostly from among the marginal segments of society, as is evident among Evangelical Baptists in the Soviet Union and Romania, because their theology presents a sharp ideological alternative to the official Marxist teaching, which leaves many people untouched.

The Attitudes of Churches Toward Socialism

The question of the model of the church activity is of intrinsic interest, but its importance is heightened by the fact that the Communist Parties made an effort to eliminate all other political, social, intellectual, economic, and even sports organizations which had independence of the Communist Party. The churches remained *de facto* the only major institution which espoused an ideology other than Marxism. It was soon perceived by the Communists that the churches might be used as an instrument of resistance against its mode of organizing society. The same insight occurred to those who wanted to show their disapproval of the established order; they would sometimes support the churches not for religious reasons, but because they wanted to express an unfavorable attitude toward the government. When one adds to this the undeniable fact that there were very few Communist sympathizers among the active church members and church leaders, it becomes evident that the churches were, from the outset, counted among those who would oppose Communist policies. This posture can be labeled "religion against socialism" or even anti-socialist religion.

That "religion against socialism" is still the prevalent form of church attitude needs no documentation. The first years of Communist takeover were especially characterized by a sometimes bitter and violent confrontation. The state resorted to repressive measures causing martyrdom and great devastation institutionally and individually.

The Marxists judged the impact of religion upon social policies as altogether negative. For them the only question was what was the most effective way of confronting the churches. Tactical approaches differed. In some instances the major church in a country was attacked so mercilessly that the smaller churches got the message that resistance was fruitless and they were cowed into silence. This was the case with the Catholic Church in Hungary and Czechoslovakia where the most bitter resistance against the new socialist society came from the side of Roman Catholics. In other instances the policy was to make an example of a smaller church to show how ruthless the attack could be, thus providing a lesson to the larger church to avoid confrontation. That was the case in Bulgaria where the state targeted its attack on the four small Protestant churches and succeeded in intimidating the Bulgarian Orthodox Church.

The second possible posture is "religion indifferent to socialism." According to this approach, the life of the church goes on without either showing active resistance or embracing the new social order. This is usually a form of accommodation which considers all social orders as temporary in nature, while the church has an abiding sense of mission and will survive this social order as it has, for instance during the Roman or Byzantine Empire, the Turkish rule, and so forth. Many Eastern Orthodox Churches have assumed this posture of tacit acquiescence coupled with the hope of divine deliverance. The church avoids any explicitly political posture, neither directly aiding nor resisting socialism. At best, some church leaders will declare from time to time that certain socialist policies are not inimical to church teachings or that they may be in accord with a long held church position, e.g., on curbing personal greed or trying to bring peace. The latter issue, i.e., working for peace, is by far the most mutually acceptable social issue on which a politically non-involved church and the state can find a common platform. In most socialist societies the churches have been encouraged by the government to work for peace as it was hoped that by careful influence the church's position could be channeled to be inoffensive or in tune with the government's foreign policy.

The third form of accommodation may be called "religion in socialism," or religion within socialism. This particular phrase was coined by the leaders of the Evangelical (Lutheran) Churches in East Germany as they struggled to find a theologically and socially productive relationship to socialism. They rejected the former two models as they felt that it led to a mentality of being an alien in one's own land. Indeed, many East Germans were in a spiritual emigration, looking forward to German reunion which would free them from the Soviet-type socialist imposition. Others in East Germany aggressively urged a much more intimate endorsement of socialism, a "religion for socialism," which is to be described below. With the phrase "the church within socialism," it was hoped to communicate the acceptance of the fact that the social system for the foreseeable future was a socialist one and that wishful thinking would not change it. Thus the church accepts this as its mission, namely to work in this very socialist society without nurturing illusions about escape to the West or some magic disappearance of socialism. Within this socialist system the church has a task of humanizing it and interacting with it in whatever manner possible. This approach has made it possible for the churches in East Germany to continue a number of their social and charitable institutions (e.g., hospitals, old people's homes, youth fellowships), and occasionally made the churches able to speak out against certain social policies (e.g., universal military conscription or pre-military education in the schools).

"Religion for socialism" is a minority approach among churches in Eastern Europe, but it has its adherents. Their motivation and actions vary considerably. Some are simply opportunists or careerists. But others are theologically or socially sensitive people who were shocked by the church's reactionary policies of the past when the church may have been an accomplice of pro-Nazi policies, or sided with the privileged classes, giving no heed to the poor and downtrodden. In their opinion the past behavior of the churches requires total repentance on the part of the churches. Socialism is seen either as an instrument of punishment by God, or more frequently as God working outside the realm of the churches, even by means of a hostile atheistic social system, to bring about greater social justice and harmony than the previous society. Many protagonists of this view of "religion for socialism" perceive the world to be shaped through the struggle of two social systems—capitalism, which they see as being on its way out, and socialism, which they believe to be the wave of the future. There is no third way, they say. Thus one must decide for socialism (East Germans call it "partisanship"), because socialism means progress, peace, justice, equality, dignity, etc. Sitting on the fence is as bad as being for capitalism, according to this view. The first to vigorously espouse such views in East Europe was the famous and controversial Czech theologian Joseph Hromádka, who swayed many young theologians in his church (the Czech Brethren) and outside to follow him on this path of bold acceptance of socialism with the attempt to gain credence in socialist society, so that eventually the church could serve it more effectively.

The Hungarian Reformed bishop Albert Bereczky pioneered a similar approach in Hungary, leading the Reformed and Lutheran Churches, after some bitter inner-church battles, into a posture of officially giving their support, usually without critical perspective, to the present social system. That attitude earned those church leaders who were deemed reliable by the government certain privileges, including representation in the parliament, analogous to the one they had in pre-socialist times, or clergy salaries being paid by the state. But the price has been that this church leadership self-censored expressions of dissent. The first time when either internal opposition to this course or popular resentment against such policies surfaced was during the 1956 Hungarian Revolt. At the time, nearly all the vocal proponents of "religion for socialism" were quickly demoted from their positions, only to be reinstated shortly after the crushing of the revolt. Since 1984 a small group of clergy and laity in the Lutheran Church of Hungary have voiced their dissent against the collaborationist policies of their bishops.

There is also the group of younger clergy, born since the establishment of socialism, to whom socialism is the only social system they have experienced. For a number of them, there is no feeling of guilt or sentimental wishing for the return of the past. While they accept as normal the life of the church under socialism, they also tend to be critical, not so much of the system per se, but of the shortcomings in the implementation of socialist ideals. They are more likely to feel more secure in questioning day to day policies. Usually they lack the zeal or idealistic enthusiasm of their older colleagues, yet they do not even contemplate what it would be like if socialism were not the system in their country. Many of them think that socialism has made some advances which should not be given up. If they oppose concrete issues it usually does not mean that they oppose socialism; rather they tend to oppose a specific perversion or malpractice of socialism. One can see such an attitude among the many youthful Christians who were involved in the upheavals in Hungary, Czechoslovakia, and Poland.

It may come as a surprise to many that there is one more model on this scale which one can loosely tag as "socialist religion." That should be a contradiction in terms, but it is not. Perceptive analysts have noted long ago that Marxism may turn into a "pseudo-religion" for some of its adherents. Now, many Marxists even recognize that one may have a "religious" attitude toward socialism. One Marxist wrote of "black clericalism" being supplanted by "red clericalism" or "atheist clericalism."[4] While in most instances such "socialist religion" is evaluated negatively by both Marxists and non-Marxist thinkers, it is quite evident that socialism can elicit a kind of response on the part of some of its followers, which usually characterizes religious movements, though, in the opinion of many, it is idolatrous religion. Therefore, one must use this category very carefully and in a nuanced way. It should be granted, however, that there is such a phenomenon as "socialist religion" and note, as most analysts do, that it is most developed among the socialist bureaucracy *(apartachiks)*. If this is correct, then religion indeed continues to have a most profound social impact under socialism (e.g., in the form of Stalinism, Maoism, or any other "cult of personality").

Not all churches can easily be categorized into this typology. The Roman Catholic Church in Poland, which undoubtedly has the greatest social impact of all East European Churches, may be perceived by different people as fitting different categories. Many have seen the Roman Catholic Church as the staunchest social opponent of the branch of pro-Soviet socialism that is dominant in Poland. Its moral authority is derived from its unflinching protection of certain rights and ideals. Others attribute the success of the Polish Roman Catholic Church to its wisdom of not playing an overtly political role but, instead, maintaining its distance from or neutrality to the socialist system itself, as well as its passionate identification with Polish national interests, which sometimes produces policies in support of the governing party and sometimes advocacies of opposition causes. Finally there are those who may perceive the Polish Roman Catholic Church as having come to terms with life within socialism and pursuing a course of critical acceptance, embracing certain features of the new social reality but lashing out at others.

Currently the first three models are the most widely utilized, though it would not be wise to attempt to quantify this generalization beyond an educated estimate that perhaps the largest number of religious people vaguely opted for the second model of "religion indifferent to socialism," for it is the one least demanding and, under conditions of bureaucratic totalitarianism, the one most favored by the structure of the system. In the estimation of this author, the most creative option is "religion within socialism," which is based on the presupposition that religion can operate under a variety of social systems and that it cannot merely adapt itself to it, but engage critically in the process of social transformation, depending on concrete political circumstances. This view holds that no given social system is inherently "Christian," but that the more basic issue is how any social system is made to serve fundamental human needs, including spiritual ones. The option "religion for socialism" likewise has produced some thoughtful (as well as some naive or sinister) theological reflections which value those features of socialism most in accord with the great humane religious strivings and promotes their implementation instead of systems of injustice.

If one were to ask which of these models is most effectively influencing social policies, no clear answer could be given. It is not so much the model itself which determines the influence, but a whole network of historical, national, political (foreign and domestic), economic, and other reasons. A church's intransigent opposition to socialism may either relegate it into obscurity or catapult it into the focus of opposition, depending on factors such as the power of the Communist party, the success or failure of economic policies, international relations, national identification, etc. Should, for instance, the Yugoslav federation get into political jeopardy and Croatian separatism become a more potent movement, the Roman Catholic Church may be perceived as protector of the Croatian national values and will increase its influence. On the other hand, should the federation succeed and the Catholic church be unable to adjust itself to this reality, it may be relegated to the role of a minor nuisance on such issues as abortion laws. Much depends on a church's perceptive judgment not only of the political moods of the country, but also the sense of what is more ultimately right or wrong for both the people it represents and those it does not represent but cares for.

I also venture to express the judgment that the only option doomed not to have long-range social effects is a non-critical support attitude. While in the short run this policy may yield some practical results in, for instance, being able to intervene on behalf of individuals imprisoned or persecuted or in softening the impact of this or that decree, in the long run a position which is merely conveying the views of the policy-makers is neither respected by the promoters (because one did not completely join them), nor by the critics or dissenters or even the passive part of the population, because they perceive the group as being compromised, as being "bought off" or being duped. In any case, a Christian who can say "yes" to a society can meaningfully do so only if she or he can also say "no." Merely saying "yes" does not make distinctions between God and Caesar. Both potentially and in actuality, that is the core of the issue of the social impact of Christians in a society which tends to require absolute allegiance to Caesar. The very fact that Christians (and other religionists) do not share this allegiance makes religion both potentially and in actuality an autonomous source of social influence.

Areas of Greatest Impact

Now, one may ask in what fields, or in what areas does religion tend to show the greatest and most constant impact on public policy?

In Eastern Europe, in addition to the traditional impact on ethnic or national policies, one may say that a concern for the implementation of ethical or religio-ethical values has the greatest impact and is appreciated even by those rarely willing to praise religion.

When one considers the question of the relative power of Marxist ideology, religion, and nationalism, it is important to observe that, of the three, nationalism is the most potent force. While some people are ready to live and die for the Communist ideology, this cannot be said of the majority. Many people undoubtedly should be willing to make the supreme sacrifice of life or death in the name of their religion, but they, too, are not in the majority. Nationalism (and in the multinational states ethnicity of the component national units) is probably the most potent motivator for the largest number of people. The universal claims of religion and the internationalist claims of Communist ideology have both had to make allowances for the influence of nationalism. The Communists have realized that national Communism is a potent factor among socialist states and parties. The churches have long been willing to maintain a very close relationship with the nationality of their territory. Both church and state must come to cope with the impact of nationalism and both have often sought to demonstrate their own loyalty to it and, likewise, attempted to cast doubts in regard to the loyalty to the national idea on the part of their adversary. The government finds itself often at odds with a church's impact and attempts to counteract it, being, however, quite aware of the potent effect that the churches can have in a volatile nationalistic conflict situation. The policies of a church can either accelerate or diminish the national enmity. The government is usually quite aware of the power of the church or churches in this area and takes it into account in its legislative and implementing policies.

Another area of the impact of religion is in the social and individual ethical matters. While this is an area in which churches have exerted customary influence over the centuries, in socialist societies of Eastern Europe the ethical impact of the churches has been heightened. Two factors coalesced to bring this about: One is that rapid industrialization and urbanization brought about a nearly total breakdown of the traditional interpersonal and social links which reinforced the norms and mores of the prior era. This left many people adrift. On the other hand, Marxism has not paid a great deal of attention to the development of ethical norms and inculcating them into the population despite frequent appeals to socialist morality. In fact the predominant practical approach to ethics among Communists was a pragmatical approach that tended to relativize all norms subject only to the ultimate goal of their victory.

With large segments of the population set adrift and without constraints, many institutions suffered, including the family, economic enterprises, and the government itself. Low working morale, sabotage, laziness, theft, bribes, nepotism, lack of personal integrity and civil courage were among the results, which harmed productivity and the living standard. Marxist leaders noticed that religiously motivated people often resisted such temptations more effectively than others. They welcomed the church's appeals to its members to stick to the ethical norms, since the government would profit from it. Thus, for instance, the government welcomed the endorsement of the Hungarian Protestant Churches of its agricultural policies of collectivization, urging peasants to cooperate for the national welfare. The Roman Catholic bishops and clergy frequently appealed to a higher work ethic among Polish workers, being, however, careful to balance it with criticism of bureaucratic misdoings. This is one of the reasons why that Church became so successful as a mediator between the government and the Solidarity labor union. In East Germany the Protestant Churches appealed to young people and others to go to the farms and help farmers with the harvest when the government requested such voluntary labor. But the government rejected the use of Christian labor brigades who set out to work in the fields and celebrated a shared communal meal interpreted by participants as Holy Communion.

Sometimes the churches' ethical teachings reflect only the traditional way of doing things and can be seen as an obstacle by the state in making needed social changes. Thus for instance, certain cultural mores and superstitious practices which were associated with religion continue to be advocated by certain church members or leaders. These may be "faith healing" in preference to medical attention, avoidance of certain foods or rejection of public education. In an atheistic state where the propaganda attempts to portray the conflict as a conflict between science and religion it may be to the advantage of the government to caricature all religion as associated with traditional superstitious folkways and values.

Sometimes the religio-ethical values of a church may take an oppositionary character to the intended policies of the government. This has been the case with the Roman Catholic Church concerning divorce laws, abortion, and birth control laws, not unlike conflicts in the West. The government maintains that this is a mixing of the church into political issues contrary to the principle of separation of church and state; the churches maintain that it is the protection of human rights. One needs to mention parenthetically that Marxist convictions are often totally pragmatic. In Hungary, for instance, a liberal abortion law was passed only to be quickly rescinded when the birthrate was deemed insufficient.

While some of the religious impact in the sphere of ethics occurs in conflict with Marxist notions, this is not always the case. There is room for dialogue and mutual influence or complementarity. Marxism has a more developed theory of work and its creative place in human development. On the other hand religion has tended to promote responsible attitudes toward work. In Poland, for instance,

Christians and Marxists engaged in dialogue on the nature and dignity of work. Dialogue on ethical issues is only in its inception, but if it were to be pursued it could prove beneficial to both parties.

Another area for cooperation is the struggle for peace and disarmament. Without judging the genuineness of the Communist desire for peace, the proclaimed policy of the Communist governments is peace with justice (on their terms, of course). The countries of Eastern Europe have been frequently involved in devastating wars culminating in World War II. The population genuinely craves peace. Therefore it is not hard for the churches to recall that it is their task to strive for peace and justice. It is irrelevant at this point whether the Communist governments may be using their churches for certain propaganda purposes. The point is that, at least externally, the goals seem to be parallel. While the churches rarely had the freedom to take an explicitly critical attitude toward their own government's policies, at least in some instances the church appeals are directed toward all governments to end the arms race and in particular to ban nuclear weapons. Since conscription is universal in Eastern European countries, the Churches have shown no endorsement of pacifism, as they hasten to point out, and have not been voicing defense of conscientious objection. The only exception to that is that some young Christians in East Germany have voiced their objections to performing military duties and that some local churches and some church leaders have cautiously defended their young members when they resisted induction or formed independent peace movements. The fact that this disturbs the government is probably a greater testimony to the abnormal fear of the Communist government of any dissent than to the actual power of the churches to alter state policies.

If being a humane person or a humane society is of value to the churches then the most encompassing influence that the churches could have would be to bring a "human face" to socialism, as the Czechoslovaks, in 1968, coined the phrase. Whether that is actually possible remains yet to be seen; previous failures do not preclude that possibility for all eternity. An analysis still needs to be made whether contemporary forms of socialism are capable of becoming the kind of liberating societies which Marx dreamed about, but certainly some improvements are possible. In a few instances churches have consciously worked in that direction.

In societies in which the government overstresses unity and strives to have complete consensus on all issues, attempting to deny pluralism, the churches have prevented full assimilation and uniformity. In the past it was easier for religions to identify themselves with social forms; but since Communism fosters an atheist society, such syncretism is very hard. This guarantees at least some degree of diversity and differences of approach in a given country and is a very distinct factor in the minds of the policy-makers, who experience this as a hurdle for their plans of uniformity.

The influence of a new kind of spiritualism has been noted among the intellectuals and the young in some places in Eastern Europe, notably in the Soviet Union as described by Alexander Solzhenitsyn and Mihajlo Mihajlov. Its impact is not yet measurable, in the estimate of this author. It has a more latent than active impact. Another latent impact is that of the popular religious leaders, such a *startsi* (ascetic, monastic old men living in seclusion but revered by the masses for their holiness) and certain bishops, who might, in case of a crisis, provide suitable leadership for dissenters. The population often accords great respect to clergy, in particular to higher clergy. This is especially true in rural areas. The bishops of the Orthodox Church, for instance in Romania, may have an entire village, including the Communist officials, go out spontaneously to greet them upon arrival; such a welcome may not be accorded to government officials, even with considerable prior preparation. The Slavic term *vladika,* meaning ruler, is still conventionally applied to many Orthodox bishops. A similar respect is enjoyed by Roman Catholic hierarchs. In Hungary some of the higher clergy are still members of Parliament. While this does not mean that they have outright political power, it does serve as a sign of recognition in their society. They are accorded V.I.P. status at receptions and airports, and in the media.

In two of the Eastern European countries the religious press plays a certain independent and influential role. In Poland this press was particularly vigorous and has never been totally curtailed, even during the martial law period. They publish journals, magazines and even weekly newspapers (e.g. *Wieź* and *Tygodnik Powzsechny*). During liberal periods, such a press becomes particularly active in providing alternate interpretations. In Yugoslavia the religious press was nearly eliminated after the Communist takeover, but was revived in the 1960s. Currently it is so independent that it criticizes, sometimes in veiled and sometimes in open ways, the government, in response to which certain publications are occasionally banned. The religious press was also vigorous in Czechoslovakia during the "Prague Spring" but is now so tightly controlled that it is innocuous. The Hungarian, Romanian, and East German religious publications seem to have no political influence. The other countries have very limited or no religious press.

Two countries have political parties or organizations with political representation in the parliament. In East Germany the Christian Democratic Union is guaranteed a fixed number of seats in the legislature. Right after the war it conceived of itself as potentially independent, but soon thereafter defined itself as a vehicle of implementation of the "scientific" views of the ruling Socialist Unity Party (Marxist). Currently it is not providing any alternate options. However, leading personalities of this party often occupy important, even highest offices in the land, e.g., supreme court justice, president of the parliament, etc. In Poland, several Roman Catholic lay organizations, namely "Znak," "Pax" and the "Christian Social Association" have a designated number of their leaders (not more than five each) in the *Seym.* In some instances these deputies have abstained from voting for government policies. A few even voted against the government, which caused much agitation and sometimes replacement of the "errant" deputies. No such political groupings exist in other Eastern European countries.

Schools are another potential influence in society. For that reason a sharp separation of schools from the church was advocated by the Communists and carried out in Eastern Europe. Nearly all church schools became public. The exception, again, is Poland where the Catholic University in Lublin is the only such private institution in Eastern Europe. In addition, there are two other academies which, likewise, train students not intending to be ordained as clergy. In other countries the schools are mostly theological seminaries or preparatory religious schools, though in Hungary a few high schools were left in church hands.

It is common knowledge that there were no independent labor unions in Eastern Europe until the creation of "Solidarity" in Poland in 1980. The impact of the Roman Catholic Church on this independent union movement is fairly well known. Here the labor union leaders included among their demands the demand for more religious liberty and the use of mass media for communicating religious ceremonies and sermons. Prayers and priestly counsel, including consultation with the highest clergy, including the bishop primate of Poland, were frequent. "Solidarity" was the largest mass movement in Poland's history and the Roman Catholic Church played a very central role in that movement. One can regard this as the high watermark of political and social influence of a church in Eastern Europe under a Communist regime. After the banning of "Solidarity," the Church's role did not diminish, as it remained the only institution not controlled by the government.

Finally, one should mention a unique source of social influence of churches, namely the election of a Pole, Karol Wojtila, as the pope. That surprising election was hailed as a sign of recognition to the Polish Roman Catholic Church not only by all Polish Catholics, but also by many Communists. It is impossible to measure precisely the impact which this election and the subsequent papal visits to Poland have made on the Polish events of the 1980s, but a significant measure of impact is undeniable. Millions of Poles repeatedly poured out their admiration and affection toward Pope John Paul II and the Catholic Church in spontaneous, orderly public assemblies and pilgrimages. The papal support of "Solidarity" and greater openness of Polish society has influenced the course of events, and has demonstrated the central role of the Catholic Church in Polish national life. The attempted assassination of the pope had no lasting effect, which it undoubtedly would have had had the attempt been successful. As it is, the Polish government must always calculate what the role of the pope and the Church is going to be in any development which affects the country. A lesser invigorating impact of the "Polish Pope" is also noticeable in other countries, such as Czechoslovakia and Yugoslavia.

Source of the Churches' Influence

The churches are still the single largest mass organization in each Eastern European country and this undoubtedly contributed to their impact, although the Communist Party has worked out a fairly effective domination of society as a minority movement.

Size is enhanced by the perception that the religious institutions are among the very few institutions permitted to function in a Communist society. Thus, as noted above, the churches sometimes draw the support of dissenters and other dissatisfied people. When at an Easter Midnight Liturgy in Tbilisi, Georgia (USSR), the church is crowded with young males between 15 and 30, that is probably less an expression of religious fervor and more a Georgian nationalistic demonstration against central government policies of Russification. If, at the grave-site of Alojzije Cardinal Stepinac in

Zagreb, thousands of people place flowers or candles, they are not merely coming to pay respect to a dead prelate, but are making a statement about Croatian nationalism and defying the government which attempted to crush Stepinac. The crosses made of flowers in Warsaw since August of 1982 are obviously more a symbol of resistance to the military rule than they are purely religious symbols. The significant fact is that these resistances are taking on distinct religious symbolism.

Another reason for the impact of religion is the power of tradition in a world that shows little appreciation for traditions. Religion appears to be one of the few stable elements in a rapidly changing world. Many are yearning for stability and security and are hoping to find it in institutions which have tended to show stability and sought to conserve value.

The churches have also tended to help individuals in time of need and have placed some emphasis, particularly the Protestants, on personal salvation. The bureaucratic totalitarianism which emerged in Eastern Europe as a result of the interaction of Marxist ideology and modern industrialization, urbanization, and secularization seems to show very little interest in the individual and the individual's problems. Where shall a person go when haunted by fear, doubt, anxiety, loneliness, rejection, loss of dignity and respect? Or where shall a person celebrate the festive elements of life, such as birth, puberty, marriage, and death? To whom shall one unload a troubled conscience? Secular society has not provided enough avenues for personal concerns and the churches continue to fulfill an important function.

Many people feel the need for change or transformation, as they are not happy with themselves as they are. Perhaps they are adrift or unfulfilled. Again, society does not provide for such needs, in fact less so than in the West, because psychology and analysis are not generally available. Many people have experienced the great transformational power of God in some aspect of church life to such a degree that they consider it the central experience or experiences of their lives. The result is that they place supreme or absolute allegiance in what is for them the ultimate source of all good. To them other goals, such as class struggle, victory of the proletariat, leadership of the Communist Party, the great future society, or anything else that may be held up as of supreme value, always come under God's ultimate rule. Religious people have most effectively refused to raise the lesser values of life to the level of ultimacy.

Their faith in God helps them to judge these lesser claims and keep their demands in a different perspective. This appears to be the very core of religion's influence. From the government's perspective this is a grave threat because it seems to lessen loyalty on the part of a considerable number of their citizens. Churches have consequently been accused of unpatriotic, traitorous behavior. This was the explicit charge in a number of show trials in the late 1940s and early 1950s. Roman Catholic and other churches with a strong foreign connection have been additionally accused of betraying the state to the Vatican, or the U.S.A. or some other foreign power.

The churches have normally affirmed their loyalty to the state and recognized the government as legitimate, but nevertheless maintained that God's law has primacy over state law, when the two are in conflict. Since much of Eastern European legislation discriminates against religion, prohibiting or restricting many traditional religious activities, many religious people do indeed perceive a conflict between their duty to God and their duty to the state. Under great duress in times of intense crisis, such as during 1956 in Hungary, 1968 in Czechoslovakia, and the 1980s in Poland, for some religious people the tension becomes unbearable and they turn against the government, actively or passively. Thus religion may directly turn against the state, which it is unlikely to do in more stable times.

Implications for U.S. Policy

From the above, it is obvious that it is dangerous to generalize about the influence of the churches upon social policies of the Soviet Union and Eastern Europe. One should neither overemphasize nor underrate their influence. The role of the Catholic Church in Poland is not an accurate measure of the secular role of other churches. But, on the other hand, neither is the Russian Orthodox experience the best criterion. The impact varies from country to country and from church to church. For policy decisions, one must be knowledgeable about the concrete situation.

Nor is one to give unqualified support for the aims of every church, with the justification that anything that tends to break the monopoly of the Communist Party is to the advantage of the U.S. or the West. There are some religious groups whose aims may be even less in accord with one's own perceived interest than that of the Communist Party. If some of these groups were to have their intentions implemented, grave instability would result not only in that region, but elsewhere as well. On the other hand the correct path is to defend the religious liberties as a fundamental human right for every group, even those with whose aims one may not be able to agree. In that respect one should voice support for their rights, but not necessarily for their aims.

The links between nationalism and religion should not be lost sight of. As pointed out above, nationalism is sometimes a more powerful motivator in Eastern Europe than either religion or ideology. But when ideology, for political reasons, suppresses nationalism, a church may appear to be the only channel through which nationalism can express itself. Some of the churches have either instinctively or deliberately recognized this and made use of it for their own benefit. This is, after all, not a new trend, but a centuries old tradition, where a church was the defender of national interests in time of crisis. A nuanced and cautious approach should be made lest one encourage the rise of nationalism in order to weaken Communist ideology. The Communists themselves tended to underestimate the power of nationalism only to discover that national Communist ideologies brought about Communist polycentrism, leading to several breakaways and several unsuccessful attempts at breakaway from Soviet domination. Soviet domination and attempts at Russification have not only embittered the other Eastern European socialist nations but also the non-Russian nationalities in the Soviet Union. The churches have sometimes benefited from these nationalistic strivings. But nationalism is a very dangerous ally; it can result in murderous and destructive tendencies which can be encouraged only at everyone's peril. If human life is important, then U.S. policy will not indiscriminately encourage local nationalism.

The U.S. should not use the churches of Eastern Europe for narrow political aims. The churches are attempting to work out their own identity and mission under extremely difficult circumstances. One way in which they have been hampered by their own governments has been the accusation of being in alliance with "American imperialism." There is, indeed, a broad sympathy among church people in Eastern Europe, as among much of the general population, for the West and for the U.S. in particular. This is the type of goodwill rarely found even among U.S. allies, and it must not be lightly gambled away by crude exploitation. The worst possible result would be that the government accusations would be justified and the churches would suffer even greater curtailment of their rights than they do presently.

Under no circumstances should approaches be made to Eastern European church leaders and members for intelligence purposes. The benefits of such an approach would be very small because practically none have access to the kind of classified secrets of interest to intelligence agencies, while the long-range losses to the churches would be catastrophic.

The goodwill of church people is of immeasurably greater worth to the U.S. than any short-range political advantage that could be gained from manipulating a church. The best policy would appear to be the same as the one used domestically, namely the separation of church and state; as in the U.S.A., the U.S. government can be friendly to the churches but keep a strict line of demarcation. The U.S. can show support of the churches, especially those particularly badly treated, by intervening in their behalf (e.g., the support of Soviet Jews or Pentecostals, for whom even highest state officials of the U.S. government intervened with the Communist government officials). But if this is not done judiciously one may achieve the opposite effect, namely getting them into greater trouble and persecution than heretofore, when they are explicitly perceived as domestic enemies.

Christians in the Soviet Union and Eastern Europe do have an alternate world view from the Communists. But it should not be concluded that all Christians are against their social or governmental system. Some Christians are very enthusiastic in their support of their government and of the socialist system. Others are merely nationalistic; in a time of crisis, many would defend their country out of patriotism though they may have little love for its social system. And undoubtedly there are also those who feel totally trapped in their present situation and would do almost anything to get away, including emigration or siding with rebel forces or an outside force in case of war. Some of these people may be explicitly pro-U.S.A., others are not necessarily so. Their right to emigrate should be supported as a principle. Should some attempt to use criminal means, e.g., hijack a plane, they should not be dealt with more leniently by Western countries than similar lawbreakers at home. A safe guideline to follow would be the implementation of the U.N. Universal Declaration of Human Rights and the Helsinki Accord.

Finally, U.S. churches should be allowed to engage in lively contact with Eastern European churches. The practice of denying U.S. visas to those church leaders in Eastern Europe who are supportive of their government is an abhorrent practice which gains few friends for the government's action either at home or abroad. It only makes it look as if the U.S. government is no better in that respect than the Communist governments. One is not to suppose that U.S. church leaders are unable to discriminate between those who are obediently toeing their government's line and those who represent more genuinely their church's mainstream. In order to keep contacts, one must meet both those who are pro-government and those who are moderate; that may lead to later contacts with the dissidents as well. When détente prevails and when contacts are not imperiled, there is more room for exercising religious and other freedoms. When pressure is applied on the Soviet Union and other Eastern European governments either in general or explicitly in support of the churches, a boomerang effect sets in and the churches find themselves more restricted. It is not surprising that the church members and leaders of Eastern Europe almost unanimously favor détente; they definitely profit from it. On the other hand it is also obvious that at least some of them appreciate a firm U.S. position because they fear that, if the U.S.S.R. has its own way without resistance, the Communist slogan about the withering away of religion will ultimately come. Thus a U.S. policy which supports religious liberties at home and abroad is one of the brightest rays of hope for these who are anxious about the future of the churches in their countries and on a worldwide basis.

NOTES

1. Kenneth S. Latourette, *A History of Christianity* (New York: Harper & Brothers, 1953), pp. 94–95.
2. Bohdan Cywinski, *Rodowody Niepokornych* (Warsaw: Wiéz, 1971).
3. *Ibid.,* pp. 262 and 263. Cited from Szymon Chodak, "The Secular role of the Catholic Church in Present-Day Poland," in *Nationalities Papers,* 10:2 (Fall, 1982).
4. Esad Ćimić, *Čovjek no raskršću* (Sarajevo: Svjetlost, 1975), pp. 147 ff.

12

People and the Church Versus the State: The Case of the Roman Catholic Church in Poland

SZYMON CHODAK

There is a large city square in the capital city of Poland which before World War II was called Jozef Pilsudski Square.[1] It was renamed Adolf Hitler Platz under the Nazis. After 1945, in commemoration of the victory over the Nazis, it was renamed Victory Square; the name remains. Following the imposition of General Jaruzelski's military rule in December 1981, the square turned into a battlefield for a different victory: day after day, for several months, the people of Warsaw erected there a huge floral cross, a monument to the outlawed Solidarity union movement. On some days the cross bore the portrait of the interned Solidarity leader Lech Wałesa. On other days it was adorned with the now famous red on white inscription, *Solidarność.* Every night, the police removed the flowers. Every day the people returned and rebuilt the cross. Eventually, the police and the dreaded ZOMO security forces, with their clubs, tear gas and water cannons, came at noon, when the crowd was praying and singing hymns. The flowers were trampled over and the crowd was forcefully dispersed. Then the authorities erected a high grey fence around Victory Square to prevent the people of Warsaw from gathering and rebuilding it with flowers again. The fence—the Jaruzelski victory monument—now stands in the heart of Warsaw like that other wall stands in the center of Berlin. The fence is symbolic not only of confrontation, but of the long, ongoing struggle between the Solidarity movement, backed by the Catholic Church, and the government of Poland, backed by the Soviet Union.

In Poland the Roman Catholic Church has succeeded in preserving its traditional influence and giving new meaning to traditional values and norms, while acquiring a new role in contemporary society. In attempting to preserve both its religious and its nationalistic hold on society, the Polish Church has supported causes which earlier had been those of the secular left-wing intellectual opposition and the nationalistic forces. Even though it remains conservative on many issues, to large sections of the Polish society the Church stands for freedom of expression, association and equality, and defense of national identity and traditions. Defense of the right to worship thus has evolved into the defense of freedom of thought and expression and into the broader spectrum of human rights. Without becoming a political party or competing for political power, the Polish Church has taken on the role of a unique, nonpartisan umbrella institution that defends the right to profess ideals differing from those imposed by the State. Because of this position vis-à-vis the State, the Church has won an unprecedented popularity and respect among the Polish population.

Previous, periodic rebellions took place in Poland in 1956, 1968, 1970 and 1978. In those instances only certain sections of the population were involved. The election of Karol Wojtyła to the Papacy and his subsequent visit to Poland in the Summer of 1979 engendered a situation where all forces that opposed the State became united, and involved the entire population in all kinds of anti-governmental activities. Widespread strikes erupted in Gdansk, Silezia and Bydgoszcz. The workers not only demanded higher wages and opposed food price increases, but also called for, and won, a number of unprecedented political concessions. These included the right to form unions free of Party control, the right to strike, and the right of workers to voice their opinions on the division of national income for consumption and for investment, and on wage and price policies—all matters which, until then, had been determined by the Party alone. They also demanded, and were promised by the government, an easing of censorship of essential published information, as well as media access for their representatives and the Church. Peasants joined in with their demands to establish a Peasant Solidarity Union. The government, which refused at first to allow such an organization, had to relent and accept this demand also.

What began as merely a struggle against food price increases in some sections of the population, a struggle for freedom of religious practices in another section, and for intellectual freedom in still other parts of society, evolved into a major ongoing struggle for the transformation of the system of government and of social conditions. This situation is unprecedented in Communist-ruled countries. The Soviet Union could, of course, have quelled this rebellion by sending its troops and K.G.B. forces into Poland. The price it would have paid for this would have been so high, however, that it has not dared to do to Poland what it did to Czechoslovakia and Hungary. The Soviets have entrusted this job, for the moment, to General Jaruzelski and the military.

During its heydey, when it still was legal in December 1981, ten million people, including a large number of Party members, belonged to the first independent union in the Communist countries, *Solidarność.* During the August 1982 demonstrations, the fully equipped security forces, in some instances army units, were positioned all over the country to face possible demonstrations. Still, in about 60 cities people came out in mass to face the police formations. Regardless of the way it is evaluated, and to whom the victory is attributed, it was proof that the massive support for Solidarity has not vanished. Poland has thus become a Communist country where farmers are not collectivized, where the Church, which has never accepted the control of the Party, enjoys wide support among the intellectuals and the masses; and also a country where workers, most of the population, are involved in permanent rebellion—in some periods openly, in others, subdued and passively.

Just because the Solidarity organization has been outlawed and many of its leaders imprisoned, the rebellion cannot be considered totally defeated. In a sense a victory did occur. For the first time in history, albeit for only sixteen months, the Communist regime had to accept the unthinkable, the existence of an organization involving millions of people, not controlled by the Party. What these people did not dare to say to each other for decades, was said aloud and in public during these sixteen months. Out of this exchange of ideas, a new more mature understanding of their condition and a new spiritual solidarity was born. This, as Lech Wałesa wrote in 1985, cannot be erased. The spirit of solidarity evoked by the events of the rebellion persists as part of the national tradition.

The rebellion also was a victory for the Roman Catholic Church. Left-wing intellectuals of the Committee of Social Self-Defense (K.O.R.) cooperated in this struggle with Catholic intellectuals by advising workers at striking plants. Crosses were erected at many sites where strikers were protesting not only against workers', but intellectuals' conditions, as well. Priests prayed in workshops and factories. Striking women in factories sang religious songs. The first thing that Wałesa, leader of the striking workers, did after the victorious conclusion of negotiations with the state representatives, was to go to Warsaw and see Primate Wyszynski. When asked about the meaning of the crosses at their plants, the workers explained that most of them were believers. Yet the cross was regarded not merely as a religious symbol, but as a symbol of the workers' position; the working class, they believe, is crucified in Poland.

The workers, although believers, were not simply blind followers of the Church. The strikers rejected the archbishop's call for moderation during the course of the strike and for acceptance of the government's offer. The Church, though venerated, was also expected to represent public sentiment. The Church is aware of this. In a sense, it is acting in its traditional nationalistic role, which developed during the 19th century when Poland was ruled by Russia, Prussia, and Austria. It also is playing a new role developed in accordance with its interpretation of the decisions of policies reached by the Second Vatican Council.

The Julian Character of the Roman Catholic Church in Poland

The issue, as seen by Catholics and non-Catholic intellectuals and some part of the clergy in Poland, can be outlined as follows: Since Christianity became the official religion under Emperor Constantine in the 4th century, the Church participated in the exercise of political power, at first in Rome and Byzantium, and then elsewhere in Europe. In spite of occasional conflicts and disruptions in relations between the monarchy and the clergy, the Church enjoyed many benefits from this participation. Some aspects of this exercise of power, however, are presently considered to have been disadvantageous to the Church and inconsistent with its religious mission. As a participant in the official structure of power and bearer of ethical values, the Church was part of the establishment. It had to protect the existing social order and political power structure and this could not always be regarded as ethical from a Christian position.

In the course of the 20th century, the Constantinian period came to an end. The Roman Catholic Church, like other churches, has been increasingly excluded from the exercise of political power and from decision-making processes, not only in Communist, but in most other countries as well. It has lost control over education and welfare services. During the Vatican Council's meetings, and even more so in Poland later, some of the clergy began to express opinions that the Catholic Church not only must accept separation from the state but, in turn, must declare its own separation from the establishment in general, and particularly from the state and corporate structure. They felt that the church had a moral obligation to defend social justice, the right of individuals to protect their individuality, and other essential rights. They called for the church to condemn the materialism and social injustice perpetrated by capitalism, socialism and the contemporary state. The Council recognized this change. It adopted, however, a modest formula in defining its position. In paragraph 76 of the *Constitution on the Church in the Modern World,* the Council declared that "the Church, by reason of her role and competence, is not identified in any way with the political community nor bound to any political system. She is at once a sign and a safeguard of the transcendent character of the human Person."[2]

The new situation was also discussed in many documents released by the Council, particularly in the *Constitution on the Church in the Modern World.*[3] This document, and its implications for state-church relations, was reviewed with great interest by the Polish Catholic press and was analyzed in a number of books which appeared in Poland.[4] Both the hierarchy of the church and the Catholic *intelligentsia* searched for a model of state-church relations and were keen to establish the identity of the church vis-à-vis the state, and particularly the communist state.

The Polish Church has a long history of resisting the encroachment of the State. For a hundred and fifty years, in areas under Russian occupation, it operated under the restrictions of the Tsarist regime, which regarded it as an alien nationalist force. The tsars claimed the right to appoint the highest posts of the clergy. They wanted full control of all links between the Catholic Church and the Vatican. At one time, they even demanded that the Church substitute Russian for Latin as the official Church language. After World War II, under the Communist regime, the Church was pushed out of public life, restricted to ritual performances only, restricted in building new churches, forced to pay heavy property taxes, harassed in various ways, and accused of serving foreign enemies.

The Polish Church was one of the first large national Roman Catholic Churches forced to confront a Communist state, in which the government claimed exclusive control not only over political and economic affairs, but in the sphere of education, family life, and moral standards as well. This situation was well outlined in a recent article:

> As for the communists, their Marxist-Leninist doctrine demanded clear repudiation of any sort of religious ideology; the law of history and not the grace of God laid the foundation for the dictatorship of the proletariat. The communist leaders had every reason to announce war on the Church. But there also were good reasons for declaring only cold war. The Church had a coherent, uniform organization, not inferior to that of the Communist Party, and in addition it had a large social basis which the communists lacked. The communists had for the time being to tolerate the independence of their implacable opponent, but by no means did they intend to maintain this situation forever.[5]

Fighting the new encroachment of the state in all spheres of life, the Church began to oppose policies that restricted its influence and that reduced individuals to interchangeable participants in state agencies in what to the Church seemed a morally and culturally devastating environment. Unexpectedly, even to itself, perhaps, the Church took on a role it had not held at any other place or time.

At first, the Church was only reacting and defending itself against restrictions. But gradually the Church began to initiate a more systematic action in defense of its principles and activity. Eventually, the leadership of the Church began to raise moral issues important to society, but conflicting with the Party's policy. While getting involved in such activities which, evidently, contained political implications, the Polish Church refused to act as political opposition in the strictly political meaning of the word. Whether this was intended or not, and whether the leadership of the Church accepted it or not, by asserting its religious, cultural, and moral role in society it performed the role of the principal opposition in society. Because it formed the only legally available organization outside the all-embracing state and because it promoted a different morality and different value standards, it was perceived as an alternative to the State. Because the Church was excluded from political activities, was persecuted, and yet had to speak out against the immorality of state bureaucracy, discrimination against believers and non-Party members, it began to represent, at first, the social and political strivings of believers, and eventually of the left-wing Democratic and New Socialist movement as well. In spite of the fact that the Church continued to cling to its conservative tradition, it was regarded as being progressive and, indeed, had to support the movement for democracy. It was thus transformed into a vehicle of revolt. This was similar to the situation in the 19th century. Then, under the partition of Poland, the Church was regarded as the principal institution of national identity and unity, as well as the abode of national consciousness. It is still viewed as acting in this capacity.

In our times, however, it is said that the Church has changed. It does not represent the Constantinian tradition but a new Julian tradition in the Church's history.

Julian Apostate, nephew of Constantine I who ruled the Roman empire from 361 to 363, in an effort to restore the culture of antiquity, attempted to destroy the Church by excluding it from participation in the power structure. He did not institute a systematic persecution of Christians, yet as a result of this exclusion from political power, the Church was forced to act in a different role than it did under Constantine. Using the analogy of ancient times, the Polish writer Bohdan Cywiński, has coined the concept *Julian Church* to denote the features of the Church when it was forced to act under the conditions of the post-Constantinian period. Deprived of its political position in society, it sustains its position by winning respect through its moral authority. According to Cywiński:

> the Julian is exactly the opposite to the Constantine situation. Instead of cooperating, the secular and ecclesiastic authorities are in conflict. The Church is put in a position in which she has no option but to be in opposition. She is devoid of political power but is recognized by the society as its principal moral authority. This provides her with a new source of strength. . . . Persecuted and abandoned by opportunists, the Julian Church is nevertheless residing at the highest ethical altitudes in the eyes of the public. She is surrounded by glory and applause. The Julian tradition is beautiful and durable.[6]

Cywiński further pointed out:

> the Julian is not a Church which on its own volition gave up the participation in power. To the contrary, she is rancorous and bitter that she was excluded from participation of it.[7]

What is even more important is that in this new moral capacity, the Church does not necessarily identify itself with the society whose moral authority it represents. Rather, the Church stands aloof and expects society to identify itself with the values and striving of the Church. This, Cywiński points out, is obviously very different from representing and reflecting the values and hopes of the people. But at the same time it wins the support of the masses because it is persecuted. Cywiński also asserts that the Julian Church claims to have a monopoly on moral righteousness. As a result, it refuses to recognize and to cooperate with other groups that oppose the State. This was the case in ancient Julian times. It also is the case in present-day Poland, where the Church has been forced into the role of an opposition that refuses to accept secular groups who call themselves opposition and who fight the state.

It must be observed that, to some extent, this situation has changed recently. The secular, and frequently socialist or left-wing, opposition in Poland, recognizing the ethical authority of the Church among the masses, views the Church as the leading force of dissent. Regardless of its objections to the Vatican's and the Polish clergy's position on matters such as family planning and birth control, where the Church takes a conservative stand, the secular opposition stands on the side of the Church on the principal issue at present—opposition to the all-controlling state. Again, partially against the explicit wishes of some members of the clergy, the Church has been transformed into the patron of all opposition forces. It warns against violence but is obliged to forgive individuals who fight the oppressive state, even if they turn to open rebellion. It calls for moderation, but should the workers and peasants have to face the police or the Soviet army, the Church would have to support them against the establishment.

It also must be observed that the Polish Catholic Church has become the high moral and social authority of society, not only because it is no longer a part of the organization of power and state, and is in the Julian position, but as a result of a number of other factors. First, in Poland, not only was the Church excluded from exercising power, but the opposition-minded individuals were prohibited from forming a legal opposition, and, therefore, turned to the persecuted Church and used it in their struggle. Second, in contrast to other churches in Eastern Europe whose role and prestige in society are presently declining, the Polish Church has become more militant in its religious, ethical and political activities. As a result, the Church actively promotes a strong moral and ideological challenge to the Party and the State. Finally, the Church has been led by the strong-willed Archbishops Wyszynski, Wojtyła, Kaczmarek, Klepacz, and others who have fearlessly opposed the State, and, therefore, became influential and charismatic figures in society. Because they challenged the State on moral grounds rather than on strictly political terms, they won social approval and were able to enhance religiosity as well.

Peculiarities of Polish Religious Behavior

Elsewhere in Europe, particularly in Britain, France and the Scandinavian countries, no more than five percent of the population attend church on an average Sunday. Even in the traditionally religious Latin countries of Southern Europe, the number of active Catholics is rapidly dwindling. This decline has been attributed to growing urbanization, industrialization, the spread of secular education, dissolution of traditional communal localities, abandonment of antiquated norms, and other similar causes. Yet in Communist Poland, which has rapidly become industrialized and urbanized and has one of the world's highest percentage of university graduates and those who are involved in contemporary intellectual concerns, the churches are usually crowded on Sundays. To be sure, in their daily habits, most Poles do not seem to be more religious than, for instance, Italians or other Catholics in Europe. On the whole, they are not fanatical about religion. In this strongly Catholic country, the rate of divorce is one of the highest in Europe. Birth control and abortion are widely practiced. There is ample evidence that, to some of the Polish people, participation in religious acts is important for truly religious reasons. To others, however, it provides the means through which they can manifest their nationalist feelings. To still others, the Church is an institution through which they can express their opposition to the government's inadequacy in solving the country's economic and social problems, as well as to its dependence on the Soviet Union.

As in the 19th century, the Catholic Church now constitutes the anchorage of national tradition. It provides the link with the civilizational entity of the West, to which the *intelligentsia* as well as the masses feel they belong culturally and psychologically. Poland is Catholic not only because most Poles are christened at birth and marry in the Church, nor because many attend Mass, but mostly because they identify themselves as belonging to a Roman Catholic civilization; because they profess a Roman Catholic world-outlook and ideology. They may not subscribe to the Vatican's position on birth control or other issues any more than is done elsewhere in Europe, yet they regard the Pope, the Polish Primate, and the leading bishops as their true national spiritual leaders. Even the Party must now accept this as reality.

Most Poles are unhappy with the government and the political system not only because of the standard of living or because the government's policies are wasteful and inefficient, but also because they feel that theirs is a government imposed by the Soviet Union, and therefore not truly their own. As mentioned above, the Church is perceived as the alternative. To most of the population, the Church represents the ideology of truth, human dignity, freedom of belief and thought, righteousness, and other noble standards. But again it is not a blind following. The Church is and will be esteemed only as long as it represents the sentiments of the population. This became quite evident during the recent labor unrest. The population strongly protested against the Church's reconciliation attempts during the strikes. The Church must relentlessly oppose the system to earn respect and support.

Religiosity in Polish conditions has a different meaning than elsewhere. Different religions offer differing roads to salvation; in some instances by means of purely ritual activities, in others by asserting the importance of ethical achievement, and in still others through one's work in God's vineyards. At times, the way is through involvement in politics. In today's Poland, religiosity can be characterized as an emotional syndrome in which the beliefs in God, pursuance of religious ritualistic practices, nationalism, anti-Soviet and anti-government sentiments, attachment to traditions, sublime idealism, and idealistic preference for noble ethical values and norms are closely interwoven and transposed into each other.

Three forms of religiosity seem to appear in the contemporary situation in Poland. The distinction is schematic and simplifying but still useful for analytical purposes. Thus, let us distinguish three forms of religiosity, identified as (1) ritualistic; (2) spiritual; and (3) ideological:

Ritualistic Religiosity. Ritualistic religiosity consists of outward manifestations and observances of rules as well as participation in ceremonial events prescribed by the doctrine and liturgy of the faith.

Max Weber has written that

> a religion of salvation may systematize the purely formal and specific activities of ritual into a devotion with a distinctive religious mood, in which the rules to be performed are symbols of the divine. In such a case the religious mood is the true instrument of salvation.[8]

Weber further points out that, as a result of the emphasis put on rituals, religions tend to become routine and are frequently devoid of true spirituality. Weber goes on to say that

> Consequently—in his opinion—the possession of an essentially ephemeral subjective state is striven after, and this subjective state—because of the idiosyncratic irresponsibility characterizing, for example, the hearing of a mass or the witnessing of a mystical play—has only a negligible effect on behavior once the ceremony is over. The meager influence such experiences frequently have upon everyday ethical living may be compared to the insignificant influence of a beautiful and inspiring play upon the theater public which has witnessed it.[9]

In those rather rare instances when occasional devotion induced by rituals escalates into a piety that extends to everyday living, ritualistic piety most readily takes on a mystical character.

As elsewhere, religiosity in Poland is often routine and sporadic. In this country, however, religious observances have taken on a nationalistic character. Many participants in Church activities in Poland would have difficulty separating their religious and nationalistic emotions. As a result of this process, a phenomenon that is different from the one described by Weber is occurring. Devoid of true religious piety, ritualistic observances acquire a patriotic meaning as strong as deeply religious devotion. To these people the Holy Mary—patron of Poland—and the Motherland Poland amalgamate into one sacred tradition. Others consciously participate in religious activities in order to demonstrate their opposition to the godless and, in a sense, foreign state.

Even though the entire phenomenon has political significance, three categories of people can be distinguished among those who attribute importance to ritualistic religious observances in Poland: (1) those who observe religious observances occasionally; (2) those who observe rites regularly; and (3) those who observe religious rites to indicate and demonstrate their political and ideological interest.

For the first category, as in the West, most Poles who live their lives with little attention to strict observances of religious norms, arrange to have religious rites on important life-occasions, such as christening of the newborn, marriage and death. Some do it because they wish to continue the tradition, others because the religious act marks this special occasion more ceremoniously. Still others accept religious rites in order to please their religious relatives. It is estimated that, on the whole, at least 95 percent of the Polish population arrange religious rites to christen newborn children and on the occasion of death. Approximately 85 percent marry in churches besides having legal civil marriages. About 60 percent attend churches on Sundays at least once a month. According to a study by Bishop Pluto, up to 40 percent of believers who attend church feel that it is right to practice birth control, and only 60 percent seem to agree that divorce is immoral and unacceptable for the Roman Catholic.[10]

According to another writer, "95% of the population of Poland is Catholic (total population 33 million in 1972), and about 75% of them are practicing Catholics (in the rural areas from 75% to 90%, in the cities 60% to 75%)."[11]

Should no other than ritualistic meaning be attributed to church practices, they would have, as elsewhere, the primary importance of routine. In Poland, however, and to some extent in other East European countries, a different meaning must be attributed even to strictly ritualistic participation in church activities. In instances where individuals participating in religious acts are Party members or hold important positions in the administration, they commit an act of disloyalty to Party authorities and have to do it at the risk of impairing their career advancement because of the strong recommendation by the Party against such involvement. The routine is then transformed into insubordination. An act of little more than ritualistic importance in other circumstances becomes an act of ethical disobedience with political significance.

Regarding the second category, the majority of regular citizens who do not subordinate their lives to goal-oriented career achievements take part in religious observances in due course and without regard to how this would affect their promotions. To these people it is an act of tradition if not routine, a due paid to their religious communities and to God; if not an act of religious piety, then a sort of religious insurance-payment to be observed for their own and their family's well-being. Even these acts take on a different dimension when the government is involved in extensive efforts, at great cost, to reduce the religious involvement of its citizens.

Though the state attempted to discredit the clergy by various accusations of deception, immorality, and anti-patriotism, the population nevertheless expressed attachment and trust in the clergy. Thus this should be seen as a political phenomenon.

Finally, certain people, especially youth and non-religious *intelligentsia,* take part in religious observances solely for political purposes—to demonstrate their opposition to the State and to express support for opposition forces. Recent events, such as the election of Karol Wojtyła to the Papacy, and the labor unrest of 1981, enhanced the position of the political opposition, causing more of this group to attend churches. Some of the people who attend churches for political reasons eventually become true believers as well.

The essence of religiosity is supposed to be spiritual. *Spiritual religiosity* means a deep and conscious belief in God, eternal salvation, and other teachings of the faith as well as observance of religious norms in regular daily practices. A good part of the Polish population can be characterized as religious in the spiritual sense of the term. Within any society, spiritually religious people comprise a minority within the large religious community who attribute importance to religious observances. A large number of Poles annually participate in pilgrimages to Jasna Gora in Czestochowa and in other special religious ceremonies and pilgrimages organized by the Church. Many of these are deeply religious people who attribute importance to spiritual matters. But today, not only believers but even some groups of atheists and non-believers march for nine days, 350 kilometers, in such pilgrimages, to demonstrate their solidarity with religious people. The vast body of religious Catholic literature that discusses issues of spiritual religiosity, ethics and matters of doctrine is in great demand; this is an even stronger indication of the concern of the population under the present regime. Poles were not only born Catholics, but had to choose to be Catholic against the advice of the Party and against other "realistic" considerations. People join the persecuted Julian Church, therefore, with feelings similar to those of the early Christians.

The term *ideological religiosity* is employed to denote displays of religious behavior that reflect not only general ethical values but a peculiar ideological attitude that first emerged under Tsarist rule, then during the Nazi occupation, and which has largely reemerged under Communist rule.

In order to discuss ideological religiosity, one must deal with concepts which in Western literature carry a fairly fuzzy connotation. One must distinguish between "dissidents," "opposition" and the wider and less institutionalized "protest movement." Since these phenomena overlap, this distinction, important as it is, has only a relative validity. Tadeusz Szafar astutely points out that "Dissenters and dissidents can exist only within the 'church' or at least within the 'religion,' not outside it and in total opposition to it. Such terms might thereby be legitimately used in relation to a Sakharov or a Medvedev, but not to a Solzhenitsyn or Bukovsky."[12] When speaking of dissidents, one speaks of rebellious intellectuals who, in quest of human rights, freedom of expression and social justice, act within the Party in the hope of transforming it into a democratic, socialist institution. Others act outside the Party but still make it more efficient and do serve the needs of the people. Some of the dissidents are eventually forced to reject the system and to act within the wider movement of spontaneous opposition and mass protest. They become anti-communist or anti-state activists.

In 1979–81, dissidents and rebel activists who felt that the system must be changed, started the publication of numerous uncensored and, therefore, illegal ideological and political periodicals, pamphlets and leaflets.[13] They have established one major and a number of smaller publishing houses which released several hundred uncensored books. They have operated an underground university in private apartments and churches. Some well-known professors from state universities and the Academy of Sciences taught in this unique school that was modelled on the "flying universities" during Tsarist and Nazi times, when Polish universities were forbidden.

Opposition within the system is obviously not allowed under the Communist regime.[14] The Church, the independent "Solidarity" union, and then also the union of agricultural producers—and, in fact, all the various dissenting groups—make a great effort to assert that they do not challenge the role of the Party or constitute a political opposition. Nevertheless, an unstructured opposition, in the sense that it opposed past and present policies and practices of the Party, emerged. In 1980, according to some observers, the opposition was comprised of three forces: (1) the Church and the movement supporting it; (2) the democratic *intelligentsia* organized around the Committee of Social Self-Defense (K.O.R.); and (3) the nationalist groups most manifestly represented by the Movement for Defense of Human and Civil Rights (R.O.P.C.I.O.). Others consider *Solidarity* to be the principal opposition to the Party. Spontaneously interacting in the perceived common interest, these movements condemned undemocratic and unsocialistic practices of state bureaucrats. The workers and the wider protest movements, involving millions of people, are not only dissident or opposition.

They are involved in a class-like struggle against the ruling bureaucratic and privileged elite.

The Church does not promote any official ideological or political program. Its position, represented by the leading clergy, is mostly intended to reflect the values of Catholic ethics. Rather than express any opposition, the late Primate Wyszynski and other eminent bishops admonished "our brothers Communist who rule us" against breaking their own law in disregarding the nation's constitution. They criticized the government for ineptitude in administration and for engaging in ill-advised programs to increase the power of the State, or for no apparent reason at all, instead of for the welfare of the people. At the same time, the Church cautioned against the use of violence and called the people to accept the political realities determined by the geopolitical situation of Poland constantly under the threat of foreign intervention. The Church also denounced materialism, hedonism, common cynicism and dishonesty engendered under bureaucratic rule and the frequently practiced discrimination against churchgoers.

To the Polish people, disenchanted with the idea of political and social revolution advocated by Party-*apparatchiks,* and by those who reject both capitalism and socialism, and who abhor growing *etatization* and bureaucracy, the Church proposes a new alternative. It calls for a moral revolution in which each individual would raise his/her own ethical *milieu* and thus the entire ethical *milieu* of society. In short, the Church does not compete for power and does not advocate a change of system, although it would evidently welcome it. It is, therefore, not an opposition in the competitive sense. It opposes the Party in power as a moral authority of the nation. Yet, as was mentioned above, the Church stops short of calling for political rebellion. At this point it becomes an unwilling ally of the Party; an ally of the Party that can live with widespread dissatisfaction but is afraid of riots and possible disobedience of the police and army, should these forces be ordered to quell a major popular uprising that may also provoke Soviet intervention.

Catholic Lay Groups

Apart from the Church itself and the various groups related to K.O.R., R.O.P.C.I.O., and other organizations, one must mention a number of so-called "clubs," discussion societies that represent different shades of Catholic ideology and act legally within the system. Clubs began to appear as early as the late 1940s, after World War II. They were tolerated by the state in the hope that in due course the party would transform them into its own agencies to control Roman Catholic public opinion. Two such clubs, representing quite distinctive orientations, first emerged: *Pax* and *Znak* [Sign]. *Pax* was established by Bolesław Piasecki and a group of other former members of the *Endecja,* the pre-war Polish Falangist extreme rightist party. At a time when other non-Communist parties and independent organizations were disbanded and suppressed, this organization of former extreme rightist authoritarians and chauvinists was not only allowed to develop but to own factories and run other businesses in order to finance its operation. For years, *Pax* was paying its employees the highest salaries in Poland. It is widely believed (and in the early 1960s the official Polish press dared to allude) that this was possible only because *Pax* was actually a front organization for, or at least operated under the patronage of, the Soviet K.G.B. *Pax* has not given up many of the ideological objectives of Roman Dmowski, founder of the pre-war *Endecja,* enemy of Marshal Piłsudski (the man who established and ran the between-war regime), and of all centrist, liberal and socialist groups. During the 1950s and up into the 1980s, it strove to implement some of the old Falangist goals, this time in close cooperation with the Soviet Union. Their objective was promoted in a program claiming to represent a "truly national realistic approach." The main idea of it consisted, and still consists, of Catholic and Communist cooperation in building a new order at first in Poland and then, by extension, everywhere else. If it was dissatisfied with the existing state of affairs at all, *Pax* was resentful of only one major mistake of the Party. In their opinion, the Polish United Worker's Party did not involve *Pax* in the actual exercise of power. In a superb book, *Współrzadzic czy nie kłamać?* [To Jointly Rule or Not to Lie?], published in Polish, Andrzej Micewski, himself a former active member of *Pax* and later of other Catholic clubs, wrote that *Pax* and *Znak* stood for so distinctively different Polands, that in avoidance of any confusion, one should not even discuss the two visions in one book together. He chose to discuss the two groups in separate parts. He described *Pax* as an offspring of the pre-war Polish Falangist movement. Piasecki is characterized as a man who, in order to be part of the ruling elite, would be willing to serve any force in power. With an articulated revulsion, Micewski summarizes *Pax*'s program, as one calling to serve God best by serving the

Church, the People and the Party which is building socialism. Contemptuous of masses, Piasecki felt that the populace is just obliged to follow the leader, because the leader alone knows in which direction to march. The Party was suspicious of this program, because its declared objective was to serve God. Primate Wyszynski characterized Piasecki's program as "a journey to God without God." Claude Naurois wrote about it in a book entitled *Dieu contre Dieu.*[15] Distrusted and even condemned by the Church and the wider circles of Catholic public opinion, *Pax* has not been able to win the Party's real trust either. The Party supported *Pax* or asked for its support only at a time when it attacked *Znak,* other Catholic groups, or the Church leadership as a whole, and whenever it wanted to contrast the "unpatriotic" Catholics with the good and "patriotic ones," supporting the Party. Now, once more, without Piasecki, who died recently, *Pax* activists are beginning to play a more important role than usual.

Znak was established in Cracow, soon after World War II, as a group cooperating with the Catholic weekly *Tygodnik Powszechny.* Frequently harassed, and at times strongly restricted and even banned, it nevertheless managed to persevere in promulgation of Catholic ethics, in defending the cause of human rights, and in propagating ideas akin to those of French philosophers Camus and Maritain, existentialists such as Marcel and Heidegger, and views of Tillich. At a time, when *Pax* embraced totalitarianism and labeled it Catholic statesmanship, *Znak* stood for Catholic humanism. It accepted the fact that the Communists are and will remain in power for the time being. Instead, however, of engaging in the power game under such conditions, it called for a "positivist" and not "romantic" way of action. ("Romantic" was the traditional 19th-century Polish way to struggle for the preservation of Catholic ethics and national culture.) Viewing Communist politics as immoral, at least until 1965, *Znak* wanted to be only an observer, which occasionally voiced protest against the most immoral of deeds. It believed that by practicing differently from the Party's standards of ethics, and continuing the Polish cultural tradition, the Church, in fact, in spite of the Party's domination, generated a situation which allowed for some pluralism. Acting under the slogan, "Not to Lie Regardless Of The Cost To Be Paid," *Znak* defended students and intellectuals after the 1968 unrest, and workers during and after the 1970 and 1976 troubles.[16]

Eventually, during the late 1950s and the 1960s, splinter groups of *Pax* formed other clubs: *Wiez* and the so-called *Centre for Documentation and Social Studies* (ODISS). These new groups adopted the ethics and philosophy of *Znak,* but aspired to a more active role in politics than *Znak* members strived for. Still later, during the 1970s, *Znak* itself was split into two wings, one willing to cooperate with the Party more than the other, which stayed with the more no-compromise position.

The main purpose of Catholic clubs was to provide a forum for discussion for groups interested in religious and cultural issues, as well as to provide the Catholic public with its own press. Each of the clubs published a journal; some published weeklies. *Pax* built a press empire. It published journals, weeklies and even a daily paper. The clubs organized discussion groups. They were allowed to have a few representatives in the Polish *Seym,* the formal rubber-stamp national assembly. And to create confusion, although this representation was comprised of members of all clubs and not of *Znak* only, it was called and recognized as a faction of *Znak.*

The faction could exercise close to no influence in the decision-making process; the *Seym,* as a whole, has little actual power. Still, it provided certain possibilities. After the tumultuous events in 1968, 1970, and 1976, during the adoption of the new Polish Constitution and the emergence of Solidarity, some members of this faction voiced protest over a number of issues. In 1981, after the establishment of Solidarity as an independent union, K.O.R., the Left intellectuals' group, dissolved itself. Its members accepted different active roles in the Solidarity organization. Many members of *Znak, Wiez,* and *ODISS* acted likewise. All these people, Catholics and non-believers alike, were later interned. Some, accused of crimes not yet specified, will be tried soon.

The impact of Catholic clubs in unifying the opposition forces in Poland was spectacular. These legally independent Catholic organizations provided shopwindows for ideas and ideals of the Church, Catholic as well as non-Catholic, Left-Wing, socialist, humanist and other opposition forces.[17]

Communist Policy; Church Policy

Over the years, the policy of the Polish Party-State vis-à-vis the Church has changed several times. At first, the Party launched an all-out frontal attack against the Church. Some Church property, particularly in the new, western provinces was seized. Restrictions were imposed on certain Church activities. The Church was forbidden to erect new church buildings and chapels. Members of the clergy were persecuted and given jail terms under different accusations. During the fifties, the Primate was exiled to a convent where he spent a number of years in isolation. Occasionally, in times of crisis, the Party-State sought reconciliation with, and even the support of, the Church. It promised to ban further persecution, to allow the building of new churches and to forbid discrimination against believers.

Another policy involved the penetration of the church hierarchy and developing the so-called "priest-patriots" movement, an internal Church opposition to the Episcopate, or inducement of splits of other kinds within the clergy. In return for this opposition and the implementation of the government's instructions as well as participation in state-initiated policies, some priests were promised and given beneficial favors. Favoring some club members and harassing others, the government succeeded in causing rifts within Catholic clubs and, more recently, in imposing a *Znak* representation in the *Seym,* which is more inclined to cooperate obediently with the Party. It did not succeed, however, in changing the attitude of the wider membership of these groups. This became especially evident during autumn and winter of 1980 when many members of Catholic clubs, particularly of *Znak* and *Wieź,* were involved in the formation of the new independent union.

The mass strikes and labor unrest during the winter 1980/81 caused the Church to develop a new function. It became a mediator between the Party and the emerging independent union. As a result, a sort of triangular relationship emerged between the Party, Solidarity, and the Church. Some observers were prone to regard it as a surrogate for, or a beginning of, a three-party system. Yet as long as the Soviet Union has a strong say in Polish affairs, the Western type multi-party system even composed of two or three parties—all accepting Soviet domination and socialism—will not be allowed. To win over the Church to its side and to placate Catholic public opinion a little known Catholic activist of *Znak,* Jerzy Ozdowski, was recently even appointed to the post of vice-premier, a position which bears little power in practice. Further, the government no longer prohibits building of new churches. Although the Party has not changed its position on church attendance, it does not punish its regular members for it either. And it promises more benefits to the Church if it cooperates.

The Polish Church at the Crossroads

The Roman Catholic Church is now at the crossroads. Leaders of the Church who for three decades have led the battles and opposed the state have become quite old. Primate Josef Cardinal Wyszynski and a number of others have died. Karol Wojtyła is in Rome. A new, until recently little known bishop, Josef Cardinal Glemp, has been appointed to the Primacy. A new generation of higher clergy took over. Not all of these new leaders of the Church are as strongly militant in opposition to the State as was the previous generation. Some among them feel that Poland is destined to be part of the Soviet block and nothing can be done about it. They are looking for new solutions, possibly some sort of cooperation, in which, in return for their Party's acquiescence to greater freedom for the Church, the Church would offer shepherding of the masses more to the liking of the State. *Pax* has been calling for such cooperation for a long time. Churches are full of believers, numerous young believers among others. But when the new archbishop Glemp called on young people not to allow themselves to be "manipulated" by "very irresponsible people" he got two responses. He delighted the Party press, which praised him as cautious, realistic and wise. But he also got a response in the underground press, which circulates widely in spite of all efforts of the police to put it down. It referred to him as "comrade Glemp," the way one addresses the party *apparatchiks,* indicating contempt. As Nina Darnton reported in *The New York Times Magazine* (June 6, 1982): "Glemp was chosen specifically because of his ability to compromise, his political savvy and his calm and modest demeanor, coupled with his strength of character."

But youth and the workers do not wish to have a Church willing to compromise. They applaud when Glemp and other archbishops call for the restoration of civil rights and the revival of the suspended, and then finally legally forbidden Solidarity union and other dissident and opposition groups. And they turn away when Glemp or others call for a compromise and the acceptance of the existing reality which no rebellion can change. They resent the clergy deploring activities of the demonstrators even when they deplore the action of the police and the government as well.

Which road will the church take? Continue on her Julian path or choose a new Constantinian road, now under the control of General Jaruzelski or under an even more hard-headed General Kiszczak, the chief of the Polish security forces and police?

The Church is being credited for the support it lent to the opposition movement and, most recently to the workers during the stormy days of 1980 and 1981, when the Soviet army was poised on the Polish border. But critics point out that even in those critical days the Church acted quite inconsistently. A Polish writer, published in the West under the pen name B.M., pointed out that in the recent conflict the Church played the role of mediator between the state and the union, but did not always act as it did in the past, when it opposed the state. In his opinion, the Church

seems to have fallen into the communist trap in agreeing to participate in the secrecy on affairs which should have been maintained public. She is being ruthlessly manipulated and misinformed by the Party and the State administration. In these very decisive moments in Polish history, the supreme moral Authority of our nation has chosen to perform a role too small in social activities. This could have a very adverse effect not only on the position of the Church in society but on the very fate of the nation as well.[18]

This opinion is shared by Klempski (1981) and other observers. Some criticism is even stronger. Stanisław Małkowski, a priest in Poland points out in a recent edition of the Parisian *Kultura:*

I have the feeling that our Primate seems to be more lenient toward authorities than he is toward society. How can I explain this to myself? I think that the Primate speaks to Christians as a father does and to pagans as a diplomat does . . . Besides, he sometimes treats the two quarreling sides in a way that some grownups treat two struggling kids. He tells that he wants silence and peace without looking into it who is right and who is wrong and who started it all.[19]

Małkowski continues:

The hidden evil must be revealed. Poland is facing the danger of an alliance (perhaps only a temporary one) between the two authorities (the Church and the State), an alliance to be concluded above the heads of people and against the society. The authorities of the state strive for the consummation of such an alliance. Yet, they treat the Church in such a contemptible manner and society with such a loathing and hatred that, thank God, they will not be able to attain what they want. The Church is too much bound by the Gospel and with the people to commit such terrible treason. As John Paul II said "the Church wishes to remain free facing the two systems opposing each other in the modern world; she must stand for the human cause."[20]

He warns that the Church could lose a large part of the youth and the *intelligentsia* as it lost various groups and entire strata in other societies when it disregarded the wishes of the people. The Church seems to be aware of this. One day it calls for moderation in protest. The next day it calls for harmony, criticizes the opposition activists, and expresses some sympathy for the Party's predicament. Still on another day, Archbishop Macharski of Cracow or some other archbishop, or even Glemp himself, appeal to the authorities to release political prisoners and restore to Solidarity its rights and to let the people feel more free. At the end of September 1982, the Church is making such appeals to the State authorities.

Since the beginning of this century and until World War II, the Polish *intelligentsia* and by extension the entire nation was split into a right-wing minority following the *Endecja,* the centrist nationalist or Catholic-oriented bourgeois and peasant majority, and another, left-wing minority, divided into all shades of socialism. After the Communist takeover, the division into rightist and leftist and the center persisted to an extent for some time. Then, however, the Church began to play a more prominent political role as the unofficial opponent of the Party. At first the church only tried to defend her rights and domains of influence. Soon, the Church felt obliged to speak up in defense of imprisoned students and laid-off workers who were protesting food shortages and price increases on essential commodities. The Church became the first propagator of *détente* and initiated a dialogue with the German Church on Polish-German relations when the Cold War was still in progress. Eventually it emerged in its present Julian role.

The traditional division into right and left and centrist changed as well. Both camps of the right and left became internally split. Part of the extreme right, as the example of *Pax* shows, now supports the ruling Party and the regime. Although the present regime claims to be socialist and employs a Marxist ideology instead of a unique derivative of conservative Catholicism and nationalism, to these people the regime represents an implementation of their own ideals. By "working from inside" and cooperating with the Party, they hope to transform it into a system which would be even more to their liking. Other rightists and nationalists, however, oppose the regime. The Left has become divided too. At first it embraced the new system. Gradually, a new dissident Polish Democratic Left opposing bureaucratic Communism came into being. These anti-dogmatic leftists refused to be alienated within their own society. They have found new meaning in church traditions and rituals. Mostly non-religious, they nevertheless associated with the Catholic Church as the Church of the people. They discovered that they speak the same language and share many ideas as do *Znak* and *Wieź* people. They marched together in the front lines of the Solidarity ranks.

The Polish Church, then, has been forced to change. Perhaps quite unintentionally, at first, it emerged in a new role as a moral authority of all society that opposes the State, a role traditionally performed by rebels and revolutionary movements. It even won the acclaim of many left-wing intellectuals, who used to criticize it and oppose it in the past. Western observers, accustomed to different ideological divisions, are still puzzled by this situation. How could radical leftists support the conservative, although to a certain extent changed, Church? Antoni Słonimski, one of the most respected poets and writers of the liberal left in post-war Poland, who in the past staunchly attacked the Church as the mainstay of capitalism and conservatism, explained most succinctly why the attitude of the left toward the Church has changed. "Before the War, the Church was reactionary and Communism represented the forces of progress. At present, it is just the opposite."[21] Adam Michnik, a former party activist, then a rebel and advisor of Wałesa, writes:

> The history of men is a history of striving for truth. Because it is a right as well as a duty to live in truth and in pursuance of truth, those who share the anti-totalitarian concern, regardless of their nationality or religion, join forces together. The value of truth-pursuance is deeply rooted in both the Christian declaration of faith and the secular literary tradition. Both of these traditions have developed a strong concern about the growing of the State domination. Christian doctrine has developed a strong argument against the omnipotency of the State as well as against all kinds of other "*statelatrian* impositions." Analogous theories appeared in the secular literature concerned with freedom (one can refer to classical works by the liberal John S. Mill or to the writing by Karl Marx as exemplary on the issue). In spite of this parallel and objective convergence of ideas, in the past, Christians and writers of the secular Left did not develop a feeling

of sharing of those ideas and therefore did not join forces. This is changing at the present however.[22]

He further writes that, in the present situation, when the very existence of human civilization is endangered by all-devouring bureaucracies and state-systems that transform their members into thoughtless robots who believe neither in God nor in freedom and dignity, the intellectual forces of Catholicism and of the radical left must unite their efforts in defense of more vital interests than those that divided them until now.

The Polish *intelligentsia,* and, by extension, the entire population is now more and more divided into two ideological camps. The dividing issue is different from the issues that divided society in the past. On the one hand, there are those who accept the omnipresence of the state, and succumb to its dictates and, on the other hand there are those who, because of their belief in God or desire for freedom and independence, reject the tutelage of the state. Those who support the state are in a minority. They have the police and the army on their side. They know, however, that they cannot trust their soldiers and the regular party members. The other minority is small too, because it is comprised of the most daring, those who are willing to go to jail, if necessary, or to die in the streets and prisons. Such people are, almost always, in the minority. The majority looks suppressed, subdued, and their concern is how to live. They are forced to work hard and they get little in return. The stores are empty. People have to stand for hours in long lines to obtain essentials. They have learned that no government in the West is going to help them. They walk in the streets at the time when the news is being broadcasted to indicate that they do not wish to hear it. They build floral crosses. They go to churches and pray. When the battles erupt in the streets, they come out. Some join those who demonstrate. The Church does not feel comfortable in this new, constantly worsening situation and polarization of forces. It has changed in the past. It may have to change again.

Church–Solidarity–State 1986

Four years have passed since this article was written. What has occurred in the Church–Solidarity–State relations during these years?

Nowadays, people in Warsaw bring their flowers to the grave of murdered priest Jerzy Popieluszko at the St. Stanislaus Kostka Church instead of Victory square. This church where he used to preach is now regarded as a national religious shrine. Most Solidarity leaders, released from internment under an amnesty law, are now imprisoned again. After a five year hunt, in May 1986 the security forces captured Zbigniew Bujak, the most prominent undergound resistance leader. Lech Wałesa is allowed to stay out of prison, but is kept under strict surveillance by security forces. Solidarity continues to operate as a two-tier network composed of underground regional and factory cells and an above-ground group of activists and advisers, all recognizing Lech Wałesa and the Interim Coordination Commission (TKK) as the union's supreme authority. The Party-state refuses to recognize Wałesa and his organization as representing anyone.

Deprived not only of the freedom won in Solidarity days, but of hope to regain it in the foreseeable future, forced to endure conditions within which nothing can be improved, the society has slipped into a state of permanent psychological shock. Poland has the dubious distinction of having the most polluted natural environment in the world. Dilapidated and poorly maintained homes can be seen all over the country. The state, which owns these buildings, does not have the means to repair them. Food and other commodities are in short supply. Without drugs, hospitals advise patients to obtain them on the black market. Paid ludicrously little, people do the minimum at work. Many feel that they are living in a gigantic lunatic asylum under guard by the military. Underground, and in some instances legally produced literature, music and art convey the pain, awareness of collective powerlessness, helplessness, hopelessness and despondency experienced by these people. The police are unable to eradicate the flood of underground publications.

The Church evidently does not have a concerned plan of action. It can only react to the situation. The Church called for release of political prisoners, but otherwise carefully avoided situations in which it would be identified with political opposition. Cardinal Glemp and bishops close to him are trying to develop a compromise with the Party-state within which the Church would retain influence and the position acquired in many conflicts since the War. The leadership of the Church avoids confrontations and does not express a militant enough opposition as the Solidarity forces and society at large expect it to take. On the other hand, Bishop Tokarczuk and a number of other priests take a more uncompromising position. They preach that the Church's duty is to fight evil both big and small. They argue that since the communist authorities have broken the terms of agreements many times in the past, they cannot be trusted. Tokarczuk is regarded as patron of the young defiant clergymen speaking out against the regime regardless of the consequences. Popieluszko, murdered by security forces, was one of them. The Church is trying to silence others; Malkowski and Nowak, who continued to preach against the state, were transferred to remote parishes.

Priest Popieluszko's funeral was attended by 250,000 mourners. At the trial of his killers, the prosecutor, and the government press blamed the Church for his death, claiming that it was guilty of harboring "unruly and politicking clerics." A campaign of anti-Church propaganda, harassment and repression against priests was started simultaneously with the trial. It led to a "war of the crosses." During the Stalinist period, the government strictly forbade the display of crosses and other religious symbols at schools. Crosses reappeared on school walls again under Gomulka's rule, and especially during the Solidarity days. Now, referring to a 1961 decree, the government ordered a total ban on crucifixes in school. Students in certain schools organized sit-in strikes and protest meetings against the removal of crosses. This was an issue to which the Church could not react with silence. The Main Church Council and the 199th Plenary Conference of the Polish Episcopate, convening in Warsaw March 28 and 29, issued communiques urging Catholics to defend the display of religious emblems in public places. The war went on for several weeks and eventually ended in a compromise. Crosses were retained only in special reading rooms of some schools, but not in regular classes and were removed from most other schools.

For several years now, the Church has tried to conclude an agreement with the state over two recognitions. The Church wants (1) to have an officially recognized legal status and (2) state acceptance of its right to manage the Church-sponsored Agricultural Fund involving foreign donated monies. In response, the state demands that the Church accept its control over the nominations to Church positions and to adjust more "to the conditions of the socialist system." If concluded, such an agreement, would open a new chapter in the history of Church-State relations in Poland. The issue is this:

would the Church be transformed into yet another transmission belt of the Party to the masses, as churches in other East European nations have been, or would it retain its role as a platform for freedom striving forces of the nation?

NOTES

1. This article is an updated and thoroughly revised version of a paper presented to the Annual Meeting of Sociology of Religion, Toronto, in 1981, published under the title, "The Secular Role of the Catholic Church in Present-Day Poland," in Nationalities Papers 10:2 (Fall 1982). Reprinted by permission of *The Journal of Ecumenical Studies.* All translations from the Polish were done by the author.
2. *The Teaching of the Second Vatican Council* (Westminister, Maryland: The Newman Press, 1966), p. 636.
3. Walter Abbott, S.J., ed., *Lumen Gentium. The Documents of Vatican II* (New York: Herder and Herder, 1966), pp. 199–340.
4. Andrzej Bardecki, *Kosciół Epoki Dialogu* (Warsaw: Znak, 1968); Andrzej Bardecki, *Prezłom* (Warsaw: Znak, 1970); Karol Wojtyła, *Upodstaw odnowy. Studium o realizacji Vaticanum II* (Cracow: Polskie Towarzystwo Teologiczne, 1972).
5. Anna Kaminska, "The Polish Pope and the Polish Catholic Church," *Survey* 24 (Autumn, 1979) no. 4, p. 205.
6. Bohdan Cywinski, *Rodowody Niepokornych* (Warsaw: Wiez, 1971), p. 262.
7. *Ibid.,* p. 263.
8. Max Weber, *The Sociology of Religion,* trans. Ephraim Fischoff (Boston: Beacon Press, 1964), p. 151.
9. *Ibid.,* p. 152.
10. B.P. Wilhelm Pluta, "Małżenstwo, rodzina i wartości Boże," *Wieź,* No. 1 (1981), p. 81.
11. Karol Borowski, "Secular and Religious Education in Poland," *Religious Education* 70, no. 1 (1975), p. 70. These and other estimates of Polish religiosity were developed with the use of a questionnaire distributed partially in Poland, partially among the emigree community in the U.S.A. and Canada.
12. Tadeusz Szafar, "Contemporary Political Opposition in Poland," *Survey* 24, no. 4 (Autumn 1979), p. 40.
13. Jakub Swiecicki, "Polskie periodyki poza cenzura," *Kultura,* No. 10/397 (1980).
14. Szafar, "Political Opposition."
15. Claude Naurois, *Dieu contre Dieu?* (Paris: Saint Paul, 1956).

16. Andrzej Micewski, *Wspolrzadzić czy nie kłamać? Pax i Znak w Polsce 1945–1976* (Paris: Libella, 1978), pp. 161–197.
17. Additional information on these groups can be found in Richard Sharpless, Paul Mojzes, Stephen Lammers, "Polish Concerns, Soviet Apprehensions," *OPREE* 1, no. 7 (December, 1981), pp. 1–9.
18. B. M., "Kryzys totalny," *Kultura,* No. 11/398, p. 531.
19. Stanislaw Malkowski, "Strzały z bunkra 'endokomuny' (kula w plot)" *Kultura* No. 7/418–8/419, pp. 110–112.
20. *Ibid.*
21. Found in Adam Michnik, *Kosciol, Lewica, Dialog* (Paris: Instytut Literacki, 1977), p. 98.
22. *Ibid.,* p. 88.

13

Liberation Theology and the Political Order in Latin America

FRANK K. FLINN

The history of the world is nothing but the unfolding of the idea of freedom.

—G. W. F. Hegel

Introduction: Modernity, Religion and the Political Order

The present government in Israel refers to the West Bank region as Judea and Samaria—geographical designations which are derived from the Bible. The revolution in Iran has sent political analysts to the books in order to discover the social and political differences between Shiite and Sunni Moslems. At the second Latin American Bishops Conference (CELAM II), in Medellín, Columbia, in 1968, the bishops announced the church's duty of "solidarity with the poor." In the United States, coalitions of Christians and others lobbied to overturn, or at least thwart, the U.S. Supreme Court decision *Roe v. Wade* (1973) because they believed that the human fetus bears the image of God from the moment of conception.

I cite the above facts, not so much because they are incontestable, but because they confuse us, both conceptually and emotionally. Their mere occurrence produces *ad hominem* arguments ("Communists have infiltrated the Latin American Roman Catholic Church") or unrestrained bouts of stereotyping ("The Moral Majority is nothing but a bunch of 'rednecks'"). Obviously, emotional arguments and self-blinding stereotypes will not guide us toward a reasonable assessment of events like those noted in the first paragraph. We need to dig deeper to discover the source of our confusion in dealing conceptually and practically with religious events which directly impinge on the political order. *The source of our confusion, I suggest, lies at the very heart of modernity itself.*

Modern political theory begins with a conscious break with the perennial philosophical and theological tradition. Henceforth, reason alone was to accomplish what heretofore had been accomplished by reason in conjunction with revelation, i.e., by Athens and Jerusalem. Though there are important differences in modern theories of the state, they are all in agreement that the ancients aimed too high, i.e., that they took their bearings from humanity's final end or how humans ought to live. The philosophers of Athens thought that humanity was directed to a life of virtue in the "best regime," and the prophets of Jerusalem believed that humanity was called to righteousness in the Kingdom of God. In their attempt to overcome the political problem and to sidestep, as it were, the recalcitrant problem of fallen human nature, the moderns turned their attention—and ours, too—away, from final causes to efficient causes,[1] from virtues to the passions, from the god-like aspect of human nature to the beast-like, from piety to satisfaction, from imaginary ideals (Utopias) to hard-nosed reality. The modern enlightenment of "realism" may indeed be enlightenment, but it is from below rather than from above.

The ever widening gulf between reason and revelation, philosophy and theology, politics and religion, however, had one cankerous flaw. In the words of Leo Strauss, the modern turn to realistic expectations brought on "a lowering of the standards."[2] This lowering has never been more explicit than in a text from Chapter 15 of Machiavelli's *Il Principe*—a text to which the subscript *Hic incipit modernitas* may well be added:

> For many writers have constructed imaginary republics and principalities which have never been seen nor known actually to exist. But so wide is the separation between the way men actually live and the way they ought to live, that anyone who turns his attention from what is actually done to what ought to be done, studies his own ruin rather than his preservation.[3]

It is on this foundation that Machiavelli recommends new modes and new orders for an entirely new kind of prince—one who is prepared to mix vice with virtue or, more accurately, vice with a reputation for virtue in order to preserve himself in power. He turns our attention away from the imaginary Best City of Plato which exists only as a "pattern laid up in heaven" (*Republic* 592b), and from Restored Jerusalem which exists only in the word of the Lord's promise (Isaiah 60:1–22), to the grubby, but real, political cutthroating which reigned in the Italian principalities of his time. With the qualified exception of Immanuel Kant, this text is approvingly quoted or referred to by almost all major thinkers of the modern era. Beginning with Francis Bacon, the moderns in varying degrees concurred that the ancients made "imaginary laws for imaginary commonwealths, and their discourses are as the stars, which give little light because they are so high."[4] After Machiavelli, political philosophy was to take its bearings from the "Is," not the "Ought."

Modern political philosophy assumes that human passions cannot be elevated by the rhetoric of Virtue or Justice. It grounds itself, therefore, on a minimalist hypothesis or extreme case that all human beings are by nature vicious unless forced to be good.[5] It collapses the classical distinction between necessity (the "Is") and the good (Plato, *Republic* 493a–c), thereby claiming that the good could emerge from necessity through the emancipation of the socially malleable passions. That emancipation takes various forms: fame and glory (Machiavelli), power (Hobbes), acquisitiveness (Locke, Smith), recognition (Hegel). Though the moderns rejected the Utopian thought of Jerusalem and Athens, they nonetheless affirmed the Utopian belief that the emancipation of the passions would be historically redemptive or, in the words of Adam Smith, that a man in the pursuit of selfish gain would be "led by an invisible hand to promote an end which was no part of his intention."[6]

It is in the context of the emancipation of the passions that we can detect the diminution of the importance of religion in modern political philosophy. The theory of the state of nature, upon which all modern political theory is founded, is a rationalized and rationalizing substitute for the biblical account of the creation of humanity in a state of innocency (= state of nature), the fall through disobedience, and restoration to a state of grace.[7] In Hobbes' *Leviathan,* the state of nature stands not in opposition to the state of grace, but to the state of civility.[8] Nor does it imply a state of innocency, but, rather, a condition wherein brutish passions prevail and which can be overcome and "humanized" by entering the social contract. Behind the famous modern distinction between nature and culture lies hidden the less flattering distinction between bestiality and humanity. For this low but solid estimation of human nature, Hobbes was beholden, like his mentor Francis Bacon, once again to Machiavelli. The Florentine ingeniously replaced the imitation of Socrates, who looked single-mindedly at the highest and god-like part of the soul for the construction of the just city, and the imitation of the Christ, the God-Man, who single-mindedly looked toward the Kingdom of his Father, for the imitation of Chiron, the centaur Beast-Man, who legend tells us was the instructor of war-like Achilles.[9]

In his founding of the just city in speech but not in deed, Socrates argued that there are three aspects of the soul, to which correspond three classes in the city, which must be accounted for: a desiring part *(epithymia)* which leads to money-making; a spirited part *(thymos)* which is war-like; and a reasoning part *(logismos)* which is god-like and meant to govern the whole and restrain the other two parts (*Republic* 419a–445e).

Because of the low estimation of human nature in modern political philosophy, the moderns omit an account of the reasoning part of the soul in their description of the origin of the social contract. Prepolitical humanity is a vicious brute at its worst (Machiavelli, Hobbes), or a rather stupid and unimaginative animal endowed only with feeling and a sentiment of compassion, at its best (Rousseau).[10] Reason, it was hoped, would emerge as the accidental by-product of the historical process. For analogous reasons, the moderns also omitted the biblical teaching that humanity bore the image of God. Machiavelli charged that the Christian emphasis on contemplation, along with the cultivation of the virtues of humility and lowliness, led to "the effeminacy of the world" and attached human loyalty to a "disarmed Heaven."[11] In place of the other-worldly fatherland and heavenly citizenship, Machiavelli hoped to reinstitute the civil religion of the Romans, in which religion and patriotism coincided because the gods of religion were also gods of the State. Otherworldly (= imaginary) religion was to be passed over in favor of this-worldly (= real) religion because "all the institutions which set man at odds with himself are worthless."[12] The secret wish of the most radical modern thinkers was that other-worldly or supranatural religion would evanesce, giving way to "the religion of the citizen," to use Rousseau's phrase, in which "sentiments of sociability" would replace religious dogmas and the only negative commandment would be "no intolerance."[13] Yet even this seemingly liberal platform of tolerance concealed a most intolerant proviso. Rousseau concluded his *Social Contract* with the recommendation that "anyone who dares to say 'Outside the church there is no salvation' should be expelled from the state."[14] Thus the "irrational" intolerance of supernatural religion, which often led to fanatical religious wars, was replaced by the more "rational" intolerance of political excommunication.

Despite the anti-religious undercurrent of most modern political theory, most moderns were not so foolish as to think that the emancipation of the passions could be left unchecked. As human nature was malleable, the passions could be shaped and directed in socially useful ways by the clever ordering of institutions.[15] The ancient sacred restraints of negative commands, which were addressed to the formation of character, gave way to the "socialization" of animals into humans by means of secular virtues embodied in society itself. Thus Hobbes sought to replace fear of the Lord with the fear of violent death, while Rousseau sought to put compassion in place of love of neighbor, and tolerance in place of piety. The secularization of virtue is no better symbolized than in Rousseau's *Émile,* the tap root of all modern educational theory, wherein the author supplants the Bible with Daniel Defoe's *Robinson Crusoe.*[16] Allan Bloom describes Defoe's adventure book as a "kind of Bible of the new science of nature."[17] Crusoe is a pre-Adamic Boy Scout thrust into pure nature with a moral and religious *tabula rasa.* There are no Greek or Roman heroes for him to emulate; there is no Eden to remember, nor any salvation to look forward to. Rousseau's primordial natural man is guided solely by an interest in comfortable self-preservation.

In summary, modern political philosophy was of the opinion that political virtue could be sustained without otherworldly supports. If religion was to have a social role, then it was only in the form of this-worldly civil religion, which hopefully would instill sentiments of patriotism and social solidarity. If supranatural religion still had a place in modern political theory, it was only in the form of "the religion of the private person" which had "no specific connexion with the body politic" but was "wholly spiritual, concerned solely with the things of heaven."[18] This conception of religion as inner feeling or sentiment gave impetus to the privatization of religious meaning and its association with freedom of thought rather than freedom of action. We see this conviction epitomized in Thomas Jefferson's declaration "I am a sect myself" and Thomas Paine's proclamation "My own mind is my own church."[19] This line of thinking terminates in Alfred North Whitehead's dictum: "Religion is what the individual does with his own solitariness."[20] Such a dictum not only blunts the social cutting edge of the prophetic aspect of religion but also deprives the mind of the necessary conceptual equipment for prudently judging and acting on religious events which, despite the theoretical separation of religion and politics, nonetheless continue to impinge on the political order.

Yet, in pointing out the lacunae in modern political theory, there can be no doubt that the moderns were great lovers of liberty. The love of liberty passed over into the Americas. Whether by chance or by providence, North America was spared the vehement attacks on revealed religion which lay beneath much modern political theory. This circumstance was no doubt due to the doctrine of the separation of powers which was mediated through Locke and especially the judicious Montesquieu.[21] The ideal of the separation of the executive, legislative and judicial powers lays the groundwork for the separation of church and state, while preserving the liberty of both.

In contrast with early modern political thinkers, the American federalists did not entertain a political philosophy that aimed at the whole, undivided person or state. They were content to let power be divided and at loggerheads, looking not at the best political order possible but at the political order which allowed for the most improvement. As a concession to the moderns, the federalist writers admitted that representative democracy offered a gradual cure to "men of factious nature" and not simply the best regime.[22] The idea of division of power was applied to the various sects. In his *Notes on Virginia* (1787), Jefferson stated, "Difference of opinion is advantageous in religion. The several sects perform the office of a *censor morum* over each other."[23]

Nonetheless, the long litigation over the interpretation of the separation of church and state reveals that there is confusion about the meaning of that separation. In principle, the First Amendment maintains that there can be no formal *civil religion* in the United States, that is, a religion which is established and supported by the government. Conversely no religion can be disestablished by the government. This disentanglement of religion and politics, however, does not mean that religion cannot be *public,* as some claim, for freedom of religion is indissolubly bound up with freedom of speech and freedom of assembly. Today there seems to be much confusion about the distinction between the civil and the public aspects of freedom of religion. If this confusion is coupled with the prevailing tendency to see religion, or at least supernatural religion, as a strictly private affair, and with the similar tendency to see religious congregations as "voluntary associations" with no institutional bite, the indirect benefit of religion on the public order will be imperilled and the ogre of an implicit state religion will raise its ugly spectre.

The chief benefit of the separation of church and state has been to remove from religion the power of physical coercion, thereby avoiding the violent fanaticism that led to religious warfare. Conversely, the First Amendment severely restricts government authority over matters religious ("Congress shall make no law . . ."), thereby preventing the state from becoming tyrannical. Obviously, religion cannot protect its own sphere if it is restricted to the privacy of conscience. To the extent that religion can have a direct influence on the general public, it has a political role but not, it should be emphasized, a civil function in the State. The doctrine of the separation of powers when applied to church and state implies that the state's tendency to claim sovereignty over all spheres of existence can be checked and balanced only by the countersovereignty of institutional ecclesiastical religion.[24] It is no accident that the civil rights movement in the United States sprang from institutional ecclesiastical religion. It was only on the basis of a prophetic vision of a New Jerusalem that the nation could become conscious of the injustice which mere civil justice deals out to the poor and the oppressed.

Yet even the ideal of the separation of church and state is not without its ambiguities. There is a dispute between strict separationists, who hold to Jefferson's image of an impregnable "wall" between church and state, and accommodationists, who appeal to Madison's image of a "line." Wilson Yates has suggested the more realistic image of a "border," with closed and open sectors, respectively prohibiting absolutely and cautiously allowing crossings and interactions between church and state.[25] It would be unwise to attempt to universalize these models. In countries like Iran there is now a coincidence of the Shiite interpretation of the Quran and the constitution of the state. In some European countries, there is separation of church and state along with state support of certain churches' institutions. In Latin America the Catholic Church has always continued to see itself as responsible for the political order. In the Latin American context the image of an osmotic "membrane" would be the more appropriate way to describe the relation between church and state.

When one looks back at the project of modern political philosophy, one is constrained to confess that, despite their claim to Realpolitik, the moderns, with few exceptions, upheld a most unrealistic picture of religion and its effects on the political order. According to Machiavelli and Rousseau, revealed religion could have no effect on the political order because it was strictly "heavenly" or "supranatural." "A society of true Christians," wrote Rousseau, "would not be a society of men."[26] Yet the claim of a religion like Christianity is to establish a *communio sanctorum* in the here-and-now in anticipation of the coming Kingdom of God. The prayer of the *ecclesia* "Let thy Kingdom come on earth as it is in heaven" is not an otherworldly prayer but a demythologization of any claims to ultimacy on the part of the earthly *civitas.* Secondly, the modern reduction of the origin of the political order to one or more of the passions simply cannot account for the scope of the life-world of the political. Certainly a soldier in the defense of country and home forgoes "comfortable self-preservation." In this circumstance even the moderns appeal to something higher than mere existence—freedom, honor and even God—thereby coming into contradiction with the premise of their reductive political philosophy. The lowering of the standard necessarily entails the resurrection of the standard because it is not by bread alone that things political are sustained. Hence, Thomas Jefferson, heir to the modern tradition, taught the necessity of "natural *aristoi*" or those guided by virtue in order to offset the venal appetites of the masses.[27]

The failure of modern political philosophy was to hypersupernaturalize the political effects of revealed revelation. The concrete historical impact of religious belief on this-worldly political reality is perhaps nowhere more discernible than in the Christian iconographic tradition which passes from the Byzantine Christos Pantocrator, crowning the Holy Roman Emperor with the assistance of the Apostles Peter and Paul, to the humble medieval Christ Crucified, whose wounds are inflicted by the Christian virtues of Humility, Piety and Wisdom, and, finally, to the Cristo Liberador as depicted by Juan Orozco in the Baker Library of Dartmouth University in 1938.[28] In Orozco's mural, the background is strewn with tumbled canon and fallen statues. Behind the figure of the Cristo the cross lies supine. The Cristo stands defiantly erect with a transfixing, fierce gaze, his left arm raised in a clenched fist and his right wielding an ax. To this awesome painting Rosenstock-Huessy has appended a phrase from Augustine's Epistle 38: *Crux ipsa crucifigenda est* (The cross itself has to be crucified). One glimpse at this mural is enough to convince the viewer that here the supernatural has invaded the historical process.

What is Liberation Theology?

Liberation theology is a recent formulation of Christian theology. Classically, Christian theology has been articulated in terms of the three articles of the Christian creed which enunciates the belief (1) that God is the creator of heaven and earth, spirit and matter; (2) that redemption is made needful through the fall of humanity away from the original purpose of creation and comes through Jesus Christ; and (3) that the sanctification and consummation of humanity results from the outpouring of the Holy Spirit on the church and the arrival of the Kingdom of God on earth. In sum, Christian theology is composed of the three doctrines of creation, redemption and sanctification (or consummation). Though there has always been a tension between the spiritual and physical in Christianity, with the concurrent tendency to spiritualize and supernaturalize the content of the creed, the notions of God-created matter, the incarnation of God in human flesh, the Kingdom of God on earth and the resurrection of the flesh make it preeminently clear that, *pace* Machiavelli, Christianity can in no way be labelled an exclusively "otherworldly" religion.

Not all Christian theologies, however, have fully accounted for all three articles of the creed and their interrelations. Irenueus of Lyon, the first Christian theologian, explained the heart of Christian teaching in terms of two doctrines, creation and restoration. Calvin broke down the creed into the topics of creation, redemption, sanctification and the church.[29] Luther, by contrast, introduced a dialectical tension between the doctrines of creation (Law) and redemption (Gospel), thereby foreshadowing the dialectical character of later German thought.[30] Karl Barth, the most influential Protestant theologian of the twentieth century, subordinated the doctrines of creation (God above us) and sanctification (God within us) to the doctrine of redemption in Jesus Christ (God with us), which he describes as "the fountain and light by which the other two [i.e., the first and third articles of the creed] are lit."[31] These theological formulations exemplify the different ways Christian theology has been clarified in order to meet specific historical situations and crises.

When we turn our attention to a phenomenon like liberation theology, we can see immediately that it puts strong emphasis on the doctrine of redemption over and above the doctrines of creation and sanctification. Barth turned to the second article of the creed (God's "no" to the old Adam and "yes" to the new humanity bestowed in Christ) because the theology of the orders of creation *(Ordnungstheologie)* was being transmogrified by Nazi theologians into an apology for "blood and race."[32] Similarly in traditional Latin American Catholicism, the theology of creation had been invoked to support the permanence of oligarchic regimes and the status quo. At the other end, the theology of sanctification in traditional Catholic circles had been deflected from its dialectical anchor in this world and its concerns into a quest for "eternal rewards," thereby relegating questions of social justice and human rights to a secondary status.

Liberation theology is not simply a theology of redemption; redemption is seen not so much in terms of justification (Luther) or restoration of the original life-giving power of creation but specifically as liberation. Liberation theology looks toward the loosening of God's poor and oppressed people from the shackles of bondage. The key liberation text is Exodus 3:7–8:[33]

> The Lord said:
> I have indeed seen the misery of my people in Egypt,
> I have heard their outcry against their slave-masters;
> I have taken heed of their sufferings,
> And have come down to rescue them from Egypt's power,
> And to bring them up out of that country
> Into a find broad land, a land flowing with milk and honey.

This text about the deliverance of Israel from bondage provides the background both for liberation Christology (the teaching about Christ) and liberation ecclesiology (the teaching about the church's role in the world).

The liberationist Christ is not primarily the Logos (Word) of creation, as in much early Christian theology, nor primarily the God-Man, as in late medieval theology, but savior and liberator who leads his people out of physical, mental and spiritual bondage. In the official ecclesiastical document "Justice" at the Medellín conference, the bishops declared that God

> . . . in the fulness of time, sends his Son in the flesh, so that He might come to liberate all men from the slavery to which sin has subjected them:

hunger, misery, oppression and ignorance, in a word, that injustice and hatred which have their origin in human selfishness.[34]

Salvation, then, is not simply "spiritual" or the guarantee of supernatural bliss in "heaven," but the outcome of the historical process for attaining political, economic and social well-being. Secondly, liberation looks to the active ministry of Jesus Christ. Where much modern Christology works within the horizon of the "gospel within the gospel," i.e., the biblical texts on the death and resurrection of Jesus, liberation also includes within its horizon the Jesus of Nazareth, who says to the poor and the lame "Take up your pallet and walk."

In accord with this political understanding of the work and ministry of Christ, liberation ecclesiology does not stress the church as a hierarchical institution, nor as a "mystical body" for the dispensation of sacraments, but the model of the church as servant to the poor and herald of socioeconomic justice.[35] On the other hand, it would be incorrect to say that liberation rejects earlier models of the church. Rather, the more traditional models of the church as institution, mystical body and sacrament are both preserved yet transformed under the prophetic imperative "to bear witness to its message and to use its prophetic word of annunciation and denunciation in an evangelical sense."[36] The mission of the church is not so much as an institution to preserve traditional societal structures, but as a "catalyst in the temporal realm in an authentic attitude of service."[37] Liberation theology, therefore, introduces a note of dialectical eschatology into ecclesiology. While recognizing the relative autonomy of temporal institutions under the principle of subsidiarity, the bishops at both the Medillín and Puebla conferences envision a critical role for the church which has both positive and negative aspects. On the positive side, it is the annunciation of the "Good News" of freedom from bondage. On the negative side, it is the denunciation of injustice which embraces both self-criticism (e.g., the one-sided identification of the clergy with the interests of the ruling classes)[38] and criticism of social structures which do not serve the common good.[39] Like the prophets of the Old Testament, liberation theology approaches the future with the word of judgment on unjust structures in society and the word of promise for the time when peace and justice will reign on earth and not just in heaven.

A definition of liberation theology would state that (1) it is an Exodus-type theology (2) which places strong emphasis on the doctrine of redemption or salvation as freedom from physical, mental and spiritual bondage and (3) which views the function of the church as a prophetic catalyst for the attainment of justice on the earth so that the Kingdom of God may reign. This definition, though adequate in its basic points, does not, however, exhaust all the characteristics of liberation theology.

Characteristics of Liberation Theology

Although liberation theology arose in Latin America and speaks to a specific Latin American situation, it has had wide influence not only in the Third World but also in the Second and First Worlds. One can point, for example, to black liberation theology, to feminist liberation theology, to the use of liberationist theme in the anti-nuclear movement in Europe, and to solidarity movements with the Third World.[40] It cannot be my purpose to discuss these offshoots of and parallels to liberation theology, except occasionally to note where they converge or diverge from the chief characteristics of the liberation movement in Latin America. In general, there are five characteristics of the liberation theological movement in Latin America.[41] All of them have direct bearing on the political order.

Justice The question of justice is in the forefront of liberation thought. "Justice" is the title of the first document issued at the Medellín conference in 1968. Yet the very meaning of justice is under dispute. In nations where contractual liberalism has come to prevail, justice in its primary sense is attached to individual civil rights and these rights precede duties. In this understanding of justice there are perfect (individual) rights but no perfect (social) duties.[42] The one indubitable natural right is the right of self-preservation. The duties which arise result from entering contracts. Thus, justice has come to mean the habit of fulfilling one's contracts. The Roman Catholic tradition has never abandoned the classical tradition which looks not primarily toward origins, but toward ends or possible perfection. Thus justice proceeds from the end of the law and the end of the law is unequivocally defined as the "common good."[43] Justice means, first and foremost, that which serves the common good. This notion in no way denies individual rights, but, rather, sees those rights as deriving from the fulfillment of obligations to the common good, of which the individual constitutes a part. Even in traditional Latin American Catholicism this notion of corporate justice never lost its appeal. From one aspect, liberation theology is the attempt to move the corporate sense of justice from right to left and from high to low, thereby bonding it with concrete actions, inducing social solidarity and the preferential option in favor of the poor and oppressed: "The Christian quest for justice is a demand arising from biblical teaching. All men are merely humble stewards of material goods. . . . We have faith that our love for Christ and our brethren will not only be the great force liberating us from injustice and oppression, but also the inspiration for social justice, understood as the whole of life. . . ."[44]

Conscientization. The second attribute of liberation theology is bound up with the word conscientization. The practice of *conscientização* was first associated with Brazilian adult education programs in the 1960s under the populist *Movimiento de Educação de Base,* and first made known to North Americans through the educator Paolo Freire's *The Pedagogy of the Oppressed* (1970) and *Education for Critical Consciousness* (1973).[45] Conscientization is the educational process of becoming critically aware of the personal, social, political and economic circumstances of life through dialogue and reciprocity, with the aim of changing reality through critical praxis. Freire is convinced that the democratization of culture can take place only through conscientization. Freire contrasts critical with naive and fanatical consciousness. Naive or magical consciousness "superimposes itself on reality"; fanatical consciousness "adapts to reality." Critical consciousness, on the other hand, represents "things and facts as they exist empirically, in their causal and circumstantial correlations."[46]

At the Medellín conference, the Latin American bishops gave official sanction to the educational use of conscientization in church circles because they saw it as "indispensable to form a social conscience and a realistic perception of the problems of the community and of social structures."[47] In most base communities (see below), conscientization has an *evangelical* basis. In the community of Our Lady of Solentiname, the Sunday reading of the scripture served as the focal point for the critical evaluation of social conditions.[48] Solentiname was an example of hermenuetics *de base,* in which all the members of the congregation had the opportunity to reflect on the gospel and to interact with each other's reflection. In some instances, however, conscientization turns in the direction of Marxist social analysis of class struggle.[49]

Praxis. Hand-in-hand with the notion of conscientization is the commitment to praxis. Praxis is not simply motion, nor individual action, but "reflective action" which maintains theory and action in interplay through dialogue and reciprocity.[50] Liberationists think that both church and state structures in the just society will emerge not simply on the base of pure theory, doctrinal teaching or intellectual critique, but through the dialectic of theory and praxis in concrete historical situations, which in Latin America means the plight of the poor and the oppressed. Furthermore, praxis is not determined by "projects and programs" sent down from above, or from the developed nations to the undeveloped, but emerges from within local communities in accord with the local community's own critical reflection of what needs are.

Latin American liberationists break away from European theologizing, which they think is tied in too closely with the "bourgeois Enlightenment" of the 19th century and which attains reconciliation between religion and society only on a theoretical level.[51] Likewise, they reject the North American pragmatic approach. The Alliance for Progress inaugurated by President John Kennedy, for example, employed a *developmental* model to Latin American problems, but for the Latin Americans themselves, "development" has meant the advancement of U.S. economic interests, increased militarism ("National Security"), and the expropriation of resources. As the bishops at Puebla noted, " . . . since the decade of the fifties, and despite certain achievements, the ample hopes for development have come to nothing. The marginalization of the vast majority and the exploitation of the poor has increased."[52] The failures of one-sided theory and one-sided practice have since moved the Latin American church further in the direction of liberating praxis, through which programs, needs and cooperation are defined *de base.*

There has been much rhetoric about liberation praxis in Latin America. Most often, the charge of Marxist analysis comes to the fore. Arthur McGovern, a first-hand observer of Latin American base communities, counters that "borrowing from Marxist analysis does not mean advocating Marxist-Leninist tactics," i.e., a single vanguard party, dictatorship of the proletariat, centralized state control, armed revolution, etc.[53] In McGovern's observation, analysis is scripture-based and the type of community organization is on the pattern pioneered by Saul Alinsky in the United States.

Solidarity. A fourth aspect of liberation theology is the notion of solidarity with the poor and the oppressed in their quest for social justice. When North Americans hear the word "solidarity," they immediately associate with the free trade union movement, e.g., in Poland. In Latin America, solidarity means much more than this. The theological conception of solidarity stems from the biblical notions of God's uniting with the people for their deliverance, and God's particular care for widows and orphans, the poor and the oppressed. It is also linked with the Christology of the poor Christ who announced:

> The spirit of the Lord is upon me; therefore He has sent me to bring glad tidings to the poor, to proclaim liberty to captives, recovery of sight to the blind, and to release prisoners, to announce a year of favor from the Lord (Luke 4:18–19).

In his 1965 encyclical letter *Populorum Progressio* (§43), Pope Paul gave special attention to the need of social solidarity on the national and international levels. At the Medellín and Puebla conferences, the Latin American bishops discussed at length the factors militating against social solidarity: disparity in international commerce, alienation of capital out of the Third World, multinational corporations, exacerbated nationalism, the arms race and consumptionism.[54] The growing economic disparities from Medellín (1968) to Puebla (1979) led the bishops to state in even stronger terms the church's "preferential option for the poor," although the Puebla documents are careful to say this is a preferential but not exclusive option.[55]

Base Churches. The principle instrument by which the liberation message is being transmitted in Latin America is through base church communities, known in Spanish as *communidades eclesiales de base* (CEBs) or, more simply, *iglesias de base.* The CEBs are cooperative community cells which are larger than families and smaller than parishes. The institution of base churches adds something new to the traditional Roman Catholic categories of family, parish, religious orders, clergy and hierarchy. The stated goals of the base churches are evangelization, conscientization and social action.[56]

Estimates place the number of base churches as high as 150,000.[57] From the practical side, they have had enormous influence in Latin America. Internally, the base churches introduce a horizontalization of church structures in keeping with the communal and collegial ideas of Vatican Council II.[58] The idea of the base church reaches beyond the distinction between clerics and lay persons. Externally, the base churches have been the chief means for fostering social action and for advocating economic, social, political and religious rights in opposition to the "National Security" policies of many Latin American regimes.[59] Although the model of the base church has arisen to meet the needs of the church in an "underdeveloped" situation, the model is spreading to other parts of the Christian world.[60] European theologian Johann Baptist Metz advises against relativizing the base church model. He sees it, rather, as an advance model for the universal church, moving away from the model of a church caring *for* the people to the model of a church *of* the people.[61] Whatever else may be said, the base church movement in Latin America is the medium through which the dialectic of theory and practice is passing into concrete reality. Its ecclesiastical, social and political importance cannot be underestimated.

The above summary of the characteristics of liberation theology, both in its theoretical and practical aspects, cannot hope to be exhaustive, but it does present the essential features of a theopolitical tide in contemporary theology which will have enormous and far-reaching effects on the political order in Latin America, perhaps in the world. This sketch needs to be amplified with some notes on the historical background to the theology of liberation.

Historical Background: Before Medellin and After Puebla

One often hears the charge that liberation theology is nothing but the radical "marxizing" of Catholic theology in Latin America. There can be no denying that there are Marxist-like aspects in liberation thought. First, there are similarities between the liberation method of *analysis* (conscientization) and Marx's ideology critique, both of which are applied to the conditions of oppression and alienation on local, national and international levels. However, as was pointed out above, similarity in *analysis* does not entail a similarity in *tactics.* Though there have been liberation-type movements which have joined hands with Marxist political parties (e.g., the Christians for Socialism in Chile), the main thrust of liberation theology, in general, and the base churches, in particular, has been to steer clear of partisan politics.[62] Secondly, to see liberation movement simply as a Fifth Column of Marxist "infiltrators" is to overlook the more important theopolitical fact that both the Medellín and Puebla documents censure capitalistic liberalism, for its "practical atheism," as well as Marxism, for its "militant atheism."[63] Thirdly, the stress on *praxis* is without doubt akin to Marxist praxis. Yet liberation in the main has eschewed revolutionary praxis centered on a party elite in favor of evangelical praxis which moves in the direction of community organization, cooperatives and grassroots self-help. To the minority upperclass, any sort of community organizing may appear as "revolutionary" and, therefore, evoke the charge of "Marxist."

The above three factors (analysis, tactics, praxis), however, reflect only one side of the rise of liberation theology. The other side is seen in the growing concern on the part of Roman Catholicism in general and the papacy in particular about the effects of modernization and rationalization on human life in late industrial societies. This concern is already in evidence in Leo XIII's encyclical *Rerum Novarum* (1891) which both upholds the right to private property and legitimates the trade union movement. The focus on social concerns is continued in Pius XI's *Quadragesimo Anno* (1939), which established the principle of subsidiarity, i.e., that higher collectivities should not usurp the initiative of lower ones unless the common good calls for it, and in John XXIII's *Mater et Magistra* (1961) and *Pacem in Terris* (1963), both of which dealt with the unequal distribution of wealth in the world. While the popes have always upheld the right to private property, John XXIII in *Pacem in Terris* (§§ 21–22) stressed that this right "derives from the nature of man" and that "there is a social duty inherent in the right of private property."

All of the currents of the church's social concerns came to fruition in Vatican II's *Gaudium et Spes* (1965), the universal church document which is most frequently cited at the Medellín conference. What is important to note is that all church teaching has been inspired by the tradition of the common good which has never been abandoned but, rather, gradually reinterpreted in light of 19th century political restorationism, early 20th century accommodationism (pluralism), mid-20th century developmentalism, and, finally, late 20th century liberationism. The impetus in the direction of the liberationist reinterpretation of the common good was advanced by Paul VI's bold *Populorum Progressio* and *Evangelii Enuntiandi* (1974), which were addressed directly to the Latin American situation and which championed the notions of solidarity and the subordination of free trade to social justice, while scoring the inequities in international trade, human rights, and oppressive political and economic systems.[64]

While it is fair to say that there are convergences between Marxist analysis and liberationist conscientization, the theologians and bishops who have promoted the liberationist viewpoint have not needed to cite Marx either for method or content. Thus, at both the Medellín (1968) and Puebla (1968) conferences, all positions and arguments are sustained by citations of conciliar, papal and episcopal documents. While Marx recognized that "religion is the sigh of the oppressed creature, the heart of a heartless world and the soul of soulless conditions," he nonetheless asserted that it was also "the *opium* of the people" which promised "imaginary flowers" that blossomed under an "illusory sun."[65] Marx thought that religion would wilt in the fiery furnace of criticism. What he could not imagine was that religion itself could become critical religion, giving voice to the sigh of the oppressed and exposing the soulless conditions of modern society. In liberation theology, religion itself has become critical not only in the otherworldly, but also in the this-worldly sense.

Medellín (1968). Medellín represents the commitment of the church to the realities of Latin America. With its liberation christology and ecclesiology it established a theology of the "signs of the times," thereby replacing a preservationist model of the church with a prophetic model. It announced the "preferential option for the poor" not only as an ideal but as the practical way to alleviate the conditions of inequality and oppression. The official recognition of the base churches laid the groundwork for their eventual dissemination throughout Central and South America. Its declarations were strong and forceful, presenting the image of an active church, alive in its tiniest cell and its widest expanse.

Medellín came as a surprise, not only to the church at large, but to the Latin Americans themselves. It drew its inspiration not only from the activist bishops, like Dom Helder Câmara, Cardinal Lorscheider and Bishop Oscar Romero, but also from the most articulate liberation theologians, like Gustavo Gutierrez, Jon Sobrino and José Comblin. For many moderate and conservative church leaders, however, Medellín raised the spectres of Marxism, revolution, social unrest, heresy, etc. Those fears gathered momentum as the third Latin American Episcopal Conference at Puebla began to approach.

Puebla (1979). Between Medellín and Puebla several historical developments took place. On the one hand, the Medellín reforms were put into effect, especially with the widespread growth of base churches. Then, too, the political, social and economic conditions in Latin America became worse. Almost everyone admitted that the Alliance for Progress had failed and that it had served the interests of the First World rather than fostering the social and economic conditions for democracy in Latin America.[66] On the other hand, the church witnessed the death of Paul VI and the sudden elections of John Paul I, who died quickly, and of John Paul II. Also, moderate and conservative bishops were elected to leadership roles in the Latin American Episcopal Conference, most notably Archbishop Alfonso Lopez Trujillo.

A notable feature of Puebla was the considerable ecclesiastical maneuvering which went on behind the scenes. A document of consultation was prepared beforehand in conjunction with Cardinal Baggio of the Roman Curia.[67] Theologians, so much in evidence at Medellín, were to be excluded from the actual proceedings. There were even charges that the CIA was secretly supporting the efforts of certain conservative factions. The press, too, was permitted only controlled access, with the result that contradictory reports were issued daily. The fundamental tension was between those who wanted to stick to the developmental approach and those who wanted to confirm the liberationist model worked out at Medellín.

When all is said and done, the realities of Latin America prevented Puebla from being the undoing of Medellín and the overall thrust of the theology of liberation. In the words of Jon Sobrino, Puebla ended up being "a quiet affirmation of Medellín."[68] In some areas it even went beyond Medellín, especially in the declaration on the rights of indigenous peoples, human rights in general, the status of women, dialogue with workers' movements, the ideology of "National Security" regimes, the neocolonialism of multinational corporations, and consumptionism. Secondly, certain factions were hoping that John Paul II would bolster their positions. Indeed, the pope's opening address pointed in the direction of traditional doctrinal Christology,[69] but the pope who arrived in Mexico was not the same pope who departed. The departing pope, in his Address to the Indians of Oaxaca and Chiapas—the report was that he rewrote the speech after experiencing the conditions of the poor in

Mexico—spoke of "prolonged sufferings and unsatisfied hopes," of "plunder" and "exploitation," of "expropriation" in the name of the common good. Echoing Paul VI's Address to Peasants (Columbia, 1968), John Paul II declared his "solidarity" with the poor and professed that there is "a social mortgage on all private property."[70] The post-Puebla claim was that the pope said something to satisfy all sides. The truth seems to be that the pope changed or, rather, declared his allegiance to the direction already taken by his predecessors, John XXIII and Paul VI. If anything, the pope's departing speech meant Medellín, far from being condemned as an aberration from orthodoxy, had itself become the new church tradition for Latin America. Together, Medellín and Puebla mean that the theology of liberation has become an integral part of church teaching with implications far beyond Latin America.

Critical Implications for Religion and Politics

Perhaps the most important reality to acknowledge about liberation theology in the Latin American context is that it is here to stay and will have lasting effects on the political order. The attempts at Puebla to blunt or mollify the liberationist message, and the failure of those attempts mean, if anything, that liberation now constitutes an integral part of the church tradition in late 20th century Latin America. Together, Medellín and Puebla point to the cutting edge of politics and religion in Latin America.

Secondly, it is equally imperative to recognize that, for the most part, the Latin American nations have never gone through a constitutional separation of church and state. Although there now exist accords of tolerance toward Protestants and other denominations, the preferred status of Roman Catholicism as the religion of popular culture remains intact. The only difference—and it is a major difference—is that from the grass-roots up, the Roman Catholic Church in Latin America is disengaging from preservationist stance and assuming a liberationist posture toward both spiritual and temporal matters.

Any critique of liberation which does not take into account the above realities will simply be misguided. On the other hand, this does not mean that liberation theology ought to be immune from critique. Indeed, what it most needed is a two-pronged critique which assesses (1) internal weaknesses in liberation theology and (2) the shortcomings of misapprehensions of liberation thought and practice from outside the liberation movement.

Critique from Within. Before I give specific critiques of liberation thought in general, one thing needs to be said. Paul Ricoeur has emphasized that immediate or "naive" faith is no longer accessible to modern man. If faith is to survive and to keep open the possibility of a "second naiveté," it needs to subsume and overcome the critique of religion as manifested in that troika of demystifiers, Marx, Freud and Nietzsche.[71] Liberation theology is one manifestation of critical faith in post-modernity. Whether it is able to subsume the critique of religion while overcoming it without being overcome by it, is a question perhaps no one can answer. That there are dangers to this enterprise, no one can doubt. Yet, we are reminded of the poet Friedrich Hölderlin's words in the poem *Patmos:*

> Near and
> Hard to grasp is The God
> But where danger is,
> There, too, the redeeming grows.

The main question I put to liberation theology is the question of its *incompleteness.* The liberationist emphasis on redemption as an historical process leaves lacunae in the theology of creation and the theology of consummation, the other two aspects of Christian theology. In all philosophies of freedom, nature becomes the neutral "object" or "raw material" for human historical action. Yet the so-called "objective" view of nature and humanity has led to exploitation of both without a sense of sacred restraints on or limits to freedom. The ecological crisis, present even now in certain areas of the "undeveloped" world, points up the necessity that liberation must also be thought in tune with restoration of both humanity and nature.[72] On this score, there is much that liberation theology can learn from the "natural" theology of creation in the traditions of the Indians of the Americas.

The other aspect where liberation seems to fall short, is on the question of the traditional third article of the creed, i.e., *eschatology.* David Tracy notes that Gustavo Gutierrez subjects the sociopolitical category of "development" to critical reflection and comes up in favor of "liberation." However, Gutierrez fails to perform the same critical reflection on the eschatological symbols, Utopian visions and proleptic fulfillments which characterize so many theologies of the future.[73] The point is that the images of the future in much Christian theology in general and of liberationist theologies in particular remain vague and nebulous, i.e., abstract. Secondly, Tracy questions a too-rapid move into praxis in the dialectic between theory and practice. Authentic praxis calls for critical, theoretical reflection on the meaning of Christian symbols in our present context. In agreement with Paul Ricoeur, Tracy contends that "the return to symbols and, through symbolic meaning, to *praxis* be achieved through, not around, the most critical reflection upon those symbols."[74] In effect, the liberation project represents an incomplete critical faith with respect to the critical reappropriation of the eschatological symbols of the tradition.

From another perspective, it would seem that in all the vast amount of analysis devoted to the phenomenon of oppression, the liberationists have not given sufficient attention to what Simone Weil calls *the mechanism of oppression.* Critical social analysis, Weil stated, has shed some light on the origin of oppression, but it has failed to explain "why oppression is invincible so long as it is useful, why the oppressed in revolt have never succeeded in founding a non-oppressive society."[75] Here we can point to the Reign of Terror that followed the French revolution and the repressive regime that followed the Russian revolution. Theologians of praxis seem not to have given sufficient reflection to one of their favorite analytical notions, the Hegelian *Aufhebung,* which means negation, preservation and elevation at the same time.[76] Conscientization that limits itself to the mere negation of the present conditions of existence can determine what liberation is *from* much more easily than what it is *for*. Secondly, the prevalent critique of "bourgeois consciousness" does not make clear just what is to be *preserved* as the lasting good of the bourgeois revolution of the 19th century. Freedom of religion, freedom of the press, the right to vote in fair elections, etc., were all freedoms accomplished by the much vilified bourgeois revolution. Although many individual bourgeois freedoms have been tainted by commercialized individualism and isolationism, a leap into excessive collectivism would be both undialectical and oppressive. Even the critical political theologian Johann Baptist Metz has written: "A new coalition between politics and religion is required, for only then is a post-bourgeois humanity possible that results neither in negating the individual nor in undialectically rejecting the bourgeois history of freedom."[77] Finally, I do not see how the elevation or sublation in the Hegelian *Aufhe-*

bung can take place unless the dialectic of contradiction and conflict in some way opens upon a dialectic of complementarity in which individual and society, labor and capital, church and state can reciprocally transform one another. Too often, the rhetoric of contradiction has led not to transformative reconciliation, but to the annihilation of one of the poles opposition. An *Aufhebung* that does not allow for the moment of transcendence can look forward only to the cyclic repetition of contradiction and not to the authentic regeneration, recapitulation, and renaissance of all the types of humanity which history has brought forth.[78]

The final question that liberation theology raises is whether it is prone to *co-option* either by violent revolutionary struggle or by partisan politics. It is important to know that liberation movements have taken many directions. Basically, there are four types: (1) revolutionary, as represented by Camilo Torres, the revolutionary guerilla priest; (2) Marxist, as represented by the Christians for Socialism party in Chile during the early 1970s; (3) social-populist, as represented by adult education programs, cooperatives, rural reforms throughout Latin America; and (4) evangelical, as represented by the base churches.[79] Each of these types deserves comment. Despite the enormous publicity given to Camilo Torres, who was killed in guerrila action in 1966, he represented a party of one. All forms of violence, armed and institutional, were scored in the documents of Medellín and Puebla.[80] The vast majority of the Latin American bishops and theologians who can be classified as liberationist see that revolutionary violence is incompatible with the church's preferential option for the poor and look to the models of Mahatma Gandhi and Dr. Martin Luther King for a path of nonviolent struggle.[81] Secondly, the Christians for Socialism party flourished chiefly during the government of Salvador Allende in Chile, but since 1975 has not had much influence. Thirdly, the social-populist efforts in Latin America have had considerable church support, but the real question is whether most of these projects are aimed at community organization rather than at political party formation. Finally, the evangelical model, centered in the base churches, has been the most favored and most effective direction taken by the Latin American church community. In most instances, the base churches are associated with community organizing projects on a local scale. The realization of communal life through such programs as work cooperatives has had to contend not only with the fatalism and isolation of the peasants, but also with government accusations that such efforts are covert political activity. One thing that seems certain is that the boundaries between the political arena, religious action and communal interests are under contention in Latin America.

Critique from Without. The critique of liberation movements by moderate and conservative factions within the Latin American church has been covered in the preceeding pages. Although the rhetoric of that critique is flagged with terms like "Marxist" and "socialist," the fundamental difference hinges on whether or not the developmental model espoused in both ecclesiastical and political circles during the 1950s and 1960s served to foster the establishment of democratic institutions and social justice in Latin America. It was the perceived failure of the developmental model that motivated the turn to a liberationist position, both within and without the church in Latin America. The critique of liberation movements and liberation theology coming from the First World, and from the United States in particular, is rooted in a belief that the developmental model, as framed by a consumer society, is still viable for Latin America. The failure of North American foreign policy toward Latin America stems in great part from the failure to perceive that the developmental model is increasingly becoming unacceptable to Latin Americans themselves. Ignorance of the causes and consequences of the failure of the developmental model accounts for most of the weaknesses in the critique of liberationism coming from outside Latin America.

The first order of business is to understand the depth of the *failure of developmentalism.* Hopes for a gradual or developmental emergence hinged on the success of Christian Democratic parties in Latin America, massive economic assistance from North America and Europe, the growth of labor unions, and the growth of democratic institutions (free elections, independent judiciaries, etc.). In all of these efforts, the cooperation of Latin American Catholicism was at first considered essential. These hopes were illusions. The principal cause of those illusions in the United States is that, while the United States may be a *political* democracy internally, in its foreign relations it has been a narrowly *commercial* democracy.

In foreign relations, *freedom of trade* has prevailed over other freedoms, especially political, social, religious, and human rights freedoms. From the beginning, such programs as the Alliance for Progress, AID (Agency for International Development), AIFLD (American Institute for Free Labor Development) and the IMF

(International Monetary Fund) were limited in vision by this free trade bias. The First World countries may have been able to import raw products from and export finished goods to Latin America, but they failed to foster the *political* and *social* institutions which enhance democratic justice. Without entering into the bitter debate about the subversive role of the CIA-Defense establishment in the manipulation of many of the Alliance for Progress agencies, we can say that the commercial bias of almost all efforts to modernize Latin America led a multinational stranglehold over the Latin American economies, the export of medicines and pesticides banned even in the First World, gross imbalance in trade, and the attempt to transform Latin America into a consumer society. In reality, the developmental model was a trickle-down theory applied to Latin America, which neglected to take into account grass-roots efforts at rural education, self-help, trade-union formation, cooperative movements, etc. The attention given to the commercial suprastructure in Latin America entailed blindness to the political and social infrastructure. In Latin America, even founders of the Alliance for Progress began to doubt the turn of events. Raul Prebish, Argentine economist and a father of the Alliance for Progress, expressed the doubt in the following way: "What is good for the consumer society is not necessarily good for development."[82] The doubt expressed at the end of the 1960s became a full-blown critique by the beginning of the 1970s. In *A Theology of Liberation* (first Spanish edition, 1971), Gustavo Gutierrez wrote:

> *Developmentalism* thus came to be synonymous with *reformism* and modernization, that is to say, synonymous with timid measures, really ineffective in the long run and counterproductive to achieving a real transformation. The poor countries are becoming more clearly aware that their underdevelopment is only the by-product of the development of other countries, because of the kind of relationship which exists between the rich and the poor countries. Moreover, they are realizing that their own development will come about only with a struggle to break the domination of the rich countries.[83]

The rich commercial democracies were now faced with a contradiction. The failure of the measures to "modernize" Latin America and "integrate" it into the consumer system can be attributed to unrestrained economic self-interest of commercial democracies. The failure was double. Not only did the developmental model lead to the comparative underdevelopment of Latin American autonomy, but also to a massive blindness on the part of the powerful democracies to the fact that their international commercial self-interests were in conflict, if not contradiction, with the social and political ideals of democracy itself.

The failure of developmentalism motivated the fateful turn toward *militarism* and what have been called *National Security states.* In the United States this turn was signalled in Nelson Rockefeller's recommendation that the United States look to the "new military" who have experienced "exposure to the fundamental achievements of the U.S. way of life . . . through military training programs which the U.S. conducts in Panama and the United States."[84] Not only does the Rockefeller report place its hopes on the "new military," it also openly mistrusts labor, the church and student movements because their "idealism" makes them "vulnerable to subversive persuasion and to exploitation as a revolutionary means for the destruction of the existing order."[85] If nothing else, *The Rockefeller Report on the Americas* sounded the death knell of the Alliance for Progress which had looked to the cooperation of government, the church and labor unions for bringing about agrarian reform, literacy programs, and the betterment of living conditions for the general populace. Despite the brief interlude of the Carter human rights foreign policy, the Rockefeller policy of a preferential option for the military prevailed in the 1970s. This gave encouragement to the growth of National Security regimes throughout Latin America—regimes which came into divisive conflict even with moderate church leaders. As recently as 1982, Thomas O. Enders, Assistant Secretary of State for Inter-American Affairs, listed the order of priorities in U.S. policy as (1) military assistance, (2) economic assistance, (3) trade and investment measures, (4) commitment to democracy and (5) human rights.[86] What is significant about this set of priorities is that the commitment to political democracy is now subordinated to commercial interests and military measures. Absent from the list are agrarian reform, popular education, support for communal cooperative efforts, and cooperation with church and labor.

The turn to the militarism represents an amazing *narrowing of options* both for Latin America and for the United States and other countries which have an interest in the Americas as a whole. Even if the First World countries deem the current Latin American unrest as the work of Marxist-Leninist infiltration, the military option locks foreign policy into a stereotypical response which falsifies both the complexity and the variety in the Latin American situation and the liberation movements themselves. A flexible response to Latin America would mean a tolerance toward a mixed economy, socialist on certain national levels, cooperative on local levels, joined with private enterprise which does not seek to dictate the total political landscape. A flexible response would also recognize in the *communidades eclesiales de base* elements which are very similar to the voluntary associations, farmers cooperatives, rural and urban organizations programs which Alexis de Tocqueville saw as crucial to the formation of democracy in North America. And, certainly, a flexible *democratic* response would not put military and economic interests above the political, social, labor and religious needs of which Latin Americans are becoming critically conscious. A foreign policy which is oblivious to or rides roughshod over the critical faith now emerging in Latin America will find itself walled-in inside a communicative vacuum. Latin America no longer wants or needs to be a recipient of First World largesse, but to be the principal active participant in its self-making. The society it seeks is far more participatory and communitarian than has emerged in the commercial and consumerist democracies which have prevailed up to the present. It would be well for us to listen carefully to the final words of the Latin American bishops at the Puebla conference:

> We must create in the people of Latin America a sound moral conscience, a critical-minded evangelical sense vis-à-vis reality, a communitarian spirit, and a social commitment. All that will allow for free, responsible participation, in a spirit of fraternal communion and dialogue, aimed at the construction of a new society that is truly human and suffused with evangelical values. That society must be modelled on the community of the Father, the Son, and the Holy Spirit; and it must be a response to the sufferings and aspirations of our peoples, who are filled with a hope that cannot be disappointed.[87]

NOTES

1. "The final cause rather corrupts than advances the sciences," Francis Bacon, "The New Organon" II.ii, in *The New Organon and Related Writings,* ed. Fulton H. Anderson (Indianapolis: Library of Liberal Arts, 1960), p. 121.
2. Leo Strauss, *On Tyranny,* rev. and enl. (Ithaca: Cornell University Press, 1963), p. 110, n. 5.

3. Nicolo Machiavelli, *The Prince,* trans. A Robert Caponigri (Chicago: Henry Regnery, 1965), pp. 84–85.
4. See, e.g., Bacon, "The Advancement of Learning" II.xxiii.49, ed. *Encyclopaedia Britannica,* 1952, p. 94b; Thomas Hobbes, *Leviathan* II.xxxii, ed., Michael Oakeshott (New York: Collier, 1962), p. 270; Benedict Spinoza, "A Political Treatise," I.5 in *A Theologico-Political Treatise and A Political Treatise,* trans. R. H. M. Elwes (New York: Dover, 1951), p. 289; Jean-Jacques Rousseau, *The Social Contract* III.vi, trans. Maurice Cranston (Baltimore: Penguin, 1968), p. 118; Georg W. F. Hegel, *The Philosophy of History,* trans. J. Sibree (New York: Dover, 1956), pp. 35, 403.
5. Machiavelli, "Discourses on the First Ten Books of Titus Livius," I.iii, *The Prince and the Discourses,* intro. by Max Lerner (New York: Modern Library, 1950), p. 117; Rousseau, *Social Contract* I.vii, p. 64.
6. Adam Smith, *An Inquiry into the Nature and Causes of the Wealth of Nations* (New York: Modern Library, 1937), p. 423.
7. See Leo Strauss, *Natural Right and History* (Chicago: University of Chicago Press, 1953), p. 184.
8. *Leviathan* I.xiii, pp. 98–102.
9. *Prince* XVIII, p. 94.
10. Rousseau, "Discourse on the Origin and Foundations of Inequality," *The First and Second Discourses,* ed. Roger D. Masters (New York: St. Martin's Press, 1964), pp. 115–17.
11. Machiavelli, *Discourses* II.ii, p. 285.
12. Rousseau, *Social Contract* IV.viii, p. 181.
13. *Ibid.,* p. 186.
14. *Ibid.,* p. 187.
15. As the Is replaces the Ought, so institutions replace character and mass "education" supplants the quest for wisdom. See Leo Strauss, *What is Political Philosophy? and Other Essays* (Glencoe: Free Press, 1959), pp. 36–37, 40–41.
16. Rousseau described *Robinson Crusoe* as "the best treatise on an education according to nature," *Èmile,* trans. Barbara Foxley (London: Everyman's Library, 1911), p. 147.
17. Allan Bloom, "The Education of Democratic Man: *Emile,*" *Daedalus* 107:3 (Summer, 1978), p. 139.
18. Rousseau, *Social Contract* IV.viii, pp. 182–3.
19. According to Robert N. Bellah, Jefferson and Paine epitomize modern religion with its "notion that each individual must work out his own ultimate solutions and that the most the church can do is provide him a favorable environment for doing so," "Religious Evolution" in *Reader in Comparative Religion: An Anthropological Approach,* 2nd ed., ed.William A. Lessa and Evon Z. Vogt (New York: Harper & Row, 1965), p. 86.
20. Alfred N. Whitehead, *Religion in the Making* (New York: New American Library, 1974), p. 16.

21. Charles, Baron of Montesquieu, *The Spirit of Laws* XI.vi, trans. Thomas Nugent (New York: Colonial Press, 1900), pp. 151–62; *The Federalist* (New York: Modern Library, n.d.), no. 47, pp. 312–20.
22. *The Federalist,* no. 10, p. 59.
23. Thomas Jefferson, *Writings* VIII, 401, ed. H. A. Washington (New York: Taylor & Maury, 1853), quoted from *Sources of the American Republic,* vol. 1, ed. Marvin Meyers, Alexander Kern and John G. Cawelti (Chicago: Scott, Foresman, 1960), p. 278.
24. See Herbert Richardson, "Civil Religion in Theological Perspective" in *American Civil Religion,* ed. Russell E. Richey and Donald Jones (New York: Harper & Row, 1974), pp. 178–82.
25. Wilson Yates, "Separation of Church and State: Civil Religion and Crossings at the Border," *Hamline Law Review,* 1978:1, pp. 67–105.
26. *Social Contract,* IV.viii, p. 182.
27. Letter to John Adams (October 28, 1813), quoted from *Sources of the American Republic,* vol. 1, p. 275.
28. Eugen Rosenstock-Huessy, *Out of Revolution: Autobiography of Western Man* (Norwich, Vt: Argo, 1966), pp. 482, 484, 501 and nn., pp. 763–65.
29. The four books of Calvin's *Institutes* are divided according to these headings. See François Wendel, *Calvin* (London: William Collins, 1963), pp. 120–21.
30. See esp. Luther's Preface to the New Testament in *Martin Luther: Selections From His Writings,* ed. John Dillenberger (Garden City, N.Y.: Doubleday Anchor, 1961), p. 14.
31. Karl Barth, *Dogmatics in Outline* (New York: Harper Toarchbooks, 1959), p. 65.
32. See Ronald F. Thiemann, "Toward a Theology of Creation: A Response to Gustav Wingren," in *Creation and Method,* ed. Henry Vander Goot (Washington: University Press of America, 1981), pp. 119–21.
33. See esp. Gustavo Gutierrez, *A Theology of Liberation: History, Politics and Salvation* (Maryknoll, N.Y.: Orbis, 1971), pp. 155–156.
34. CELAM II 1.3; see also CELAM III 1183. All references to the Conferencia Episcopal de Latinoamerica held at Medellín, Columbia, in 1968 (CELAM II) and at Puebla, Mexico, in 1979 (CELAM III) will follow this format. The official English translation of the Medellín documents are contained in *The Church in the Present-day Transformation* (Bogatá: General Secretary of CELAM, 1968), vol. 2, Conclusions. The official English translation of the Puebla documents are contained in *Puebla and Beyond,* ed. John Eagleson and Philip Sharper (Maryknoll: Orbis, 1980), which also contains the addresses of John Paul II in Mexico, 1979, and several important commentaries.
35. See Avery Dulles, *Models of the Church* (Garden City NY: Doubleday, 1974), pp. 71–96. Dulles discusses the current operative models of the church as institution, mystical communion, sacrament, herald and servant. Liberation theology centers on the models of the church as herald (or prophet) and servant.
36. CELAM III 1213.

37. CELAM II 1.22.
38. CELAM II 14.2.
39. CELAM III 317–18.
40. Much firsthand information on the Latin American is coming from U.S. based solidarity groups. See, e.g., James McGinnis, *Solidarity with the People of Nicaragua & Peru* (St. Louis: Institute for Peace and Justice, 1982).
41. See E. Schillebeeckx, "Befreiungstheologie zwischen Medellín und Puebla," *Orientierung* 43:1/2 (Jan. 15/31), pp. 6–10, 17–21; English redaction, "Liberation Theology between Medellín and Puebla," *Theology Digest* 28:1 (Spring, 1980), pp. 3–7. Schillebeeckx enumerates four characteristics: justice, conscientization, solidarity and concrete action. I include also the base church communities.
42. See Strauss, *Natural Right and History,* p. 181–87.
43. "Consequently, since the law is chiefly ordained to the common good, any other precept in regard to some individual work, must needs be devoid of the nature of law, save insofar as it regards the common good. Therefore every law is ordained to the common good," St. Thomas Aquinas, *Summa Theologica* 1a.2ae, q. 90. art. 2, resp.
44. CELAM II 1.5.
45. On the early phases of the *Movimiento Educação de Base* in Brazil and other education for consciousness efforts in Latin America, see Frederick C. Turner, *Catholicism and Political Development in Latin America* (Chapel Hill: University of North Carolina Press, 1971), pp. 69–77. Freire's work in education for critical consciousness has had a significant impart on pedagogical theory and practice in North America. See esp. Thomas Groome, *Christian Religious Education* (San Francisco: Harper & Row, 1980), pp. 175–77.
46. Paolo Freire, *Education For Critical Consciousness* (New York: Seabury, 1973), p. 44.
47. CELAM II 1.17; see also CELAM III 77, 1220. In popular educational practice conscientization is communicated by the three steps of SEE-JUDGE-ACT: seeing how poverty can blind one to the effects of oppression in the family, the community and the world; judging the situation according to the Word of God, especially in light of Jesus' words: "He has anointed me to set at liberty the oppressed" (Lk 4:18); and acting within the community to bring about change. See Gregory Joeright, O.F.M., "I will send you to liberate my people," *Franciscan Missionary Union Mission News* 24:1 (Jan.-Feb., 1983), pp. 2–3.
48. Ernesto Cardenal, *The Gospel in Solentiname* (Maryknoll: Orbis, 1976), 2 vols. In 1977 the island community of Our Lady of Solentiname was turned into a military barracks by the Somoza government. Ernesto and his brother Fernando, a Jesuit priest, joined in with the Sandinista revolution. Both today are ministers in the Nicaraguan government. The events surrounding the military takeover of Solentiname were very influential in turning the Nicaraguan Catholic community in favor of the revolution. See Penny Lernoux, *Cry of the People* (Garden City NY: Doubleday, 1980), pp. 85–107.

49. Arthur McGovern SJ, "Liberation Theology in Actual Practice," *Commonweal* 110:2 (Jan. 28, 1983), pp. 46–49. McGovern found more influence of Marxist analysis in Mexico and Nicaragua than in Peru.
50. Groome, *Christian Religious Education,* p. xvii, n. 1.
51. There is a growing tension between certain Latin American liberation theologians and European liberationists. See José Miguel Ponino, *Doing Theology in a Revolutionary Situation* (Philadelphia: Fortress, 1975). As Brazilian Bishop Pedro Casadáliga states: "It seems to me that these European theologians spend a lot of time thinking but perhaps not so much living. They want to think for others but not live with others, specifically the poor," quoted in Alan Neely, "Liberation Theology in Latin America: Antecedents and Autochthony," *Missiology: An International Review* (July, 1978), p. 366.
52. CELAM III 1260.
53. McGovern, "Liberation Theology in Actual Practice," p. 47.
54. CELAM II 2.9–11; CELAM III 311–15.
55. This option does not imply exclusion of anyone, but it does imply a preference for the poor and a drawing closer to them," CELAM III 733. Schillebeeckx questions whether the preferential option is not susceptible to exclusivist class struggle: "The Kingdom [of God] knows no 'historically' chosen social class as sole bearer of universal salvation" ("Liberation Theology between Medellín and Puebla," p. 6).
56. CELAM II 15.10–11; CELAM III 617–57.
57. Joseph Gremillion, "The Significance of Puebla for the Catholic Church in North America" in *Puebla and Beyond,* p. 318.
58. The doctrine of church collegiality was enunciated in the Vatican II document *Lumen Gentium* (§ 23). See Walter Abbott SJ, ed., *The Documents of Vatican II* (New York: America Press, 1966), pp. 44.
59. See CELAM III 547–50; Lernoux claims that the doctrine of National Security emerged out of military training programs that had direct and indirect U.S. assistance, *Cry of the People,* pp. 142–45, 155–202.
60. See esp. Johann Baptist Metz, " 'Wenn die Betreuen sich andern': Vision von einer Basiskirche," *Reformatio* 29:9 (Sept., 1980), pp. 550–61; English redaction, "Base-church and Bourgeois Religion," *Theology Digest* 29:3 (Fall, 1981), pp. 203–6; Robert McAfee Brown, "The Significance of Puebla for the Protestant Churches in North America," in *Puebla and Beyond,* pp. 330–46; Gremillion, above, n. 57.
61. Metz, "Base-church and Bourgeois Religion," p. 204.
62. On the Christians for Socialism, see Lernoux, *Cry of the People,* pp. 306–7.
63. CELAM II 1.10; CELAM III 546.
64. For an analysis of the evolution of Roman Catholic social teaching in the 20th century, see Joseph Gremillion, *The Gospel of Peace and Justice* (Maryknoll: Orbis, 1976), pp. 3–138.
65. Karl Marx, "A Contribution to the Critique of Hegel's Philosophy of Right," in *Early Writing* (New York: Vintage, 1975), p. 246.

66. See esp. Jerome Levinson and Juan de Onís, *The Alliance That Lost Its Way* (Chicago: Quadrangle, 1970), pp. 77–212; Lernoux, *Cry of the People,* pp. 203–80.

67. See Moises Sandoval, "Report from the Conference," in *Puebla and Beyond,* pp. 28–43.

68. Jon Sobrino, "Los documento de Puebla: serena affirmaçión de Medellín," *Sal Terrae* 67:3 (Mar., 1979), pp. 191–204; English redaction, "Puebla: A Quiet Affirmation of Medellín," *Theology Digest* 28:1 (Spring, 1980), pp. 13–16.

69. John Paul II, Opening Address at the Puebla Conference 1.2, in *Puebla and Beyond,* p. 59.

70. John Paul II, Address to the Indians of Oaxaca and Chiapas, *Puebla and Beyond,* p. 82. The pope later clarified the confusion about his stand on liberation theology in the encyclical *Redemptor Hominis* (1979) and, in a papal audience, announced that there is "reason for a theology of liberation on a universal scale." See Lernoux, *Cry of the People,* pp. 425–32.

71. See Paul Ricoeur, *The Symbolism of Evil* (Boston: Beacon, 1967), pp. 347–57; *Freud and Philosophy* (New Haven: Yale University Press, 1970), pp. 20–36; "The Critique of Religion," *The Philosophy of Paul Ricoeur,* ed. Charles E. Reagan and David Stewart (Boston: Beacon, 1978), pp. 213–22. See also Frank K. Flinn, "The New Religions and the Second Naiveté," *Ten Theologians Respond to the Unification Church,* ed. Herbert Richardson (New York: Rose of Sharon/Unification Theological Seminary, 1981), pp. 43–59.

72. Theologies which stress history over nature and redemption (Christology) over creation have the tendency to reduce material creation to the status of a "neutral" or "technical" means, thereby opening the door to an exploitive relationship between humanity and human nature itself. See the critique of Barth's christocentrism in Gustav Wingren, *Creation and Gospel* (New York: Edwin Mellen, 1978), pp. 56–69.

73. David Tracy, *Blessed Rage for Order* (New York: Seabury, 1978), pp. 237–50; see Gutierrez, *Theology of Liberation,* pp. 21–42.

74. Tracy, *Blessed Rage for Order,* p. 248. As the ancients placed theory and contemplation above action and praxis, so the moderns tend to put action and praxis above theory and contemplation. Tracy seeks to maintain the reciprocity of theory and praxis through critical reflection. See also Jürgen Habermas, *Theory and Practice* (Boston: Beacon, 1973), pp. 1–40.

75. Simone Weil, *Oppression and Liberty* (Amherst: University of Massachusetts, 1972), p. 58. Just as there is much self-delusion about oppression in modern thought, there is also, according to Weil, much deception about the nature of true liberty: "True liberty is not defined by the relationship between desire and satisfaction, but by a relationship between thought and action" (p. 85).

76. Hegel, *Logic,* trans. William Wallace (Oxford: Clarendon, 1975), VII. 96. (note), pp. 141–42; *On Art, Religion, Philosophy,* ed. John Gray (New York: Harper Toarchbooks, 1970), p. 181. See Tracy, *Blessed Rage for Order,* pp. 247–48.

77. Metz, "Base-church and Bourgeois Religion," p. 205.

78. Rosenstock-Huessy, *Out of Revolution,* p. 735.
79. See Schillebeeckx, "Liberation Theology between Medellín and Puebla," pp. 5–6.
80. CELAM II 2.15–19; CELAM III 508–9, 532, 534.
81. Lernoux, *Cry of the People,* pp. 447–48.
82. *Ibid.,* p. 313.
83. Gutierrez, *Theology of Liberation,* p. 26.
84. *The Rockefeller Report on the Americas* (Chicago: Quadrangle, 1969), pp. 32–33.
85. *Ibid.,* p. 30.
86. Thomas O. Enders, "Commitment to Democracy in Central America," *Department of State Bulletin* 82:2085 (Aug., 1982), p. 76.
87. CELAM III 1308.

14

The Political Significance of Latin-American Liberation Theology[1]

RICHARD L. RUBENSTEIN

The 1973 appearance of the English translation of *A Theology of Liberation* by Gustavo Gutierrez introduced North America to perhaps the most influential theological voice to emerge from Latin America in recent decades.[2] This book and the writings of other Latin American liberation theologians marked a radical departure in both the motive for writing and the content and method of theology.[3] Unlike traditional theologies, including the North American "radical theology" of the 1960s, Latin American liberation theology has a practical political objective, the revolutionary transformation of Latin American society, by force, if necessary. Although liberation theology takes issue with the atheism of Marxism, it shares many of Marxism's political objectives. On almost all political and social issues, liberation theologians are far more likely to side with the Marxists than with those who regard capitalism, in spite of its problems, as offering humanity a freer and a more hopeful future.

The genuinely radical character of the new theology can best be understood by a comparison of its methods and motives with those of traditional Euro-American theology in the modern period. In a very important sense, skepticism and doubt have been the parents of modern theology. The theologian has normally regarded his vocation to be the defense of his religious tradition against the skepticism of the unbeliever and the temptation to unbelief of the believer. Thus, a principal function of theology has been dissonance-reduction. Theology seeks to foster dissonance-reduction when significant items of information regarded as credible by the believer are perceived to be inconsistent with established religious beliefs, values, and collectively sanctioned modes of behavior.[4]

This function became especially important as a result of the Enlightenment of the eighteenth century. The fundamental insight of the Enlightment is that humanity has come of age, that it requires no transcendent authority but only the free and unconstrained use of reason to understand the world and to shape a felicitous human destiny. Immanuel Kant has characterized the Enlightenment as follows:

> The Enlightenment represents the emergence from immaturity. Immaturity is cradled in the incapacity to make use of one's own understanding without another's guidance. . . . *Sapere aude!* Have the courage to make use of your understanding! This is the motto of the Enlightenment.[5]

Some of the more practical consequences of the Enlightenment were spelled out succinctly by Hegel:

> Right (i.e., law) and [Social] Morality came to be looked upon as having their foundation in the actual present Will of man, whereas formerly it has referred only to the command of God enjoined *ab extra*. . . . [6]

Of necessity, the Enlightenment's legitimation of the autonomous use of reason as the hallmark of mature humanity was problematic for religious tradition. The Roman Catholic Church claimed that in matters of faith and morals, it is humanity's divinely certified "teacher of truth." Although the Church encourages free enquiry in science and technology, there is a point beyond which it cannot go in permitting the use of autonomous reason in matters of faith.

As is well known, in the case of Protestantism, the Bible rather than the institutional Church is regarded as the ultimate source of authority. The Bible, however, is the record of God's action in history, especially the history of Israel, culminating in God's incarnation in the person of Jesus Christ. As the Danish religious thinker Soren Kierkegaard has pointed out, faith in the God of history can sometimes leave the believer with the unpleasant choice of either rejecting the teachings of Scripture or his own commonsense view of the way of the world. In the nineteenth century, the conflict was broadened to one of faith versus science, as is evident in the still unresolved conflict between the biblical account of creation and the scientific theory of evolution. As the Enlightenment initiated a cultural movement which could—and for many people did—lead to a cultural, ethical and intellectual posture of radical unbelief. When Nietzsche's Madman proclaimed the "death of God," he was giving expression to a fundamental tendency of the Enlightenment.

In the face of so radical a challenge, it became necessary for both Catholicism and Protestantism, and at a later time, Judaism, to train a cadre of intellectual professionals known as theologians whose function was to demonstrate that science and reason could be reconciled with religious faith. Since modern culture, especially in the capitalist West, has been characterized by the progressive rationalization of both the economy and society, it has been a fundamental task of post-Enlightenment theology to attempt some kind of harmonization of religion and modernity. This should not be interpreted as meaning the wholesale surrender of religion to modernity. There have been a variety of attempts at accommodation and adjustment. The late H. Richard Niebuhr succinctly described three principal strategies as being Christ and culture, Christ against culture, and Christ above culture.

It should, however, be obvious that the task of theology was directed to a very limited audience. As the dean of liberation theologians, Gustavo Gutierrez, has pointed out, modern theology has been a class-bound discipline of interest primarily to the bourgeois, middle-class audience which has been chiefly responsible for fostering the Enlightenment in the first place.[7] It has been the consensus of historians and other scholars that the Enlightenment gave expression to and advanced the class interests of the capitalist bourgeoisie. By insisting that autonomous reason, unconstrained by traditional values, was all that was required to maximize human well-being, the Enlightenment liberated trade, finance, commerce, science and industry from the limitations which had previously impeded economic development. The Enlightenment fostered a free market in goods and services as well as a free market in ideas.

The task of theology was thus both class-bound and fundamentally intellectual in character. The best of the twentieth century's theologians can deepen our understanding of religion but they neither can nor propose to do more. Theirs is a work of analysis and synthesis. It is at this point that the liberation theologians make their most original and problematic contribution. Gustavo Gutierrez has argued that theology must have both a radically new method and a new constituency. Instead of attempting to resolve the intellectual problems of the well-educated, middle-class nonbeliever, theology must immerse itself in and attempt to solve the questions of the *nonpersons,* those who have been excluded from a meaningful role in Latin American society because of their extreme poverty and their superfluity to the productive processes of modern industrial capitalism.

According to Gutierrez, the problem of modern bourgeois theology was expressed most incisively by Dietrich Bonhoeffer in a now-famous letter written on June 8, 1944, while in a Nazi prison: "How can one speak of God in a world come of age?" Gutierrez argues that, while that question may be of overwhelming importance to a privileged stratum of the educated bourgeoisie of the Northern Hemisphere, it has no meaning to those people who according to Gutierrez, are the true subjects of Christian theology, those Latin Americans who have been made nonpersons by capitalist neocolonialism and neoimperialism, the poor and the marginalized. In Latin America, the challenge to theology does not come from the nonbeliever but from those whom capitalist society refuses to recognize as persons at all, namely, " . . . the poor, the exploited, the ones systematically and legally despoiled of their humanness, the ones they scarcely know are persons at all."[8]

Liberation theology's unreserved identification with the cause of the poor is a relatively new development in Latin America. For centuries, the Church has been the most conservative political force in Latin America. Until recently, neither the Church's leaders nor her intellectuals could be said to identify themselves, as does Gutierrez, with the underclass. Far from seeking to overturn established social hierarchies, the Church counselled a submission, obedience and resignation in this world which was made bearable by the hope of salvation in the next. It is precisely the cause of these nonpersons that liberation theology takes as its project.

In contrast to the bourgeois nonbelievers and potential nonbelievers who were the audience of traditional theology, the nonpersons of Latin America do not question religious faith. Uprooted from their traditional moorings by the twin processes of modernization and urbanization and cast into some of the world's most miserable urban and semi-urban slums, these people hold onto Christianity as the ultimate defense against the indignity, meaninglessness and hopelessness the modern world would inflict upon them. They are not troubled by the theological and intellectual doubts fostered by the Enlightenment. Their misery embodies something never recognized by bourgeois liberals with their faith in reason, science and progress, namely, that the Enlightenment had a terrible night side, the fact that scientific and technological progress could simultaneously result in an ongoing population explosion, millions of human beings rendered vocationally redundant because of the rationalization of production in agriculture and industry, and the creation of state institutions capable of eliminating any group defined as unwanted by political authorities.

According to Gutierrez, the nonpersons' question "will not be how to speak of God in a world come of age, but rather how to proclaim God as Father in a world that is inhumane."[9]

For Gutierrez, it is meaningless to answer that question intellectually. It can only be answered by "liberation praxis," the practical, revolutionary activity whose objective is the abolition of the economic and social injustices and the material exploitation that have rendered the poor nonpersons. For the Christian this involves taking sides with the poor in their class struggle against their domestic and foreign class enemies.

Lest there be any mistake concerning the intellectual roots of Gutierrez's liberation praxis, he explicitly links it with the young Karl Marx's call in his celebrated *Theses on Feuerbach* (1845) for a revolutionary praxis whose objective was to be the destruction of the bourgeois-capitalist world.[10] In the *Essence of Christianity* (1841), Ludwig Feuerbach had attempted to demonstrate that the idea of God is the objectivated expression of man's image of his own perfected self.[11] Marx found no fault with Feuerbach's conclusions, but he insisted that Feuerbach had failed to ask the most important question, namely why did man feel compelled to project an image of his perfected self into an imaginary realm? For Marx the answer was obvious: The contradictions and failures of the actual world compelled men to seek consolation of an imaginary, supra-mundane world. According to Marx, when men understood the imaginary character of such a supra-mundane world, the real task had only begun. It was not enough for reason to understand the alienated character of the real world. Reason's basic task was to transform that world into a context of human fulfillment through revolution. Until now Marx argued, "The philosophers have only interpreted the world in various ways; the point is to change it."[12]

Just as Marx argued that *theoria* must give way to *praxis* in philosophy, Gutierrez insists upon a comparable transformation in theology. For Marx the task of philosophy is revolution; for Gutierrez and his theological colleagues, theology has an identical task. Moreover, Gutierrez explicitly identifies Marx's *Theses on Feuerbach* as the intellectual source of his call for a liberation praxis.[13]

It would, however, be a mistake to dismiss Gutierrez as offering warmed-over Marxism in theological guise. Gutierrez is a world-class religious thinker who received his training in the sixties at one of Roman Catholicism's greatest intellectual centers, Belgium's University of Louvain in Belgium. He is a serious theologian who has endeavored to elucidate the scriptural basis of his radical theology. Moreover, when he insists that theology involves deeds more than words, he is mindful of the hundreds of priests and bishops who have suffered arrest, torture and even murder because of their opposition to right-wing governments.[14]

For Gutierrez, the death which made the greatest impression was that of his fellow student at Louvain, Camilo Torres, a priest from a prominent Colombian family. Torres studied sociology at Louvain, where he became convinced that only violent revolution could change the system. He joined Colombian guerillas and was killed on February 15, 1966, in his first battle with the Colombian army. Although Gutierrez disapproved of Torres' decision to join the guerrillas, his death profoundly moved the theologian. Gutierrez has written:

> The year 1965 marked a high point in armed struggle in Latin America and hastened a political radicalization even of persons who had hoped to find other avenues for their revolutionary activity. Camilo Torres and "Che" Guevara symbolized so many others—anonymous, committed, setting a seal on the Latin America process, raising questions and exerting definitive influence in Christian circles.[15]

Thus, in addition to its intellectual and theological seriousness, liberation theology can claim that, in contrast to the traditional theologians who pursue comfortable careers in prestigious universities and seminaries, liberation theology has martyrs who have offered their lives as testimony of its truth. No other contemporary Christian theological movement can make that claim.

The theological legitimation of liberation theology is dependent upon a "militant" rereading of the Bible. In that reading, God is seen as revealing himself in history. Of crucial importance is God's self-revelation as Israel's *liberator* from slavery and oppression, "an event that will be read and reread again and again, to shed light on other historical interventions of Yahweh."[16] According to Gutierrez, the Bible's fundamental teaching about God is that he "*takes sides* with the poor and liberates them from slavery and oppression" [italics added].[17] The Bible teaches that it is not enough to know

God intellectually as liberator. Gutierrez asserts that "to know God as liberator *is* to liberate, *is* to do justice" and to do justice is to act on behalf of the poor.[18]

In Gutierrez's reading of Scripture, the New Testament deepens and intensifies the Old Testament teaching that our relationship with God is inseparable from our relationship with the poor. The New Testament teaches us that Jesus Christ is "precisely *God become poor.*"[19] The kingdom proclaimed by Jesus is a kingdom of justice and liberation established on behalf of the poor in which the rich and the powerful can have no place. In our world, characterized by radical injustice and exploitation, there is only one way to proclaim the Good News of Christ's liberation, to take sides with the poor in order to crush a "system of oppression" and to "lead to a classless society." Gutierrez goes so far as to declare that the "God of the Masters" is not the God of either the poor or the Bible. On the contrary, the God of the poor "considers the rich blasphemers because they speak of God in order better to oppress the poor."[20]

Gutierrez's preference for the poor has special relevance in the arena of international economics and politics. According to Gutierrez, the Third World, of which Latin America constitutes a major part, is as much a victim of exploitation and domination in the international sphere as Latin America's poor have been within their own continent. Relying heavily upon a questionable Marxist analysis of underdevelopment, the liberation theologians tend to see Latin America's economic and political plight as due to the continent's "economic, political, and cultural dependence" on capitalist power centers in the Northern Hemisphere led by the United States. The terrible poverty of Latin America's masses, the extraordinary wealth of its overprivileged upper-class minority, and the system of political terror which has been necessary to keep the system from exploding are all seen as the direct consequence of the "external neocolonialism" imposed upon Latin America by the capitalists of the Northern Hemisphere.

Liberation theology is thus profoundly anti-American and deeply hostile to the bourgeois capitalist world. It manifests no comparable hostility to the Communist world. This animus is expressed even in discussion of purely theological issues. As noted, liberation theologians regard their work as constituting a radical break with traditional Western theology, which they typically characterize as bourgeois and implicitly condemn as spiritually impotent. For example, Enrique Dussel, an Argentine theologian, tells of an encounter he had with a German theologian: "I was telling him that we were now reflecting on the whole matter of liberation. . . . But do you know what was really uppermost in his mind . . . ? Hans Kung's book on papal infallibility. Europeans are down to splitting hairs whereas the problem that occupies us right now is liberation."[21]

The idea that their thought constitutes a theological equivalent to liberation from colonialism is often expressed. Dom Pedro Casaldalgia, a Brazilian bishop, has written that he was "indignant that certain European theologians denigrate liberation theology. When finally there emerge among us some theologians with the capacity and desire to think for themselves, other theologians from Europe arrive to cut them short. . . . It seems to me that these European theologians spend a lot of time thinking but perhaps not so much living. They want to think for others but not live with others, specifically the poor."[22] Liberation theologians thus tend to regard their rejection of European and North American cultural and theological dominance as a precursor of the end of capitalist economic dominance.

Socialism is the political system by which liberation theologians would overcome this dominance. Gutierrez calls for "a society in which private ownership of the means of production is eliminated." He also calls for an end to the "division of society into classes."[23] With few, if any, exceptions, liberation theologians prefer socialism to capitalism. Father Juan Luis Segundo, one of the most important liberation theologians, has expressed this preference: "There is no perfect solution. The only way is for us to choose between two oppressions. And the history of Marxism, even oppressive, offers right now more hope than the history of existing capitalism. . . . Marx did not create the class struggle, international capitalism did."[24]

One searches in vain for a serious discussion of the failings of the Soviet system or of the mass crimes committed in the name of socialism from the Russian Revolution to the present. Even the oil crisis of the 1970s, which did so much to distort the economies of Latin America, is blamed on "international capitalism" rather than on the OPEC cartel.[25]

One can with considerable justice speculate that the silence of the liberation theologians on the subject of the mass murder and the homelessness instigated by Communist regimes may be due to a certain reluctance to regard such violence as altogether criminal. By insisting that faith in Christ mandates identification with the cause of the poor, by rejecting any possible reform of capitalism, and by denying any connection between the God of the rich and the God of the poor, liberation theology offers, perhaps unwittingly, a powerful theological legitimation for the merciless elimination of those who obstruct a classless society. Atheistic Communism legitimated its elimination of "objective enemies" in the name of an unrealized secular future. Liberation theology identifies the opponents of socialism as enemies of God, a far more dangerous legitimation. In any event, the classes targeted for state terror by Communist regimes, the bourgeoisie and their allies, are precisely those whom liberation theologians have identified as rejected by the God of the poor. Admittedly, liberation theologians are humane men and women for whom the idea of totalitarian terror is repugnant. Nevertheless, given their identification of the cause of God with the cause of the poor, one wonders how liberation theologians would comport themselves if they had control of a state apparatus. How would they deal with middle-class professionals and businessmen who felt they earned the right to their status and possessions and had no intention of passively accepting state-enforced downward mobility? Would the liberation theologians regard them as enemies of God and treat them accordingly? Would they encourage their emigration *en masse,* as did Fidel Castro and the leaders of Communist Vietnam? Not surprisingly, Catholic intellectuals in countries dominated by the Soviet Union exhibit no enthusiasm whatsoever for liberation theology. As we shall see, in view of Pope John Paul II's Polish nationality, that is a fact of considerable importance.

Another source of disquiet concerning liberation theology is the flawed character of its analysis of Third World problems. As noted, liberation theologians argue that the problems facing their societies are largely a consequence of neocolonial exploitation by Northern Hemisphere capitalism, especially that of North American multinational corporations. One need not enter into the substance of their analyses to note that, in blaming the United States and international capitalism, they fail to ask why the societies of non-Communist Asia have succeeded so well in coping with the problems of modernization and development that they are in a position to challenge the developed nations of Europe and America for worldwide technological and financial preeminence. The Asian societies were devastated at the end of World War II. Additionally, South Korea had to endure the further travail of the Korean War. The countries of Latin America were largely untouched by World War II. Since the war, the Asian states have been subject to economic, social, and demographic problems not unlike those confronting Latin America. Yet, there are few contrasts more striking to the visitor to non-Communist Asia than that between the Philippines and Taiwan. In many ways, the Philippines shares the religion, the Spanish colonial history, and the overwhelmingly difficult economic and social problems of Latin America. Many Philippine Catholics also share a strong commitment to liberation theology. For many decades after the end of the war, both Taiwan and South Korea were at least as dependent upon the United States as the Philippines or any Latin American nation. Yet the story of their economic progress is far more encouraging than that of the nations of Latin America.

It is surprising that liberation theologians have had so little to say about the extraordinary development of Asian capitalism. Their failure suggests that the theologians are far more the prisoners of ideology than they and their North American admirers are prepared to recognize. Their claim that the northern capitalist world is largely to blame for Latin America's problems would be far more credible had they taken non-Communist Asia into account. Their omission to do so further suggests that were they ever in possession of political power, the followers of liberation theology would be so far more prone to blame others than to criticize themselves should their program fail. Because of their assimilation of political categories to a theology of history, those whom the liberation theologians held responsible for their failure could expect little mercy or compassion.

It may seem strange that we express such apprehensions concerning men and women who have manifested so much compassion for the poor, on many occasions even at the sacrifice of life itself. Regrettably, the history of religion offers us little reason for comfort concerning the behavior of well-intentioned, armed utopians who are convinced that they have been divinely certified to overturn existing social hierarchies. But, one may ask, would not a society created by such dedicated religious men and women be preferable to harsh regimes which have governed much of Latin America in recent years? That question has been answered so effectively by Ambassador Jeanne Kirkpatrick that we can do no better than to call to memory what she has written on the subject:

Generally speaking, traditional autocrats tolerate social inequities, brutality and poverty while revolutionary autocracies create them.

Traditional autocrats leave in place existing allocations of wealth, power, status, and other resources which in most traditional societies favor an affluent few and maintain masses in poverty. But they worship traditional gods and observe traditional taboos. They do not disturb the habitual rhythms of work and leisure, habitual places of residence, habitual patterns of family and personal relations. . . . Such societies create no refugees.

Precisely the opposite is true of revolutionary Communist regimes. They create refugees by the millions because they claim jurisdiction over the whole life of the society and make demands for change that so violate internalized values and habit that inhabitants flee by the tens of thousands in the remarkable expectation that their attitudes, values, and goals will "fit" better in a foreign country than in their native land.[26]

Ambassador Kirkpatrick could have added another contrast between authoritarian and revolutionary regimes. Authoritarian regimes can be replaced by more moderate, democratic regimes without violent revolution. The history of modern radical revolutionary regimes offers no such assurance.

Ambassador Kirkpatrick wrote the previous paragraphs in 1979 before the world learned of the hideous abuses involved in the disappearance and murder of thousands of Argentine citizens. There was nothing traditional about the methods used by military regimes in Argentina, Brazil, Chile, and Uruguay in suppressing left-wing opposition. Nevertheless, there is an important respect in which even these regimes can be reckoned as traditional: It was possible to replace the right-wing, military regimes in Argentina and Brazil without violent revolution. The same was also true of Spain.

Spain, so long governed by Francisco Franco, now has a socialist Prime Minister, Filippe Gonzales. Informed Spaniards of both the right and the left are generally agreed that such a development would have been impossible had not Franco unintentionally laid the groundwork by the restoration of the monarchy under King Juan Carlos. The king has given the Spanish government an aura of legitimacy that has made it difficult, if not impossible, for a right-wing military coup to take place. It is the monarchy that makes possible a government led by the Socialists. There has been a cultural and economic revolution in Spain, as is obvious to anyone who has seen the contrast between Spain today and the country a decade ago, but it was not a revolution based upon class warfare, as was the

Leninist seizure of power in the Soviet Union and as would be a revolution based upon the principles of liberation theology. This does not mean that liberation theologians, with their emphasis on freedom from oppression, envisage a revolution supported by all of the now familiar instruments of totalitarian power. Nevertheless, their objectives, the abolition of private property, a classless society and a massive redistribution of resources, could only be achieved by a social revolution in which sustained state terror would be an indispensable component. And, to repeat, the supporters of such revolution would be sustained by the awesome conviction that their efforts were an expression of God's activity on behalf of and identification with the poor. Ironically, the poor would suffer most because a classless society would eliminate both the classes and the incentives necessary for economic progress in a technological era.

If the liberation theologians have been insensitive to Marxist terror, the same cannot be said of Roman Catholicism's first Polish Pope, John Paul II, who can hardly be described as indifferent to the fate of the poor. We cannot enter into detail concerning the evolution of the Vatican's attitude to liberation theology, save to note that in 1978, four months after he had been elevated to the pontificate, Pope John Paul II came to the city of Puebla de las Angelas, Mexico, to initiate the Third Conference of the Latin Episcopate. The most important element in the agenda at Puebla was a reevaluation of the strong endorsement of liberation theology issued by the bishops who had participated in the Second Conference a decade earlier at Medellin, Colombia. Ever since Puebla, there has been debate concerning the extent to which the Pope rejected liberation theology.

Perhaps one of the most important indications of the Vatican's attitude can be discerned in the elevation of the most important Latin American antagonist of liberation theology, Archbishop Alfonso Lopez Trujillo, to the cardinalate. Cardinal Lopez Trujillo was formerly secretary general of CELAM, the Latin American Episcopal Conference. In preparation for Puebla, Lopez Trujillo's staff prepared a 214-page preliminary consultative document which was extremely critical of liberation theology and of the pro-liberationist elements in the bishops' statement at the earlier Medellin conference. Because of the opposition of many bishops at Puebla, the anti-liberationist tone of the preliminary document was moderated in the final document. Nevertheless, Lopez Trujillo's position has apparently been adjudged to be the official position of an increasingly conservative official Church. There have been other signs of the Vatican's rejection of liberation theology insofar as it contains unacceptable Marxist elements. Joseph Cardinal Ratzinger, the Prefect of the Sacred Congregation for the Doctrine of the Faith, has denounced liberation theology and has criticized, by name, Father Jon Sobrino, a Spanish Jesuit working in El Salvador, who is one of its most important exponents. In a related development Pope John Paul II has condemned Nicaragua's "popular church," a collection of individuals and religious institutions that support the pro-Marxist Sandinista regime.[27]

Undoubtedly, the attitude of the Vatican will cause many advocates of liberation theology to have second thoughts about their commitments. Nevertheless, as noted, liberation theologians have attached great importance to their liberation from European theological colonialism, and they are not likely to be permanently deterred by anything the Vatican says or does. Catholicism is too deeply interwoven with Latin American civilization for a total breach between the theologians and the Vatican ever to occur. Still, there are many ways in which even the most radical elements in the message of liberation theology can be communicated in seemingly orthodox religious language.

As far as the United States is concerned, it is difficult to avoid the conclusion that liberation theology constitutes a long-term ideological menace, and, by now, the U.S. should have learned that ideology is very important. By blaming the United States for Latin America's problems, liberation theology ascribes a demonic identity to our country. Liberation theologians do not call the United States the "Great Satan," as do the followers of the Ayatollah Khomeini. Nevertheless, by identifying the classless society as the kingdom of God and by further identifying the United States as its principal enemy, the satanic ascription is implicit. In a major economic or social crisis, that ascription could easily become explicit.

The United States cannot be expected to solve the monumental economic and social problems confronting Latin America or the rest of the Third World, nor can it reduce significantly the social costs involved in the modernization of their economies. Moreover, it cannot and should not attempt to outbid the utopian promises of the Marxists or the liberation theologians. Undoubtedly, an important reason why the Vatican was bound to assume a posture of hostility toward the socialist and utopian elements in liberation theology is that the Church has had almost 2,000 years in which to learn how difficult it is to overturn economic and social hierarchies, and how terrible the cost can be when such attempts succeed.

If America has a constructive role to play in Latin America, it is the modest but effective task of helping our neighbors to increase their productivity, a subject about which liberation theologians are almost completely silent. We have the knowledge, the skill, and the experience for such aid. Liberation theologians have contemptuously rejected such assistance in the past as "reformism." Instead, they have focussed their complaints on the necessity for a domestic and an international redistribution of resources. In what is in essence an ongoing debate, we must remind the liberationists that the success of non-Communist Asia was not based upon redistribution but upon gains in productivity. Those Asian countries who utilized the power of the state to effect a wholesale redistribution of resources have been the least successful in providing a better life for their citizens. If Latin Americans are tempted by liberation theology to imitate the methods of socialism, they will only achieve a comparable result. The Soviet Union may have its own reasons for sustaining the economy of Cuba, but it is doubtful that it would or could sustain the economies of the more populous nations of Latin America. When compared with the promises of socialism, America's assistance may appear modest and undramatic. Nevertheless, we are in a far better position to help Latin America toward realistic economic and social progress than anything the religious or secular parties of the left can offer.

NOTES

1. This paper was published as a monograph by the Washington Institute for Values in Public Policy in 1985.
2. Gustavo Gutierrez, *A Theology of Liberation* (Maryknoll, N.Y.: Orbis, 1973).
3. Among the works on liberation theology available in English are: Jose Miguez Bonino, *Theology in a Revolutionary Situation* (Philadelphia: Fortress Press, 1975); Bonino, *Christians and Marxists* (Grand Rapids: Erdmans, 1976); Enrique Dussel, *History and Theology of Liberation: A Latin American Perspective* (Maryknoll, N.Y.: Orbis, 1976); John Eagleson and Phillip Scharper, *Puebla and Beyond: Documentation and Commentary* (Maryknoll, N.Y.: Orbis, 1980); Alfredo Fierro, *The Militant Gospel* (Maryknoll, N.Y.: Orbis, 1976); Alain Gheerbrant, ed., *The Rebel Church in Latin America* (Penguin Books: Harmondsworth, Middlesex, 1974); Rosino Gibellini, ed., *Frontiers of Theology in*

Latin America (Maryknoll, N.Y.: Orbis, 1979); Gustavo Gutierrez, *The Power of the Poor in History* (Maryknoll, N.Y.: Orbis, 1983); Gary MacEoin and Nivita Riley, *Puebla: A Church Being Born* (New York: Paulist Press, 1980); Jose Porfiro Miranda, *Marx and the Bible* (Maryknoll, N.Y.: Orbis, 1974); James V. Schall, S.J., ed., *Liberation Theology in Latin America* (San Francisco: Ignatius Press, 1982); Juan Luis Segundo, *Liberation of Theology* (Maryknoll, N.Y.: Orbis, 1976). Note the preponderance of works published by the Maryknoll Fathers and Sisters. According to Michael Novak, "the headquarters of liberation theology in the United States, and perhaps in the entire world, are located [at the] . . . international center of America's most active missionary order, the Maryknoll Fathers and Sisters." Michael Novak, "Liberation Theology and the Pope," in Schall, *Liberation Theology,* p. 281.

4. On the dissonance-reduction function of theology, see Richard L. Rubenstein, *The Age of Triage* (Boston: Beacon Press, 1983), pp. 131–33.
5. Immanuel Kant, "What is Enlightenment?" (1784) in Carl Friederich, ed., *The Philosophy of Kant* (New York: Modern Library, 1949), p. 132.
6. G. W. F. Hegel, *The Philosophy of Hegel* (New York: Dover, 1956), pp. 440–41.
7. Gutierrez, *The Power of the Poor,* pp. 56–7.
8. *Ibid.,* p. 57.
9. *Ibid.*
10. Marx's theses on Feuerbach are found in Karl Marx and Friedrick Engels, *The German Ideology* (New York: International Publisher, 1947), pp. 197–99.
11. Ludwig Feuerbach, *The Essence of Christianity* (New York: Harper & Row, 1957).
12. Marx and Engels, *German Ideology,* p. 662.
13. Gutierrez, *The Power of the Poor,* p. 59.
14. See Penny Lernoux, "The Long Path to Puebla" in John Eagleson and Philip Scharper, *Puebla and Beyond* (Maryknoll, N.Y.: Orbis, 1980), p. 190.
15. Gutierrez, *The Power of the Poor,* p. 190.
16. *Ibid.,* p. 6.
17. *Ibid.,* p. 7.
18. *Ibid.,* p. 8.
19. *Ibid.,* p. 13.
20. *Ibid.,* p. 19.
21. Alan Neely, "Liberation Theology in Latin America: Antecedents and Autochthony," *Missiology: An International Review* (July, 1978), p. 366.
22. Dom Pedro Casaldalgia, "Perdidas y ganacias de la Iglesia in America Latina," *Christus* (Mexico City, August, 1978), pp. 23–27.
23. Gutierrez, *The Power of the Poor,* pp. 37–8.
24. This passage is cited by Michael Novak, "Liberation Theology and the Pope," in Schall, *Liberation Theology in Latin America,* p. 283.

25. Gutierrez, "The Historical Power of the Poor," in *The Power of the Poor,* p. 85.
26. Jeanne Kirkpatrick, "Dictatorships and Double Standards," in Schall, *Liberation Theology,* p. 188.
27. For this information, the author is indebted to the as yet unpublished paper of Rev. Enrique T. Rueda, "The Marxist Character of the Theology of Liberation Theology."

15

Religion, Politics and Economic Competition: The Case of the United States and Japan

RICHARD L. RUBENSTEIN

The essays in this book explore the influence of religion on politics in regions as diverse as North America, the Middle East, Eastern and Western Europe, and Latin America. Although the selection is wide-ranging, no attempt has been made to cover every community. Instead, a representative sample has been offered of the ways in which religion both affects and is effected by contemporary politics.

There is, however, an important instance of the interaction of religion and politics which ought to be of special interest to Americans, namely, the case of Japan. In his introductory essay, Huston Smith observes that, like politics, religion is fundamentally concerned with power. In the ancient Near East, for example, the religious and political realms originally knew no distinction. Political authority was sacralized through the institution of divine kingship.[1] Americans nurtured by a culture rooted in the Bible are likely to regard that institution as an archaism of little relevance to the modern world. Certainly, no political institution is further removed from the American political tradition. Nevertheless, the institution of divine kingship has awesomely affected American history as a consequence of the way Japan entered the modern world.

When in 1853 Commodore Matthew Perry's Black Ships initiated the process which culminated in the opening of Japan to trade and diplomatic relations with the West, it was obvious to the Japanese that they were incapable of defending themselves. A rapid and effective program of modernization was indispensable for the Japanese to acquire the organizational, economic, industrial and military capacity to remain an independent nation. The Samurai elite realized that the Tokugawa Shogunate, which had institutionalized the old feudal order, had to be replaced by a rationalized, centralized modern state. A crucial impediment to the abolition of the old order was the feudal system of privileges and obligations, and the code of loyalty which bound the Samurai to their local lords.

The Meiji "restoration" of 1868 laid the foundations of modern Japan. The Samurai elite responsible for the restoration of imperial authority were genuine revolutionaries. They deliberately destroyed a six-hundred year old political tradition which had failed to meet the challenge of the forcible opening of Japan by the Western powers in the 1850s. Unlike their 1789 French revolutionary counterparts, Japan's elite succeeded in rationalizing the economy and society of their country with a minimum of domestic violence or alienation of elite classes and institutions. Utilizing a seemingly conservative strategy, namely the Shinto doctrine of the Emperor's divinity, to legitimate a radical social and political revolution, the elite was able to create a strong central government, abolish all estate distinctions, eliminate warrior privileges, open military service to commoners hitherto forbidden to possess arms, and establish a system of universal public education. By contrast, Europe's modernizing revolutions have involved regicide and the transformation of traditional elites and institutions into enemies of the new political and social order. Shinto enabled modernization and political centralization to be carried out under conditions of far greater social cohesiveness than was the case elsewhere.[2]

The doctrine of the Emperor's divinity was crucial to the creation of both a strong, centralized government and Japan's modern economy. Feudalism was based upon the Samurai's unconditional loyalty to his lord. By subordinating all other loyalties to loyalty to the Emperor, State Shinto enabled the Samurai to transfer their allegiance from local feudal leaders to the imperial leader of the new centralized state and, of greater importance, to those politicians and bureaucrats who successfully claimed to speak on his behalf. This was a precondition of successful modernization, in an era of heavy industry requiring large-scale capital investment. Thus, Japanese modernization involved the blending of one of the most archaic religio-political institutions known to man with the imperatives of economic, political and industrial rationalization.

Shinto's role in Japan's modern wars is undeniable. All of Japan's modern wars have been holy wars fought in the service of Japan's divine-human sovereign. The role of Shinto in contemporary Japanese business and technology is no less important, albeit less well understood. Writing for a Japanese audience in *Shukyo Shimbun,*

Honda Soichiro, founder of the Honda Motor Company, has observed,

> . . . the people who shoulder the responsibility for the Japanese economy are also genuinely Japanese in the sense of being worshippers of the Japanese deities. These people are guided in their work by economic rationality, and they pray to the *kami* for the safety and prosperity of the enterprise communities over which they preside.
>
> Such Shinto belief is hidden at an unconscious level in the minds of the Japanese people and is the spiritual ground of belief tacitly controlling this industrial society.[3]

Among the leading corporations that have Shinto shrines at their headquarters, branches and industrial establishments are the Sanwa Group, Toyota, the Mitsubishi Group, Hitachi, Toshiba, and Matsushita. The shrines, known as *kamidana,* are the village shrines of the new business communities. With the destruction of the old village life of preindustrial Japan, membership in a large-scale business enterprise has become the functional equivalent of the old village. Just as the agrarian villagers were united in seeking prosperity and fertility from the local *kami,* (the multiple divine spirits venerated at the village shrines), so today members of the same corporation are united in veneration of the guardian *kami* of their company.[4] Groundbreaking ceremonies for new factories usually involve a lengthy Shinto ritual, as was the case at the 1985 groundbreaking ceremonies for Mazda's new automobile factory in Michigan. Even where Japanese corporations enter joint ventures with American corporations, groundbreaking ceremonies are likely to involve a Shinto ritual. Gerald Greenwald, Chairman of the Chrysler Motors division of the Chrysler Corporation, reported in an interview in *Barron's* that a Shinto priest officiated at the groundbreaking ceremony of the new factory jointly owned by Chrysler and Mitsubishi in Bloomington, Indiana.[5] Konosuke Matsushita, founder of the giant Matsushita Electric Company (Panasonic, Quasar), and one of this century's preeminent Japanese business leaders, has served for many years as president of the Worshippers of Ise Shrine, Japan's most sacred shrine. Unfortunately, few, if any, Western writers on Japanese business have noted the power of Shinto to forge an attitude of collective unity within large corporations. The advantage this unity gives Japanese business over its American rivals, with their adversarial relationships, should be obvious.

Nor is Shinto's influence absent from advanced science and technology. For example, when "Sakura 2," Japan's first communications satellite was launched, three leading scientists from the Tanegashima Space Center visited Chichibu Shrine to pray for the success of the venture. For centuries, Chichibu Shrine has been dedicated to the god of the stars. At the Shrine, *Ame-no-minaka-nushi,* (the one who reigns in the heavens) and *Yakokoro-omoikane-no-kami* (the god of wisdom) are especially venerated.[6]

One of the reasons Shinto is so little noticed as a factor in Japanese business and politics is that it is so all-pervasive that it is sometimes barely noticed. Between 1872 and 1946, State Shinto was classified as a government institution. Its values, including veneration of the divine-human sovereign, were inculcated as moral instruction rather than as religious teaching. State Shinto was thus made binding on all Japanese. It served to create a sense of national identity with religious devotion to the Emperor as the cornerstone of an enlarged, sacred, national community. One contemporary Japanese author, writing under a Hebrew pseudonym of Isaiah Ben-Dassan, has argued that all Japanese, whether Buddhist, Confucian or Christian adhere to the religion of "Japanism," with the non-Shinto traditions functioning as subcults of the indigenous religion.[7] In reality, Shinto is the religion of "Japanism."

To the extent that "Japanism" is a religion, in spite of the American-imposed 1946 constitution, with its disestablishment of State Shinto and its rejection of Emperor worship, the religious, political and economic realms can never be discrete. Thus, economic activity has a very different meaning for Japan than it does for the West. Japanese capitalism has never been American-style "private enterprise." At the time of the Meiji Restoration, the Samurai elite did not foster the introduction of modern capitalism for the sake of personal gain. They were not engaged in *private* enterprise. Their fundamental concern was *political,* namely, national defense. The elite understood that only by the most rapid modernization could Japan retain its political independence. Because of the doctrine of the divinity of the Emperor, the political and the religious realms were inseparable. The relationship between economic, military and political power was clearly understood and was summed up in a popular slogan: *fukoku kyohei,* rich country strong army. In the modern era the Japanese have never lost sight of the relationship between economic power and their nation's standing in the world.

There is a religious component to the current Japanese-American economic competition. Japan is the world's most successful nation with non-Christian roots. Even the Soviet Union has Christian roots. Marxist atheism is grounded in the very biblical tradition which Marxism negates. By contrast, Shinto can be seen as the polar opposite of the biblical tradition. The idea of a divine king is alien to Americans, both Jewish and Christian. As noted in chapter 2, the biblical injunction, "Thou shalt have no other gods before me" (Ex. 20:3) was originally as much a political as a religious statement. Its targets, in addition to the gods and goddesses of ancient Near Eastern mythology, were the divine kings of Egypt and the Canaanite city-states.[8] When, in 1945, the victorious Americans insisted upon the denial of the Emperor's divinity, they were acting in a manner which accorded with their age-old biblical tradition. Nevertheless, by compelling the Japanese to disavow their Emperor's divinity, the Americans had, perhaps unwittingly, demanded of their defeated enemy a religious, as well as military, capitulation short of executing the Emperor as a war criminal. It was perhaps only fitting that the victors demanded a religious capitulation to what had been a holy war. Nevertheless, a victorious power that demands such a capitulation would be well advised to recognize the nature of its action, especially if it wishes to retain the long-term fruits of victory.

There are important resemblances between the way the Emperor has functioned in Japanese society, at least until 1946, and the way Pharaoh functioned in ancient Egyptian society. Both Japan and Egypt were sacralized kingdoms with dynasties of extremely long and stable duration. By asserting the divine origin and divine nature of their respective sovereigns, both Egyptian and Japanese society, until 1946, bestowed upon their members a sense of "cosmic" security unattainable in the secular societies of the modern West. There was, and probably still is, far less anomy in Japanese than Western society.[9]

Moreover, there is evidence that the current Emperor's disavowal of his own divinity, known as *ningen sengen,* remains problematic for important sectors of the Japanese public. When the Americans insisted on the renunciation, they were naturally thinking in biblical terms. Their idea of God as an omnipotent Creator was very different from the Japanese understanding of the Emperor as a living *kami.* According to Motoori Norinaga (1730–1801):

> The word *kami* refers, in the most general sense, to all beings of heaven and earth that appear in the classics. More particularly, the *kami* are the spirits that abide in and are worshipped at the shrines. In principle human

beings, birds, animals, trees, plants, mountains, oceans—all may be *kami*. According to ancient usage, whatever seemed strikingly impressive, possessed the quality of excellence, or inspired a feeling of awe was called *kami*.[10]

Norinaga's view has been regarded as an authoritative definition of the meaning of *kami,* save for his restriction of *kami* to "spirits that abide in and are worshipped at shrines." *Kami* can include flora and fauna that are not enshrined. Only those *kami* possessed of human-like powers are introduced to shrine worship. Thus, there are for the Japanese a multiplicity of *kami,* and the distinction between the gods and men is often blurred. The Japanese Emperor was never divine in the sense understood by Americans. He was divine in a very different Japanese sense.

Two million, five hundred thousand Japanese soldiers and sailors died for the sake of the Emperor they regarded as a living *kami*. They are enshrined as *kami* in Tokyo's Yasukuni Shrine on Kudan Hill. Their number now includes Japan's wartime Prime Minister, Hideki Tojo, who took his own life rather than submit to the sentence of death by hanging imposed upon him by the International Military Tribunal for the Far East. For right-wing Japanese, denial of the Emperor's divinity is almost tantamount to declaring that the millions who fell in his service died in vain.

Yasuhiro Nakasone is the first post-war Prime Minister to visit Yasukuni Shrine while in office, although many other high government officials have visited the shrine on government time and at government expense. Nakasone claims his visits are those of a private person. Nevertheless, right-wing Japanese have seen in his visits a symbolic reaffirmation of the State Shinto system. The Prime Minister's "private" shrine visits inevitably elicit the question of whether they anticipate official visits by future Prime Ministers of an ever more powerful and self-confident Japan, determined once again to reassert her indigenous traditions. In 1986 Japan became the world's leading creditor nation. That nation's extraordinary success has intensified Japanese pride in their indigenous traditions. The voices currently calling for a return to the traditions forcibly abandoned at the end of the war are growing in number. The year 1945 was a trauma from which Japan has yet fully to recover. That nation was compelled to renounce hallowed traditions which had given meaning and structure to her national life. Such a renunciation is hardly likely to be the last word. Should the divinity of the Emperor ever be reasserted in a revised constitution, it will almost be as if the ancient conflict between Yahweh, the transcendent God of biblical monotheism, and Pharaoh, the God-king of Egypt, had been resumed in the cultural aspects of the ongoing Japanese-American economic rivalry.

Lest we appear to overemphasize the religious aspect of trade rivalry, let us recall that many Koreans turned to Christianity between 1905 and 1945 when Japan attempted forcibly to impose State Shinto on their occupied country. Today Korea has East Asia's largest Christian population; Japan has the region's smallest. Moreover, during the period of Japanese occupation, Koreans tended to favor conservative Protestantism, with its assertion of the sovereignty of a transcendent, monotheistic Creator God and its emphatic rejection of the institution of divine kingship. In response to Japanese attempts to impose State Shinto, Koreans in large numbers turned to Shinto's polar opposite.

There are times when a single, improbable, unexpected incident can illuminate the subterranean forces at work in the life of a nation. The 1970 suicide of Yukio Mishima, perhaps Japan's most celebrated post-war writer, may have been such an event. Mishima's suicide offers a hint that renunciation of the Emperor's divinity remains unacceptable to some very influential Japanese. Many students of contemporary Japan have dismissed Mishima's suicide as nothing more than the bizarre ending of a bizarre personal life.[11] Nevertheless, the deed may have had an importance which transcends the writer's mixed personal motives. In the opinion of Donald Keene, a preeminent authority on modern Japan, Mishima is destined to become "the most famous Japanese of all time."[12]

In 1968, Mishima organized a small, extreme right-wing, anti-Western, private militia known as the *Tate no kai* or Shield Society. Both Mishima and his young followers were fervently committed to the remilitarization of Japan and Emperor worship. In a recent article, Henry Scott Stokes, Mishima's biographer, argues that the suicide was meant to be Mishima's faithful rebuke to the Emperor he worshipped, as well as a militarist and an anti-Western gesture.[13] As Stokes points out, in Mishima's novel, *Voices of the Heroic Dead,* a chorus of dead kamikaze pilots chant, "Why did the Emperor have to become a human being?"[14] As noted above, by denying his own divinity, the Emperor had in effect disavowed the millions of men who had died in his name, an issue stressed by Mishima. Nevertheless, as a loyal subject, Mishima could not openly reprove his imperial master. Suicide was the only path open which would permit him to express his dissent without disloyalty. Mishima's suicide was thus both an extraordinarily dramatic affirmation of the Emperor's divinity and a simultaneous rebuke of the Emperor for having surrendered spiritually to General MacArthur.

On November 25, 1970 by threatening to kill General Kanetoshi Mashita, whom Mishima's followers had taken prisoner, and then commit suicide, Mishima compelled all 1,000 soldiers of the Ichigaya base of the Self Defense Forces to be assembled to listen to his last speech. The speech was delivered from the balcony of the garrison's Headquarters Building. While Mishima spoke, his followers released copies of his last manifesto. Mishima then went inside and committed *seppuku,* the traditional ritual of *hara–kari.* Mishima's manifesto read in part:

> Our fundamental values, as Japanese, are threatened. The Emperor is not being given his rightful place in Japan.
>
> We have waited in vain for the *Jieitai* to rebel. If no action is taken, the Western powers will control Japan for the next century!
>
> Let us restore Nippon to its true state and let us die . . . We will show you a value which is greater than respect for life. Not liberty, not democracy. It is Nippon! Nippon, the land of history and tradition. The Japan we love.[15]

Stokes, *New York Times* bureau chief in Tokyo from 1978 to 1983, has characterized Mishima's suicide as "a spiritual *coup d'ētat*" and "the single most startling news event in the postwar history of Japan." To repeat, whatever may have been the murky congeries of personal motives that brought Mishima to his end, the act itself contains the raw materials for an enduring religio-political myth. Nothing waters the tree of religion so effectively as the blood of martyrs. And, the whole point of Mishima's act was to affirm the indissoluble union of Japanese indigenous religion and politics.

As extreme as were Mishima's widely publicized views concerning religion and politics, the writer was not a fringe agitator devoid of mainstream support. On the contrary, the quality of support enjoyed by Mishima underscores the importance of his highly symbolic ritual death. Mishima enjoyed the support of Eisaku Sato, Prime Minister from 1964 to 1972, and Yasuhiro Nakasone, Japan's current Prime Minister. Upon hearing of Mishima's suicide, Sato declared, "He must have been out of his mind." Nevertheless,

Sato's government permitted the *Jieitai,* the Japanese Self-Defense Forces, to train Mishima's private militia in the armed forces training facilities on Mt. Fuji. Nakasone was Minister of Defense at the time and thus directly responsible for the unprecedented and unconstitutional state support given to Mishima's private army. Moreover, both Sato and Nakasone had served as Ministers of MITI, the Ministry of International Trade and Industry, before becoming Prime Minister. More than any other agency of the Japanese government, MITI has been responsible for the Japanese "economic miracle."[16] Moreover, Sato was the younger brother of Nobusuke Kishi, Prime Minister from February 1957–July 1960.[17] Kishi had served as the Minister of the Ministry of Commerce and Industry (MCI), MITI's predecessor, in the wartime cabinet of Prime Minister Hideki Tojo. When MCI became the Ministry of Munitions on November 1, 1943, Kishi became Vice-Minister, that is, the Bureau's functioning chief. As a minister in Tojo's cabinet Kishi signed the declaration of war against the United States. Before resuming his political career in postwar Japan, Kishi spent almost four years in prison as an unindicted Class A war criminal. It should be obvious that Mishima's support came from some of the most influential Japanese leaders of this century.

When Mishima attempted in his last speech to awaken support for his program of Emperor worship and rearmament, he was met with derision and incomprehension by the assembled soldiers. There was less derision when the manner of his death became known. He had testified with his life to values once held by the overwhelming majority of Japanese and still held today by a minority of his highly influential countrymen. By his death, Mishima demonstrated that the issue of the Emperor's divinity remains alive in postwar Japan.

In chapter 2 we noted how the fundamental religious institutions which have given shape to Western culture, and most especially American civilization, originated in a profound polemic against and rejection of the institution of divine kingship in Egypt, Mesopotamia and Canaan. As noted above, there is no institution more antithetical to the political ideals of biblical religion. When the Prophet Samuel grew old, Scripture reports that the elders of Israel approached him and said:

> You are now old and your sons do not follow in your footsteps; appoint for us a king to govern us, like other nations (I Sam. 8:5).

The "other nations" the elders had in mind were, of course, Egypt and Mesopotamia, with their sacralized political institutions.

Upon hearing the request, Scripture depicts Samuel as praying to God and receiving His unambiguous reply:

> The Lord answered Samuel, "Listen to the people and all that they are saying; they have not rejected you, it is I whom they have rejected, I whom they will not have to be their king. They are now doing to me what they have done to me since I brought them up from Egypt: they have forsaken me and worshipped other gods (I Sam: 8:7–8).

This passage can be seen as one of the foundation passages of American democracy. There has always been a tension between the biblical insistence that all human institutions are to be judged in the light of the supramundane Creator to whom men owe their ultimate allegiance and the institution of monarchy, an institution which is always under the temptation to ascribe ultimacy to the political realm. When monarchy is sacralized, such ascription is legitimated in the most powerful way known to men. In our own era the sacralization of the royal institution was fundamental to Japan's extraordinarily successful entry into the modern world. As noted, the extent to which that institution has been *effectively* desacralized in Japan remains a matter of considerable doubt.

We have also noted Motoori Norinaga's definition of the *kami* as including "human beings, birds, animals, trees, plants, mountains, oceans." Put differently, Shinto is both animistic and polytheistic. As such, it constitutes the strongest possible antithesis to biblical monotheism's affirmation of one, unique sovereign Creator as well as the Scripture's persistent tendency to desacralize both the natural and the political orders, a tendency identified by Max Weber as the "disenchantment of the world" *(Entzauberung der Welt)*.[18] According to Weber and many other social theorists, the biblical "disenchantment of the world" was an indispensable precondition of the rationalization of the economy and society which are characteristic of Western capitalism. In essence, the Protestant insistence on the radical sovereignty of God, salvation by faith alone and the authority of Scripture so redefined the sacred as to facilitate the abandonment of the hierarchical world of medieval feudalism and entry into the modern world of bourgeois-capitalist, functional rationality. By contrast, Japan's entry into the modern world involved a redefinition of the sacred in which the institution of divine kingship subordinated all feudal loyalties to the requirements of a centralized modern state led by Japan's sacred sovereign.[19] Japan thus presents the image of a thoroughly modern, extraordinarily competent high-technology civilization whose ethical and political foundations rest upon a religious consciousness totally at odds with that of the West.

In their book on Japanese management, Richard Tanner Pascale and Anthony Athos have observed that the differences in values that determine managerial style between Japan and the West are rooted in differences in religion. They observe:

> In contrast to China and Japan, Western societies evolved separate institutions with separate spheres of influence: the Church emerged as the custodian of man's faith and spiritual life while governmental and then commercial institutions were given the role of providing for man's worldly existence.[20]

If, as Pascale and Athos argue, the separation of political, religious and economic institutions characteristic of the West did not take place in Japan, a position with which this writer is in accord, then *what appears to the average American as an economic challenge is in reality a profoundly religio-political challenge.* Lest there be any misunderstanding, this writer does not currently anticipate a scenario in which a remilitarized Japan inspired by State Shinto once again attempts to dominate the Pacific world by force of arms. Nevertheless, there is more than one way to alter power relations so that the power of command flows from one nation to another. The present Japanese-American economic competition is in actuality a multidimensional contest in which religion, economics and politics are all inextricably bound together. The real issue in the conflict is which nation and which civilization will dominate the world's richest and most productive region, the Pacific rim, in the twenty-first century. As a result of his encounters with Japanese academics and leaders, this writer can report that the Japanese are confident the twenty-first century will belong to them.

Elsewhere in this volume, Leo Sandon and Lonnie Kliever have discussed the rising political influence of Evangelical Protestantism and Fundamentalist Christianity in the United States. As the religio-political dimension of the Japanese challenge becomes clear, it is very likely that Evangelical Protestantism and Fundamentalism will become even stronger forces in American cultural and political life. They are, after all, the most "indigenous" expressions of American religion. In the face of an external challenge, it would not be unnatural for Americans to turn to those traditions that constitute the spiritual roots of our civilization. Perhaps the most intriguing question for American politics and civilization is whether individualist, American Protestantism's spiritual and cultural resources can provide the nation with the leadership necessary to meet the most profound, multi-dimensional, long-term challenge the United States has ever faced. It has not been difficult for Protestantism to provide the leadership necessary to meet the weaker challenge of Marxist collectivism. The Soviet Union is hardly a model of a successful society. It remains to be seen how well the stronger challenge of Japan can be met.

NOTES

1. On the institution of divine kingship, see Peter Berger, *The Sacred Canopy* (Garden City: Anchor Books, 1966), pp. 113ff.
2. On the role of Emperor worship in the modernization of Japan, see T. C. Smith, "Japan's Aristocratic Revolution," *Yale Review,* 50:3 (Spring 1961), pp. 370–383.
3. Honda Soichiro, "Shinto in Japanese Culture," *Nanzan Bulletin,* No. 8/1984, p. 30. This article originally appeared as "Bunka no naka no Shinto," *Shukyo Shinbun* (February 1 and March 1, 1984).
4. *Ibid.*
5. Richard Rescigno, "Godzilla and the Big Gorilla: Chrysler is Gearing Up to Fight the Competition," *Barron's* (May 26, 1986), p. 25.
6. Honda Soichiro, "Shinto," p. 26.
7. Isaiah Ben-Dassan, *The Japanese and the Jews,* trans. Richard L. Gage (Tokyo: John Weatherhill, 1972), pp. 107ff.
8. Chap. 2, p. 7.
9. See Berger, *Sacred Canopy,* p. 114.
10. Cited by Ueda Kenji, "Shinto" in Hori Ichiro et. al., eds. *Japanese Religion: A Survey* (Tokyo: Kodansha International, 1972), pp. 37–8.
11. See John Nathan, *Mishima: A Biography* (Boston: Little, Brown and Company), 1974.
12. Cited by Henry Scott Stokes, "Lost Samurai: The Withered Soul of Postwar Japan," *Harper's Magazine* (October 1985), pp. 55–63.
13. *Ibid.*
14. *Ibid.*

15. Mishima's suicide is described by Henry Scott Stokes, *The Life and Death of Yukio Mishima* (New York: Ballantine Books, 1974), pp. 24–37. *Jieitai* refers to the Self-Defense Forces.
16. On MITI, see Chalmers Johnson, *MITI and the Japanese Economic Miracle: The Growth of Industrial Policy, 1925–1975* (Stanford: Stanford University Press, 1982).
17. Kishi was adopted into another family, hence the difference of name. Details of the adoption can be found in Dan Kurzman, *Kishi and Japan: The Search for the Sun* (New York: Ivan Obolensky, 1960).
18. See Max Weber, "Science as a Vocation," H. H. Gerth and C. Wright Mills, eds., *From Max Weber: Essays in Sociology* (New York: Oxford University Press, 1946), p. 139.
19. On the redefinition of the sacred in Protestantism and Japanese religion see, Robert Bellah, *Tokugawa Religion: The Values of Pre-Industrial Japan* (Glencoe: The Free Press, 1957), pp. 8–9.
20. Richard Tanner Pascale and Anthony Athos, *The Art of Japanese Management: Applications for American Executives* (New York: Simon and Schuster), p. 23.

NOTES ON CONTRIBUTORS

Edward Azar is Professor of Government and Politics and Director of the Center for International Studies at the University of Maryland. His recent publications include *United States-Arab Cooperation* (1985) and *International Conflict Resolution* (1986).

Michael Berenbaum is the Hymen Goldman Lecturer in Theology at Georgetown University. He has taught at Wesleyan University and has served as Deputy Director of the President's Commission on the Holocaust, where he authored the Commission's *Report to the President.* Dr. Berenbaum is the author of *The Vision of the Void* (Wesleyan University Press) and other works. He has won national awards for his work in journalism and in television and has published widely in the fields of modern Jewish thought, the holocaust, Israel, and contemporary politics. He also heads a Washington-based consulting firm.

Szymon Chodak is Professor of Sociology at Concordia University in Montreal, Canada. His career has included teaching at the University of Warsaw in Poland, the University of Accra in Ghana and the University of Dar es Salaam in Tanzania. He is currently visiting professor at the Institute of International Studies at the University of California in Berkeley. Dr. Chodak is the author of numerous books and articles dealing with political parties in Western Europe, African political systems and the theory of societal development. He is currently completing a book entitled *The New State,* discussing Western societies and etatization.

Frank K. Flinn is a Consultant in Forensic Religion, serving as an expert witness on questions of church and state. He is also Editor of *New ERA Newsletter* and Senior Consultant to the Sun Myung Moon Institute. He edited *Hermeneutics and Horizons* and has contributed essays to *George Grant in Progress, The Return of the Millennium,* and *Phenomenology in Practice and Theory.*

William R. Jones is Professor of Religion and Director of Black Studies at Florida State University, having formerly served as Associate Professor and Coordinator of Black Studies at Yale Divinity School. He is a theologian with numerous publications in the areas of black theology and religious ethics including *Is God a White Racist?*

Lonnie D. Kliever is Professor of Religious Studies at Southern Methodist University. He has previously held appointments in philosophy at the University of Texas of El Paso and in religion at Trinity University and the University of Windsor. Dr. Kliever is a philosopher of religion and culture with special interest in secularization, modernization and religion. His publications include *Radical Christianity, H. Richard Niebuhr,* and *The Shattered Spectrum.*

Farhang Mehr is Professor of International Relations at Boston University. He is a former president of Pahlavi (Shiraz) University and has taught law and political economy at the University of Tehran and the National University in Iran. Dr. Mehr served as governor for Iran in OPEC for several years. He has authored numerous articles and books concerning labor laws, social security and state-owned corporations.

Paul Mojzes, a native of Yugoslavia, is Professor of Religious Studies at Rosemont College in Pennsylvania. He was educated at Belgrade University Law School, Florida Southern College (A.B.) and Boston University (Ph.D.). He is the coeditor of the *Journal of Ecumenical Studies* and the editor of *Occasional Papers on Religion in Eastern Europe.* He writes frequently on religious developments in Eastern Europe.

Wellington W. Nyangoni is the Chairman and Professor of International Politics in the Department of African and Afro-American studies at Brandeis University in Waltham, Massachusetts. In addition to numerous articles, he has published the following books: *Ambiguities of National Security Symbols in U.S. Foreign Policy Formulation* (1979), *United States Foreign Policy and the Republic of South Africa* (1981), and *Africa in the United Nations System* (1985).

John K. Roth is the Russell K. Pitzer Professor of Philosophy at Claremont McKenna College. A specialist in American philosophy and religion, he has been Fulbright lecturer in American studies at the University of Innsbruck, Austria. He has also served as visiting

Professor of Philosophy at Doshisha University, Kyoto, Japan. Among his publications on life in the United States are *The American Religious Experience* (with Frederick Sontag); *The American Dream* (with Robert H. Fossum); and *American Dreams.*

Richard L. Rubenstein is the Robert O. Lawton Distinguished Professor of Religion at Florida State University and president of The Washington Institute for Values in Public Policy. He is the winner of the *Portico d'Ottavia* literary prize in Rome, 1977, for the Italian translation of *The Religious Imagination.* He has authored or edited ten books, including *After Auschwitz* (1966), *My Brother Paul* (1972), *The Cunning of History* (1975), *The Age of Triage* (1983), and *Modernization: The Humanist Response* (1985).

Leo Sandon is Director of American Studies at Florida State University. He was the founder and Executive Director of the Institute for Social Policy Studies, 1974–79. Dr. Sandon has received the AMOCO Foundation Award for excellence in undergraduate teaching. He has authored over eighty monographs, articles and review essays, and coauthored a widely used textbook, *Religion in America.*

Arvind Sharma is currently Senior Lecturer in the Department of Religious Studies at the University of Sydney, Australia. He has also taught at Temple University in Philadelphia, McGill University in Canada and the University of Queensland in Australia.

Huston Smith is Professor of Religion, Emeritus, at Syracuse University. He has also taught at the Massachusetts Institute of Technology and Washington University in St. Louis. He is the author of six books which include *Forgotten Truth, Beyond the Post-Modern Mind,* and *The Religions of Man,* which has sold over two million copies. His special field is comparative philosophy and religion.

Index

Index

Index

Index